A BRONTË COMPANION

A BRONTË COMPANION

Literary Assessment, Background, and Reference

F. B. PINION

BARNES & NOBLE

BOOKS

10 East 53d St., New York 10022
(a division of Harper & Row Publishers, Inc.)

First published 1975 by
THE MACMILLAN PRESS LTD
London and Basingstoke

Published in the U.S.A. 1975 by
HARPER & ROW PUBLISHERS, INC.
BARNES & NOBLE IMPORT DIVISION

ISBN 0–06–495573–7

Printed in Great Britain

TO CATHERINE
(C.F.P.)

Contents

PART III

Appendixes

List of Plates

Plates are reproduced by courtesy of the Brontë Society (7, 8, 9, 12, 14, 15, 19, 22, 24a); the Burnley Public Libraries (26b); the governors of Casterton School (6a); the National Portrait Gallery (13, 16, 27); the Scarborough Public Libraries (24b); Walter Scott (Bradford) Ltd (17b); and the governors of Woodhouse Grove School (2).

Nos. 18b, 18c, 25a, and 26a originate from Louis Ambler, *The Old Halls and Manor-Houses of Yorkshire*, London, 1913; 11 and 25b from the Grant edition of the Brontës, Edinburgh, 1907; 5, 10a, 20, and 28a from the Haworth edition, London, 1899 and 1900; 18a from John Horner, *Buildings in the Town and Parish of Halifax*, 1835; 21 from Frederika Macdonald, *The Secret of Charlotte Brontë*, London, 1914; 3 from Frederick Ross, *The Ruined Abbeys of Britain*, London, 1882; 4 and 17a from William Scruton, *Thornton and the Brontës*, Bradford, 1898; 28b from Clement Shorter, *The Brontës, Life and Letters*, London, 1908; and 1, 6b, and 10b from J. A. Erskine Stuart, *The Brontë Country*, London, 1888.

Maps and Illustrations
in the Text

Illustrations 5 and 6, by T. Mackenzie, from Elizabeth Southwart, *Brontë Moors and Villages*, London and New York, 1923, are reproduced by courtesy of the Bodley Head.

Abbreviations

A.	*Agnes Grey*
J.	*Jane Eyre*
P.	*The Professor*
S.	*Shirley*
T.	*The Tenant of Wildfell Hall*
W.	*Wuthering Heights*

G.	Mrs Gaskell, *The Life of Charlotte Brontë*
H.	(ed.) C. W. Hatfield, *The Complete Poems of Emily Jane Brontë*. The numbers refer to the poems, not the pages.

BST.	*Brontë Society Transactions.* The Roman numerals denote annual numbers.
NCF.	*Nineteenth-Century Fiction.*
PMLA.	*Publications of the Modern Language Association of America.*
TLS.	*The Times Literary Supplement.*

Dates in parentheses, e.g. (12.1.48), give references to Brontë letters.

When references are given without full bibliographical information, (e.g. 'Lord David Cecil' or 'Simpson, 59'), *this implies that details of the relevant essays or works are to be found in the Select Bibliography.*

Preface

Most of this book is based on a study of the Brontë writings, including the poetry and early prose; by far the largest section is devoted to literary assessment. The biographical introduction is an important part of the background. Special attention is given to Patrick Brontë; the lives of the Brontës which follow have been presented separately for more convenient reference, and with the minimum of repetition.

Modern biographers have done justice to Patrick, but Brontë biography is still apt to include 'apocryphal' elements. They concern Branwell; the relation of his sisters to him and to each other in his last years; and, even more critically perhaps, Aunt Branwell.

The topographical background of most of the Brontë novels is of great interest, but traditional ascriptions may be found which do not tally with literary evidence. How far actual people contributed to Charlotte Brontë's characters can be assessed with some degree of certainty from her letters; it will be found, for example, that important links existed initially between Mary Taylor's brother Joseph and Ellen Nussey and the Robert Moore and Caroline Helstone of *Shirley*.

Literary influences on the writings of the Brontës provide a more significant background. Among these Byron must take precedence; accounts of his life, Thomas Moore's biography in particular, were a creative source not only for Charlotte Brontë in her Angrian fiction and *Jane Eyre* but also for Emily in *Wuthering Heights* and Anne (a neglected author) in *The Tenant of Wildfell Hall*. Emily's literary inspiration owes much, it will be seen, to Shelley.

The most valuable reference books for me have been the four volumes of the Brontë letters published for the Shakespeare Head

Press by Basil Blackwell; they have proved to be quite indispensable. I owe much detail to several articles in *The Brontë Society Transactions*, and to Winifred Gérin's *Charlotte Brontë*, especially with reference to Brussels. Other acknowledgments are made elsewhere in the course of this book.

Permission has been kindly given by the Columbia University Press to quote from C. W. Hatfield's edition of *The Complete Poems of Emily Jane Brontë* (New York, 1941), and by Basil Blackwell, publisher, to use the text of the Shakespeare Head Brontë for quotations from the Brontë letters, the miscellaneous writings, and the poetry of Charlotte, Branwell, and Anne Brontë, and also to reproduce an illustration from the same edition. These sketches by Branwell Brontë are included with the further approval of the Brotherton Library.

I am indebted to the University Library of Cambridge, the Huddersfield Central Public Library, the Sheffield Central Public Library, and the University Library of Sheffield for information, maps, and books. For assistance in a number of ways I am grateful to Mr P. J. Allott, Professor J. O. Bailey, Mr D. W. Bromley, Mr B. E. Coates, Miss Beatrix Collingham and Mrs R. F. Pearce of the British Council, Miss Brenda Davies of the British Film Institute, Mr R. H. Fairclough, Mrs Mabel Ferrett of the Red House Museum, Gomersal, Mr W. C. Kerr, Mrs Edith M. Kitching, Mrs Shirley White of the B.B.C., and Dr Tom Winnifrith. To Miss Amy Foster, archivist at the Brontë Parsonage Museum, I owe a great debt for her courtesy in answering inquiries on several occasions. Special acknowledgments are due to my wife for her patient scrutiny of the text, and to Mr T. M. Farmiloe and Mr H. W. Bawden for their co-operation on behalf of the publishers.

PART I

Chronology

1826 Plays, leading to Angrian stories and chronicles, begin

1831 Charlotte sent to Miss Wooler's school at Roe Head (January)

1832 Finishes at Roe Head in May

1833 Ellen Nussey visits Haworth in the summer

1835 Charlotte becomes assistant teacher, and Emily, a pupil, at Roe Head (July). Anne replaces Emily, and Branwell visits London (October)

1836 Ellen Nussey's family moves from Rydings to Brookroyd (towards the end of the year)

1837 Miss Wooler's school transferred to Heald's House (June). Emily engaged as assistant and teacher at Law Hill in the autumn. Anne withdrawn from school for health reasons (December)

1838 Branwell sets up as portrait painter in Bradford, and Charlotte leaves Miss Wooler's school (May)

1839 She rejects Henry Nussey's offer of marriage (March). Anne becomes governess at Blake Hall, Mirfield (April), and Charlotte at Stonegappe (May). Charlotte returns (July). William Weightman appointed curate at Haworth. Charlotte and Ellen Nussey at Easton House Farm and Bridlington. Anne dismissed (December). Tabitha retires to her sister's

1840 Branwell becomes tutor at Broughton-in-Furness; dismissed in June. Appointed clerk at Sowerby Bridge station (August)

1841 He moves to Luddenden Foot (April). Charlotte becomes governess at Upperwood House, Rawdon, and Anne at Thorp Green Hall (March). Charlotte resigns in December.

1842 Charlotte and Emily travel to Brussels (February). Branwell dismissed (end of March). William Weightman dies of cholera (September). Aunt Branwell dies (end of October). Charlotte and Emily return (November)

1843 Charlotte leaves for Brussels, and Branwell takes up his post as tutor at Thorp Green Hall (January). Tabitha returns early in the year

1844 Charlotte returns from Brussels (January).

1845 Mr Nicholls appointed curate (May); Anne resigns from Thorp Green (June); Branwell hears of his dismissal (July). Charlotte at Hathersage (June–July)

1846 *Poems by Currer, Ellis, and Acton Bell* published (May). *The Professor, Wuthering Heights*, and *Agnes Grey* sent to a publisher (July). Mr Brontë's eye-operation in Manchester; *Jane Eyre* begun (August)

1847   *Jane Eyre* published (October). *Wuthering Heights* and *Agnes Grey* published (December)

1848   *The Tenant of Wildfell Hall* published (June); Charlotte and Anne visit London (July). Branwell dies (September). Emily dies (December)

1849   Anne dies at Scarborough (May). *Shirley* published (October). Charlotte's second visit to London

1850   Visits London, Scotland, and the Lake District, where she meets Mrs Gaskell. Stays with Harriet Martineau at Ambleside (December)

1851   Mr Taylor proposes. Charlotte visits London (May–June) and stays at Mrs Gaskell's on her homeward journey. *Villette* begun

1852   Illness, and holiday at Filey. *Villette* finished (November). Mr Nicholls proposes

1853   Fifth London visit; *Villette* published (January). Mrs Gaskell makes her first visit to Haworth (September)

1854   Charlotte engaged to Mr Nicholls. Married in June

1855   Death of Charlotte (31 March). Mr Brontë invites Mrs Gaskell to write an account of his daughter's life and works (June)

*   *   *   *   *   *

1857   *The Professor* and Mrs Gaskell's *The Life of Charlotte Brontë* published

1861   Death of Patrick Brontë

1894   First meeting of The Brontë Society (President: Lord Houghton)

1895   The first Brontë Museum opened. The Brontë Society Publications (now known as Transactions) begin

1928   The Brontë Parsonage Museum opened

Patrick Brontë

There is much in the Brontës which cannot be adequately appreciated without a knowledge of the life and character of their father. Only in recent years have amends been made by scholars to Patrick Brontë. In the popular mind, he still lingers as a rather grim despotic creature, a caricature of reality. He had his crotchets, but he was a conscientious, kind, and unusually tolerant parent; all the real evidence we have suggests that his children were lively and happy at home. His reputation was guilelessly damaged by Mrs Gaskell, who came to her biographical task with certain preconceptions. Rumours retailed by Lady Kay-Shuttleworth[1] had already created her image of Patrick, and she turned a willing ear to any supportive Haworth gossip, though almost all of it related to a period so remote that little first-hand knowledge of it could have been available to the most thorough researcher.

Not enough is known of Patrick Brontë, particularly with reference to his critical adolescent years in Ireland and to his family life as a widower at Haworth, to present him in the round; yet there is sufficient evidence to show that he was not merely a man destined to be more sinned against than sinning but one worthy of respect, sympathy, and even of admiration, particularly for his bearing in the face of suffering and detraction. His magnanimity and comparative selflessness at the age of eighty suggest that, in his eyes, misrepresentation was unimportant compared with the blows he had suffered in rapid succession at two stages of his life, and that nothing was to be

---

[1] See *The Letters of Mrs Gaskell*, pp. 124–5 (25.8.50). Further reference is made to this edition on p. 356. Mrs Gaskell's revision of her biography is the subject of Appendix 1, pp. 367–70.

gained by contesting the world's judgment when he had soon to face his Creator's. His subsequent defence of Mrs Gaskell against her critics stemmed, no doubt, from gratitude that she had contributed so much to the recognition of Charlotte's genius.

The eldest of a large family, he was born on 17 March 1777 at Emdale in the parish of Drumballyroney, County Down. It was the day of the patron saint after whom he was named. His father, Hugh Brunty, was a labourer who had moved north from Drogheda a year or so earlier and, according to an almost legendary tradition, won the heart of a beautiful girl from Ballynaskeagh; they were married against the wishes of her parents, who were indignant when she renounced her Catholic faith. The Bruntys lived in pleasant pastoral country north-west of the Mourne Mountains, first in what contemporaneously would have been called a 'rude' cottage; it was thatched, had only two rooms, and no laid floors. As the family increased, they moved to larger houses in the neighbourhood. There is nothing to indicate that their status improved very much. From England Patrick sent his mother gifts of money, and all his brothers and sisters were equally remembered in his will.

How much assistance in his early education he received at home is conjectural. His parents' books were restricted to *The Pilgrim's Progress*, the Bible, and *Poems* by Robert Burns. The story runs that he worked first for a blacksmith, then as a weaver; and that he bought books, including *Paradise Lost*, with his savings. At the age of sixteen he was teaching in a Presbyterian Church school at Glascar Hill, and it is highly probable that the minister, Andrew Harshaw, helped him with his studies and lent him books, including classical texts. So convinced was Patrick of the value of education that he initiated evening classes, and took older boys on rambles among the Mourne Mountains in the summer holidays. For him, as for Cowper and many contemporaries, the beauty of nature was a revelation of God's handiwork. Wesley's hymns had a great hold on him.

At the age of twenty-one, Patrick moved to the church school at Drumballyroney, and became tutor to the minister's sons. Whether this change of post was dictated by the discovery that he had to belong to the Established Church in order to graduate at Oxford or Cambridge is uncertain. It seems likely that the Reverend Thomas Tighe had discovered his prowess as a teacher and, being persuaded that he was the right kind of man for the Church, had encouraged him to read theological books and aim at taking a degree. Tighe belonged to an important family, and had been a great friend of John Wesley. He was influential, and undoubtedly helped to secure Patrick Brunty's admission as a sizar to St John's College, Cambridge, in the autumn of 1802. Tighe had been a student there from 1771 to 1775.

In all probability Patrick helped his family financially during his years as a teacher; he left home for St John's with no more than seven pounds at his disposal, and was glad to receive soon after his arrival a gift of five pounds from a distant friend. Was it because poverty stared him in the face, and he did not want his humble origins to be known, that Patrick took advantage of the variations in his family name to alter the college registrar's entry from 'Branty' to 'Brontë'? Snobbery could be cruel and humiliating, but how could a dependent sizar, with his fees reduced in return for certain duties, benefit from such a change of patronymic even if it recalled the title bestowed a few years earlier on Nelson by the King of Naples? (Thereafter, even at Cambridge, he signed his name with an accent of one kind or another.) Patrick had to make his own way, and he succeeded. His tall impressive figure, his seniority, and his determination earned him some respect, no doubt, just as his ability, sincerity, and geniality won him friends within a circle generally restricted by class or pursuits. We cannot assume that because he trained in the college army corps with a student who became Lord Palmerston that he hobnobbed with the rich. His poverty was undoubtedly a social barrier, but it was also a spur to success. He won a number of small exhibitions or scholarships, and his prizes bear witness to his pride in having 'always kept' in the first class. There is evidence that he did some coaching to eke out his funds. Medicine was one of his earlier studies but if he ever had any uncertainty about his career, it did not last long. 'There is reason to hope that he will be an instrument of good to the church, as a desire of usefulness in the ministry seems to have influenced him hitherto in no small degree', wrote Henry Martyn, Fellow of St John's, in 1804, when he was urging William Wilberforce to give Patrick financial help. The result of his appeal was an annual allowance of twenty pounds. Martyn was curate to Charles Simeon, vicar of Holy Trinity, Fellow of King's, and founder of the Church Missionary Society. It was a propitious time for Patrick, in close relation to a group inspired by evangelical fervour. Unlike Henry Martyn, however, he did not accept the challenge to take up missionary work in India. After graduating, and offering himself to the Bishop of London as a candidate for Holy Orders, he became a deacon in 1806, and was appointed curate at Wethersfield in Essex. The vicar was a friend of Charles Simeon and other leading Evangelicals.

Before he began his dutes, Patrick returned home for the first and last time; his first sermon was preached at Drumballyroney. He was twenty-nine, but he persuaded his father to write a certificate testifying that he was twenty-eight, and to sign it 'Hugh Brontë' in conformity with his own signature. He had heard that it was unusual for priests to be ordained over the age of thirty. It was after more than a year's service at Wethersfield that he was ordained a priest of the Established Church at the Chapel Royal of St James, Westminster, on 21 December 1807.

At Wethersfield he fell in love with Mary Burder, a girl much younger than himself. It is generally thought that their engagement was opposed by her relatives on the grounds of his social inferiority or unknown origin. At the beginning of 1809 Patrick left Essex to become assistant curate at Wellington, a mining-town in Shropshire. He continued his correspondence with Mary for at least a year, and she never forgot her disappointment when he ceased to write. His fellow-curate was William Morgan, destined to be a lifelong friend. Patrick's introduction to the widow of John Wesley's successor had consequences of the greatest importance. She had spent much on charities at Birstall before her marriage, and her husband, John Fletcher, described Yorkshire as 'the Goshen of our land'. Mrs Fletcher's influence was responsible for Patrick's appointment to a curacy at Dewsbury at the end of 1809, before Jabez Bunting (pilloried in *Wuthering Heights*) began creating local dissidence by the setting up of chapels and schools for Methodists.

At Dewsbury Patrick Brontë was popular; he carried a shillelagh and was nicknamed 'Old Staff'. Some admired him because he was handsome; many respected his ability to preach without recourse to script; others thought highly of his good deeds, his compassionate sincerity, and his habit of holding local services in working-class homes. He was most at ease with children, in the Sunday school or on family visits. The Napoleonic trade war had hit the cloth and woollen industries, and there was much unemployment and distress. Patrick's pastoral work was long remembered. More publicized, however, were his clash with the ringers who, in the vicar's absence, began a bell-practice without his permission after a Sunday evening service; the fearlessness with which he dealt with a drunkard who tried to hold up a Whitsuntide procession of boys and girls; and his action in procuring the acquittal of William Nowell, who had been imprisoned on the false charge of deserting his regiment.

In March 1811 Patrick became minister of Hartshead, four miles west of Dewsbury. So neglected was the church building that an old ash tree, rooted in the roof, thrust its branches out of the tower. Sunday School pupils from Dewsbury often came to hear him preach. He was a great walker, visiting cottages and farms on the moors. Years after his departure, he was remembered for his anecdotes. At various times he had written poems; twelve were published in 1811 as *Cottage Poems*, 'chiefly designed for the lower classes of society',

> All you who turn the sturdy soil,
> Or ply the loom with daily toil.

Patrick had no great illusions about his verse, but he made no attempt to adopt a form of basic English for his purpose, as Wordsworth had done in the more experimental poems of *Lyrical Ballads*. His hope was that his work might be 'well-pleasing in the sight of God' and 'useful to some poor soul, who cared little about critical niceties'. Patrick's partiality for the stanza which was a favourite with Burns is noticeable. The main biographical interest of this volume is that his name appeared for the first time as 'Brontë', simply because printers found the diaeresis more readily available than any other accent. So it remained.

By 1812 Luddism had spread from Nottingham into Yorkshire. Modern machinery was smashed on its way to the mills, owners were threatened, and redcoats stationed in the main towns. A former incumbent of Hartshead, Hammond Roberson, now the owner of a boarding-school at Liversedge, had used threats of damnation to dissuade mill-workers from violence. Patrick Brontë did not go so far; his sympathies were with the poor, but he condemned lawlessness. Well-wishers warned him that his life was in danger, and he bought two pistols, one of which he always carried with him; the shillelagh was inadequate in times of political agitation, when memories of the French Revolution were still fresh. The climax came when scores of workers assembled one evening after dark in a large field below Roe Head and, after being armed and addressed by agitators, made for Rawfolds Mill between Cleckheaton and Heckmondwike. They passed near Lousey Thorn, the farm where Patrick lodged. The mill-owner, William Cartwright, was prepared for them; he was unusually

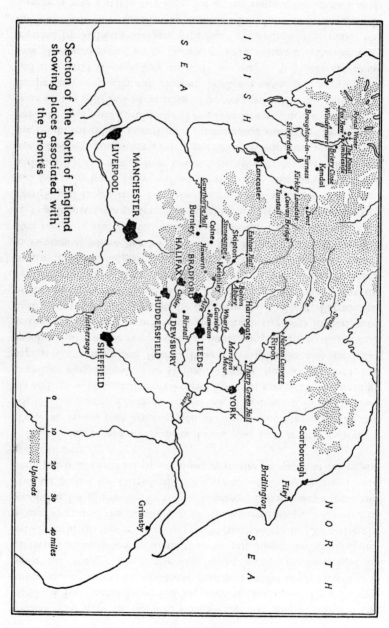

Section of the North of England
showing places associated with
the Brontës

I R I S H   S E A

Rydal Water
The Knoll
Fox How   Ambleside
Windermere   Briery Close
Silverdale
Broughton-in-Furness
Kendal
Kirkby Lonsdale
Dent
Cowan Bridge
Tunstall
Lancaster

LIVERPOOL

MANCHESTER

Gawthorpe Hall
Burnley   Colne
Haworth
Stonegappe   Skipton
Keighley   Eshton Hall   Ure
HALIFAX
BRADFORD   Wharfe   Bolton Abbey
Calder   Guiseley   Harrogate
Rawdon   Swale
Birstall   Marston   Norton Conyers
LEEDS   Moor   Ripon
HUDDERSFIELD   &   DEWSBURY   ×
Thorp Green Hall
Liddthersage
SHEFFIELD   Aire   YORK
Ouse

Scarborough

Filey

Bridlington

Grimsby

N O R T H   S E A

0   10   20   30   40 miles

Uplands

fearless and, with the help of a small military guard, repelled the attack. A few nights later, Patrick realized that some of the hunted militants had come to bury their dead in Hartshead churchyard; so concerned was he about the fate of parishioners who might be suspected of harbouring them that he put mercy before law and 'wisely held his peace'. The repeal of the Orders in Council eight weeks later, and the resumption of trade with Europe, soon created conditions for improving industrial relations. It had been a tense and exciting period for Patrick Brontë, one to which he recurred with some relish at times when reminiscing in the company of his eager-eyed children.

In Airedale, eight miles from Leeds and four from Bradford, a Wesleyan school had been opened at Woodhouse Grove in January 1812. The principal was John Fennell, a godson of John Fletcher. He and his wife Jane Branwell came from Penzance. He required an examiner and, according to William Morgan, now at Bradford, had expressed the wish that Patrick Brontë should accept the post. The appointment was for one year only, demanding no more than a visit at the end of the summer term, to examine the boys in Scripture, Latin, 'and so on'. Soon after he had accepted the post, Patrick was invited to the school; there he met Morgan, who was engaged to the Fennells' daughter Jane, and was introduced to her cousin Maria Branwell. She belonged to an important Wesleyan Methodist family in Penzance, where her brother was the Mayor. Their parents had died recently, and Maria had accepted her aunt's invitation to assist at Woodhouse Grove. Before he carried out his duties as examiner, Patrick had found time to make a number of visits; he and Maria had fallen in love. They walked by the Aire, occasionally as far as Kirkstall Abbey, where they became engaged in August. Maria was small and not altogether pretty, but she was winsome and elegant; she combined religious zeal with humour and sincerity. 'Dear Saucy Pat', she addressed him in one of her love-letters. She had written an essay on the religious advantages of poverty, an economic state which she had never directly experienced. With her annuity of £50, Patrick and she could contemplate an early marriage. A double ceremony took place at Guiseley on 29 December 1812. Maria and Patrick were married by William Morgan with Jane Fennell as bridesmaid, and the latter pair were married by Patrick with Maria as bridesmaid. In a sense it was a triple wedding, for at the same time Maria's sister Charlotte was married at Penzance.

The Brontës lived at Clough House, Hightown, at the west end of Liversedge and a mile from Hartshead Church. In 1813 Patrick's second volume of poetry, *The Rural Minstrel*, was published. Most of the poems show a religious theme with proclivities towards natural description in rather hackneyed diction. 'Lines, addressed to a Lady, on her Birth-day' were inspired by Maria. Her first child was born early in 1814, and named after her; her second, about a year later, and named after Elizabeth Branwell, who had travelled from Penzance to keep her sister company. In May 1815 the Brontës moved to Thornton, near Bradford, Patrick having exchanged livings to his financial advantage with Thomas Atkinson, who wished to be nearer the young lady he was to marry, Frances Walker of Lascelles Hall, east of Huddersfield. He had probably met her at Kipping House, Thornton, where Miss Elizabeth Firth, her cousin, lived.

Though a strong Nonconformist centre, Thornton at the time was but a small village; the main part, along Market Street, where the Brontës lived, consisted of twenty-three houses of local grey stone. The church, known as Old Bell Chapel and, like the one at Haworth, a chapel-of-ease to Bradford parish church, was situated lower down, and in a worse state of neglect than Hartshead had been. Patrick promptly took measures to secure improvements. Elizabeth Branwell stayed at Thornton for a period. *The Cottage in the Wood*, Patrick's first prose tale, was published at Bradford in 1815. This brief and simple story is supplemented with verses; its subject is the finding of wisdom. The heroine is another Pamela, the object of a rich inebriate. She rejects him, and becomes rich; he loses his wealth in riotous living and becomes converted. They fall in love, and enjoy a happy and godly life with their children. In retrospect Mr Brontë realized that the happiest years of his life had been spent at Thornton. All his most famous children were born there: Charlotte (1816), named after her aunt in Cornwall; Patrick Branwell (1817); Emily Jane (1818); and Anne (1820). Miss Firth was very friendly, and there were numerous tea-parties. Writing was a pleasant avocation; and the publication in London of his second prose tale, *The Maid of Killarney* (1818), gratified, perhaps raised, Patrick's authorial ambition. If, as seems unlikely, he took his cue for a discussion novel from T. L. Peacock, he provided plainer fare, revealing without subtlety or satire his anti-Catholicism and admiration of Wellington, his views on sermons, juries, and hanging for minor offences, and his distrust of cards, dancing, and the theatre. He preferred the songs of

Zion to amorous ditties, and was brother to Sir Anthony Absolute in his suspicion of novels.

In June 1819 Mr Brontë's ecclesiastical ambition seemed to be accomplished when the vicar of Bradford offered him the incumbency of Haworth. To take charge of a church associated with the almost legendary memory of the redoubtable Evangelical William Grimshaw, and hallowed by visits from the Wesleys, Whitefield, John Newton, and the Countess of Huntingdon, was a daunting but irresistible challenge. Unfortunately the trustees had not been consulted, and, though they wanted Patrick, honour forbad them to accept him. Their representatives advised him to resign his living at Thornton, and apply in two months' time; the Archbishop of York requested him to take charge at Haworth until the question was settled. Fully appreciating the attitude of the trustees, Patrick asked that his nomination should be withdrawn. The trustees were delighted; all that they required was to hear him preach. Mr Brontë had too much integrity to stage a performance; his answer was that they could come and hear him at any time when he did not expect them, and discover too his character, conduct, and work outside the precincts of his church. This manly reply confirmed the wish of the Haworth trustees to appoint him. He was instructed by the Archbishop to preach at Haworth, but the trustees insisted that the vicar of Bradford should consult them first. By this time the vicar had lost patience, and appointed the temporary incumbent Samuel Redhead. He had proved popular, and his appointment was ratified by the Archbishop. A sorry farce engendered by stubborn pride now reached its climax. The trustees and parishioners of Haworth were indignant at not being consulted a second time. The following Sunday, they marched noisily out of church; the next Sunday a man rode in on a donkey, face to tail, with as many old hats as he could carry. The uproarious merriment which resulted was too much for Mr Redhead. Nevertheless he tried again; this time a half-witted chimney-sweep, covered in soot, climbed up to the pulpit and endeavoured to embrace him. Mr Redhead was led out of the church with the sweep, and pitched into a pile of soot. The mob chased him between the tombstones. Luckily he managed to take refuge in the Black Bull, where the landlord, apprehensive for Redhead's life, secured his escape by clever subterfuge. In the end the vicar of Bradford agreed that the trustees had the right of appointment, and Mr Brontë's position as perpetual curate of Haworth was ratified by the Archbishop on 25 February 1820.

This was probably deemed a sufficient answer to Patrick's appeal
for a charity grant to support his family and household.

The Brontës moved to Haworth in April. Together with their
servants, the youthful Nancy and Sarah Garrs, they were conveyed in
a light, hooded waggon, followed by their possessions in seven carts.
The parish was wide, including Stanbury and Oxenhope, and had a
large population; men and youths were employed chiefly as mill-
hands, weavers, farmers, or quarriers. Turning into Kirkgate (now
Main Street), above the mills, the Brontës' drivers required sustained
efforts from the horses to keep them moving up the long steep
narrow setted street, which matched in greyness its clustered houses
and shops, on the exposed flank of a gritstone hill. Near the top there
was just room for them to turn left up a twisting lane which
straightened past the east end of the church to the parsonage above.
Beyond were the moors. For over forty years Patrick Brontë was
destined to reside there, the tower of St Michael's directly beyond the
end of his front garden enclosure, and between them, and all the
way down on the right, an open graveyard thick with tombs. When
he arrived, his hopes were high; looking back years later on the succession of blows which fate struck him twice, he might have been
justified in thinking that Kirkgate had been the road to his Calvary.
Self-pity and repining were incompatible with his character and
outlook, however.

He was not the sort of man to take his duties lightly; his printed
works show that he was diligent and scholarly in his habits; and there
can be no doubt that his family and the education of the older
children, his sermons and studies, and his parish work, kept him
fully occupied. He walked long distances on pastoral missions not
only in Haworth, Oxenhope, and Stanbury, but also to cottages and
farms on the moors and in valleys for miles around. There were
Nonconformist churches, but Patrick Brontë was tolerant, and not
disposed to offend his parishioners needlessly; his policy was not to
interfere. Unfortunately Haworth could provide little society, and no
deep friendships sprang up for the Brontës such as they had enjoyed
at Thornton.

The parsonage was no mean abode. It was built of local stone in
1779, and almost symmetrically designed. In the hall, beyond a
graceful archway, a railed stone staircase wound below a landing-
window which faced west and overlooked the moors. The room on the
right of the hall was Patrick's study; behind it was the kitchen. On

the left was the dining-room, where the children were to play and write; behind it was the peat-room (later Mr Nicholls' study). Above the dining-room was the parental bedroom, soon to become Aunt Branwell's; behind was the maids' room. The room over Patrick's study was soon to become his bedroom, later to be shared with his son Branwell; behind was a room which was Branwell's studio at one period, and Charlotte's bedroom when Mrs Gaskell visited the parsonage in 1853. Between the front bedrooms, above the hall and pedimented doorway, was a smaller room, first a nursery, later Emily's bedroom and refuge, where she often wrote poetry and communed with the stars.

At the end of January 1821, Mrs Brontë collapsed in pain. Whatever the cause, she suffered from anaemia; a Leeds specialist diagnosed cancer. A day-nurse was hired, doctors came and went, but little could be done to lessen the agony. Elizabeth Branwell arrived in May, never to return to her Penzance home, and Maria died in September, anxious about the future of her children. For the first time the wicket at the bottom of the front garden was opened to convey one of the Brontë family for burial below the paving-stones at the east end of the church.

The Brontë children were 'well brought up' and well-behaved, according to the later testimony of Sarah Garrs. 'They were very timid among strangers, but lively and cheerful in their own home. Mr Brontë was a kind and loving husband and father, kind to all about him.' He continued the education of the eldest, while Aunt Branwell was responsible for the younger children and the supervision of the house. The readiness of modern biographers to condemn her is strange; it is based primarily on the belief that she was Calvinistic in outlook, and responsible for the fear of eternal damnation which assailed Charlotte, Anne, and Branwell much later, when they were able to think for themselves. The girls grew out of it, but one is hardly surprised that Branwell, as he continually relapsed, thought that he must be among the damned. Most religious people believed in hell, but the mark of Wesleyan evangelism was a fervent belief in salvation for the penitent. There could have been no serious disagreement between Maria Branwell and Patrick on this question, nor is it likely that Elizabeth Branwell's beliefs conflicted with her sister's. It is scarcely probable that the views of Helen Burns (*J.* vi), who was, we are assured by Mrs Gaskell, 'as exact a transcript of Maria Brontë as Charlotte's wonderful power of reproducing character could give', could have been nurtured in a household where Calvinism was strong; Patrick abhorred any suggestion of it. The Brontë children were happy; disciplined at times, no doubt, but not inhibited by deep-seated fear; much to the contrary, if all the evidence is weighed.[1]

Mr Brontë made at least two unsuccessful attempts to re-marry: first, Elizabeth Firth, who remained a loyal generous friend; secondly, Mary Burder of Wethersfield, whose reply is noteworthy for its sarcasm and the writer's gratitude to providence that she had escaped marrying one who had shown his insincerity when he ceased to correspond with her in 1810. On Miss Firth's recommendation, the two eldest children, Maria and Elizabeth, were sent to Crofton Hall School, Wakefield, during the latter part of 1823. The fees proved to be beyond Mr Brontë's means, and they were withdrawn after a few months to attend a new and relatively inexpensive school for the daughters of poorer clergymen.

This was at Cowan Bridge near Kirkby Lonsdale. It seemed to have high credentials; Wilberforce and Charles Simeon subscribed to it, and Miss Currer, patroness of William Morgan's former living near Bradford, gave it her support. The school was opened in January 1824, but Maria and Elizabeth, as a result of measles and whooping-cough, were not able to attend until July. In August they were joined by Charlotte. Mr Franks, vicar of Huddersfield, and his wife (formerly Elizabeth Firth) visited them in September, the month of the great bog eruption which the three youngest Brontë children witnessed while walking with Nancy and Sarah Garrs on the moors, and which Mr Brontë made the subject of a sermon, taking it as 'a monitory voice of Divine Wisdom'. He sent Emily to Cowan Bridge in November when he heard that the Garrs were leaving. Their place was taken by Tabitha Aykroyd, a Methodist widow of fifty-four, who had just returned to Haworth after working on a farm. Except for a period of nearly three years, after breaking her leg, she lived at the parsonage, loyal and loved, almost to her death just over thirty years later. The children enjoyed her company in the kitchen; she talked of the fairies in the 'bottoms' before the factories drove them away, and told stories and strange reminiscences, all in her broad dialect.

The two eldest children knew little of 'Tabby'. In February, Maria had to be fetched home; she died of consumption in early May. At

[1] For an impressively informed vindication of Aunt Branwell, see Eanne Oram, 'Brief for Miss Branwell', *BST*. lxxiv. The evidence of Mary Taylor is relevant, G. viii, third edition.

the end of the month Elizabeth was brought home ill; hearing that there was fever at the school, Patrick set off to fetch Charlotte and Emily, found that they had been taken to Silverdale near the sea, and brought them home at once. Elizabeth died, also of consumption, in the middle of June. The two Brontës were not the only children taken home from Cowan Bridge to die, it should be added.

Almost a year later Mr Brontë brought home from Leeds, with other presents, the box of wooden soldiers which soon led to play-acting, and subsequently to the writing of stories and chronicles, activities in which all four children took part, though the initiative inevitably fell to the seniors, Charlotte and Branwell. The gradual evolution of Charlotte's prolific fiction through a prolonged period of Byronic adolescence, and of Emily's poetry within another fictional framework, provides an area of study which is far from exhausted, and a background which has an important bearing on some of the novels, especially *Jane Eyre*.

With his parochial duties, the educational programme which Mr Brontë followed at home must have been very demanding, one which only a devoted and energetic parent could have achieved. Whether Branwell attended the local grammar school for a short period is rather uncertain, but it seems clear that Patrick Brontë soon came to the conclusion that he must take responsibility for the education of all his children for some years at least. Their daily routine was as follows: breakfast together after family prayers; morning lessons in Mr Brontë's room; early lunch (Patrick dining alone in his room, and probably turning his mind to parish affairs) followed by a walk with Tabitha; then tea with her in the kitchen. In the evening, Charlotte and Emily often sewed in their aunt's room upstairs; afterwards she or their father would read to the children from newspapers or magazines, including *Blackwood's*. It was she who presented them a copy of Scott's *Tales of a Grandfather*. At an early age they discussed contemporary politics with their Tory father, and heard a number of his recollections from the period of the Napoleonic War. They had time to read and write to a considerable extent, especially when inclement weather kept them indoors; and they could borrow books whenever they pleased from Papa's shelves, including interesting additions which were on loan from the Mechanics' Institute at Keighley.

In the summer of 1830 Patrick Brontë was ill, suffering acutely from inflammation of the lungs. From that time the white silken stock which he had worn as a protection against bronchitis was wound higher and higher until it covered his chin. Perhaps this illness made him think more practically of the need to qualify his children for careers. Thomas Atkinson's wife undertook to pay for the education of her godchild Charlotte, who attended Miss Wooler's school at Roe Head from January 1831 to May 1832, and made lifelong friends in Ellen Nussey and Mary Taylor. The impressions of the former, on her first visit to Haworth in the summer of 1833, are of great interest. She was struck by Mr Brontë's kindness and 'tone of high-bred courtesy'. Miss Branwell disliked the stone floors, and clicked about the kitchen in pattens while superintending 'household operations'. She talked about the gaieties of Penzance, and presented snuff 'with a little laugh, as if she enjoyed the slight shock' she imparted. On summer afternoons, or early in the evening before tea, in winter, she read aloud to Mr Brontë. She was very lively and intelligent, and would 'tilt arguments' against him without any fear. The house was scrupulously clean and, though rather austere, suggested refinement. Mr Brontë's fear of fire 'forbade curtains to the windows'. He told stories he had heard from some of his oldest parishioners, 'of the extraordinary lives and doings of people who had resided in far-off, out-of-the-way places, but in contiguity with Haworth, – stories which made one shiver and shrink from hearing; but they were full of grim humor and interest to Mr Brontë and his children, as revealing the characteristics of a class in the human race, and as such Emily Brontë has stereotyped them in her *Wuthering Heights*'. This valuable note, like her concluding ones, must have been based on a number of visits. These final remarks stress her most vivid impression of the Brontës: 'what [they] cared for and *lived* in most were the surroundings of nature, the free expanse of hill and mountain, the purple heather, the dells, and glens, and brooks, the broad sky view, the whistling winds, the snowy expanse, the starry heavens', and the 'charm' of a 'solitude and seclusion which sees things from a distance', and which they 'shared and enjoyed with intelligent companionship, and intense family affection'.

A master had been attending the parsonage regularly to give lessons in drawing and painting; all four children showed considerable talent. Ellen Nussey noted that Branwell was painting in oils, in preparation, it was thought, for his career. Soon after her visit, a piano was acquired, and it is fair to assume that all four had lessons. Emily played with 'precision and brilliancy'; the many-talented

Branwell was enthusiastic about music, particularly in 1834, when he practised on the new church organ. Whether the girls thought of vocational qualifications in pursuing their accomplishments is not known; Charlotte and Emily became teachers at Roe Head and Law Hill respectively in 1835 and 1837.

Emily's note of November 1834 suggests a lively unrepressed atmosphere: 'Aunt has come into the kitchen just now and said Where are your feet Anne Anne answered On the floor Aunt'; 'Anne and I have not done our music exercise which consists of *b major* Taby said on my putting a pen in her face Ya pitter pottering there instead of pilling a potate. I answered O Dear, O Dear, O Dear I will derectly With that I get up, take a knife and begin pilling.' Since Ellen Nussey's departure, Aunt Branwell had given way on the subject of domestic pets. The Irish terrier Grasper was accommodated in 1831; now we hear of Rainbow, Snowflake, and Jasper (a pheasant), forerunners of a number of animals and birds, of which the best known are the mastiff Keeper (appropriated by Emily), Flossy, a King Charles spaniel presented to Anne by the Robinsons of Thorp Green, and the hawk Hero which Emily found injured on the moors.

Branwell's talents, his excitability, his lack of a regular profession, and his father's fond indulgence were too much for him. In Haworth the seeds of his undoing had already been sown. The portrait-painter William Robinson was engaged to give him regular lessons, and it was confidently expected that Branwell would be admitted to the Academy Schools. The failure of his London visit made Charlotte realize that she must do something to help her family. Hence her teaching at Miss Wooler's in part exchange for the education, first of Emily (who soon found that she could not bear to be away from home), then of Anne; hence also Emily's valiant efforts at Law Hill. Branwell lost his tutorial post at Broughton-in-Furness in June 1840. A year later, probably with Charlotte and Anne's unhappy experiences as governesses in mind, Mr Brontë and his sister-in-law discussed the possibility of setting up a school for the girls to manage at home. Miss Branwell had promised a loan. Although Charlotte had often suggested this, she had no difficulty in persuading her aunt that the money would be spent more advantageously if she and Emily could attend a school abroad to gain qualifications in foreign languages, particularly French. Mr Brontë accompanied them in February 1842 to their school in Brussels; he then visited the field of Waterloo, which he described in his first sermon at Haworth after a three weeks' absence. Wellington was his hero, and Charlotte's; and he had a great interest in military affairs, including arms.

Patrick was now almost sixty-five; for years his hair had been white and his eyesight failing. His second curate, the handsome, popular, and flirtatious William Weightman, had officiated in his absence. Mr Brontë's experience with his first had led him to state carefully what kind of new assistant he wanted; he 'could not feel comfortable with a coadjutor who would deem it his duty to preach the appalling doctrines of personal Election and Reprobation', as he considered them 'derogatory to the attributes of God'. (It is inconceivable that he would have entrusted the guidance of his young children to Aunt Branwell, or could have lived amicably with her for more than twenty years, had she held such unacceptable beliefs.) Weightman died of cholera in September 1842. In his funeral sermon, Mr Brontë praised his emphasis on the love of God rather than the fear of Hell, his visiting and cottage lectures ('a most important part of a minister's duty'), and his work in the Sunday school. They had been like father and son, 'giving and taking mutual advice'. Here Patrick could probably not help thinking of the failure of his own son, dismissed that summer from his railway post, and now helping to nurse his aunt. Elizabeth Branwell died at the end of October, before her nieces could return to see her (Anne had taken up her second post as governess). She was sixty-six; by her will of 1833, when she assumed that Branwell would qualify for a career, she left her estate, nearly £1500, equally to Charlotte, Emily, Anne, and another niece.

Mr Brontë's influence and exertions were reflected in a number of improvements in the parish of Haworth. The church acquired its first organ and peal of bells; the Sunday school in Parsonage Lane was built; and churches were erected at Oxenhope and Stanbury. Cottages were purchased for housing the destitute, and cleansing operations took place to prevent the spread of cholera. He was no bigot. In 'A Brief Treatise on the Best Time and Mode of Baptism' (1836) he wrote: 'I wish to live in peace and be on good terms with all my ministerial brethren, of *every* denomination, and to co-operate with them in every good work of charity.' One of his objections to Mr Nicholls was that his Puseyite prejudices made him intolerant. In his old age, he sometimes attended evening worship in the Wesleyan Chapel; his most memorable appearance there was at a meeting to which ministers of all denominations had been invited; he entered, almost blind, leaning on Charlotte's arm, and was led to the platform, where, with tremulous voice and outstretched arms, he recited the psalm which begins (in the more familiar words of today), 'Behold, how good and joyful a thing it is, brethren, to dwell together in unity!' After years of persistent effort and writing to Whitehall, he succeeded in obtaining better water supplies and sanitation for Haworth. He was anxious to promote the welfare of all his parishioners.

Though a diehard, from whom Charlotte inherited some of her opinions, he took both Tory and Whig newspapers (*The Leeds Intelligencer* and *The Leeds Mercury*). In politics, as in religion, modern events underline the significance of his views: 'no number of men can long benefit any undertaking by force or violence, especially in England. If men will not hear, it is because they dare not; and vociferation, and missiles, and brute force, are poor substitutes for arguments and liberality and justice.'

Anne resumed her post as governess after Christmas 1842, taking Branwell to act as tutor in the same family. Mr Brontë visited them the following spring, and came back feeling reassured. Charlotte had returned to Brussels, and Emily was his one companion. Tabitha Aykroyd was back after her three years' absence, but she spent most of her time with young Martha Brown, a diligent and faithful servant who stayed at the parsonage until not a Brontë was left. Emily continued the writing of Gondal romance in prose and poetry, but she must have spent a great deal of her time with her father, walking, playing the piano, reading to him, and discussing events. She would hear reminiscences, including stories which may have contributed to scenes in *Wuthering Heights*. Perhaps it was at this time that he encouraged her to practise firing his pistols at a target in the front garden. He admired her intrepidity and love of nature. They must have talked on many things, including religion. However independent her views they were not alien to him, and would be discussed with sympathy and toleration.

Mr Brontë's eyes were still failing, and he used a lotion, the smell of which (like a previous prescription for dyspepsia) suggested to a few village quidnuncs that, privately, he was a toper like his son. Branwell was the last of his children to return home; for the third time, at least, he had been dismissed from his post. Mr Brontë had to endure not only his son's excesses but his own inability to read, or write, or walk without a guide. Charlotte and Emily sought medical advice in Manchester, and in August a successful operation for cataract was performed. Charlotte had to stay with him for a month, during which he was confined to a dark room. By the end of September they were at home, and in a few weeks Patrick was taking church services again. He was aware that his children had been ardent scribblers for many years, but he did not know that his daughters aspired to publication until Charlotte brought him a copy of *Jane Eyre* in October 1847. He had not meddled; he trusted them. With Branwell, however, it was another matter. From drink he had proceeded to opium and laudanum. Tradition has it that his father often picked him up and carried him home. After almost setting his bed on fire, he had to sleep in his father's bedroom. He dragged out his wretched existence until September 1848. Patrick had lost hope in him, but the tragedy of wasted genius was not less hard to bear. 'My poor father naturally thought more of his *only* son than of his daughters', wrote Charlotte; 'he cried out for his loss like David for that of Absalom . . . and refused at first to be comforted.'

Patrick's fear of fire was obsessional but not without cause. In 1844 he wrote that he had buried over ninety or a hundred children at Haworth who had died because their clothes caught fire. They had all, he discovered, been wearing cotton or linen. He therefore advised the wearing of wool or silk. Not until her last years did Charlotte persuade him to have curtains, and buckets of water had been kept in the hall at night as a fire precaution. But for these, and Emily's prompt action, Branwell might have died in his stupor.

The death of Emily in December and of Anne at Scarborough the following May must almost have broken their father's spirit, whatever his trust in Heaven. 'My *dear* little Anne' was all he could say as he drew her to him, after hearing the specialist's diagnosis. Thinking of Charlotte after Anne's death, he urged her to stay at Scarborough with Ellen Nussey until she had recovered; for his sake she did not have Anne brought back to be buried at Haworth.

After an attack of bronchitis in August 1849, he walked to Keighley and back one day at the beginning of November with little fatigue despite the long climb home. 'Where is my strength gone? I used to walk forty miles a day', he complained in 1853.

Although he did not seem to resist the idea of having Mr Taylor of Charlotte's publishing firm as his prospective son-in-law, Mr Brontë was greatly offended when his curate proposed to Charlotte at the end of 1852. Arthur Bell Nicholls (who came to Haworth in 1845) belonged to an Irish family much more distinguished than the Bruntys, but Patrick regarded a mere curate, with less than £100 a year, as unworthy of his famous daughter. There were other objections, no doubt: he may not have been convinced that Charlotte was in love (and if so, he was right); moreover, Mr Nicholls was a Puseyite. The sequel has an amusing side. Mr Nicholls applied for missionary service in Australia, but would not commit himself. He took another curacy in May 1853, and won Charlotte's heart by his grief and persistent postal wooing. His successor proved to be so unsatisfactory that Mr Brontë was pleased to have Mr Nicholls back at the cost of his engagement to Charlotte. Mr Nicholls then withdrew his application for missionary service on the grounds that he suffered from rheumatism. They were married a few weeks later, in June 1854. Patrick would not attend the service to give away the bride, but 'behaved very well in his grandiloquent manner' at the wedding-breakfast which followed. He was not quite a Mr Woodhouse; it was sensible to have the Nicholls at the parsonage after their honeymoon. Whether Charlotte's death the following March had been foreseen when Mr Brontë opposed her marriage is doubtful; his anxieties undoubtedly grew during her pregnancy. Martha Brown related how, after the specialist had given up hope of Charlotte's recovery, Patrick walked into the kitchen and reminded her of his affirmation that the marriage was inadvisable because Charlotte was physically unequal to its consequences.

Whatever reservations he had, Mr Brontë was more than satisfied with his curate's conscientious attention to his parish duties. He himself preached about once a month. In August 1855 he lost his sexton John Brown, Martha's father and Branwell's friend. At the suggestion of Ellen Nussey, without whose letters from Charlotte the task would have been impossible, he had invited Mrs Gaskell the previous June to write his daughter's biography, and put an end to the unauthorized and inaccurate articles that were already appearing about her, himself, and other members of his family. Mrs Gaskell had been a guest at the parsonage in 1853 (when relations between father and daughter may not have been most cordial, owing to differences over Mr Nicholls), and with amateurish zest had collected a store of impressions which were to present her host in a false light for more than a century. When Charlotte's biography appeared, however, he hailed it as a masterpiece and ignored most of the errors concerning himself. His courteous and commendatory letters to Mrs Gaskell do him great honour: 'I am not in the least offended at your telling me that I have faults – I have many – and, being a Daughter of Eve, I doubt not that you also have some. Let us both try to be wiser and better as Time recedes and Eternity advances.' Subsequent letters to that in which the misinformed biographer protested most sincerely, 'I did so try to tell the truth', redound to his selfless magnanimity. Mrs Gaskell thought he acted 'like a brick'.

He preached his last sermon in the summer of 1860. In October Mrs Gaskell asked if she might call with her daughter; they found him confined to bed. Margaret (Meta) Gaskell's account of the visit does the writer and Mr Brontë more credit than her mother's.[1] The following winter Patrick suffered from bronchitis; he was tended by Martha Brown, and died on 7 June 1861, at the age of eighty-four, the last link with eighteenth-century evangelicalism in the history of St Michael's, Haworth. Crowds collected in the churchyard to see the coffin borne into a church full of mourners; he was buried in the family vault within the altar rails, by the side of Charlotte.

Mr Nicholls did not succeed Mr Brontë. He returned to Ireland, gave up the ministry for farming, and married his cousin. In 1864 a wing was added to the Haworth parsonage, and trees were planted in the churchyard. Except for the tower (still said to be marked by Patrick's bullets), the old church was demolished. The Brontë vault was not disturbed.

[1] See J. Lock and W. T. Dixon, *A Man of Sorrow*, pp. 519–22.

Charlotte Brontë

The first day Charlotte spent at Haworth was her birthday. She was four years old, having been born at Thornton on 21 April 1816. She probably read at an early age, though for many years her writing and spelling had the appearance of being acquired rather than taught. At about the age of eight she wrote, and illustrated in water-colours, a little book, apparently for the entertainment of her youngest sister Anne. When she was sent to school at Cowan Bridge in August 1824, she could hardly remember her mother, who died three years earlier. She would be delighted to join her elder sisters, but the treatment Maria received for her untidiness, the wintry damp and cold, the poor, ill-prepared food, the outbreak of 'low fever', and the death of her sisters soon after they were brought home, seared and soured her memory. Her recollections of the school in *Jane Eyre* were vivid and, in her view, not at all exaggerated.

At home Mr Brontë continued the education of his children as best he could. Charlotte, the oldest of the young family, probably helped as Maria had done. The children played and read together; and, in their different ways and places, Tabitha Aykroyd and Aunt Branwell 'mothered' them. They were happier generally with 'Tabby' in the kitchen, though their aunt displayed a marked fondness for Branwell and Anne. With the elder girls she could be more punc-tilious, having them learn to sew at regular sessions in her bedroom, when they would have preferred their own pastimes. She and Mr Brontë read to them from books, magazines, and newspapers; together they discussed current affairs and political figures before the children had reached their teens. When the young Brontës began their plays with the wooden soldiers bought for Branwell, they soon identified themselves with politicians and explorers. From this improvised drama, countless volumes of imaginary history and romance evolved over the years. Charlotte and Branwell took the lead, and the early influence of *The Arabian Nights* is obvious; further developments were suggested by Mr Brontë's books, the Ashanti wars, and monthly numbers of *Blackwood's Magazine*. Charlotte derived stolen pleasure from her aunt's copies of *The Lady's Magazine*, still brine-stained from the storm which struck the ship conveying them and their owner on their way to Haworth (see *S.* xxii). She and her aunt thought their tales delightful, but 'one black day', finding that Charlotte was neglecting her lessons for the 'foolish love-stories' in these volumes, Papa burnt them.

The plays had generated a great enthusiasm for writing, and from the outset Charlotte's inclination had been towards the composition of stories. They show her familiarity with Byron's poetry. She was steeped in *The Pilgrim's Progress* and the Bible, and a great admirer of Scott's novels. She had read, and written, a great deal when she resumed school at the age of fourteen; and she was very short-sighted.

Thomas Atkinson's wife, Charlotte's godmother, paid the fees for her education at Roe Head. She arrived on a cold January day in 1831, looking, as her friend Mary Taylor recalled, like a little old woman; she would not wear spectacles, and gave the impression of always looking for something, 'moving her head from side to side to catch sight of it. She was very shy and nervous, and spoke with a strong Irish accent.' Although unusually accomplished as a writer, she was so unschooled in other ways that she was placed in the junior class. She was utterly miserable. Miss Wooler soon discovered her ability and promoted her. The number of pupils was small; the food was good, and great attention was paid to health. Charlotte's short-sightedness debarred her from games, but she enjoyed the walks, and soon became familiar with a beautiful part of the country that her father had known when he was minister at Hartshead. The view from Roe Head towards the Calder valley and Kirklees Park was particularly pleasing. Mrs Atkinson and Mrs Franks invited her to their homes; more often, she stayed with her school friends – with Mary and Martha Taylor at The Red House, Gomersal, or with Ellen Nussey at Rydings, Birstall. In this way she formed her first impressions of some of the most important English scenes in her novels. Such were Charlotte's assiduity and prowess, especially in literature, Scripture, French, and art, that she was awarded the three main prizes at the end of her first half-year. She left in May 1832.

When Charlotte returned to Haworth, she found that Branwell had continued the Angrian chronicles at a prodigious pace, and that Emily and Anne had set up an independent partnership in fiction. She was pleased to learn that Aunt Branwell was willing to take *Fraser's Magazine*, since there was no chance of obtaining such a periodical from the circulating library of 'the little wild moorland village where we reside'. She described her daily round as instructing her sisters and drawing from nine till twelve-thirty, sewing in the afternoon, and reading, writing, doing a little fancy work, or drawing after tea. Charlotte wished to be an artist; she 'copied nimini-pimini copper-plate engravings out of annuals' (*cf. V.* xxxv) until after infinite labour she had produced 'exquisitely faithful' copies; she was trying to *draw* stories, but concluded that she would be more successful in writing them (G. xxvii).

At the end of the summer she stayed with Ellen Nussey at Rydings; Branwell drove her there in a gig, and was so enraptured with the place that he said he was leaving her in paradise. Ellen returned the visit the following summer. By this time Charlotte had written copious instalments of Angrian romance in collaboration with the ebullient Branwell. She would have been happy to continue but, when in April 1835 Miss Wooler offered her a teaching-post at Roe Head with free education for one of her sisters as part-payment, she reluctantly decided that there was no alternative. If Branwell were admitted to the Academy Schools, as was planned, it was incumbent on her to set an example, and do what she could to reduce her father's expenses. She and Emily went to Roe Head at the end of July.

Pleasant as this school was to most girls, Emily could not endure it. She pined for home, the moors, and greater independence, returning in October to be replaced by Anne. Charlotte was unhappy. Branwell's failure may have dispirited her; as time went on, overwork, routine, and her inability to escape long into the world of fiction she had inhabited at Haworth increased her depression. At her gloomiest, she wondered if Calvinistic doctrine were true, and whether she was numbered among the damned. Withdrawn, impatient with pupils, and allowing 'sallies of ridicule which others would have ignored to rankle like venom', she felt she was not 'good enough' for her 'darling' Ellen Nussey, whom she was afraid of loving more than she loved God. A certain eroticism may be detected in her frustrations, but her journal suggests a more powerful and persistent cause for dissatisfaction. A strong wind one evening reminded her of Haworth and Northangerland; poetic impulses were stirred. Escape into the 'bright darling' Angrian dream at school is described at length in her poem 'Retrospection'. During the summer holiday of 1836 she rewrote some of Branwell's work in Byronic verse. The following Christmas she continued composing with such enthusiasm in the *Don Juan* stanza and *Childe Harold* heroics that she felt impelled to write to Southey, asking whether he would advise her to make poetry her career. His answer was courteous, dissuasive, and penetrating:

> The day dreams in which you habitually indulge are likely to induce a distempered state of mind; and, in proportion as all the ordinary uses of the world seem to you flat and unprofitable, you will be unfitted for them without becoming fitted for anything else. . . . Take care of over-excitement, and endeavour to keep a quiet mind.

Southey's diagnosis was correct. Charlotte's heart was not in her work, and she was aware of her duplicity. An amusing instance of this relates to a 'sweet August morning' in 1836 when she felt she could write 'gloriously': 'just then a Dolt came up with a lesson. I thought I should have vomited . . .' On her twenty-first birthday, Charlotte resolved to keep Southey's counsel, but Angrian scenes swam into her mind. Intermittently she managed to continue her fiction at school, and for years she was to continue it, without thought of publication. In the summer of 1837 Miss Wooler moved her school to Heald's House, Dewsbury Moor. After an illness which alarmed Charlotte and her father, and led to Charlotte's outspoken criticism of Miss Wooler, Anne was removed at the end of 1837. More lonely and frustrated than ever, Charlotte suffered so much that life became 'a continual waking nightmare'. On medical advice, she resigned, and returned home in May 1838.

In the autumn, Ellen Nussey, who had been staying in London and Bath, returned to Birstall, and lost no time in arranging meetings with Charlotte. Perhaps she had her brother Henry's interests at heart, for he proposed by letter to Charlotte the following February, only to be rejected. She did not feel 'that intense attachment which would make [her] willing to die for him'. It might be assumed that she had nourished too many Angrian flames to make a *mariage de convenance*. She was certainly no Charlotte Lucas, but in real life she refused to look at marriage through romantic spectacles, nor did she in fiction except in *Jane Eyre*. After a second proposal six months later (from Mr Bryce, a curate), she wrote to Ellen: 'I've heard of love at first sight, but this beats all. . . . I'm certainly doomed to be an old maid . . . never mind, I made up my mind to that fate ever since I was twelve years old.'

In May 1839 Charlotte followed Anne's example and became a governess. At Stonegappe, the home of the Sidgwicks, she was not a success; she resented being treated as an inferior and not as 'a living and rational being'. It was while the family were staying with Mrs Sidgwick's father at Swarcliffe near Harrogate that Charlotte visited Norton Conyers with her employers, and saw the attic where a mad woman had been confined in the eighteenth century. She gave up her post in July, never so glad to get out of a house in her life. At the end of the summer she and Ellen stayed with Henry Nussey's friends at Easton House Farm near Bridlington. Like Dorothy Wordsworth she was so overcome by her first sight of the sea that she burst into tears; its 'glories' were 'a subject for contemplation that never wearied either the eye, the ear, or the mind'. After a week in lodgings at Bridlington, they returned home. For Charlotte, these few weeks' holiday were one of the happiest periods in her life.

In the early part of 1840 the flirtatious curate William Weightman brought gaiety into the lives of the Brontë sisters. Charlotte overcame her early susceptibility, and was amused by 'Celia Amelia', as she called him. When Ellen Nussey was at Haworth for a few weeks in February and March, he paid her such attention that Emily insisted on acting as her chaperon in walks on the moors. In her letters Charlotte teased Ellen repeatedly on the subject.

In March 1841 Charlotte and Anne took up new posts as governesses, the former, after 'a world of trouble, in the way of correspondence and interviews', with the Whites of Upperwood House, Rawdon, six miles north-east of Bradford and not far from Woodhouse Grove. Charlotte was much happier there than with the Sidgwicks, though she never really cared for being a family governess. She had not yet relished being parted from her family (9.5.41):

it is indeed a hard thing for flesh and blood to leave home, especially a *good* home – not a wealthy or splendid one. My home is humble

and unattractive to strangers, but to me it contains what I shall
find nowhere else in the world – the profound, the intense affection
which brothers and sisters feel for each other when their minds
are cast in the same mould, their ideas drawn from the same
source – when they have clung to each other from childhood, and
when disputes have never sprung up to divide them.

The question of whether the three Brontë sisters should set up their
own school was discussed at the parsonage, and Miss Wooler was
prepared to let them take over Heald's House when her sister Eliza
could be persuaded to retire. At this juncture, however, Charlotte was
captivated by Mary Taylor's recommendation that she should pursue
higher 'accomplishments', particularly in languages, at a school in
Brussels such as the one attended by her sister Martha; she had no
difficulty in persuading her aunt to give her and Emily the requisite
financial aid. At length (through Ellen Nussey indirectly) they found
a suitable school, and set off for Brussels in February 1842 with Mr
Brontë, Mary Taylor, and her brother Joseph.

Mr Brontë's knowledge of London was limited. He took his party
to the Chapter Coffee House which he remembered from his visits in
1806 and 1807. Three days were devoted to museums, galleries, and
sight-seeing in London. A week after leaving home, the Brontës
reached Mme Heger's school. At the back, overlooking the garden of
the Pensionnat Heger, stood the Athénée Royal, the principal boys'
school in Brussels. The great bell of Ste Gudule, the cathedral church,
could be heard tolling time or calling to prayers daily.

M. Heger was a professor at the Athénée, but taught part of his
time in his wife's school. He had fought at the barricades during the
Belgian revolution of 1830, lost his first wife and child during the
cholera epidemic of 1833, and married his present wife in 1836. She
was five years his senior, and kept a strict eye on her school. Her
fourth child was born in July after the arrival of the Brontës. They
were received kindly, and given special privileges because of their
seniority. The number of pupils was to increase, but at this time
there were only twelve other boarders and forty to fifty day-girls.
Lessons took place from nine to twelve, and from two to four; after
dinner, one hour was devoted to studies. Charlotte thought the
institution was liberal, and a model for 'many an austere English
school-mistress' (*V.* viii). She and Emily were given excellent tuition
in French by M. Heger.

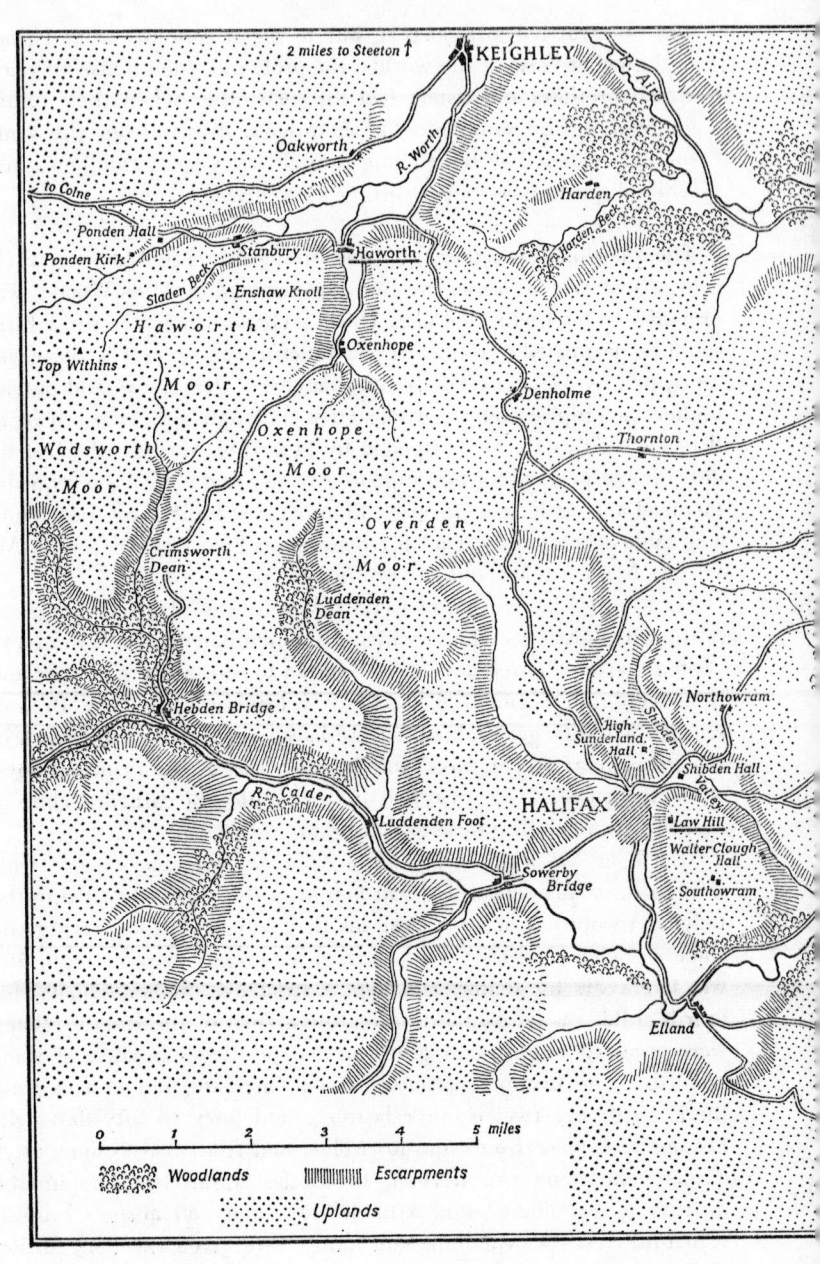

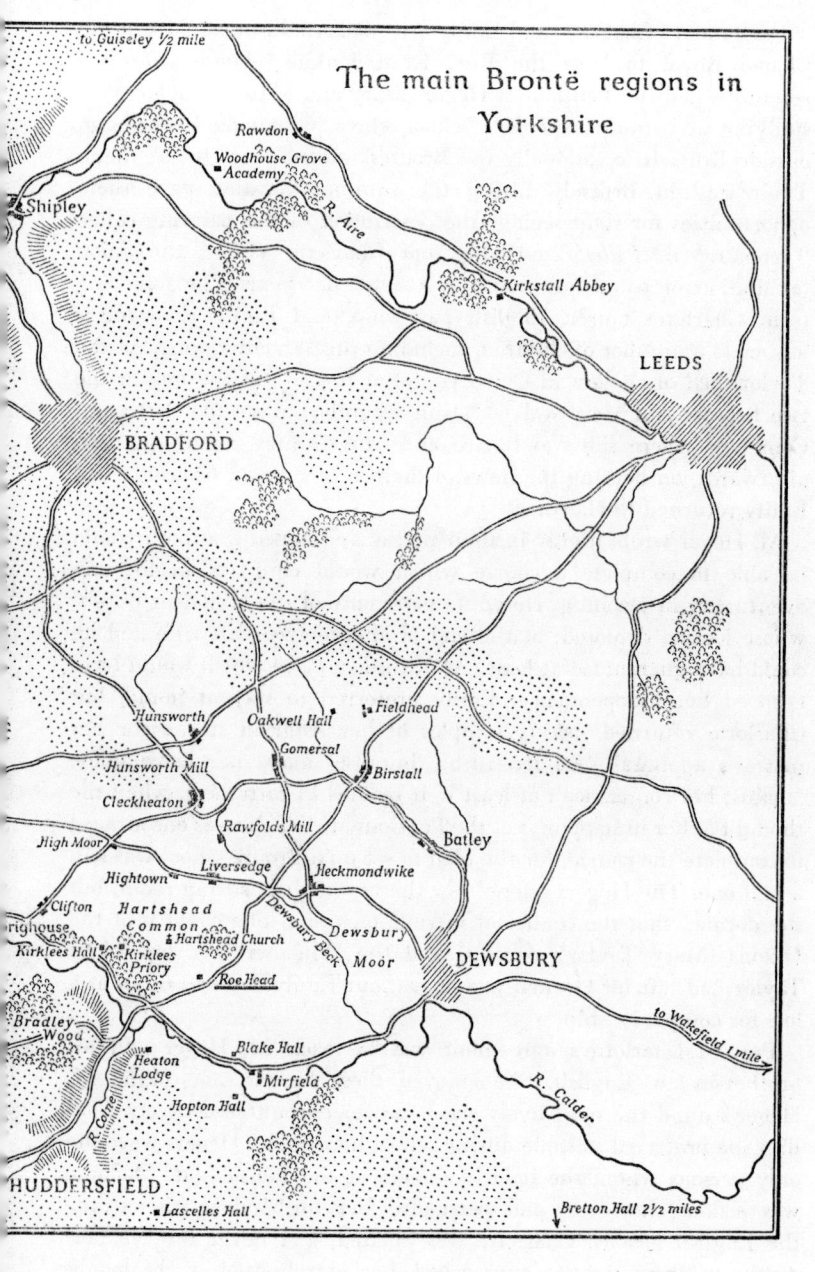

The main Brontë regions in Yorkshire

On Sundays Charlotte and Emily attended Anglican services in the Chapel Royal to hear the Rev. Evan Jenkins, whose wife had recommended the Pensionnat Heger. Mary and Martha Taylor were studying at a more expensive school, the Château de Koekelberg, outside Brussels; occasionally the Brontës walked there to see them. Their stay in Brussels during the summer vacation gave them opportunities for sight-seeing; the description of the painting called 'Cleopatra' in *Villette* indicates that Charlotte visited the Salon (exhibition of paintings) which was held that year. The following term Charlotte taught English part-time, and Emily gave music lessons to a number of children, including the Wheelwrights. Martha Taylor died of cholera in October, and at the end of the month the two Brontës and Mary walked 'about six miles' to see the Protestant Cemetery where she was buried and 'the country round it'. Soon afterwards, on hearing the news of their aunt's death, Charlotte and Emily returned to Haworth.

M. Heger wrote highly in their praise, and hoped that both would be able to complete a course which would equip them for any eventuality in teaching. He wrote paternally of the 'two dear pupils' whose loss he deplored; at the end of another year his wife and he could have guaranteed at least one of them a place which would have ensured her independence. Emily preferred to stay at home, but Charlotte returned, taking samples of her Angrian stories for her master's appraisal. 'An irresistible impulse' made her leave home 'against her conscience'; at least so it seemed in retrospect, when she thought of her unhappiness at the Pensionnat. Yet she was encouraged to complete the course, for the plan to set up a Brontë school was still a real one. The Hegers offered her the use of their sitting-room, but she decided that she could not intrude on them. She could visit the Dixons (Mary Taylor's cousins) and the Wheelwrights, but Mary Taylor had left for Germany, and without Emily she was often at a loss for companionship.

Part of Charlotte's agreement was to teach M. Heger and his brother-in-law English. She enjoyed these lessons, and found M. Heger's mind the most lively she had ever encountered. Away from him she preferred solitude during school hours. The Hegers were the only persons whom she held in esteem at the Pensionnat. Madame was jealous, however, and persuaded her husband to discontinue the English lessons. Charlotte was isolated, and never forgave her. As the summer vacation approached, her apprehension of the loneliness she had to face grew more alarming. Her friend Mary Dixon would be absent, and the Wheelwrights were to leave Brussels at the end of August. Monsieur was not indifferent and, before he and his family left for a holiday, made Charlotte a present of the works of Bernardin de Saint-Pierre. She was alone; she could not sleep; within two weeks she was exhausted and in the depths of despondency. It was at this time that she made her confession at Ste Gudule. The visit of Queen Victoria a fortnight later was a *divertissement* in a dreary period. Charlotte was bitter at the neglect she had experienced, and soon handed in her notice. M. Heger would not accept it, and she promised to remain. In December she attended a concert at the recently opened Salle de la Grande Harmonie; the King and Queen of Belgium were present. When she completed her course, she was given a certificate of attainment, but was distressed at the thought of parting; M. Heger was moved. It grieved her to grieve him, who had been 'so true, kind, and disinterested a friend', she wrote to Ellen Nussey. Mme Heger accompanied her to Ostend on New Year's Day, 1844.

At home, Charlotte was eager to set up a school: 'I desire it above all things. I have sufficient money for the undertaking, and I hope now sufficient qualifications to give me a fair chance of success.' Yet she did not wish to leave her ageing father; he was losing his sight, and she felt guilty of having been absent from home too long. She found Haworth dull after Brussels; her spirit was 'tamed down and broken'; she longed for 'active exertion – a stake in life'. In the summer plans were on foot to establish a school for the board and education of five or six pupils at the parsonage, and a prospectus was issued. There was no response, and by the end of the autumn it was recognized that the scheme was abortive. Writing, which she would have preferred, seemed out of the question, for Charlotte's eyes were so weak that she felt certain she would become blind if she wrote much.

Absence increased her regard for M. Heger. What she wrote in her first letters to him is not known, but it was not her custom as a writer to suppress her feelings. Had she been more temperate, all might have been well. It would have been wiser to address her letters to both the Hegers; Monsieur hated letter-writing. He tried to restrain Charlotte by advice, then by long silences. The effect was to excite more moving appeals, until at length in November 1845 she declared that not to correspond with him would be the loss of her 'only joy on earth'. She had lost her head rather than her heart. Her anxiety to sustain a friendship with the only man she had admired is agonizingly evident in the letters which survive. M. Heger tore them up, but Madame took care to preserve them as a proof of her husband's innocence, should it ever be required. She may have been jealous, but Charlotte was injudicious; if she had had 'a stake in life', something to achieve, she would have attached less importance to the preservation of M. Heger's friendship.

Before Mary Taylor left in March 1845 to settle in New Zealand, Charlotte stayed with her at Hunsworth. In June, after Anne had resigned her post and returned home, she travelled by train to Sheffield to keep Ellen company at Hathersage vicarage. It could have been Charlotte's home, for it was Henry Nussey's; his sister had taken charge while he was on his honeymoon. From this point, overlooking hills and valleys, Charlotte explored the moorland and ridge country which provided one of the principal settings in *Jane Eyre*. Back at Haworth, she was shocked to hear of Branwell's dismissal, and even more by his behaviour. At the end of July Anne noted that Charlotte hoped to get another situation and wished to go to Paris. Life at home gave her little incentive, only a sense of rusting unburnished while time passed by. Then the unexpected happened. By chance she discovered Emily's poems; some of them stirred Charlotte's heart 'like the sound of a trumpet'. She immediately thought of publication. Emily resisted; Anne produced her poems, and finally it was agreed that all three should contribute to a selection which Charlotte would edit. Literary ambition of a new kind was kindled, and novel-writing became a major preoccupation for all. Emily insisted on the adoption of *noms de plume*. Early in 1846 a firm specializing in religious poetry agreed to publish, provided the authors contributed over £30 towards costs. Only two copies of *Poems by Currer, Ellis, and Acton Bell* were sold. The volume appeared in May, and fair copies of *The Professor*, *Wuthering Heights*, and *Agnes Grey* were dispatched to a publisher at the beginning of July.

The Professor is closely related to Charlotte's experiences in Brussels, but the story is far from being a direct transcript. One of the main reasons for its continued rejection was its lack of 'startling incident' and 'thrilling excitement'. Charlotte was spurred to begin *Jane Eyre* in Manchester, while her father was recovering from his eye-operation in August; against her more mature judgment, she had decided to use moving and sensational effects in the hope of producing the kind of novel which she had been led to expect would suit contemporary taste. She had received such a courteous and discriminating appraisal of *The Professor* from Smith, Elder & Co. (the seventh publishing firm to consider it) that she sent them her second novel towards the end of August 1847. On his reader's recommendation, Mr Smith took it home to read one Sunday; he did not go to bed until he had finished the story. Within six weeks of its acceptance it was published. Thackeray, Charlotte's favourite novelist at this time, gave up a whole day to reading it, guessed it was written by a woman, and declared it a fine book, the first English novel he had been able to read for many a day. Its early reception was favourable, and Charlotte was gratified but level-headed; 'every nameless writer should "rejoice with trembling" over the first doubtful dawn of popular goodwill', she wrote to Mr Williams, her publishers' reader. *Jane Eyre* was republished in December, and dedicated to Thackeray. She did not know that Rochester's domestic circumstances paralleled Thackeray's in one major respect, and that the literary quidnuncs of Mayfair had lightheartedly alleged that her novel had been written by his governess.

The trickery of Emily and Anne's publisher, who did not scruple to pretend that 'Ellis Bell' was the author of *Jane Eyre* and, in 1848, that 'Currer Bell' was the author of *The Tenant of Wildfell Hall*, prompted George Smith, Charlotte's young publisher, to write for an explanation. Charlotte and Anne decided to travel to London immediately; Emily preferred to be indifferent. They left on the day of the letter's arrival, walking through a July thunderstorm to Keighley, and travelling in damp clothes by the overnight train. They stayed, of course, at the Chapter Coffee House, and after breakfast went straight to Cornhill. Mr Smith remembered 'two rather quaintly dressed little ladies, pale faced and anxious looking'. They announced themselves by handing him his letter, and Charlotte informed him that they had come to prove that there were at least two 'Bells'. He asked them to stay with him and his mother, but they were too nervous to accept his invitation. They were taken to the Opera House, where they saw Rossini's *The Barber of Seville* performed by the Royal Italian Company; they dined at the Smiths', had tea at Mr Williams', visited the Royal Academy and the National Gallery, bought a copy of Tennyson's *The Princess* for Emily, and returned home five days after leaving it, laden with books from Mr Smith, and utterly fatigued.

Branwell died in September, and Emily in December 1848. At Charlotte's request, Ellen Nussey came to Haworth, and was there in the New Year, when consumption was diagnosed in Anne. Often Charlotte felt 'like one crossing an abyss on a narrow plank'. She devoted herself to Anne, and accompanied her with Ellen Nussey to Scarborough in May. Anne's wish to see the sea could not be resisted, weak though she was. They took rooms at the Cliff lodgings where Anne had stayed with the Robinsons, and there she died. To spare her father anguish, Charlotte decided that Anne should be buried at Scarborough. Mr Brontë recommended that his one remaining daughter should stay by the sea for her health, and, after another week at Scarborough, she and Ellen spent a fortnight at Filey and Easton. Back at the parsonage she had only her father, Tabitha and Martha, and Keeper and Flossy as companions. She was determined to face up to the agony of loneliness, and find release in her work. *Shirley* had been laid aside, and then continued at intervals; when Anne was dying, it had helped to distract Charlotte from 'dark and desolate' reality. The novel was finished by the end of August.

It was published at the end of October, when she was at Brookroyd with Ellen Nussey. By this time the secret of the Brontë authorship was out; Charlotte had concealed it even from Ellen. Some of her friends were pleased. Miss Wooler thought no worse of her, but Mrs Atkinson, convinced that *Jane Eyre* was a wicked book, did not wish to see her again, and some 'ecclesiastical brows lowered thunder' at her. She accepted her publishers' invitation to London, had new dresses made for her visit, and stayed with the Smiths at 4 West-bourne Place. She visited the Wheelwrights, and found that they had already identified her as the author of *Shirley*: in Hortense Moore they recognized Mlle Haussé of the Pensionnat Heger. At the Smiths' Charlotte was introduced to Thackeray, but she was not made for society, and her shyness was an embarrassment to her host. She called on Harriet Martineau; saw Macready in *Macbeth* and *Othello*, and did not care for him; visited the new Houses of Parliament, the National Gallery, and an exhibition of Turner's water-colours, which delighted her more than anything else she saw; and made a great impression on James Taylor, the 'little man' who ruled the firm of Smith, Elder & Co.

Early in 1850 news of Charlotte's fame reached Haworth. Martha Brown came in very excitedly, and informed her that she had 'been and written two books, the grandest books that ever was seen'. Mr

Nicholls roared with laughter over the curates at the opening of
Shirley, and was delighted to discover that he had been favourably
introduced at the end. Her father thought that Charlotte might like
to read the letters he had received from her mother; it was a strange
experience, both 'sad and sweet', to find her mother, whom she could
hardly remember, living in papers 'yellow with time' and revealing
'a mind of a truly fine, pure, and elevated order'. In March Sir James
Kay-Shuttleworth and his wife called; they had invited Charlotte in
January to be their guest at Gawthorpe Hall, their home on the other
side of the Pennines, but she had been too shy to accept. She travelled
by train to Burnley, and was relieved when the three-day visit was
over. Sir James, after a medical training, had made his name in
education. In his retirement he wished to be an important society
figure, and it was with this in mind that he invited Charlotte to join
him and his wife for the London season. The plan failed, owing first
to Mr Brontë's illness, then to his own. A sunny May induced
Charlotte to walk on the moors. Everywhere she was reminded of
Emily and Anne:

> My sister Emily had a particular love for them, and there is not a
> knoll of heather, not a branch of fern, not a young bilberry leaf,
> not a fluttering lark or linnet, but reminds me of her. The distant
> prospects were Anne's delight, and when I look round she is in the
> blue tints, the pale mists, the waves and shadows of the horizon. In
> the hill-country silence their poetry comes by lines and stanzas into
> my mind: once I loved it; now I dare not read it . . .

So she wrote to James Taylor, and the result was an invitation to the
Smiths' new home in Gloucester Terrace during the height of the
London season. She made many visits, and was taken to a Sunday
service at the Chapel Royal, St James's, to see the Duke of Wellington;
she thought him 'a real grand old man'. Mr Smith had her portrait
sketched by George Richmond. She had a slight skirmish with George
Henry Lewes for his anti-feminist criticism of her novels. Thackeray
called, and she was 'moved' to discuss his literary shortcomings;
nevertheless, she was his chief guest at his house in Young Street,
where many celebrities were invited to meet the author of *Jane
Eyre*. The evening was a failure; Charlotte was too self-conscious and
inexpert to slip into the facile *causerie* of a London literary group.

George Smith clearly enjoyed Charlotte's company, for he wished
her to meet him and his sister in Scotland, and do some sight-seeing

there, when they travelled north to bring their young brother home from school. Charlotte accepted the last part of their tour, visiting Edinburgh, Melrose, and Abbotsford. The latter names, by their association with Sir Walter Scott, spelt music and magic to her, and Edinburgh compared to London was like poetry to prose. Not long after her return, she stayed with the Kay-Shuttleworths at Briery Close, near the upper end of Lake Windermere; there she met Mrs Gaskell. Charlotte could have enjoyed the beauty of the scenery had she been alone, but she was not at ease in Sir James's company as they drove round in his carriage with Mrs Gaskell. During the three days they were together, Mrs Gaskell heard much of the story of her life, and found it wellnigh incredible; she liked Charlotte, described her as 'very little and very plain', but found in her 'a charming union of simplicity and power'.

Charlotte sent Mrs Gaskell a copy of *Poems by Currer, Acton, and Ellis Bell*, disparaging her own, praising the vigour of Emily's, and recognizing the truth and simplicity of Anne's. Mr Williams wished to know if her sisters had left anything which should be included in a definitive edition of their works. She admitted that it would be easy to compile a volume from their papers, but found their scruples and wishes such an interdict that she extracted only twenty-five poems, eighteen by Emily. How supreme her own scruples were is not known, but she found too much religious melancholy in Anne's poems, and hardly thought it 'desirable to preserve' *The Tenant of Wildfell Hall*.

For the edition of *Wuthering Heights and Agnes Grey* which appeared near the end of 1850, with a selection of the 'best literary remains' of Ellis and Acton Bell, Charlotte wrote a memoir and preface. She had revised the poems, mainly to efface the Gondalian links, and tempered the gruff Doric of Emily's novel. Altogether this editorial work had been so worrying and exacting that she was delighted to accept an invitation from Harriet Martineau to stay at her home near Ambleside just before Christmas. The Knoll would have been Liberty Hall for Charlotte had not Sir James Kay-Shuttleworth insisted on calling in the mornings to take her for drives. She found great happiness in Harriet's company and conversation, and was gratified to discover that the account of the Duke of Wellington her hostess had just written coincided with her own views on the idol of her youth. At Fox How, she met Matthew Arnold, who talked 'of her curates, of French novels, and her education in a school in

Brussels'; she found his manner foppish, but 'ere long a real modesty appeared under his assumed conceit'.

In the solitude of Haworth, Charlotte could find no inspiration for writing, and the early months of 1851 are remarkable mostly for the postal attentions of James Taylor and his visit while on his way from Scotland, before leaving as his firm's representative for five years in India. His regard for her was obvious, but Charlotte was repelled by his advances, and decided that he was 'second-rate'. Her father took to him, and Charlotte formed the impression that he would not be opposed to their marriage when Mr Taylor returned from India. Perhaps the time-interval made Mr Brontë feel safe; he was now seventy-four. When she went to London in May to stay with the Smiths, he was afraid that marriage was in the wind. She heard Thackeray give his second lecture on the English humorists, and was displeased at first because he had introduced her to his mother as 'Jane Eyre'; she had hoped to escape attention. At the Smiths' the next day she took him to task for his indiscretion. She heard the remainder of the lectures, but was distressed at the light-hearted way he treated Fielding. She saw the tragic actress Rachel in two performances, and thought she was possessed by a fiend. 'She and Thackeray are the two living things that have a spell for me in this great London – and one of these is sold to the Great Ladies – and the other – I fear – to Beelzebub.' Charlotte made numerous visits in London, five, somewhat reluctantly, to the Great Crystal Palace Exhibition in Hyde Park; her last was to Richmond on 25 June. She travelled home via Manchester, where she had promised to meet Mrs Gaskell.

In their new home at Plymouth Grove, outside the city, the Gaskells were accustomed to entertain, but Mrs Gaskell knew Charlotte well enough not to invite other guests during her first visit. Charlotte was happy, and captivated by the younger girls, Julia especially. At home, she began *Villette*. Miss Wooler stayed for ten days at the parsonage in the early autumn, and this visit gave the Brontës unusual pleasure. The illness of Tabby, Martha, and Mr Brontë in October interrupted Charlotte's writing; poor health, sleeplessness, depression, and dread of consumption made things worse. It was a relief to her and her publisher to know that a doctor had pronounced her lungs and chest sound, and ascribed her pain to inflammation of the liver. At the end of May 1852 she went to Filey for a month's holiday, staying at Cliff House, as she had done with Ellen Nussey after Anne's death. For at least six to eight months she had made little progress with *Villette*, but it was resumed by August and finished in November.

In December came the shock of Mr Nicholls' proposal. Charlotte was upset at her father's treatment of him, and George Smith's insistence on her being in London for proof-corrections afforded her a welcome escape. Yet the work was very exacting, and Charlotte had no time for social engagements; her decision to see the *real* rather than the *decorative* side of London in January 1853 – prisons and hospitals, for example – is significant. The old ties of friendship between author and publisher had weakened; her presentation of George Smith and his mother in *Villette* had not improved their relationship. Charlotte refused to alter the ending, and insisted that there should be no French translation. Nevertheless, a pirated edition did appear in 1855, and its effects on the Hegers may be seen in Madame's refusal to interview Mrs Gaskell in 1856.

In May Mr Nicholls' visible distress when administering the sacrament upset Charlotte and other women in the congregation. He left Haworth eleven days later, but began writing to her in July; by autumn they corresponded regularly. She was very unsettled, and welcomed Mrs Gaskell's first visit to Haworth in September.[1] It was not a propitious time for Charlotte's biographer to form impressions of the relations between father and daughter; Mr Brontë in no way approved of Mr Nicholls as his future son-in-law or of Charlotte's sympathy for him. Fearful lest she might leave home, he consented to their correspondence; when Mr Nicholls stayed at Oxenhope[2] in January 1854, they met often. The new curate having proved to be unsatisfactory, Mr Brontë received Mr Nicholls at the parsonage in April, and all opposition to the marriage was withdrawn. Her father was so kind, so anxious to atone for his earlier antagonism that Charlotte at times felt she could cry to think that she had not been

[1] Martha Brown told Mrs Gaskell how Charlotte, Emily, and Anne had formed the habit after evening prayers of walking one after the other round the table in the dining-room parlour until eleven o'clock, and how her heart ached to hear Charlotte continuing the practice alone. Every night, after escorting Mrs Gaskell to her bedroom above, she went down and began 'that slow monotonous incessant walk. . . . She says she could not sleep without it – that she and her sisters talked over the plans and projects of their whole lives at such times.' *The Letters of Mrs Gaskell*, September 1853. See Charlotte's letter of 23.6.49.

[2] With the vicar, the Rev. J. B. Grant, original of Mr Donne in *Shirley*.

able to gratify his pride more in her choice of a husband.[1] For her, a curacy of £90 a year, and most of the Church of England work in a large parish, Mr Nicholls had sacrificed the opportunity of a much more lucrative living. Charlotte regretted that he was not an intellectual, and hoped that his Puseyism would not make him intolerant; perhaps it would do him good, she thought, to meet Mr Gaskell, a Unitarian minister. The wedding took place on 29 June; the crisis precipitated by Mr Brontë's last-minute refusal to attend was surmounted when it was discovered that it was permissible for Miss Wooler to give away the bride. The married couple travelled via North Wales (where Charlotte found some of the scenery superior to anything she remembered in the Lake District) to Dublin, thence to Cuba House, Arthur Nicholls' family home at Banagher on the Shannon, then to Kilkee with its 'stupendous' cliffs overlooking the Atlantic, and on to Killarney. They were met by three of Arthur's relatives in Dublin, where they visited his university (Trinity College) and its library; at Cuba House, it became very apparent to Charlotte that her husband's relatives and friends were country gentlefolk. In the Gap of Dunloe, she was thrown from the back of an unruly horse. From Killarney they proceeded to Glengariff and Cork, and then back to Dublin. Charlotte was anxious to reach home, after hearing that her father was unwell. They were back on 1 August.

Arthur was worried when he discovered Charlotte's incaution in her letters to Ellen Nussey, and urged her to burn them. His health had improved remarkably since marriage, and he grew dearer to Charlotte as the months passed. Parish affairs took up much of his time, and she was glad that she was able to help him. Sir James Kay-Shuttleworth came over in September to meet Mr Nicholls, and liked him so much that he offered him the new living at Padiham near Gawthorpe Hall. Acceptance was out of the question as long as Mr Brontë lived. At the end of November Charlotte walked with Arthur on the moors; after half a mile he suggested that they should visit the waterfall. She had often wished to see it in 'its winter power', and she enjoyed the spectacle; unfortunately it began to rain, and they returned home 'under a stormy sky'. Charlotte caught cold, and was unable to accept Ellen Nussey's invitation to Brookroyd, a long-projected visit which never took place. The Nicholls were unable to decline an invitation to Gawthorpe Hall in January, but the wet

[1] *The Letters of Mrs Gaskell*, p. 280.

weather there and imprudent walks in thin shoes aggravated Charlotte's cold, and she was quite ill after her return home. Writing to
Laetitia Wheelwright on 15 February 1855, she said she had been
confined to her bed for three weeks. She was pregnant, prostrated
with fever and sickness, and had lost all appetite. An improvement
was followed by a relapse. Recovering consciousness towards the end,
she noticed 'her husband's woe-worn face, and caught the sound of
some murmured words of prayer that God would spare her. "Oh!"
she whispered forth, "I am not going to die, am I? He will not
separate us, we have been so happy"' (G. xxvii). She died in the early
hours of 31 March, at the age of thirty-eight.[1] After Patrick Brontë's
death in 1861, Mr Nicholls left for Banagher, taking with him
Brontë portraits and manuscripts, Charlotte's dresses and drawings,
Mr Brontë's dog Plato, and Martha Brown. He became a farmer,
married his cousin, Mary Bell, in 1864, and lived until 1906.

[1] The certified cause of her death ('Phthisis – duration two months')
has been disputed by Philip Rhodes, Professor of Obstetrics and Gynae-
cology, who attributed it to '*hyperemesis gravidarum*, the pernicious
vomiting of pregnancy', which appears to be excessive only in neurotic
women (*BST*. lxxxii).

Branwell Brontë

It can reasonably be assumed that, when their fourth child was born on 26 June 1817, the Brontës were delighted to have a son. He was christened Patrick Branwell after his parents. At home he was 'Branwell'; outside he was called Patrick. High hopes were held for 'Little Bany', as he called himself at an early age. He scarcely remembered his mother, who died when he was four. For three years his eldest sister Maria was dear to him; he remembered her long afterwards, and how his aunt held him up to look at her, as she lay coffined with flowers above her head. The loss of Elizabeth shortly afterwards meant that he turned to Charlotte for companionship, though he was a great favourite with his aunt.

It is thought that Branwell was enrolled at the local grammar school in his eighth year but that he did not stay long. The teaching and curriculum were poor; Branwell was delicate and, if he attended, was probably ragged and bullied because of his 'carroty' hair and outbursts of temper. Emily's view, as Mr Brontë told Mrs Gaskell, was that when her brother would not listen to reason he deserved whipping. His father was much more kind-hearted, and taught his precocious son Greek and Latin, ancient and modern history, and much more. The children were voracious readers, and had the freedom of his bookshelves. *Blackwood's Magazine* was Branwell's 'chief delight' when he was still a child, and he long recalled the fascination of contributors such as James Hogg and Professor Wilson. His interest in the Napoleonic Wars, the travels of Mungo Park, further accounts of African exploration in *Blackwood's*, current fighting in Ashanti, and some of John Martin's magnificently evocative pictures, helped to turn the Brontë children's plays (which began with the wooden soldiers bought for Branwell in 1826) into serial fiction of conquest and grandeur. Branwell's planning was on an epic scale, and his collaboration with Charlotte lasted for years. The military exploits of his imagination out-Homered Homer. He produced instalments of *Branwell's Blackwood's Magazine*, but Charlotte was interested in other matters than bloodshed and war, and soon took over the editorship. His enthusiasm for *Ossian* and his talent in verse-writing and other arts were amusingly satirized by Charlotte in the miniscule magazines which they compiled. He appeared as Young Soult, a descendant of Old Soult, whom the English had learned to admire for his gallantry when Sir John Moore was buried at Corunna. The blank verse of 'Caractacus', a two-act dramatic poem which he wrote in two days in June 1830, gives evidence of a facility for imagery not unlike that of an unfledged Shakespeare. Books borrowed from the Heatons of Ponden Hall supplied new ideas; he read Chateaubriand's *Travels* in translation; and the title of Beaumont and Fletcher's *Hermaphrodite* was so fascinating that it was adopted for a time as a term of opprobrium in the verbal contests between brother and sister.

Charlotte's departure for Roe Head in 1831 left Branwell free to develop new ideas for the Glasstown serial. Among them may be seen his interest in the Haworth boxing-club. He was lively in company, and, having little spending-money, soon had recourse to cadging and borrowing. He was often at the Black Bull, and more often with the family of John Brown, the sexton. At one time Brown, more than anyone else, was blamed for Branwell's later degeneration, but there is little evidence to substantiate the charge. Mr Brontë held the Browns in high esteem, and later depended on John to exert a steadying influence on his excitable and self-indulgent son. Branwell's education had done little to prepare him for the outer world.

He was happiest with Charlotte, and walked more than thirty miles there and back to see her one day at Roe Head. Ellen Nussey noticed their 'perfect accord' when they visited Rydings in 1832; he was 'as dear to Charlotte as her own soul'. This young genius, destined (it was thought) to be a painter, was unable to mix in a socially superior society, as was shown by the outing to Bolton Abbey, Wharfedale, where he and Charlotte travelled by gig to meet Ellen Nussey and her brothers, and dine at the Devonshire Arms, in September 1833. His father was too sanguinely proud of him, too engrossed in his own duties and reading, and too unrealistic, to ensure that his son came to terms with life and qualified for a career. Branwell translated his experiences and reading into a world of his own creation. He made himself a hero in his own eyes, and there was no one to bring him to his senses. Charlotte's caricature of him in the new Angrian character of Patrick Benjamin Wiggins is penetrating but not at all serious, part of the riotous literary fun they shared; 'Benjamin' suggests that he was the apple of his father's eye.

From their earliest years the Brontë children had sketched and painted. In 1834, when Branwell was enthusing over music, and especially over playing the new church organ, Mr Brontë took them to an annual exhibition in Leeds which included works by the sculptor J. B. Leyland and the portrait-painter William Robinson. The latter was engaged to give lessons at the parsonage, with special attention to Branwell. By 1835 the young artist was looking forward to his admission to the Academy Schools in London, and to joining the great world which he had imagined entering as Captain Henry Hastings. Branwell's account of his visit was written in his history of Angria in 1836, but all the evidence indicates that he went to London in 1835, when Charlotte and Emily were at Roe Head. At the age of little over eighteen, he set off on his two-day coach journey, but his euphoria and courage seem to have ebbed away as he approached his goal; no doubt he felt inferior once again, and completely out of place in the city. He could not summon up resolution to enter the Academy (then at Somerset House) or to deliver any of the letters of introduction he carried. Paralysed by indecision, he leaned over a parapet, gazing at the Thames traffic, until he was a prey to 'aimless depression'. He did some sight-seeing, and spent some of his evenings at the Castle Tavern in High Holborn, kept by the famous pugilist 'Tom Spring'; here, according to one witness, Branwell was eloquent and much at home. When he returned to Haworth, he alleged that he had been robbed before he left London. What a contrast to his father – ambitious, principled, energetic, and determined to succeed – when he left Ireland for Cambridge!

He had twice offered his services to *Blackwood's Magazine* without reply. The death of James Hogg excited renewed hope, and in December 1835 he wrote again. 'Read what I write', he began. 'And would to Heaven you could believe it true, for then you would attend to and act upon it.' His letters were kept as curios, believed to be written by a madman. The poetry he wrote from 1835 to 1838, influenced largely by Scott and Byron, contains some of his best and most moving work.

There was not much to occupy him usefully outside the parsonage. He was secretary of the Haworth Temperance Society (of which his father was president) and a member of the Masons, for whom he occasionally acted as secretary. As a Sunday school teacher he was noted for impatience with slow pupils. His literary pretensions increased. Twice again he addressed the editor of *Blackwood's*. With the first letter, he sent his 'Misery' poem as a specimen for insertion; the second indicated that he was 'in possession of something, the design of which, whatever might be its execution, would be superior to that of any series of articles which has yet appeared in "*Blackwood's* Magazine"'. 'Do you think your Magazine so perfect that no addition to its power would be either possible or desirable?' he asked. In January 1837 he sent a sample of his poetry to Wordsworth. 'Surely, in this day, when there is not a *writing* poet worth a sixpence, the field must be open, if a better man step forward.' There was no response to any of his brash appeals.

The Hastings story which he continued became his confessional. Clearly there was criticism at home; he was drinking too heavily. The prose fragment known as 'Percy', in which Branwell presented one of his Angrian characters in a Haworth moorland setting and inn, reflects the company he was keeping. There is a tradition that he took a post as usher in a school near Halifax, and gave it up after a term; almost inevitably this provokes the question whether he was dismissed from such a post. In May 1838 he set up a studio in Bradford, where, it has been thought, his father's friend William Morgan could keep an eye on him. He lodged with the Kirbys of 3 Fountain Street. Mrs Kirby's niece remembered him well: he was short and slight in person; few people, apart from sitters, visited him; Charlotte came for a day, and her 'sisterly ways' were noticeable. Branwell went home at weekends, sometimes by coach to Keighley, sometimes walking across the moors. He was at home on 9 June when Mary and Martha Taylor were at the parsonage. 'They are making such a noise', wrote Charlotte, 'I cannot write any more. Mary is playing on the piano; Martha is chattering as fast as her little tongue can run; and Branwell is standing before her, laughing at her vivacity.'

While at Bradford, he met Hartley Coleridge, the sculptor J. B. Leyland, who remained his friend for life, and other artists such as the mezzotintist and engraver W. O. Geller, who had studied in London under John Martin. As time went on Branwell's work declined, and it is thought that J. H. Thompson may have helped to finish some of the portraits which are now considered his best. He spent a great deal of his time at inns and hotels, and earned the repute of being a brilliant conversationalist. How he managed financially is not known, but it is likely that he finished in debt. He was back at Haworth in May 1839, and very soon had begun a revision course in the classics with his father; it did not last very long. Charlotte also was at home, and her portrayal of Hastings at the time shows that, though she knew Branwell's faults, she had not yet lost faith in him. It was at this juncture, we are told, that he began to take opium, after reading De Quincey's *Confessions*. On the last day of the year, he left home to act as tutor to Mr Postlethwaite's sons at Broughton-in-Furness. He spent the night at the Royal Hotel, Kendal, where he celebrated New Year's Eve and took 'a half year's farewell of old friend whisky', according to the high-spirited letter, plentifully laced with braggadocio, which he wrote the following March to regale John Brown and other Haworth friends. It sheds an interesting light on the Byronic role Branwell pictured for himself *vis-à-vis* the ladies.

Branwell's new duties were not very exacting, and he had time to translate some of Horace's odes. He sent two of his translations and a poem to Hartley Coleridge for appraisal; the result was an invitation to Nab Cottage, once De Quincey's home, by Rydal Water. Perhaps Coleridge's hospitality, and the excitement engendered by his advice to complete the first book of the *Odes*, went to Branwell's head. He began to neglect his tutorial duties, ignore his good resolutions, and come home late, sometimes the worse for drink. In June he was dismissed, but was astute enough to persuade his father to write to Mr Postlethwaite, requesting his return home. There he met Mary Taylor again, and probably fell in love with her, as Charlotte seemed to admit (20.11.40): 'Did I not once tell you of an instance of a Relative of mine who cared for a young lady till he began to suspect that she cared more for him and then instantly conceived a sort of contempt for her?' (A similar development is admitted by Lockwood in the opening chapter of *Wuthering Heights*.) Branwell soon completed his Horace translations, and became very friendly with William Weightman, with whom he went shooting on the moors.

At the end of August he was appointed assistant clerk at the railway station about to be opened at Sowerby Bridge, on a new stretch of line connecting Leeds with Hebden Bridge, before the final link-up with the line from Manchester to Littleborough. In Halifax, two miles away, he had friends, including Leyland and the painter Wilson Anderson. According to William Heaton, a local poet, Branwell was

blithe and gay, but at times appeared downcast and sad; yet, if the subject were some topic that he was acquainted with, or some author he loved, he would rise from his seat, and, in beautiful language, describe the author's character, with a zeal and fluency I had never heard equalled. His talents were of a very exalted kind. I have heard him quote pieces from the bard of Avon, from Shelley, Wordsworth, and Byron, as well as from Butler's 'Hudibras', in such a manner as often made me wish I had been a scholar, as he was.

Branwell was promoted early in 1841, and at the beginning of April made station-master at Luddenden Foot, one mile further up the line towards Hebden Bridge. His salary was increased from £75 to £130 a year. Luddenden churchyard probably had an early interest for him, for there the body of William Grimshaw had been buried in his wife's grave, after being carried south over the moors from Haworth. On Sundays Branwell walked with Leyland and his new friend Francis Grundy in the beautiful steep wooded valleys and over the moors above, becoming familiar with Luddenden Dean, Midgley Moor and Wadsworth Moor, Hardcastle Crags, Crimsworth Dean, and Hebden Dale. In Luddenden there was little of interest. Branwell wrote poetry, and had some published in *The Halifax Guardian*, but he resorted more and more for relief to the Lord Nelson Inn. He may have been drawn sometimes to the important circulating library housed there, but convivial company, which could have included Liverpool Irishmen working on the railway, undoubtedly proved more attractive, despite the pious hopes which he expressed in verse. He neglected his duties until, at the end of a year, in March 1842, he was dismissed after a deficit of just over £11 had been found in his accounts.

Fortunately his sisters were absent when he returned home. He suffered from illness and depression, the effects of dissipation and shame. Weeks later, he informed Grundy that he was 'far superior' physically and mentally to 'that miserable wreck you used to know under my name', and capable of enjoying company 'without the stimulus of six glasses of whisky'. The death of William Weightman, and of Aunt Branwell, who had always been kind to him, upset Branwell very deeply. When Emily returned from Brussels to stay

The vicarage at Dewsbury where Patrick Brontë lodged

Patrick's first home after his marriage: Clough House, Hightown, Liversedge, a mile from his church at Hartshead

[1]

Woodhouse Grove Wesleyan Academy in 1812 or soon after. Here Patrick Brontë met Maria Branwell

Patrick and Maria became engaged at Kirkstall Abbey by the River Aire near Leeds

The parsonage at Thornton where Charlotte, Branwell, Emily, and Anne Brontë were born

The Old Bell Chapel, Patrick Brontë's church at Thornton

The parsonage and church at Haworth, as they were in the time of the Brontës

[5]

The Clergy Daughters' School at Cowan Bridge in 1824 or a little later

Tunstall Church, two miles away, where the girls attended Sunday services. They had their lunches in a room above the porch

The Rev. William Carus Wilson, founder of the Clergy Daughters'
School

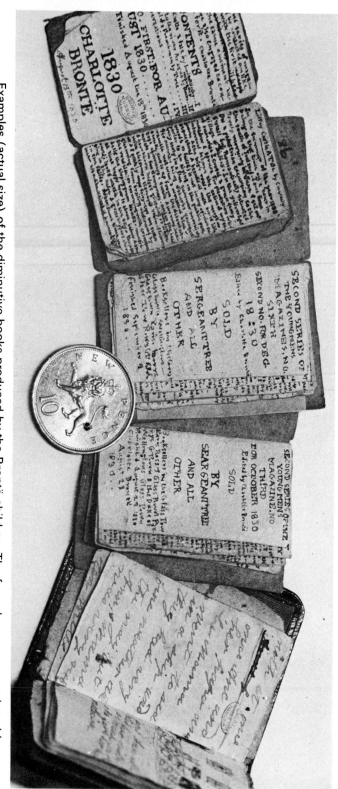

Examples (actual size) of the diminutive books produced by the Brontë children. The four above were produced by Charlotte. The three on the left belong to the second series of *The Young Men's Magazine;* on the right is an illustrated book which Charlotte may have composed at the age of eight (see p. 26)

Sketches by Branwell Brontë: the Duke of Zamorna and Alexander Percy

Miss Wooler's school at Roe Head

Rydings, Ellen Nussey's home at Birstall

The Red House, Gomersal, home of the Taylors and the 'Briar-mains' of *Shirley*

Rawfolds Mill, the scene of the Luddite attack which Charlotte Brontë used with reference to 'Hollow's Mill'

Hammond Roberson, a predecessor of Patrick Brontë at Hartshead. His opposition to Luddism cast him for the part of Mr Helstone in *Shirley*

at home, he was able to take up the post Anne had found him as tutor in the Robinson family at Thorp Green Hall (about midway between York and Ripon). It was his duty to teach an only son, who was almost eleven. *Agnes Grey* suggests that Anne had not been successful with this boy, and Branwell probably knew that to be a successful tutor he had to please an indulgent mother. Perhaps Mrs Robinson allowed herself to be fascinated by his genius and eloquence; she may have been so delighted with him that Branwell, wholly inexpert in a lady's flattery, and a prey to his excitable imagination, was soon convinced that she was in love with him. The truth seems to be lost irrecoverably. Only in the conclusion of the affair have we a few undisputed facts; beyond them it is impossible to tell where fiction begins or ends. How Branwell spent his time, and where, are a mystery; there is no evidence that he wrote much poetry at Thorp Green.

In July 1845, when his son joined the family at Scarborough, Mr Robinson wrote Branwell, who had returned to Haworth, a letter of dismissal. What disclosures led to this very sudden action, and by whom, must remain conjectural. We have only Branwell's story; his father and Charlotte believed him, and may have had what they regarded as convincing confirmation from Anne. It is doubtful, however, whether the story he told them coincided at all points with that revealed in his letters to Leyland and Grundy.

He asserted that Mrs Robinson had loved him from the first: in October 1845 he informed Grundy that for nearly three years he had daily experienced 'troubled pleasure soon chastised by fear'; in January 1847, four years after his first arrival at Thorp Green, he claimed that he and the lady had been intensely in love with each other during the whole of the intermediate period. The wildness of this exaggeration need not be emphasized, but we are still left to guess from what reality Branwell's self-delusion sprang, how far he could have been the victim of paranoiac fantasies, and how guilty he was of invention to cover up disgrace and deceive his friends. Did Mrs Robinson send over her coachman to inform Branwell that by her husband's will she would lose all her fortune if she married him? Did the doctor who attended Mr Robinson state that his wife's conduct was the cause of his death? Did Mrs Robinson send Branwell money at intervals? These are some of Branwell's most critical allegations. Mr Robinson's will shows the falsity of the first, and there is no evidence of the slightest discord between the Robinsons just before his death. Whatever the truth, there can be little doubt that Branwell had become habituated to fictive excuse; and it is not impossible that he worked on the credulity of his friends to borrow money for carousing, on the expectation he created of marrying a rich widow.

Branwell's dismissal made him seek refuge in drink and drugs; he was so distraught that his father persuaded John Brown to take him to the Welsh coast for a holiday. When he returned, Branwell began writing a novel for distraction. With characteristic hyperbole, he claimed that it was 'the result of years of thought', but all he achieved was the uneven fragment 'And the Weary are at Rest'. It presents himself and Mrs Robinson in the Angrian characters of Percy, Earl of Northangerland, and the heroine, Maria Thurston. The Thurstons' home is transferred to the Haworth moors, and Percy arrives at the beginning of the grouse season. Maria is a 'neglected' lady, terrified of her jealous husband. Then follows a farcical gallimaufry of Nonconformist scenes and observations, arising from Percy's hope that Mrs Thurston will hear of his religious zeal, and be convinced of his sincerity. She yields to his embrace. They leave the house for the shrubbery, and return, her 'raven tresses' in disarray. She cannot help herself, she says; her husband's neglect is her excuse, but she is as God formed her. 'I am Thine with whom to do what Thou pleasest – but I am another's also!' the inartistic fragment ends. Its climactic coincidence with one of the main events in *The Tenant of Wildfell Hall* suggests real and imaginary possibilities; Anne's shrubbery story may have been based on what she had heard from Branwell. There is a difference in the fictional accounts, however: Anne believes the lady was principally to blame; Branwell fancies himself as the seducer. How far, it might be asked, was he betrayed by his erotic imagination?[1]

He remained at home, often in a state of stupor. Emily thought he was 'a hopeless being'; he was capable of extorting money from his father on pretence of paying debts, and spending it at the Black Bull. According to a letter he wrote to J. B. Leyland (28.4.46), Branwell found his family unsympathetic:

> Home thoughts are not, with me,
> Bright, as of yore;
> Joys are forgot by me,
> Taught to deplore!

[1] See 'Further Thoughts on Branwell Brontë's Story', *BST*. lxxii.

> *My* home has taken rest
> In an afflicted breast
> Which I have often pressed,
>   But – may no more!

It was better to be dead. Such were his feelings, as he addressed an imaginary drowned corpse in the poem 'Real Rest':

> Thou longest not with one well loved to be,
> And absence does not break a chain with thee;
> . . .
> But, in exchange for thy untroubled calm,
> Thy gift of cold oblivion's healing balm,
> I'd give my youth, my health, my life to come,
> And share thy slumbers in thy ocean tomb.

The story goes that when Mr Robinson died, Branwell's joyful expectations were cut short, for the widow lost no time in sending her coachman over to warn him not to see her again; after his departure, Branwell was found in a fit on the floor of the Black Bull. Three weeks later, in June 1846, Charlotte wrote that he sometimes threatened to kill himself if his father did not give him money. Once, after retiring early, drink or opium overpowered him, and he let slip the periodical he was reading. It fell by the lighted candle, and he was found insensible with his bed curtains on fire. Emily immediately brought up one of the buckets of water kept in the hall as a fire precaution, and extinguished the flames. Thereafter he had to sleep, or spend his nights (for he often slept by day), in his father's bedroom. 'In the mornings young Brontë would saunter out, saying, with a drunkard's incontinence of speech, "The poor old man and I have had a terrible night of it; he does his best – the poor old man! but it's all over with me" (whimpering, "It's *her* fault, *her* fault").'[1]

Claims for his debts kept coming in, and his deterioration continued. His poetical efforts were short-lived, and he appeared to know nothing of his sisters' literary success.[2] He refused church attendance and the consolations of religion, but there was a change of heart just before

[1] G. xiii, 1st edition.
[2] F. A. Leyland thought he did.

his death on 24 September 1848. Six weeks later Mrs Robinson married the aged widower Sir Edward Dolman Scott.

A local rumour that Branwell stood up to die, his pockets full of Mrs Robinson's letters, was converted by Mrs Gaskell into unforgettable legend.[1]

[1] See p. 368.

Emily Jane Brontë

Of the Brontës it is Emily who, through her works, is most associated with Haworth and its moorland scenery. Little is known of her life. She was born at Thornton on 30 July 1818. Though she was 'the pet nursling of the school', the deep and overriding attachment to home which she seems to have felt all her life may have taken root at Cowan Bridge when she was only six. She and Anne participated in the creative drama initiated by Charlotte and Branwell in June 1826, but they must have found it impossible to maintain a lively interest in the fictional writing which ensued. The fascination of Arctic scenes, which may have originated in Bewick's introduction to the second volume of his *History of British Birds*, to be fostered by accounts of Parry's voyages, influenced Emily and Anne when they decided to set up in partnership, and leave Branwell to go his way, in 1831. Charlotte was at Roe Head, and Gondal fiction may have evolved from Anne's taking her place as Emily's bedroom companion, the two improvising play serials just as Charlotte and Emily had done.

Emily enjoyed listening to Tabitha Aykroyd in the kitchen, where she was often to be found in later years, baking or helping to prepare meals, a book propped up for study or reading whenever time allowed. It was 'Tabby' who came to the rescue when Emily broke off a branch of her father's favourite tree in the front garden, a flowering cherry which she had to climb for concealment one Oakapple Day, in the Brontë children's enactment of Charles II's escape. Tabby's application of soot to the gash in the trunk was not reassuring, for the children were unhappy until they had confessed. She took them for strolls, and they heard many stories from her in broad Yorkshire dialect. Emily was never happier than in the moorland country above Haworth. Its features and detail appear continually in her poetry, and it provided the setting for *Wuthering Heights*.

In her recollections of her stay at Haworth parsonage in the summer of 1833, Ellen Nussey described Emily as lithesome and graceful, the tallest of the Brontë children.[1]

> Her hair, which was naturally as beautiful as Charlotte's, was in the same unbecoming tight curl and frizz, and there was the same want of complexion. She had very beautiful eyes – kind, kindling, liquid eyes; but she did not often look at you; she was too reserved. Their color might be said to be dark gray, at other times dark blue, they varied so. She talked very little. She and Anne were like twins – inseparable companions, and in the very closest sympathy, which never had any interruption.

Together, they rambled

> over the moors, and down into the glens and ravines that here and there broke the monotony of the moorland. The rugged bank and rippling brook were treasures of delight. Emily, Anne, and Branwell used to ford the streams, and sometimes placed stepping-stones for the other two [Charlotte and Ellen]; there was always a lingering delight in these spots, – every moss, every flower, every tint and form, were noted and enjoyed. Emily especially had a gleesome delight in these nooks of beauty, – her reserve for the time vanished. One long ramble made in these early days was far away over the moors to a spot familiar to Emily and Anne, which they called 'The Meeting of the Waters'. It was a small oasis of emeral green turf, broken here and there by small clear springs; a few large stones served as resting-places; seated here, we were hidden from all the world, nothing appearing in view but miles and miles of heather, a glorious blue sky, and brightening sun.

Emily's sketches of wild life and pets show talent, but her musical gifts were great. 'The ability with which she took up music was amazing, the style, the touch and the expression was that of a Professor absorbed heart and soul in his theme', wrote Ellen Nussey. Her adolescent reading may be deduced from her Gondal poems, which show a familiarity with Border ballads, Scott's poetry and novels,

---

[1] She was not tall; her coffin measurements show that she was less than five and a half feet high.

Byron, and *Paradise Lost*; in one dramatic situation after another, they breathe the resolute defiance of Byronic heroes and Milton's Satan.

Emily began her brief period as a pupil at Roe Head on her seventeenth birthday. She was never reconciled to the school, happy as it was for most girls. As Charlotte was engaged to teach, the two sisters could rarely meet on equal terms. Emily was shy, unsociable, and lonely. Timetable restraints were irksome, and one can imagine her feelings on Sundays as she made her way in a procession of girls across the fields to the church at Mirfield and thought of her favourite haunts among the moors. Charlotte saw her pining for home, and her place at school was taken by Anne after hardly three months:

Liberty was the breath of Emily's nostrils; without it, she perished. The change from her own home to a school, and from her own very noiseless, very secluded, but unrestricted and inartificial mode of life, to one of disciplined routine (though under the kindliest auspices) was what she failed in enduring. Her nature proved here too strong for her fortitude. Every morning when she woke, the vision of home and the moors rushed on her, and darkened and saddened the day that lay before her. Nobody knew what ailed her but me – I knew only too well. In this struggle her health was quickly broken: her white face, attenuated form, and failing strength threatened rapid decline. I felt in my heart she would die, if she did not go home, and with this conviction obtained her recall.[1]

Emily had Branwell for company, after his disastrous mission to London, for the greater part of two years while Charlotte and Anne remained at Miss Wooler's school. Her education was not neglected: she continued her music; she taught herself German and French; she read and she wrote. When Tabby broke her leg just before Christmas 1836, the three girls insisted on looking after her, and when Charlotte returned to school with Anne, it was left to Emily to take charge of the kitchen. This she did willingly and well; she could combine the practical with her own world of musing and dreams. Of the Gondal literature only the poems remain. Emily wrote many in 1837, and some show very strikingly an urge to express herself in tragic romance.

[1] From the short memoir which Charlotte wrote for publication with her selection of Emily's poems in 1850.

Her study of German and French may indicate a resolve to teach. Possibly news of the post she accepted in the autumn of 1837 came from Miss Wooler and Charlotte. It was at Law Hill, a stoutly built, rather grim-looking three-storeyed stone house, with excellent out-buildings (one converted into the main classroom) in an exposed position on Southowram Bank, high up above Halifax. The school had a good reputation, and horse-riding was taught. Here Emily came into contact with the outside world probably more than at any other time in her life. She stayed about six months[1] and, though she found some of her work drudgery and is reputed to have told her class that she preferred the house-dog to any of them, she must have found life and Miss Patchett, the principal, congenial at times. She wrote poems; she found time to walk on the hills above the Shibden valley; she may even have ridden. Possibly she meditated non-Gondalian fiction, for the story of *Wuthering Heights* has much in common with the events which led to the building of Law Hill; and High Sunderland Hall, a remarkable building a mile further north, had architectural features which Emily included in her novel.

Apart from her poems, and the transcription of one of Branwell's ('The Wanderer', an early draft of 'Sir Henry Tunstall'),[2] hardly anything is known of Emily until 1840. The arrival of William Weightman, and the return of Anne from Blake Hall, marked the onset of a livelier, and even gay, period for the Brontë girls. Weightman, though a curate after Mr Brontë's heart, was full of fun; he was also a flirtatious Adonis. He sent valentines to the Brontës from Bradford; and, when Ellen Nussey was staying with them, arranged for a clergyman to invite them to tea, before bringing them to hear his classical lecture at the Mechanics' Institute in Keighley. The four girls walked eight miles there and back, returning at midnight with their two escorts. Aunt Branwell, who had prepared hot drinks for the 'home party' only, was not at all pleased, and (as Ellen Nussey recalled) 'Mr Weightman, who enjoyed teazing the old lady, was very thirsty. The great spirits of the walking party had a trying suppression, but twinkling fun

[1] The evidence that she was at Law Hill eighteen months is very inconclusive. More significant is the date of Emily's sketch of Keeper, 24 April 1838. The first term of the year was from January to June, and Charlotte's letter of 9 June 1838 shows that Emily was at home then. See footnote, p. 193.

[2] Not necessarily copied at Bradford, as has been thought. The date, 31 July 1838, almost certainly indicates when Branwell completed the poem at Bradford.

sustained some of them.' It was Emily's insistence on chaperoning Ellen and Weightman on moorland walks which earned her the sobriquet of 'The Major'. She had adopted the mastiff Keeper, her father's new house-dog, soon after her return from Law Hill. Her method of teaching him not to lie on beds shows an amazing combination of fearlessness and ferocity; she pummelled his eyes with her bare fists, and then bathed them tenderly. Brutal though the punishment was, it worked, and he was always devoted to her. Ellen Nussey remembered how she 'would delight in shewing off Keeper, make him frantic in action and roaring with the voice of a lion – it was a terrifying exhibition within the walls of an ordinary sitting room'. Her intrepidity was shown when she was bitten by a mad dog, and walked into the kitchen and cauterized the wound herself.

In 1841 she was once again the only one of the family at home with her father and aunt. Tabby had been compelled by lameness to retire to her sister's, and her place had been taken by Martha Brown, the sexton's young daughter, who always remembered Emily's kindness to her. Emily's quadrennial[1] birthday note of 1841 shows that the plan to set up a school under the management of Charlotte, herself, and Anne, had her unequivocal support. She felt it her duty to help her father pay the debts he had incurred to qualify them, Branwell particularly, for careers. With this in mind she agreed to accompany Charlotte to Brussels. Under M. Heger she worked assiduously at French, showing greater aptitude than Charlotte, and insisting on latitude for originality in composition. Her most striking essay shows an awareness of nature's cruelty which is almost Darwinian. The beauty of a flower about to be destroyed by a grub is an image of life; it makes her almost doubt the goodness of God. Life exists on 'a principle of destruction'. Then she is reminded that, just as the splendour of the butterfly evolves from the ugly grub, this world is 'the embryo of a new heaven and a new earth' surpassing all imagination. Another exercise stresses the hypocrisy, cruelty, and ingratitude of man. M. Heger told Mrs Gaskell that he was impressed by her

---

[1] This term does not apply to the first joint note of 24 November 1834, which looks forty years ahead. Each of the other three notes or sets of notes was intended for reference four years after it was written. The first of these is another joint composition by Emily and Anne, written on 26 June, Branwell's birthday, 1837. The others were exchanged by Emily and Anne in 1841 and 1845, on the former's birthday (30 July; Anne's second was written on 31 July 1845).

originality, strength of reason, imperious will, and imaginative power. 'She ought to have been a man – a great navigator', he thought.

Despite the original plan to stay for only the first half-year, the Brontës stayed on at the Pensionnat Heger, Charlotte to teach English part-time, and Emily to teach music to a few pupils. She made rapid progress in French, German, and drawing; and her excellence at the piano was such that the finest teacher in Brussels was engaged to give her lessons. Towards the end of September, Mary Taylor found them 'content' and 'even gay', and felt they had done right to remain. After her aunt's death, however, Emily thought there was no alternative but for her to stay at home. She was sorry to find that her pet birds, including Hero, the wounded hawk she had brought in from the moors, had been given away. Tabby was soon brought back; she was good company, and still able to give some assistance in the kitchen. Emily continued her studies as best she could, the plan for a Brontë school still in mind. The dates of her poems show that in Brussels Gondal had not been forgotten, and that she returned to it with renewed zest early in 1843. Whether for amusement or as a protective precaution, Mr Brontë encouraged her to practise firing with his pistols in the front garden. He enjoyed her music so much that, after her death, he could not bear the agony of the loss her piano awakened, and had it removed from his room.

In February 1844, a month after Charlotte's return from Brussels, Emily began copying her poems in two notebooks, one kept specially for the Gondal poems. The attempt to set up a school at the parsonage failed, and by her birthday in 1845 Emily could record that neither she nor her sisters had 'any great longing for it. We have cash enough for our present wants, with a prospect of accumulation.' Aunt Branwell's legacies reconciled them to one disappointment, and they were able to turn their thoughts to writing. At the end of June 1845, soon after Anne had resigned from her post at Thorp Green, she and Emily took their first 'long journey' together, on a visit to York. During the excursion they played the parts of eight characters, all 'escaping from the palaces of instruction to join the Royalists who are hard driven at present by the victorious Republicans. The Gondals still flourish bright as ever.' That was Emily's view on her birthday a month later. Anne's was rather different: 'The Gondals in general are not in first-rate playing condition.' She wondered if they could improve; she herself had already begun a more serious kind of fiction. Despite Branwell's dismissal, Emily was in buoyant mood: 'seldom or never troubled with nothing to do, and merely desiring that every-body could be as comfortable as myself and as undesponding, and then we should have a very tolerable world of it'. During the year she wrote some of her greatest poetry.

It was in the autumn that Charlotte 'accidentally lighted on' her Gondal book, and was so impressed that her thoughts turned immedi-ately to publication. Emily was furious that her secret had been discovered, and refused to consider her sister's proposal for many days. She probably began, or resumed, *Wuthering Heights* at this time, for only one of her poems belongs to the period from 9 October 1845 to 14 September 1846, and in April 1846 Charlotte wrote to the firm which was publishing her selection of poems by Currer, Ellis, and Acton Bell, asking if they were interested in the publication of three 'distinct and unconnected tales' by these authors. By the beginning of March 1846, Emily had given up Branwell as 'a hopeless being'.

The three novels were posted to a publisher on 4 July 1846, the day that *Poems by Currer, Ellis, and Acton Bell* was published. Although one reviewer praised the 'inspiration' of Ellis (Emily), the public showed no interest. It was not until June 1847 that *Wuthering Heights* and *Agnes Grey* found a publisher in T. C. Newby. He was neither honest nor generous; he insisted on a payment of £50 and made no attempt to press on with the printing until *Jane Eyre* created a sensation in October. Proof-sheet corrections were not made, and the books were 'not well got up'. Charlotte urged her sisters to change their publisher, but they refused. Emily's independence could be stubborn. The success of Charlotte's novel made Newby advertise in a manner calculated to persuade readers that Ellis Bell had written *Jane Eyre*.

The reviewers were almost unanimous in condemning the 'dis-agreeable' and 'diabolical' elements in *Wuthering Heights*, and Emily's depression weighed heavily on the more favoured Charlotte. Nevertheless, the demand for the book grew, and Emily probably inquired early in 1848 about the acceptance of her second novel.[1] Some support for this view is found in Charlotte's 'Biographical

---

[1] It has been suggested that the work proposed was *The Tenant of Wildfell Hall*, and that Newby was confused about the identity of Ellis and Acton Bell. Newby's letter (15.2.48) implies, however, that the writer's first novel had been a success, and this could hardly be said of *Agnes Grey*.

Notice of Ellis and Acton Bell', where she says that neither allowed herself to sink under want of encouragement. 'They were both prepared to try again. . . . But a great change approached; affliction came. . . . In the very heat and burden of the day, the labourers failed over their work.' More cogent is the evidence of Charlotte's letter (7.12.48), in which she wrote that, if Ellis lived, he reserved to himself 'the right of deciding whether or not Mr Newby has forfeited every claim to his second work'. Newby had not, in fact, shown an excess of enthusiasm about it. He had counselled the writer not to complete it too hurriedly: 'if it be an improvement on your first you will have established yourself as a first-rate novelist, but if it fall short the critics will be too apt to say that you have expended your talent in your first novel'.

Of Emily's writing after 1846, only one short poem is left. Whether she or Charlotte destroyed the remainder is not known. It is a commonplace to say that she is sphinx-like in her remoteness. 'Stronger than a man, simpler than a child, her nature stood alone', Charlotte wrote. Like Byron's Childe Harold, she had not loved the world. She may have known that her life was fleeting, and have dismissed the desire of fame as a vanity. Her last outing was to Branwell's funeral. The cold she caught accelerated her decline. She refused medical aid, preferring to endure and look forward to spiritual freedom. Only just before the end did she agree to see a doctor. She died on 19 December 1848. How long she had suffered from consumption is not known; Dr Wheelhouse guessed, and wrote, '2 months' duration'.

Anne Brontë

Anne was born at Thornton on 17 January 1820, three months before the Brontës removed to Haworth. Miss Firth of Kipping House was one of her godparents, and Mr Brontë's friend William Morgan, incumbent of Christ Church, Bradford, baptized her, as he had done her three elder sisters, Maria, Charlotte, and Emily. Anne, who lost her mother when she was eight months old, was a delicate child, subject to asthma. Aunt Branwell travelled to Yorkshire for the second time in May, and remained one of the family at Haworth until her death in 1842; Anne and Branwell were her favourite children.

Without a shred of evidence, modern biographers have followed a lead in presenting Aunt Branwell as a severe Methodist with strong Calvinistic tendencies which had disastrous effects on the Brontë children. It is highly improbable that there were fundamental religious differences between her and Patrick Brontë, who remained liberal in outlook and preached a gospel of forgiveness. Anne was endowed with an unusually sensitive religious conscience. She may have read poems by William Cowper in *The Methodist Magazine* when she was young; like Branwell and her sisters, she could not forget 'The Castaway'. The general tolerance of Mr Brontë's home and her close ties with Emily would ensure that Anne was free to judge for herself in religious matters, however. 'That's right', commented Emily, when Mary Taylor argued that religion was solely a matter between God and the individual.

What Anne made at first of the plays which began with Branwell's toy soldiers is hard to imagine, but soon she was participating in the romps and shrieks which reached such a pitch on one occasion that Tabby thought the parson's children were 'all goo'in mad'. At the age of seven, when 'The Play of the Islanders' was started, Anne chose for the chief characters of her island Michael Sadler, Lord Bentinck, and Sir Henry Halford. The knowledge of these children, whether derived from their father, books, magazines, newspapers, or family discussions on events and personalities of the day, was amazingly odd and adult. Much was done, no doubt, to involve Anne; Branwell and Charlotte drew pictures to amuse her, and it may have been specially for her that Charlotte wrote and illustrated her first story. How soon the Brontë children had drawing lessons is not clear, but Emily and Anne began copying birds from Bewick in 1829; perhaps his Arctic descriptions initiated an interest which made them choose Parry and Ross as explorers in the African fiction they began to share with Charlotte and Branwell. How much they wrote, particularly Anne, is conjectural; nothing remains of their early attempts at fiction, and of the vast Gondal-Gaaldine complex of stories which they began in 1831 only the poems remain.

Ellen Nussey found her 'dear' and 'gentle' in 1833, and 'quite different in appearance from the others. . . . Her hair was a very pretty, light brown, and fell on her neck in graceful curls. She had lovely violet-blue eyes, fine pencilled eyebrows, and clear, almost transparent complexion. She still pursued her studies, and especially her sewing, under the surveillance of her aunt. Emily had now begun to have the disposal of her own time.' The two were inseparable, like twins. In 1834 they were taught music, and subsequently they received lessons in sketching and painting from William Robinson when he came to teach Branwell. Anne's sketches often show an exceptionally delicate talent and finish.

She appreciated the friendliness of Miss Wooler's school, and was a diligent pupil: but she would have preferred the company of Emily, and longed for a greater intimacy with Charlotte, which was almost inevitably denied by the awkwardnesses of the teacher-pupil relationship. Anne's godmother, now Mrs Franks, wife of the vicar of Huddersfield, invited the sisters to stay with her for a week in July 1836, at the end of their first term together: they went reluctantly, wishing to be at home. At the vicarage, they met the Walker family: they spent a day at their home, Lascelles Hall, outside Huddersfield, and found Amelia, one of the daughters who had been a pupil with Charlotte at Roe Head, unbearably affected.

At Roe Head the following winter, Anne was ill and depressed; Charlotte, distracted between irritating duties and the lure of her

Angrian dream-world, and haunted by a sinful sense of both deficiency and indulgence, was incapable of giving her much companionship or comfort. Anne therefore requested a visit from a Moravian minister at Mirfield, who found that she needed a conviction of God's love and forgiveness. Late in 1837, after the removal of Miss Wooler's school to Heald's House, Dewsbury Moor, her health was undermined once again: Charlotte, beside herself with worry and overwork, was critical, and Miss Wooler promptly wrote to Mr Brontë, who judged that it was best for both his daughters to return home immediately, before the Christmas recess. Anne did not go back to school; she was rejoined by Emily from Law Hill early in the spring of 1838, and by Charlotte in May. After her recuperation and a period of immersion in Gondal romance, Anne decided that she would be a governess; she thought she would be happy with young children. It was typical of her that she insisted on going alone; 'she thought she could manage better and summon more courage if thrown entirely upon her own resources'. Her experiences at Blake Hall, Mirfield, are reflected in the first part of *Agnes Grey*. In the face of Mrs Ingham's over-indulgence of her children, Anne could do little, and her engagement was terminated just before the Christmas holiday of 1839, after eight months' service.

All three sisters were at home in 1840, and life was the jollier for a time in the company of William Weightman. How deeply Anne fell in love with him is not clear, even from her poetry. In March 1841 she took up her appointment as governess at Thorp Green Hall, at £50 a year, twice her salary at Mirfield. Once again she was to be disillusioned. The girls were spoilt and pleasure-loving; their outlook, like their mother's, was social and self-seeking; their interest in education, their concern for principles, was never strong. There were three girls and one boy, Edmund, in the Robinson family, and all regarded the governess as an inferior. In a thinly populated country area, she was isolated. York Minster and views of the sea at Scarborough during their July holiday raised her spirits. Her birth-day note, however, states very firmly that she disliked her situation and wished to change it. Anne and her sisters hoped to set up their own school. She was still contributing to the Gondal saga, 'writing the fourth volume of *Solala Vernon's Life*'.

The fruition of her hopes postponed by the Brussels venture, Anne's main refuge from the dreariness of life at Thorp Green must have been found in writing and study. When she returned home in the summer of 1842 she found Branwell unemployed and in disgrace. It was a shock to hear in September that his friend 'Willy' Weightman was dead (he was buried in Haworth Church):

> Yes, thou art gone! and never more
> Thy sunny smile shall gladden me;
> But I may pass the old church door,
> And pace the floor that covers thee,
>
> May stand upon the cold, damp stone,
> And think that, frozen, lies below
> The lightest heart that I have known,
> The kindest I shall ever know.

Like Charlotte and Emily in Brussels, she heard too late of her aunt's illness to attend her funeral. After the Christmas holiday, she returned to Thorp Green with Branwell, who was to tutor Edmund Robinson. All seemed to bode well when Mr Brontë came to see them in April 1843. The Robinsons had presented Flossy, a King Charles spaniel, to Anne, and she brought it home probably in the summer. The plan for a school at the parsonage came to nothing, much to her sorrow; she had intensified her studies in Latin, German, and music with this in mind. Mrs Robinson's growing lack of control over her daughters, and Branwell's indiscretions, led to her resignation in June 1845. Her quadrennial note records her 'escape' from Thorp Green: if she had known when she had written her last that she had to serve four years longer there, 'how wretched I should have been; but during my stay I have had some very unpleasant and undreamt-of experience of human nature'. She always thought that Branwell was a foolish victim of Mrs Robinson's wiles.

One of the first things she did after her return home was to persuade Emily that she must see York Minster. The visit took place while Charlotte was with Ellen Nussey at Hathersage. The Gondals still flourished 'bright as ever', Emily wrote, but Anne had tacit reservations; she had begun her third volume of *Passages in the Life of an Individual*, which suggests that she was writing from her own experience and considering more serious fiction than Emily's. Charlotte made a selection of Anne's poems for inclusion in *Poems by Currer, Ellis, and Acton Bell*, the publication of which encouraged all three to write novels. *Agnes Grey*, like *Wuthering Heights* and *The Professor*, approached completion in April 1846.

Anne's view of life as a governess was darkened by the rapid degeneration of Branwell at home. 'Sick of mankind and their disgusting ways', she wrote in her prayerbook. The effects of dissoluteness preyed on her idealistic mind, and she felt it her duty to write *The Tenant of Wildfell Hall*. Published in June 1848, it was an immediate success.

Anne had suffered from colds and asthma more acutely since the winter of 1846–7. She spent most of the summer months indoors, working on her second novel – an ill preparation for the 'cruel east wind' of the winter that followed. The soaking she received on the walk to Keighley, when she and Charlotte made their sudden London visit, to repudiate Newby's cunning claim that *The Tenant of Wildfell Hall* was a second work by the famed author of *Jane Eyre*, undoubtedly contributed to her decline. Charlotte was just as uneasy about her health as about Emily's after the death of Branwell in September 1848. The loss of Emily was cruel, but it did not sap Anne's moral strength. She lived by faith and determination. Unlike Emily, she accepted medical aid. Dr Teale, a Leeds specialist, was summoned. It was too late; both lungs were affected. When he had gone, Mr Brontë came in; 'seating himself on the couch, he drew Anne towards him and said, "My *dear* little Anne". That was all – but it was understood.' Two days later Anne began the poem 'Last Lines'.

She remained patient, and appeared to improve in health. She wished desperately to live, and had hopes that a visit to the seaside would prolong her life. 'I long to do some good in the world before I leave it. I have many schemes in my head for future practice, humble and limited indeed, but still I should not like them all to come to nothing, and myself to have lived to so little purpose.' Dr Teale recommended Scarborough. Previously he had forbidden travel; his change of mind was a concession of mercy. She went, with Charlotte and Ellen Nussey, to stay where she had been on former visits,[1] calling at York to see the Minster again. She was dying, recognizably so, but insisted on walking, and driving, on the sands, alone at times. As she weakened, a doctor was called; there could be no question of

[1] At Wood's Lodgings, the main buildings shown on plate 24, with, it seems, some additional houses (to the right). Each suite had its 'housekeeper'; Charlotte had booked one (address: No. 2, The Cliff) overlooking the sea. On the evening before her death, Anne was drawn to the window by a wonderful view of the bay and castle in a sunset glow (G. xvii).

returning home. Anne was not afraid; she asked Charlotte to take courage, and died serenely and peacefully on 28 May 1849. She was buried in St Mary's churchyard, below Scarborough Castle.

PART II

Angria and Gondal

It is impossible to present a clear, consecutive picture of the early writings of the Brontës. Miss Fannie Ratchford, whose work on the subject provides the best available conspectus, studied 'in originals or copies more than a hundred manuscripts by Charlotte and her brother Branwell'. In volume they were found to equal all the previously published work of the Brontë sisters. Some of the books microscopically handprinted by Charlotte and Branwell exist only in fragments; some are lost; and all the Gondal prose of Emily and Anne appears to have been destroyed. What survives shows in particular Charlotte's evolution as a writer, and throws light on the impulses, released or restrained, which were working in the direction of her mature novels.

The Lilliputian lettering, and the diminutive proportions of the first handmade volumes in which the Brontës wrote were intended to correspond in size to the twelve wooden soldiers (bought for Branwell in June 1826) which represented the imaginary characters they played. First, with Charlotte and Branwell as Wellington and Napoleon, they used them to act out battles. Then followed, over a lengthy period, three series of plays, 'open' or 'secret' (the latter being jointly imagined by Charlotte and Emily in bed):[1] first came *Young Men*; then, influenced by the fables of Aesop, *Our Fellows*; then, in December 1827, *The Islanders*.

For *The Islanders* each of the Brontë children had three heroes;

---

[1] Though Charlotte's lettering is inconsistent, the 't' and 'd' formations in the first half of her note on the origin of the plays favour 'bed', not 'best'. 'Best plays' would not need an explanation such as we have for 'bed plays': 'Bed plays mean secret plays.'

Charlotte's were the Duke of Wellington and his two sons, Arthur and Charles. From British islands they changed the setting to a fictitious one, where Charlotte imagined a palatial school; only nobility were admitted, and children who misbehaved were confined to dungeons, rather like the cellars at Haworth parsonage. Travels such as those of Mungo Park, contemporary fighting between the Ashantis and the British, and Mr Brontë's copy of *A Grammar of General Geography*, suggested a new setting for events on a grand scale. After a battle on Ascension Island, the twelve adventurers were shipwrecked near the mouth of the Niger. So sanguinary was Branwell's appetite that the girls were allowed to restore to life any of the twelve soldiers who had been killed. Influenced by *The Arabian Nights*, the four players became protective genii: Talli(i), Branni(i), Emmi(i), Anni(i). After defeating negro forces, the heroes built a great city. Further conquests led to the establishments of four territories named after the children's leaders; Charlotte's was still Wellington, Branwell's was now Sneaky, and Emily and Anne had chosen the Arctic explorers, Edward Parry and John Ross. The four states formed a confederation, each with a Glass Town for its capital, named after the original city, the seat of central government, now known as Great Glass Town (later Verreopolis or Verdopolis) from the glass-like harbour which reflected its gigantic buildings.

Branwell devised a series of magazines based on *Blackwood's*. One announced a forthcoming issue on Ossian's poems, a copy of which had been presented him (Sergeant Bud) by Genius Tally on 22 May 1829. In July he relinquished the editorship to Charlotte, and began a newspaper. The next numbers appeared under the title of *Blackwood's Young Men's Magazine*. Charlotte wrote sometimes as Arthur, sometimes as Charles, the eldest sons of the Duke of Wellington; at other times she was Captain Tree. She gave Arthur the title of Marquis of Douro (which Wellington gained in 1814); when he became her hero, she usually wrote under the nom-de-plume of Charles Wellesley. In 'Characters of the Celebrated Men of the Present Time', the Marquis has already acquired the dominant characteristics of Byron in *Childe Harold*. Some of these sketches were written at the expense of Branwell: as Young Soult, the Rhymer, he is an imaginative but poor versifier; as Captain Bud, the ablest political writer of his time, he is bombastic and tiresome despite his unsurpassed knowledge; as Sergeant Bud, his father's own son, he deserves to be hanged and his body given to surgeons for dissection.

The inference is that Charlotte and Branwell were reading the 'Noctes Ambrosianae' in *Blackwood's Magazine*, where John Wilson condemned the practice of body-snatching as a trade for the benefit of anatomical students.[1]

At the age of fourteen, Charlotte was writing short stories, some of which were dissociated from the Glass Town epic. She wrote fluently in prose and verse. Here, in the person of Albion, is the youthful forerunner of the Marquis of Douro:

> his stature was lofty; his form equal in the magnificence of its proportions to that of Apollo Belvedere. The bright wealth and curls of his rich brown hair waved over a forehead of the purest marble in the placidity of its unveined whiteness.

'The Rivals', a brief excursion in drama, begins:

> 'Tis eve: how that rich sunlight streameth through
> The inwoven arches of this sylvan roof!
> How those long, lustrous lines of light illume,
> With trembling radiance, all the agèd boles
> Of elms majestic as the lofty columns
> That proudly rear their tall forms to the dome
> Of old cathedral or imperial palace!

Charlotte found that Parrysland (Emily's realm) was predominantly Yorkshire in character, with factories, houses in rows, and roast beef, Yorkshire pudding, mashed potatoes, and apple pie for dinner. She was disdainful; her own conceptions were magnificently romantic, and her verse more and more imitative of the romantic poets, Byron above all. When she returned from Miss Wooler's for Christmas 1831, what was almost certainly a *fait accompli* was duly acknowledged; the dissolution of the partnership between the four genii was proclaimed, and Charlotte marked the occasion with a Byronic flourish ('The Trumpet hath Sounded'), recalling 'The Destruction of Sennacherib'. So Glass Town was doomed:

> Mute, mute are the mighty, and chilled is their breath,
> For at midnight passed o'er them the Angel of Death!
> The king and the peasant, the lord and the slave,
> Lie entombed in the depth of one wide solemn grave.

---

[1] This practice is referred to in a rather slight fictional sketch by Charlotte, written on 17–18 June 1830 and recently published. See *TLS.*, 23 November 1973.

Charlotte could now indulge her proclivities for romantic fiction
more freely; Emily and Anne were happier together; and Branwell
had revelled in independence for some time.

Inspired by books of travel and accounts of battles in the Napoleonic
War, he had written chronicles of the new empire in prose sometimes
enriched with sonorous Biblical echoes and Homeric allusions, and
more often characterized by a rhythmical fluency remarkable for a
boy of thirteen. He delighted in bloodshed and the horrific, and used
sudden balking tactics to heighten suspense. Arthur Wellesley had
climbed a rock to look for game, when he caught sight of the Ashantee
army moving along a valley towards the city:

> Instantly he seized his gun and, darting with the rapidity of an
> arrow, reached its gates in much less than half an hour, having
> run the whole distance of 6 miles in that space of time! When he
> had arrived, he instantly alarmed the rest, who had scarce time to
> bar the gates and man the walls before the Ashantees came on the
> city like an overwhelming torrent. But, before I proceed with my
> narrative, I must give some account of this army . . .

Similarly, but in grander style, he leads up to a historical account
of events in Europe which made the new realm militarily strong:

> We are now in the course of our History approaching times
> pregnant with events wonderful in their causes, operations and
> effects, times to which there is no parallel in the History of the
> World, events in which we behold a nation consisting at first of
> twelve young men becoming at length a nation, the greatest, the
> most powerful, most warlike and most magnificent in the whole
> world – a nation before whom Persia, Greece, Rome and England
> must hide their diminished heads and to which the whole world
> pays homage and is subject to; but before I begin to write of these
> events . . .

The Duke of Wellington, after a long absence to free Europe from
Napoleon, had returned with his army and been crowned King. This
happened on 30 November 1790!

Branwell, concentrating on fictional history, continued his saga
with 'Letters from an Englishman' who was visiting the new state.
The Tower of Nations, which 'soars from the vale and midway leaves
the storm' as if disdaining the lower world, is beyond all description.
The visitor, a London banker named James Bellingham, is saved from

being dissected alive – a reference to the murders committed by Hare and Burke, who sold their victims to the surgeon Dr Knox. It is a time of rebellion, led by Alexander Rogue. In Great Glass Town the fighting is on the same vast scale as the city, and millions are slain. Bellingham is about to be executed when relief forces arrive. His account ends with the Olympic or Great African Games, where an assembly of five to six million join in 'An Ode in Praise of the Twelves' to an orchestral accompaniment of ten thousand instruments. Rare lads and poachers, for whom Branwell is already showing partiality, are moved to tears. The Twelves are the twelve founders and leaders of the confederated states, who had rescued their land from the perils and wars inflicted by the presiding genii. Branwell's ode shows unusual power and facility for a boy who was hardly fourteen.

Charlotte resumed her fiction soon after her return from Roe Head in May 1832. 'The Bridal' describes an attempt by the mad Zenobia Ellrington on the life of the Marquis of Douro when he was about to marry Marian Hume. It was at the time of Rogue's rebellion, which Charlotte relates to industrial unrest reminiscent of events in the Roe Head region at the time of the Luddite revolt. Branwell resumed his 'Letters from an Englishman' with a new rebellion, butchery 'in the style of Bonaparte's battles', and further horrors on a spectacular scale. He anticipated Hardy in presenting 'a bird's eye' view of a field of battle from a cathedral tower. The Marquis, his eyes straining as if they would burst, and blazing with maniacal lustre, made a last desperate attempt to save the day:

> With one mighty effort he broke his bands like packthreads, seized the first sword he found with an energy that made the blood spring out at his finger nails, and threw himself on the thickest of Rogue's troops.

Rogue was shot by a firing squad, only to be resuscitated in 'The Pirate', a story of horrors at sea, concluding with his pardon and marriage to Zenobia Ellrington.

In 1833 Charlotte wrote at unprecedented length. 'The Secret' and 'Lily Hart', two stories which belong to that prolific year, were found in Washington in 1973. Rogue appears as Alexander Percy in 'The Green Dwarf', in the later part of which the influence of Scott's *Ivanhoe* is strong. It is the last story in which the Duke of Wellington plays an important part. For his villainy Percy was sentenced to death, then exiled for sixteen years. Thinly disguised, Branwell is an object of humour and ridicule; at the end, he is given a minor heroic role. The Green Dwarf, who had been Percy's evil agent, worked as a printer's devil after his return from the galleys, published 'drivelling rhymes' and 'snivelling tales', and became Captain Tree. Just as Emily Brontë wrote poems without observing the chronological sequence of the Gondal saga, taking any situation which appealed to her for her subject, so Charlotte was free to invent tales in relation to events of any period in the chronicles of the historian Branwell. Her narrative construction is naïve: 'It may be as well to connect the broken thread of my rambling narrative before I proceed further.' The disruptions continue, yet 'The Green Dwarf' builds up to a sequence of surprises.

In 'The Foundling', another ambitious story by Charlotte in 1833, Edward Sydney, the hero, was such an accomplished scholar that both Cambridge and Oxford 'opened their portals for his still on-journeying spirit'. When he had 'grasped the higher academic honours' at 'the latter temple of learning', he was called mysteriously to the new African colony. There as a senator he spoke successfully against the rebellious Rogue, and fell in love with the Marquis of Douro's cousin, Lady Julia Wellesley. Her refusal of Sir James Avon in marriage coincided with Sydney's restoration after his mysterious disappearance along with other leaders. He had been taken by the Duke of Wellington to the Philosopher's Island, where a secret society met in a vaulted subterranean college presided over by Byron's magician Manfred. It was revealed that the Marquis had been poisoned by Lord Ellrington (Rogue) and his accomplice. At the wish of the four Genii he had been restored to life; so too had his murderers at the request of Branii. The Duke disclosed that Sydney was the son of Frederick the Great, King of the Twelves, who had been slain in the battle against the Ashantees at Rossendale Hill. He was made Prince Edward of York, and married Julia.

Branwell was creating a new turn of interest in his heroine, Maria Henrietta (or Mary) Percy, daughter of Rogue. She visits the Marquis, whose poetry she admires, and he falls in love with her. The Marchioness conveniently dies (though later Charlotte refers to her as living and forlorn). Charlotte realized that the Marquis of Douro needed a different type of wife to accept his Byronic temperament and retain his affection.

The elevation of Rogue to the earldom of Northangerland, and the marriage of his daughter to the Marquis resulted in a reconciliation between the most powerful parties in the confederation. Branwell had insisted on a Napoleonic invasion; as a reward for his defeat of the French, the Marquis was given a large province to the east. It was called Angria, and its capital Adrianopolis was built on the Calabar river. In turn the Marquis became Duke of Zamorna (from the city of Zamora, on the Duero – the Douro river – in Spain), King of Angria, and Emperor Adrian. Here is Charlotte's picture of him:

> Keen, glorious being! tempered and bright and sharp and rapid as the scimitar at his side when whirled by the delicate but vigorous hand that now grasps the bridle of a horse to all appearance as viciously beautiful as himself. O Zamorna! what eyes those are glancing under the deep shadow of that raven crest! They bode no good. Man nor woman could ever gather more than a troubled, fitful happiness from their kindest light. Satan gave them their glory to deepen the midnight gloom that always follows where their lustre has fallen most lovingly. . . . All here is passion and fire unquenchable. Impetuous sin, stormy pride, diving and soaring enthusiasm, war and poetry, are kindling their fires in all his veins, and his wild blood boils from his heart and back again like a torrent of new-sprung lava.

Charlotte's 'The Spell' is a story of gramarye influenced by Scott. A dwarf seems to have mysterious power. Zamorna recovers when almost, it appears, at death's door; and his wife's jealousy is proved idle on the discovery that he has a married twin brother who is his double. The son of Zamorna and Marian has died, and we are given a vivid picture of the loyalty of his nurse, Mina Laury, to the Duke.

In 'The Wool is Rising', which Branwell completed in June 1834, we meet Edward and William Percy, sons of the Earl of Northangerland. He had ordered their death at birth, but they had been secreted away. After many hardships and attempts to improve their fortunes, Edward set up as a woolcomber in Verdopolis with his brother William and a Timothy Steaton. In a short time they were so successful that they bought a mill. At this juncture Edward assumed the management, and William (who was to marry one of the six rich Seymour girls of 'The Spell') and 'the mean and grovelling Timothy' became his subordinates. All this Charlotte recalled when she planned the opening of *The Professor*.

Among the less ambitious but more amusing of her writings at this time are some trifles which turn to Haworth for relief. The place-names are hardly disguised. Lord Charles Wellesley, making a series of calls in Verdopolis, proceeds from Thornton Hotel to Howard Square, and there the conversation suggests a rebuke to Branwell for associating with low company at the Black Bull. His portrait in Patrick Benjamin Wiggins is unmistakable. He has 'a bush of carroty hair so arranged that at the sides it projected almost like two spread hands', and a pair of spectacles on 'a prominent Roman nose'. He tells Lord Charles that he was 'born partly at Thorncliffe, that is after a fashion', but was a native of Howard, 'a great city among the Warner Hills'. Lord Charles tells him that it is 'a miserable little village, buried in dreary moors and moss-hags and marshes', and questions whether it has anything 'nearer an hotel than that wayside ale-house you are now eyeing so longingly'. Wiggins says that his sisters are honoured in having him as a brother: they are Charlotte, [Emily] Jane, and Anne. Charlotte is eighteen, 'a broad dumpy thing'; Emily, sixteen, 'lean and scant'; and Anne, 'nothing, absolutely nothing'. Reference is made to the installation of the organ at Haworth Church in May 1834. One feels, amid all the romantic Byronism that emerged from Charlotte's 'divine silent unseen land of thought', there was a vein of high-spirited farce and comic satire which she could have used to good effect in her novels. She concludes 'My Angria and the Angrians' with 'an earthquake of exultation' from the cannons announcing the birth of twin sons to the Duchess, and a celebratory song which begins and ends:

> Hurrah for the Gemini! blessed be the star!
> That shone on the streams of the blue Calabar,
> When the hills of the East and the woods of the West
> Bore light for their banner, and flame for their crest,
> As the wind its glad tidings exultingly blew,
> That if Rome had one monarch, our Angria has two!

Branwell was busy with his history of Angria when Charlotte went to teach at Roe Head in the summer of 1835. He was working up to civil war, and kept his sister informed about the course of events. On a stormy evening in February 1836, her thoughts turned from the dining-room where she sat to 'the war-shaken shores of the Calabar'; lost to her surroundings, she saw 'the defiled and violated Adrianopolis shedding its lights on the river from lattices whence the invader looked out'. Branwell wrote as Captain Henry Hastings, but only fragments of his chronicles have survived. Despite the warnings of his First Lord of the Treasury, Zamorna had formed an alliance with the Earl of Northangerland. A political crisis was suggested by contemporary events in England after the resignation of Peel in May 1835. While at home for Easter 1836, Charlotte, writing as Charles Townsend, contributed 'Passing Events' to the account of the Angrian crisis. It is a miscellany of prose and poetry, in a remarkable variety of styles. Lady Julia is now the wife of General Thornton, whose Doric accent is plainly Yorkshire. Mina Laury is intent on following her master to battle; hearing his voice, she 'sped like a roe over the sward' to his room, and took off his helmet:

> The Duke smiled faintly as her little fingers played about his chin and luxuriant whiskers, and then, the load of brass and sable plumage being removed, as they arranged the compressed masses of glossy brown ringlets, and touched with soft cool contact his feverish brow. Absorbed in the grateful task she hardly felt that his majesty's arm had encircled her waist, and yet she did feel it too, and would have thought herself presumptuous to shrink from the endearment. She took it as a slave ought to take the caress of a sultan, and obeying the gentle effort of his hand, slowly sunk on to the sofa by her master's side.

A change of scene takes us to a Wesleyan chapel, where we meet Timothy Steaton, with his brow expressive of nothing beyond 'low scowling depravity', and hear the preacher pray in a mode that suggests that Charlotte had recently attended a Wesleyan service at Haworth.

When war was inevitable, Zamorna had threatened to strike where he could hurt Northangerland most, at the heart of his daughter, the Queen. She insisted on being escorted incognito by Warner from Verdopolis to meet her husband in Angria. Warner tries in vain to change Zamorna's heart, and tells him Calvinistically that he has 'no place among the elect of God'. He then announces that there is a lady in the next room to see him. Zamorna is furious to find that she is his wife but, despite his ire, knows that there is nobody he loves more. In the last of Charlotte's shifting scenes, we learn that Zamorna has been defeated. Branwell found gratification in presenting horrible war scenes after the fighting. Zamorna was banished to Ascension Island, and his wife lay dying. A poem in Byronic *ottava rima* which was written by Charlotte in July 1836 consists of a monologue by

Zamorna on deck; he recalls Mary, and how at Marseilles a flower-girl, who proved to be Mina Laury, had contrived to come on board and sail with him. At home again, after Christmas, Charlotte wrote another poem, 'Well, the day's toils are over', in which Zamorna lamented the death of his wife Mary.

About the same time, she wrote another story, 'The Return of Zamorna', which evinces greater independence in fiction. Mary Percy is not dead; she believes her husband is. Then comes a note which shows that he is alive, in Africa. The scene changes. 'Reader you are amongst the Olympian Hills' (there are several addresses of this kind, especially at the opening of the story, which remind us of one of the irritating features of Charlotte's novels). Here the loyal Warner is roused by the baying of Zamorna's favourite stag-hound, an enormous, shaggy, leonine creature, which had accompanied him in exile. With it is Mina Laury, who tells Warner that her master is at Ardsley Hall. Great fear is expressed at Ellrington House, especially among Northangerland's mistresses, when news arrives of the triumphant advance of the Angrian army. Mary Percy thinks of Zamorna and how she had stolen from the apartment where she now sits to meet him in the garden before their marriage. She hears someone enter from the garden, springs to the door of her room, and dashes down the staircase into the small dark hall:

> She encountered a tall figure scarce visible in the gloom. Furs and ample drapery enveloped it. It caught her yielding form on its airy descent, surrounded, shadowed her with the folds of sable, clasped her to a warm throbbing bosom and impressed on her lips, one long fervent ardent kiss.

The story shows a growing tendency towards realism in descriptive scenes and dialogue, often in the vernacular. Zamorna and Roswal are forerunners of Rochester and Pilot.

'Julia' was finished at the end of June 1837. It is a succession of rather comical scenes, English in character rather than African, with little connection or unity. Julia, the wife of General Thornton, is hardly the central character; the poet Henry Hastings (Branwell) is the subject of ridicule for his vanity in the presence of ladies; and Percy is met at a Wesleyan chapel (as in 'Passing Events'). There is much here that seems parochial and topical. The most lively events occur at the end. After fondling the young and seductive Caroline Vernon, the Duke of Zamorna is visited by her mother Louisa, Percy's mistress, who creates a scene and is reconciled in such a way that the Duke is amusingly compromised. A former opera-singer and ballet-dancer, Louisa foreshadows Rochester's mistress, Céline Varens.

Branwell's history of Angria and his collateral writings continued, but Charlotte's efforts were confined to holiday periods. She finished 'Mina Laury' in January 1838. It is a complete and exciting story, told directly, without any intermediary narrator, and conveying deep passion. The trend from heroic romance to more quotidian situations continues, especially in the opening scenes. Northangerland, Zamorna, and their wives speak as if they were at Alnwick, the home of the Percys in England. The mixture of dialogue and narrative shows a sustained liveliness. The wintry scenes are English; when she began the story, Charlotte could have been writing from her observations at Haworth. 'Mina Laury' shows the Duke's duplicity. When he takes his leave for a week, the Duchess is very jealous. Mina Laury at her secret home near Hawkscliffe refuses Lord Hartford as a suitor, much as she is beholden to him for saving her life in the civil war:

> I saw my present master when he had scarcely attained manhood – do you think, Hartford, I will tell you what feelings I had for him? – no tongue could express them – they were so fervid, so glowing in their colour that they effaced everything else – I lost the power of properly appreciating the value of the world's opinion, of discerning the difference between right and wrong – I have never in my life contradicted Zamorna – never delayed obedience to his commands – I could not! he was sometimes more to me than a human being – he superseded all things – all affections, all interests, all fears or hopes or principles. Unconnected with him my mind would be a blank – cold, dead, susceptible only of a sense of despair. How I should sicken if I were torn from him and thrown to you! Do not ask it – I would die first.

An exciting scene follows when Hartford outside his home stops the horses of Zamorna's carriage, presents pistols, and insults the Duke. A duel is sparked off, and Hartford is wounded. Near Miss Laury's a carriage overturns, and the occupant, a lady, is brought in. She asks Mina her name, but both conceal their identities. Then Zamorna arrives. Asked if she would like to be rewarded for her fidelity by being married to Hartford, Mina swoons and falls, striking her head against his foot. When she recovers, he tells her what has happened and enfolds her in his arms. There is a knock at the door: the valet has discovered that the Duchess is in the house. Her explanation provides the Duke with a face-saving cue; his wife can stay the night at Hawkscliffe; and tomorrow they will return to Verdopolis.

The most important work Charlotte wrote between leaving Miss Wooler's school and taking her first post as governess is 'Captain Henry Hastings'. There can be little doubt that in this story she adumbrated her latent fears concerning Branwell. It shows a fecundity of dialogue, and a gift for scene and situation, but no advance towards narrative integration. Mystification seems to be the reason for leaving the action in abeyance for long periods. As Charles Townsend, Charlotte seems to be writing for her immediate satisfaction. Despite the Angrian references, the setting and people are English, and Yorkshire names are evident. After a number of scenes we discover that Hastings is being hunted for murder; he meets his sister at Massinger Hall, where she is a governess, teaching the Angrian beauty Jane Moore.[1] From Jane, Sir William Percy discovers the home of the Hastings; it recalls the moors and mountains west of Haworth, and even the parsonage. Charlotte is recognizable in Elizabeth, but the story demanded stronger passions in Hastings than were characteristic of Branwell in February 1839. There seems to be prescient anxiety, nevertheless, in:

> 'I thought you a promising fellow that was fit for anything – you're now just a poor d——l – nothing more.' 'And that's God's truth too' was the answer.

There is an exciting account of the attempt to arrest Hastings at Massinger Hall, which succeeds despite Elizabeth's desperate efforts to foil the police. What happened after the arrest is not known (part of the manuscript is missing). An interview between Elizabeth and Queen Mary (the Duchess of Zamorna) discloses that Hastings had made an attempt on Zamorna's life. The court-martial took place in Zamorna, the centre of which is undisguisedly a Yorkshire woollen town on a market-day. Hastings was released with demotion after turning king's evidence. Elizabeth set up a school –

> not wearily toiling to impart the dry rudiments of knowledge to yawning, obstinate children – a thing she hated and for which her sharp, irritable temper rendered her wholly unfit – but instructing those who had already mastered the elements of education.

[1] Jane Moore and Massinger Hall are forerunners of Shirley and Fieldhead.

Drawing many of her pupils from the wealthiest families in the city, she made numerous friends. She always burned, however, for 'a warmer, closer attachment', and longed for home 'till she cried passionately'. She felt romantic about Sir William Percy, who was drawn to her. One day she met him in the country, and they wandered to Scar-Chapel near Ingleside. In the churchyard was a raised tomb on which was inscribed RESURGAM. From Sir William she learned that it marked the grave of one who had loved Zamorna not wisely but too well. Percy invited her to be his mistress. Unlike Mina Laury, she appreciated the value of the world's opinion, and would do nothing dishonourable. She could not help loving him, and would gladly have been his servant. We can see that features of *Jane Eyre* are already emerging. Zenobia, Countess of Northangerland, is worried about her husband's odd behaviour and his mistresses, and the work closes with domestic scenes at Wellesley House, where we see Zamorna and his children with their grandfather Northangerland. The Duchess's absence is felt; she is jealous of Jane Moore. The Duke explains that she had interceded for Hastings, and the royal pair are reconciled once again.

In 'Julia' and 'Captain Henry Hastings' Charlotte had confessed that she had begun writing without preconceived plans. She opened 'Caroline Vernon' with the statement, 'When I concluded my last book I made a solemn resolve that I would write no more till I had something to write about.' Yet hardly 'three moons have waxed and waned ere "the creature's at his dirty work again"'. Perhaps this indicates that the work was begun when Charlotte returned from Stonegappe at the end of July 1839. Stonegappe and its surroundings are recalled in the opening Hawkscliffe scenes; so too is Mr Sidgwick's Newfoundland dog. Northangerland visits Zamorna's country residence to see his daughter Caroline Vernon. The desire to create fiction closer to life is evident in the humour of making Angrian nobility speak northern English:

> Mr Wellesley asked Mr Percy whether he meant 'to stir his stumps that afternoon or not?' Mr Percy said he felt very well where he was, but, however, as the thing must be done some day he thought they had better shog.

Louisa Vernon and her French maid converse in French, an inexcusable form of realism which Charlotte's stay in Brussels made her unwilling to relinquish. Louisa cannot forget her past grandeur as actress and favourite of Alexander Percy; she and her nerves, and her daughter, are recalled in Rochester's Céline Varens and Adèle. Now she is jealous of Caroline, who, after reading Byron, Moore's *The Life of Lord Edward Fitzgerald*, and Harriet Martineau, wishes to see the world. Four years pass, during which the heroine has not remained in 'a cataleptic condition of romantic immutability' but has acquired finish, ton, air, and elegance in Paris. There, she wishes to stay for the arrival of the King (Zamorna), but her father whisks her off to the country at home. She writes Zamorna an ingenuous letter, stating that she had not intended to tell him she cared for him, and conveying Republican sentiments acquired in France, where he was not popular. Zamorna, delighted by this 'profound and original document', after adjusting his dress, regarding himself vaingloriously in the mirror, and running his fingers thrice through his hair, took his hat and his new light lavender kid gloves, and was 'whirled away' by carriage to Waterloo Palace. His wife's suspicions, when he returns, are amusingly related. Caroline (shades of Caroline Lamb) was thinking of escape to Verdopolis in boy's clothes when she received a letter from the Duke at Freetown, a hundred miles nearer. She then took a coach to the Warners', where he was staying, and told Mrs Warner the truth, that she had come to see her guardian. When the Duke returned, she was afraid and kept in the background. The following evening he found her in the library, and soon she was in his arms. He refused to take her to Verdopolis the next day. When she at last realized that their attachment might be considered anything but that of guardian and ward, she was struck with an agony of shame. Nevertheless, the Duke persuaded her to accompany him to his retreat in a wood near Ingleside (like Ferndean?). When he returned to Verdopolis, Northangerland demanded his daughter, dashed the butt-end of a pistol in his face, and threatened legal proceedings. His son-in-law replied, 'The ship is worthless that will not live through a storm.'

It is significant that on the last page of the manuscript there is a copy of Charlotte's poem 'Life believe is not a dream', for by the end of 1839 she had decided to bid farewell to Angria; 'we must change, for the eye is tired of the picture so oft recurring and now so familiar':

I long to quit for a while that burning clime where we have sojourned too long – its skies flame – the glow of sunset is always upon it – the mind would cease from excitement and turn now to a cooler region where the dawn breaks grey and sober, and the coming day for a time at least is subdued by clouds.

She was twenty-three, and had decided to face life rather than take refuge in romantic dreams. In her later stories she had often sacrificed the splendour of romance for the ordinary in scene and dialogue. Yet the illicit pleasures of Byronism to which she had been imaginatively addicted had not entirely loosed their hold. Whether or not she gave up the writing of Angrian romances in 1839, she sent the opening of one to Hartley Coleridge for appraisal in 1840, and she was haunted by them in her loneliness at Brussels (1.5.43):

It is a curious metaphysical fact that always in the evening when I am in the great dormitory alone, having no other company than a number of beds with white curtains, I always recur as fanatically as ever to the old ideas, the old faces, and the old scenes in the world below.

Charlotte had never succeeded in achieving an artistic plot on any considerable scale; she excelled in scenes and episodes. Nor had she shaken off the hold of Byronism, though she had temporarily asserted the supremacy of Victorian morality in 'Captain Henry Hastings'. Their conflict and resolution were to provide the dramatic theme of *Jane Eyre*. Her later Angrian writings show that this was a subject for which the more mature Charlotte Brontë would have been well qualified had she never met M. Heger.

* * * * * *

Knowledge of the Gondal fiction begun by Emily and Anne in 1831 is limited to what is deducible from their poems and from a few notes in prose; as far as is known, none of it remains.

Charlotte's absence at Roe Head gave Branwell free rein; and both these factors probably provided the opportunity the younger sisters had yearned for. Their heroes, the Arctic explorers Parry and Ross, had been quite out of place in an African empire. Perhaps the new venture was launched by Emily in a series of secret 'bed' plays similar to those Charlotte began with her in December 1827.

After detecting that the relevant sentence in Emily's note of November 1834 read 'The Gondals are discovering the interior of Gaaldine' (not 'Geraldine'), Miss Ratchford (see p. 362) discovered a pencilled note by Anne in the copy of *A Grammar of General Geography* which the Brontë children had put to such purposeful account in developing their Glasstown fiction. The note was clear and precise, as one would expect from Anne. Gondal was 'a large island in the North Pacific'; Gaaldine was 'a large island newly discovered in the South Pacific'. We know that Bewick's Arctic descriptions were magic casements opening on the foam of perilous seas for the Brontë children (see *J.* i), and wonder whether M. Heger's statement that Emily ought to have been a navigator reflected not only admiration for her reasoning powers but also some awareness of her interest in maritime exploration. Anne's note indicated that Regina was the capital of Gondal, and that Gaaldine consisted of Zedora, a large province governed by a viceroy, and five kingdoms: Ula (which had four sovereigns), Alexandria, Almedore, Elseraden, and Zalona.

From Emily's poems it can be seen that Gondal was set in stormy seas. Its interior suggested the country above Haworth; if difference there is, it is one of degree. In winter the frozen moors and mountains were often shrouded in mist and gloom; in early summer flowers lit up the heather and bracken, and larks and swallows animated the scene. The climate of Gaaldine was almost tropical.

The Gondal epic followed some of the main outlines of its forerunner, largely because Emily and Anne were too immature at its inception to free themselves from the creative ideas they had shared for a long period with Charlotte and Branwell. First there was colonization by conquest; secondly, further expansion, after the discovery of Gaaldine; then there was the internal struggle for power which led to the rise of Julius Brenzaida; finally, civil war arose between the Royalists and the Republicans. On the other hand, whereas the Byronic Zamorna or Emperor Adrian is central to the Angrian literature, Emily's dominant character is Augusta Geraldine Almeda, a princess who becomes Queen of Gondal. Conjugal infidelities are romanticized in the former, but Nemesis triumphs tragically in Emily's poems.

How much of the Gondal saga was written is not known. In her birthday note of 1841, Emily wrote, 'I have a good many books on hand, but I am sorry to say that as usual I make small progress with any.' At Thorp Green, Anne was writing her fourth 'volume' of *Solala Vernon's Life*. Having agreed on the main course of events periodically, they probably wrote prose stories, as well as poems, with reference to any situation that appealed to them. Four years later the two enjoyed an excursion to York, during which they played, or imagined, the roles of 'Ronald Macalgin, Henry Angora, Juliet Angusteena, Rosabella Esmaldan, Ella and Julian Egremont, Catharine

Navarre, and Cordelia Fitzaphnold, escaping from the palaces of instruction to join the Royalists who are hard driven at present by the victorious Republicans'. Anne had written some 'articles' on 'the First Wars' and 'a book by Henry Sophona'; she knew that Emily was writing 'the Emperor Julius's Life' and some poetry, but the substance of the latter remained undivulged. The unfamiliarity of all the above fictional names except the last illustrates how little we know of 'Gondaland'. Some of its stories may have been merely played or imagined by Emily and Anne, their contexts being used perhaps for the creation of some of the Gondal poems.

Where so many lacunae exist, it seems unlikely that any attempt to reconstruct the story from the evidence of the poems can ever be completely convincing. Comparatively few Gondal poems by Anne exist; there are many by Emily, though it is sometimes impossible to determine whether she projected her own thoughts into Gondal scenes and situations, or whether situations of imaginative and dramatic appeal evoked the experience of the poems. As points in the plots were chosen regardless of chronology, and for poetic reasons alone, it is hardly surprising that some of the references in Emily's dramatic poems terminate in obscurity.

How much of the Gondal narrative can be reconstructed is one question; how far such a reconstruction could add to an appreciation of the poems is another. One welcome result of Gondal research is that readers are more circumspect in ascribing personal and biographical significance to certain poems. Some of the main features of the story are clear, but the view that the data for the reconstruction of a coherent narrative whole is inadequate seems to be amply supported by the wide discrepancies in the interpretations of the principal investigators. (See Appendix 2, pp. 371–3.)

Charlotte Brontë
Poems

Charlotte Brontë seems to have given serious attention to poetic composition from the age of thirteen. At the end of 1836, when she was only twenty, she had written considerably more than half her poetry, and it was at this time that she invited Southey, the Poet Laureate, to judge some of her poems. He replied:

> You evidently possess, and in no inconsiderable degree, what Wordsworth calls the 'faculty of verse'. I am not depreciating it when I say that in these times it is not rare. Many volumes of poems are now published every year without attracting public attention, any one of which, if it had appeared half a century ago, would have obtained a high reputation for its author. Whoever, therefore, is ambitious of distinction in this way ought to be prepared for disappointment.

He was old, cautious, and courteous, but he twice sounded a warning note in his letters of March 1837:

> The day dreams in which you habitually indulge are likely to induce a distempered state of mind. . . . Take care of over-excitement, and endeavour to keep a quiet mind . . .: your moral and spiritual improvement will then keep pace with the culture of your intellectual powers.

If Charlotte submitted her Angrian poem of July 1836, 'And, when you left me' (entitled 'Zamorna's Exile' by Miss Ratchford), for critical examination – and there is little evidence that she could have sent any verse better suited to show her merits at the time – the above advice seems particularly perceptive. Southey may have had nothing

more in mind, however, than the dreams of unfulfilled ambition.
'Write poetry for its own sake; not in a spirit of emulation, and not
with a view to celebrity; the less you aim at that the more likely you
will be to deserve and finally to obtain it', he added.

Although Charlotte rarely appears to have been inhibited by verse
forms, she is generally more successful in prose, as one of her earliest
poems might augur, though it ends disarmingly:

> And such a charming doggerel
> As this was never wrote,
> Not even by the mighty
> And high Sir Walter Scott!

Whether she writes directly or as the Marquis of Douro, the main
subject of her early poems is nature – sunrise and sunset, skies by day
and night, mountain scenes, and the change of the seasons. She loved
words such as 'tenebrous' and 'articulate', and was influenced by
eighteenth-century poetic diction. The sky is 'etherial' and 'cerulean';
woods are 'bathed in pale Luna's light'; Aurora glows in crimson
robes, unfolding radiant portals, through which issues 'Apollo's
burnished car'. At fourteen Charlotte wrote lines that resemble
Keats's warblings at a later age:

> A fresh breeze through my unclosed lattice playing
> Amid a vine's young tendrils wanton straying,
> Asked me with voice more sweet than harp or lute
> Or merry dulcimer or gentle flute
> To walk abroad and taste the balmy air
> Which violets of the vale and lilies fair
> Had filled with fragrance . . .

Recalling Byron and the degeneracy of Greece, she writes, with the
'romantic' poets in mind:

> Parnassus now uplifts her head
> Forsaken by the holy nine:
> They from her heights for aye have fled,
> And now in fair Britannia shine.

She pleads for 'a poet's power', and Nature, appearing in the form of
a woman –

> Her crown, a rugged mountain hoar
> Where plume-like trees waved solemnly

– grants her 'high request' ('But dim thy beam, and faint thy ray'),
and gives her not a laurel wreath but a violet which she must cherish
all her life. Two poems relating to Angrian portraits (dated 10 and
12 November 1830) suggest a genuine poetic gift; the first shows some
resemblance in imagery and verse to Wordsworth; the other is rather
like Herrick. Byronic echoes were to prove more persistent.

Fertile in imagery and expression, Charlotte probably had little
difficulty in producing verses, whatever the subject. Yet the breath
of poetry rarely inspires her work; it is found more often in her prose.
Her style does not belong to the highest order of that 'Parnassian'
class, of which Gerard Manley Hopkins said that, however 'beautiful
and unexceptionable', it 'does not *touch* you'. She attained versifying
competence at an early age, and made little significant advance. 'Lines
on Bewick', written when she was sixteen, is as typical in this respect
as any other of her poems, but specially interesting from the fascination his illustrations held for the Brontë children:

> There rises some lone rock all wet with surge
>   And dashing billows glimmering in the light
> Of a wan moon, whose silent rays emerge
>   From clouds that veil their lustre, cold and bright.

A year later she showed a mastery of the Spenserian stanza in 'Richard
Coeur de Lion and Blondel':

> Oh, how that wild strain o'er the river swelled
>   And mingled with its gentle murmuring!
> From the true fount of song divine it welled:
>   Music's own simple, undefilèd spring,
>   Notes rose and died, such as the wild birds sing
> In the lone wood, or the far lonelier sky.
>   Oh! none but Blondel, but the minstrel-king,
> Could waken such transcendent melody,
> Sweet as a fairy's lute, soft as a passing sigh.

She was turning more often to narrative-dramatic poems, but it was in
Angrian monologues, influenced by Byron's sentiments and later
style, that she wrote most fluently in language approximating the
cadences of speech. Elsewhere the measure is generally too regular to
be readable at length. There is far more life in Longfellow.

For some years after January 1838 Charlotte wrote scarcely any
verse:

Once indeed I was very poetical, when I was sixteen, seventeen, eighteen and nineteen years old – but I am now twenty-four approaching twenty-five – and the intermediate years are those which begin to rob life of some of its superfluous colouring. At this age it is time that the imagination should be pruned and trimmed – that the judgment should be cultivated – and a *few* at least, of the countless illusions of early youth should be cleared away. I have not written poetry for a long while.

Such was her statement in a letter to Henry Nussey in January 1841.

'Master and Pupil', written at Brussels, is partly fictitious, but clearly based on the relationship between Charlotte and M. Heger, and crucial to the climax of *The Professor* (xxiii). It is often assumed that her disenchantment when he failed to correspond after her return to England informs the undated poem 'He saw my heart's woe':

> He was mute as is the grave, he stood stirless as a tower;
> At last I looked up, and saw I prayed to stone:
> I asked help of that which to help had no power,
> I sought love where love was utterly unknown.

If so, her feelings were somewhat transmuted to suit a different context.

Among the poems which Charlotte included with her sisters' in *Poems by Currer, Ellis, and Acton Bell*, there are none of really outstanding merit. Undoubtedly the most sensational is 'Gilbert'. Though in a middle-class suburban setting, it belongs to the 'Peter Grimes' category of narrative; it blends the supernatural and the psychological, with the phantom of a drowned wife wreaking her revenge on a heartless husband, whom she drives to a ghastly suicide. Among the dramatic monologues, the most interesting are 'Pilate's Wife's Dream' and 'Apostasy' (a draft of most of the latter was completed at Roe Head at the end of May 1837). Comparison with Browning's dramatic lyrics will show Charlotte's main weakness: the language tends to be deadened by metrical regularity. Here is the ending of 'The Wife's Will:

> This evening now shall sweetly flow,
> Lit by our clear fire's happy glow;
> And parting's peace-embittering fear
> Is warned our hearts to come not near;
> For fate admits my soul's decree,
> In bliss or bale – to go with thee!

It is significant that she failed to communicate her grief in the poems she wrote on the death of Emily and Anne; they are expressions of reflection rather than of feeling. The opening stanzas of 'A Valentine' (which she probably sent to William Weightman) show greater success in a lighter mood, and sincerity of feeling and thought is communicated. There are felicities and fluencies in phrasing and movement in the poetry Charlotte wrote before she consulted Southey which make one wonder why she never succeeded in verse as she did in prose. Perhaps her letter to W. S. Williams (16.11.48), after unsold copies of *Poems by Currer, Ellis, and Acton Bell* had been reissued, affords a clue. She complained that a reviewer could not feel, or would not acknowledge, that 'the very finish and *labor limae* which Currer wants, Ellis has'. There is something curious in the attribution of finish and 'polish' to Emily Brontë's greatest poetry, which reveals a higher art, intuitive and applied, felt in movement and sound, and rarely restricted by accepted forms and metrical patterns. The result is an idiosyncratic voice or tone. Charlotte rarely achieved this, simply because her over-riding attention to metrical form cramped her style. Her later verse generally reaches a high degree of competence, but she had made little progress beyond the apprentice stage, prolonged though it was: she had not cultivated the higher artistries of poetry sufficiently to give adequate expression to the true voice of feeling. In prose, where she had learned to move more easily, she was able to reach higher poetic levels, most of all through the intensification that came from greater discipline.

'The Professor'

By the end of 1839 Charlotte Brontë had decided to renounce the 'burning clime' of Angrian dream fiction, and turn to 'a cooler region where the dawn breaks grey and sober'. Before writing *The Professor*, she had made many efforts, she tells us in her preface, to overcome a taste for 'ornamented and redundant composition' and achieve a 'plain and homely' style. These efforts had been destroyed. They did not include the fragment on which she asked Hartley Coleridge[1] to comment in 1840; this was the opening of a Percy story, which she says could have been Richardsonian in length, and about which she expressed regret at relinquishing a world peopled with 'Melchisedecs' who 'have no father nor mother but your own imagination'.

The Angrian writings contain a number of scenes which are recognizably of Yorkshire origin, even in topographical names. One of these (see p. 77) was redeveloped in the early chapters of *The Professor*, where William Crimsworth works for his brother Edward, and is spied on by the 'joined Methodist' Timothy Steighton (iii). The six Seacombe sisters (i) recall the Seymours of 'The Spell', and are forerunners of the Sykes sisters in *Shirley*; Charlotte had a local family in mind (see pp. 327–8).

When *The Professor* was begun is not clear. All three Brontë sisters had hoped to write something worthy of publication, and it looks as if Anne, the youngest, was the first to make headway with serious fiction. By the end of July 1845 she had started the third 'volume' (writing-book) of *Passages in the Life of an Individual*,

---

[1] Not Wordsworth, as in the published letters. See *TLS.*, 14 May 1970. One transitional fragment, 'Mr. Ashworth and his son', is referred to by Miss Ratchford, p. 208.

almost certainly the first draft of *Agnes Grey*. This, and the agreement to seek publication of selected poems by all three in the autumn, undoubtedly spurred Emily and Charlotte to pursue their first novels in earnest. Charlotte finished hers in April 1846, and the fair copy was ready near the end of June. It was rejected by seven publishers, but encouragement from the last led to the writing of *Jane Eyre* and its publication by the same firm. The great success of this novel made Charlotte write in December 1847 to W. S. Williams, reader for Smith, Elder & Co., urging that she should recast *The Professor* for a three-volume publication. Her appraisal of it is interesting (14.12.47):

> I found the beginning very feeble, the whole narrative deficient in incident and in general attractiveness. Yet the middle and latter portion of the work, all that relates to Brussels, the Belgian school, etc., is as good as I can write: it contains more pith, more substance, more reality, in my judgment, than much of 'Jane Eyre'. It gives, I think, a new view of a grade, an occupation, and a class of characters – all very commonplace, very insignificant in themselves, but not more so than the materials composing that portion of 'Jane Eyre' which seems to please most generally.

The full extent of her revisions is not known; she offered it again to her publishers at the beginning of 1851.[1] It was published posthumously, after further emasculation by Mr Nicholls; language such as 'God damn your insolence!' (which consorted well with Angrian romance) and a description of Yorke Hunsden to the effect that his form and countenance suggested more 'the result (?) of an amour (?) between Oliver Cromwell and a French grisette than anything else in Heaven above or in the Earth beneath' would have shocked Church dignitaries and most other Victorian readers.[2]

The final revision was probably made in the midwinter of 1850–51. Charlotte's preface refers to *Jane Eyre* and *Shirley*, and there can be little doubt, when her husband's appended note is taken into account, that she had the reception of both these novels in mind, in concluding that readers preferred romance to reality in fiction, and even 'the wild, wonderful, and thrilling – the strange, startling, and harrowing' to the story of a man who has to work his way through life as 'real

[1] See letter, 5.2.51.
[2] See M. M. Brammer, 'The Manuscript of *The Professor*', *The Review of English Studies*, 1960.

living men' do, without sudden accession of fortune or even marriage to 'a beautiful girl or a lady of rank'.

Upper-class society was outside Charlotte's range, and she had almost certainly read enough French fiction to realize the existence of a trend away from the more aristocratic heroes and heroines of Sir Walter Scott and Bulwer-Lytton towards the kind of people and experiences familiar to her. A schoolmaster had been seriously presented by George Sand, and a governess by Harriet Martineau. Charlotte's problem was lack of experience; 'is not the real experience of each individual very limited?' she wrote to G. H. Lewes when, after reading *Jane Eyre*, he warned her to beware of melodrama. Her first work, she explained, had been offered to a publisher who 'said it was original, faithful to nature' but 'deficient in "startling incident" and "thrilling excitement"' (6.11.47). When she began it, she was

> determined to take Nature and Truth as my sole guides, and to follow to their very footprints; I restrained imagination, eschewed romance, repressed excitement; over-bright colouring, too, I avoided, and sought to produce something which should be soft, grave, and true.

The great experience of Charlotte's life had been in Brussels. She had not altogether enjoyed it, but it offered more variety and interest than anything else she knew at first hand. Yet her self-imposed restraints made it difficult for her to write a story of great length in the Brussels setting. Hence the development of the incongruous industrial prologue from its Angrian origin. The case for opening the novel in England may be stronger than it is in *Villette*, since the return to England, with expectations of sending Victor to Eton in his father's footsteps, is a way of rounding off the moral success story of an industrious couple who, to quote Bunyan a trifle further than the author does in her preface, have had to toil up 'the Hill of Difficulty' before they can retire to their 'pleasant arbour' in Daisy Lane.

Whereas Anne Brontë attempted to conceal the autobiographical background in *Agnes Grey* by the use of fictitious names, Charlotte kept the Brussels setting undisguised in *The Professor* and camouflaged the story. The background is actual even to the details of William Crimsworth's search for Frances Henri, until he finds her in the Protestant Cemetery where Charlotte visited the grave of Martha Taylor. Crimsworth teaches at the pensionnat in the Rue d'Isabelle, and his classroom experiences are based on those of Charlotte, as may be seen in *Villette*: unlike M. Heger and Paul Emanuel, he does not teach at the Athénée. The master-pupil relationship which existed between M. Heger and Charlotte is to be seen in a development of the Crimsworth-Frances story. The poem by Frances, the opening of which Crimsworth overhears, and the remainder of which he insists on reading (xxiii), was written by Charlotte at Brussels in 1843; it obviously mingles fiction with her delight in gaining the approval of a taskmaster she admired –

> He yet begrudged and stinted praise,
> > But I had learnt to read
> The secret meaning of his face,
> > And that was my best meed.

M. Pelet is not a portrait of M. Heger, whose character more closely resembles that of M. Paul in *Villette*. He is hardly admirable. Despite the raptures which his jealousy causes him to simulate, his description of Eulalie, Hortense, and Caroline de Blémont (xi) proclaims the sensualist:

> Ah, there is beauty! beauty in perfection. What a cloud of sable curls about the face of a houri! What fascinating lips! What glorious black eyes! Your Byron would have worshipped her, and you – you cold, frigid islander! – you played the austere, the insensible in the presence of an Aphrodite so exquisite?

His bachelor life 'had been passed in proper French style, with due disregard to moral restraint', and he often boasted 'what a terror he had been to certain husbands of his acquaintance'. His original was the master in charge of a school-house which overlooked the Pensionnat Heger and the Athénée, but, though she remembered his appearance and manner, we must not assume that Charlotte knew him well enough to draw him to the life. The drunken scene and his sensuality reflect rather the author's attempts to establish Currer Bell's masculine identity and experience. Yet the speech of the above extract betrays its literary and Angrian descent.

Mme Heger is hardly recognizable in Mlle Reuter; she retains her surveillance as school principal, but is transformed into a coquette who has little difficulty at first in making a conquest of the inexperienced and susceptible Crimsworth. Charlotte's resentment against Mme Heger's jealous suspicions is vicariously expressed in the indifference and harshness with which he responds to Mlle's flattery and servility. As this 'crafty little politician' loses her hold on his heart, his interest in Frances Henri begins to develop in this almost linear story. It is in the heroine that Charlotte realizes the dream fulfilment of her ambition to take charge of a school; in her she depicted her ideal 'directress' – industrious, serious, and worthy of high respect, but kind and completely democratic in her indifference to rank and title (xxv).

There can be little doubt that, through her heroine, she also recalled her happiness on winning M. Heger's approval of her *devoirs* (xviii), her regret at being parted from him when she returned to Haworth (xix), and her pleasure in writing to him (xxi).

Through some of her principal characters, Charlotte expresses other views which she firmly held. As *Shirley* was to show, she was an advocate of women's rights. Frances could not think of marrying, 'to be kept' by Crimsworth and remain unemployed and depressed at home, as he, with typical masculine self-flattery, expected (xxiii). Earlier in the same chapter, his unimaginative attitude is reflected in his thoughts on old maids, 'the race whom all despise'; Charlotte's irony in Crimsworth's short-sightedness almost equals the poker-faced satire of Swift:

> self-control is so continually their thought, so perpetually their object, that at last it absorbs the softer and more agreeable qualities of their nature, and they die mere models of austerity, fashioned out of a little parchment and much bone. Anatomists will tell you that there is a heart in the withered old maid's carcase – the same as in that of any cherished wife or proud mother in the land. Can it be so? I really don't know; but feel inclined to doubt it.

It is a subject on which Frances speaks more sensibly (xxv). On the rights of married women and separation, she agrees with the author of *The Tenant of Wildfell Hall* (xxv); provoked by the disputatious Hunsden, she defends sentiment and feeling against the voice of logic (xxiv). On England, William Crimsworth is almost Wordsworthian in his denunciation of luxury and ostentation (xxi). The radical Hunsden minces no words on the poverty and disease of the ill-fed, uneducated poor, and the affluence of the upper classes, extremes which the Brontës had seen for themselves in parish cottages and the mansions where they had worked as governesses. The anti-Catholicism which Tractarianism had roused in England, and Charlotte had felt even more strongly in Brussels, is expressed very emphatically (xii, xvii), but less vehemently than in *Villette*. Even Mlle Reuter might have 'added straight integrity to all her other excellences' if she had been a Protestant. The heroine is a Protestant from Switzerland, and her aim is to live among Protestants in England.

As Charlotte has little sympathy for Mlle Reuter, it is significant that she uses her to express the common prejudice against women writers which induced the Brontës to adopt pseudonyms (xviii):

> and then I think, Monsieur – it appears to me that ambition, *literary* ambition especially, is not a feeling to be cherished in the mind of a woman: would not Mdlle. Henri be much safer and happier if taught to believe that in the quiet discharge of social duties consists her real vocation. . . . She may never marry . . . but even in celibacy it would be better for her to retain the character and habits of a respectable decorous female.

Time had passed, but anti-feminist irrationalism had not wholly changed since Charles Lamb expressed his contempt for the 'female author' by placing her below the actress in the less respectable classes of the social hierarchy.

The narrative avoids the 'exciting' and 'marvellous' (i). Its central setting is a school; and the scene in which awareness of reciprocated love is first surely felt is taken up largely with making tea (xix). The declaration of love is unromantic; one moment Crimsworth is sitting solus on a chair, the next Frances is on his knees, and held there firmly. After what seems an interminable time (during which the hero feels 'the agitation of the heart' and sees Gray's 'purple light of love' glowingly reflected on Frances' countenance), she agrees to marry him. He then draws her a little nearer his heart, and takes a first kiss, which is followed by a long silence and the peace of fathomless content (xxiii). The contrast between these prosaic, but not unmoving, scenes and the elaborate contextual romanticism of Rochester's declaration of love in *Jane Eyre* is startling.

The dissonance that Charlotte had grown to realize between the romance of fiction and the demands of reality accounts for much of the tone and atmosphere of *The Professor*. 'Novelists should never allow themselves to weary of the study of real life. If they observed this duty conscientiously, they would give us fewer pictures chequered with vivid contrasts of light and shade; they would seldom elevate their heroes and heroines to the heights of rapture . . . ' (xix). When Crimsworth learned to view Mlle Reuter with greater detachment (x),

'I am growing wiser', thought I, as I walked back to M. Pelet's. 'Look at this little [real][1] woman; is she like the women of novelists and romancers? To read of female character as depicted in Poetry and Fiction, one would think it was made up of sentiment, either for good or bad – here is a specimen, and a most sensible and respectable specimen, too, whose stable ingredient is abstract reason. No Talleyrand was ever more passionless than Zoraide Reuter!' So I thought then; I found afterwards that blunt suscepti-bilities are very consistent with strong propensities.

These propensities made him decide he could no longer work for her and M. Pelet when they are married; the situation threatened the development of 'a practical modern French novel', and he had already seen 'the results produced by a course of interesting and romantic domestic treachery. No golden halo of fiction was about this example; I saw it bare and real; and it was very loathsome. I saw a mind degraded by the practice of mean subterfuge, by the habit of perfidious deception, and a body depraved by the infectious influence of the vice-polluted soul' (xx). The allusion here is almost certainly to Branwell and his mysterious affair with Mrs Robinson.

It is therefore within the confines of 'grey and sober' reality that Charlotte depicts the 'ideal' in Frances. Like Wordsworth's wife,

> A perfect woman, nobly planned
> To warn, to comfort, and command,

but yet

> A Creature not too bright or good
> For human nature's daily food,

she has higher qualities which give stability to life:

> The reason firm, the temperate will,
> Endurance, foresight, strength, and skill.

For Crimsworth she is the 'personification of discretion and fore-thought, of diligence and perseverance, of self-denial and self-control'; the 'silent possessor of a well of tenderness, of a flame, as genial as still, as pure as quenchless, of natural feeling, natural passion'; but passion which 'burned safely under the eye of reason' (xix). Unlike other characters in *The Professor*, she has charm; Mrs Gaskell

[1] A significant word in the MS. See M. M. Brammer, *op. cit.*

thought that 'in grace of womanhood' she was not surpassed by any of Charlotte's other heroines.

The Currer Bell stance was not felicitous in Charlotte's first novel. In her attempt to assume a manly role and viewpoint (and in her sustained reaction against a romantic picture of life), she produced a bluntness in male behaviour which is cumulatively offensive and sometimes ridiculous. Edward Crimsworth's inhumanity may be regarded as exceptional and secondary; it is the hero and Hunsden who repeatedly fall short of what occasion requires. Their brusque, hard-hitting speech is often the perverse expression of friendship and humour (xxi, xxii), but their behaviour is as gauche as that of awkward adolescents. They can part for years without saying farewell, and meet again without any apparent relish for conversation (vi, xxii). After being introduced to Crimsworth's fiancée, Hunsden takes his friend by the collar, and they grapple and roll on the pavement like a pair of drunken idiots (xxiv). Their absurd lack of manners in each other's company is irritating; Hunsden is offensive in his protracted efforts to score at the expense of Frances when they first meet. He rarely lets up, and almost his final word to her borders on denigration.

> Some people, however indifferent they may become after a considerable space of absence, always contrive to leave a pleasant impression just at parting; not so Hunsden; a conference with him affected one like a draught of Peruvian bark; it seemed a concentration of the specially harsh, stringent, bitter; whether, like bark, it invigorated, I scarcely knew.

The hero possesses a similar sadistic streak; he is stern to his pupils (his dislike of them being obviously based on Charlotte's unsympathetic recollections); he hates their reading, and finds it torture to hear their 'uncouth mouthing' of his native tongue. He positively enjoys the game of balking Mlle Reuter's ingratiatory wiles; her smiles fall on a heart of stone: and her 'servility' creates disdain and 'despotism' in him (xv). Ultimately (xx) he derived

> a sort of low gratification in receiving this luscious incense from an attractive and still young worshipper; and an irritating sense of degradation in the very experience of the pleasure. When she stole about me with the soft step of a slave, I felt at once barbarous and sensual as a pasha.

Undoubtedly the author's vengeful re-creation of Mme Heger was responsible for this unpleasant streak in the hero's character.

Charlotte's inexpertise is revealed in her lack of resourcefulness for plot development. It could hardly be slighter. Much of the narrative is descriptive and unexciting. A scene such as that introducing Mme Pelet and Mme Reuter has its own interest, and an inventive writer would have made more of such characters to provide comic relief (viii). More open to criticism are the description of the Belgian countryside (vii) and the portfolio chapter which presents sketches of pupils 'pencilled after nature' (xii). Here the realism is indicative of an author untrained in the dynamics of narrative art. Her unprofessional ingenuousness may be seen again when she returns to M. Pelet: 'The moonlight walk is, I think, the last incident recorded in this narrative where the gentleman cuts any conspicuous figure' (xx). Perhaps this represents what Charlotte thought Mr Crimsworth would have written. Intended, like the opening of *The Tenant of Wildfell Hall*, to give verisimilitude, his introductory letter is more curious. As it elicited no reply, he wrote the remainder of his life-story for the benefit of the public. Yet the letter suggests he is not married: 'oh, how like a nightmare is the thought of being bound for life to one of my cousins! . . . I should be a bad husband, under such circumstances', he writes. (The context suggests a failure in tense rather than a factual oversight.) A reference to the pre-railway era in this letter and an allusion to the window-tax (vii) point to an anachronism in the French authors on Hunsden's shelves.[1] Many years were to pass, of course, before Edward Crimsworth became rich again from his railway speculations (as we hear at the close of the story).

Characteristics with which we are familiar from Charlotte's later novels are to be found in *The Professor*. The habit of addressing the reader had begun in the later Angrian fiction, but it is used more sparingly in this novel than in later works. Often it is a kind of authorial anxiety reflex, enlisting the reader's sympathetic attention at critical points (vii, xxiii). The frequent use of French dialogue is unjustifiable, despite the author's excuse that French 'loses sadly' in translation; it shows more sensibility than sense. The mirror technique for giving

---

[1] Charlotte remembered them from Mr Taylor's library at Gomersal. 'I have got another bale of French books from Gomersal . . . they are like the rest clever wicked sophistical and immoral', she wrote to Ellen Nussey on 20 August 1840; cf. *P*. xx on 'modern French novels'.

a visual impression of the hero-narrator is an obvious device (ii, ix, xxiiii). Personification is one of the most noticeable features of the style (the antithetical abstractions which show the true Mlle Reuter at the end of xv were all capitalized in the manuscript), often revealing the cast of the author's outlook and feelings: Duty and Perseverance are household gods, 'from which my darling, my cherished-in-secret Imagination, the tender and the mighty, should never, either by softness or strength, have severed me' (iv); 'Liberty I clasped in my arms for the first time', after leaving Ostend for Brussels (vii); and there, when one would have expected Crimsworth to be happy, he falls a prey to Hypochondria (as Charlotte did for long periods). Why this should happen in the novel is not clear: 'when my desires, folding wings, weary with long flight, had just alighted on the very lap of Fruition, and nestled there warm, content, under the caress of a soft hand – why did Hypochondria accost me now?' (xxiii). Reflections often take the form of an inner dialogue with personified participants, as in the unintentionally amusing debate between Conscience and Crimsworth (v), and that between Prudence and Conscience (xx), or when Imagination and Love speak to Crimsworth and tell him that Frances will not bend under Tyranny and Injustice but can be guided by Reason and Affection (xxii).

The style reflects a writer who tends to think in terms of visual imagery. Crimsworth repulses Hypochondria 'as one would a dreaded and ghastly concubine coming to embitter a husband's heart toward his young bride'. When giving up all hope of finding Frances, he is forced to loosen his grasp on expectation and submit to the discouraging thought that the current of life had swept her for ever from his reach (xix). Ten weeks after finding her, he does not know how he will be received when he visits her home again (xxiii):

> At that hour my bark hung on the topmost curl of a wave of fate, and I knew not on what shoal the onward rush of the billow might hurl it; I would not then attach her destiny to mine by the slightest thread; if doomed to split on the rock, or run aground on the sandbank, I was resolved no other vessel should share my disaster.

After introducing Hunsden to Frances, Crimsworth tells him he has seen only the 'title-page' of his happiness and cannot conceive the 'sweet variety and thrilling excitement of the narrative' (xxiv); this fanciful image or conceit is less happy than Hunsden's witty combination of sour grapes with the Tantalus myth (xxii). More interesting is the use of 'stone' and 'pillar' to indicate hard-heartedness (xiii, xv), and of the red fire on the hearth to connote happiness and love (xxiii). No wonder that William Crimsworth looked back on the evenings in the parlour of the small house where his married life began as 'a long string of rubies circling the dusky brow of the past'; 'our fire burned bright' though 'the leaden sky seemed full of drifts' (xxv). These images of stone and fire are repeated with the same overtones in *Jane Eyre*.

The seasonal background is significant and rather surprising. Spring marks the beginning of Crimsworth's infatuation with the directrice (ix); the conventional moonlight scene ends, however, with his disenchantment (xii). His discovery of the long-lost Frances is marked by a glorious sunset, followed by a rainbow dream (the most studied description in the novel, one suspects) which whispers 'Hope smiles on Effort!' (xix). In fact, however, their love is visually centred in the peaceful glow on the hearth, while outside in the darkness the tempest is wild (xix), or a cold late autumn wind blows (xxiii), or the streets are ankle-deep in snow (xxv).

This partially unromantic scenic pattern, with the wedding on a 'cold, bright, frosty day', harmonizes with the moral tone of the novel. Its emphasis is on reward for those who labour diligently and with foresight up the Hill of Difficulty (vii). Years of 'bustle, action, unslacked endeavour' brought happiness and prosperity to the Crimsworths. During this period Mrs Crimsworth revealed hidden faculties, but beneath new branches and foliage the flowers and the fragrance remained. This imagery harmonizes with the arbour near Daisy Lane where the nightingale is heard and the moon is unclouded. As the preface hints, there are suggestions of *The Pilgrim's Progress* in *The Professor*. The emphasis is on reason and self-control. Edward Crimsworth (whose marriage fails), M. Pelet, Mlle Reuter, and Hunsden, in their several ways, lack the finer qualities which make the married life of the hero and heroine a success. It is dangerous, however, to sleep in the arbour half-way up the hill; Crimsworth, voicing his fears that Victor may be spoiled, stresses his need of a grounding 'in the art of self-control'. One can be sure that Branwell was much in Charlotte's thoughts as she worked on the novel.

The Professor is activated by a moral strenuousness which is more earnest and thematic than in any of her later works, even *Jane Eyre*. The creative irritant was Branwell's ignominious decline. In contrast, the hero is a man 'of regular life and rational mind' (xix). Mlle

Reuter owes much to Charlotte's resentful recollections of Mme Heger, but her coquetry and allied duplicity may have had another source. They are rooted in a sterner reality than the immoralities of Angrian fiction. In view of the allusions to Branwell which break through the surface of the novel, the time of its composition, and the implications of its theme, it is more than probable that they originated from the impressions which Charlotte had formed, rightly or wrongly, of Mrs Robinson; if so, her utter condemnation of the latter (see her letters of 28.1.48 and 28.7.48 to Ellen Nussey) may have contributed to the cold disdain to which Mlle Reuter is rigorously subjected by William Crimsworth.[1]

[1] This conclusion was anticipated by Laura L. Hinkley, who, in *The Brontës: Charlotte and Emily*, p. 185, states that, in her pursuit of Crimsworth, Mlle Reuter derived from Mrs Robinson, 'as Charlotte believed her to be'.

'Jane Eyre'

Jane Eyre was begun in circumstances which would have disheartened most other writers. Perhaps it was her father's courage during his operation at Manchester towards the end of August 1846 which gave Charlotte new resolution. *The Professor* had been rejected; Branwell was a patent failure; and her teaching plans had come to nothing. It would be interesting to know whether she had a clear outline of the novel in mind, and whether the Gateshead episode formed the starting-point, or the slightly fictionalized reminiscences of Cowan Bridge. She could never have dreamed that in little over a year 'Currer Bell' would be famous, and that in January 1848 G. H. Lewes in *The Westminster Review* would rank *Jane Eyre* as 'decidedly the best novel of the season'. Thackeray gave up a whole day to reading it, when he should have been hard at work on another instalment of *Vanity Fair*, and told Charlotte (somewhat bitterly, she thought) that it had given her the kind of success he had worked ten years to gain.

The continued rejection of *The Professor* soon convinced her that she must forsake the 'grey and sober' for something more sensational in her new story. In *Jane Eyre* she wrote far more daringly and imaginatively, choosing a theme of great universality in its appeal, and presenting it with more sustained suspense and excitement than she ever achieved again. Most of the background and story elements were drawn from real life, however. Her impressions of Cowan Bridge were unforgettable; and an introductory episode of passionate intensity (largely imaginary) was created, partly from her experience as a governess (it was at Stonegappe that one of the boys threw a Bible at her), and partly from childhood memories, especially of illustrations in Bewick. Together with her visit to Norton Conyers, where she had seen the attic rooms in which a mad woman had been immured, and her stay at Hathersage in Derbyshire with Ellen Nussey, these gave her the material on which to weave a colourful and intricate pattern of contrasting character and imagery.[1] Additional suggestions for a story which could combine Angrian romance elements with moral restraints came from the blindness with which her father had been threatened, his recollections of Henry Martyn at Cambridge, Branwell's setting fire to his own bed at Haworth, visits to Rydings, and her impressions of society when she was a governess. From the 'burning clime' she had abandoned, Charlotte lifted the illicit loves of heroes such as the Byronic Zamorna and the Earl of Northanger-land, the madness of Zenobia Ellrington, the passion and devotion of Mina Laury, and Elizabeth Hastings' refusal to be Sir William Percy's mistress, metamorphosing them in the process of transfer to English fictional scenes at the opening of the nineteenth century.

To those scenes she gave unity primarily by the 'autobiographical' or 'confessional' technique which links experiences in different places over a number of years. Events, including the reported, are associated through memory from two chronological viewpoints: one, that of the main action; the other, that of the writer ten years after its conclusion. Blanche Ingram's fierce and hard eye reminds Jane of Mrs Reed (xvii). When she revisits Gateshead (xxi) she believes she can 'distinguish the two volumes of "Bewick's British Birds" occupying their old place on the third shelf'; the two Miss Reeds appear, Eliza almost as tall as Miss Ingram. Entering Mrs Reed's bedroom, Jane looks into a certain corner to see if the dreaded switch is still there, 'waiting to leap out imp-like and lace' her 'quivering palm or shrinking neck'. This detail and the reference to Bewick are sufficient to recall the terror of her childhood. In recounting the climax of this period, however, the fictitious writer, wiser from experience, admits that she had not been blameless, and that her rebellious temper had helped to create the Reeds' hostility; she was 'a discord', 'a heterogeneous thing, opposed to them in temperament, in capacity, in propensities'

---

[1] Mrs Gaskell believed that Charlotte had heard in 1835, when she was at Roe Head, the story of a governess at Leeds who married a gentleman, to discover a year later, after the birth of her child, that he had another wife, whose mental derangement was his excuse for his bigamous marriage. To spare the lady's feelings, this reference was omitted from the third edition of *The Life of Charlotte Brontë* (*BST*. xxxi). See Appendix 1, p. 368.

(ii). From phase to phase we see changes wrought by events in Jane's disposition, and these help to make the story more real and convincing. Rochester's account of his past raises pity in Jane as she listens; he senses it in her eyes and trembling hands (xxvii). The great value of fictional autobiography is that it is likely to produce immediacy of experience; when the action is at a standstill, and Jane reflects in her cottage at Morton, a diary-like directness is produced in the description by a change to the present tense (xxxi). The disadvantage of the method is that it is sequential rather than 'spatial'; consequently plot complication can be a resource which is held in reserve, as in *Jane Eyre* (where it is exploited to the full), while the writer concentrates on a chronological succession of scenes. In *Villette* Charlotte succeeded in presenting a more complicated plot directly, without sacrificing the advantages of 'confessional' narration.

This second method of giving coherence to the story is ingenious but less subtle, and fortunately much less to the fore. It is part of the technique which made *Jane Eyre* 'one of the finest stories in the world' for G. K. Chesterton, depending on a set of relationships which gradually emerges and, through John Eyre of Madeira, links the Reeds and the Rivers, leads to the sensational prohibition of Rochester's bigamous intent, and ultimately to the financial relief of Jane and her cousins, the Rivers. With all this we have a series of improbable coincidences which it would be hard to parallel in major fiction. They are soon forgotten; *Jane Eyre* lives, not in background ramification of plot, but in scenes which are intensely felt and vividly visualized.

Perhaps Charlotte had remembered Scott's use of the sensational in fiction. Yet she must have been as anxious over the fate of *Jane Eyre* as Hardy was over *The Mayor of Casterbridge*. The day after completing it, he was greatly relieved to find Trollope in *An Autobiography* (xii) stating unashamedly that 'a good novel' should be both realistic and sensational, and that the crucial question lies in the realization of character. Taking *The Bride of Lammermoor* and *Jane Eyre* as examples, Trollope wrote:

> these stories charm us not simply because they are tragic, but because we feel that men and women with flesh and blood, creatures with whom we can sympathise, are struggling amidst their woes. . . . Truth let there be, – truth of description, truth of character, human truth as to men and women. If there be such truth, I do not know that a novel can be too sensational.

Later (xiii) he wrote:

> I know no interest more thrilling than that which [Miss Brontë]
> has been able to throw into the characters of Rochester and the
> governess, in the second volume of *Jane Eyre*. She lived with those
> characters, and felt every fibre of the heart, the longings of the one
> and the sufferings of the other.

The topography is somewhat confusing. We know that Lowood is
the school which Charlotte attended at Cowan Bridge, and that
Morton is Hathersage; there is no attempt at disguise in the general
description and setting. Gateshead (like Stonegappe) is fifty miles
from Lowood School (v); Thornfield (like Rydings, Ellen Nussey's
home) is six miles on the southern side of Millcote (or Leeds), but a
hundred miles from Gateshead (xxi); Millcote is situated in a *county*
seventy miles nearer London than Lowood is (x); Whitcross (near
Morton) is a coach journey of thirty-six hours from Thornfield and in
a contrary direction to Millcote (xxvii–xxviii, xxxvi); and Ferndean
lies somewhere about thirty miles from Thornfield (xxxvi).

Some critics have seen a moral allegory in the principal place-
names, as if Jane Eyre's story were a kind of pilgrim's progress, with
Gateshead the head or starting-point of the way ('gate'), and Thornfield a place where she is caught in the toils of this wicked world.[1]
The moors associated with Rivers are amenable to allegorical interpretation, but it is difficult to place Lowood and Ferndean in a consistent
scheme. Rivers is compared to Greatheart, and looks forward to an
incorruptible crown (xxxviii), but Jane does not accompany him. She
prays to be shown the path (xxxv), and it leads her to Rochester.
Charlotte's moral overtones are to be found not in simple allegory, but
in her complex use of imagery.

Jane was victimized by her cousins at Gateshead. Her lasting
impression of its hostility (xxi) reflects no normal resentment but the
unusually passionate temperament of her childhood. Her loneliness
and misery are expressed in the wintry cold, the sombre sky, the
sweeping rain, and some of Bewick's illustrations: a lonely rock in a
stormy sea, a cold and ghastly moon peering through clouds at a
sinking ship, and death-white Arctic realms. In the red-room, just
before her agonizing sense of injustice provokes a seizure, she catches

---

[1] Jane's first impressions of Thornfield give a hint of this: she thought
that a fairer life was beginning, 'one that was to have its flowers and
pleasures, as well as its thorns and toils' (xi).

sight of herself in a mirror where all looks colder and darker than in reality; the face she sees is white, and the eyes glitter with fear. The room is chill, and white breaks up the general scheme of red, which was anticipated in the curtain behind which she looked at Bewick and the desolate scene outside. It images a 'heart in resurrection'; in short, Jane sees red. When she wakes up, after her attack, the fire in her bedroom appears 'a terrible red glare, crossed with thick black bars'; she is excluded from the Christmas cheer; and then Mr Brocklehurst arrives. She looks up at him, and sees a black pillar with a grim face at the top, as if he were one of the Brobdingnagians she had been reading about. After Mrs Reed's vindictive disclosures, she looks at her icy eyes, and, 'shaking from head to foot', cleanses her bosom of the perilous stuff which weighs upon the heart. Mrs Reed is afraid that Jane will have another seizure, defends herself (adopting the conventional view that children have to be corrected), protests that Jane is passionate, as she must admit, and addresses her in terms of unwonted affection. Jane's victory had tasted like wine; when she accused and menaced Mrs Reed, her mind had been like a ridge of lighted heath, alive with flame. Now the wine has a poisonous taste; the ridge seems black and blasted. She goes outside; black frost reigns, and the sky is grey with snow-clouds. In her misery, she keeps saying to herself, 'What shall I do? – what shall I do?' (There may be an echo of the opening of *The Pilgrim's Progress* here.) She has begun to feel that she needs to be saved not only from Gateshead but from something within herself.

If the prevailing tone of Gateshead is red, that of Lowood is grey and white, reflecting meanness, semi-starvation, and severity. Frost and snow are common, and the wind moans disconsolately or is bitterly cold. Only in Miss Temple's room do we see kindness in a cosy fire. Fury burns in Jane against Miss Scatcherd's treatment of Helen Burns, despite the exemplary patience and fortitude of the latter, her New Testament idealism, and her calm conviction that animosity and vindictiveness do not lead to happiness. Miss Temple is the greatest influence on Jane, who becomes more subdued and self-disciplined during her adolescent years as pupil and teacher. Service willingly accepted gives a sense of release and freedom. Only with Miss Temple's departure does Jane feel discontented, and crave for 'liberty' or, failing that, 'a new servitude' (x). Until Rochester's arrival, Thornfield does not satisfy her; she wishes to meet people, and finds relief only in imagining the life she desires (xii).

Spring flowers at Lowood had, ironically, coincided with fog and low fever. In the autumn, eight years later, Jane's first impressions of the Thornfield setting are pleasing. (The thorn trees can be taken literally; they were recalled from Rydings.) The drawing-room is luxurious, but its colours, a 'general blending of snow and fire' (xi), suggest both passion and deprivation. Rochester returns in a harsh, bitter mood on a frosty afternoon in January (xxvii); his accident on the icy road as he passes Jane is hardly propitious. The next evening as snowflakes thicken the twilight he invites her and Adèle to have tea with him in the drawing-room. They talk by the fire. Afterwards he examines three pictures Jane had painted at Lowood. One, a personification of the Evening Star, seems to prefigure love. The others are even more significant. In one a cormorant is seen on a half-submerged mast, with a gold bracelet in its beak; beneath, glancing through the waves, is a drowned corpse. The other, against an Arctic background, is a portrait of Death with reference to *Paradise Lost* (ii), where it is associated with Sin. When Rochester and Jane next converse, by the dining-room fire, he refers to himself as 'a fallen seraph of the abyss' (xiv). After she has saved him from being burnt to death, she dreams of billows of trouble under surges of joy; she thinks she can see, beyond the wild waters, a shore sweet as the hills of Beulah, but she cannot reach it (xv). The arrival of Miss Ingram makes her resolve not to think that she can be a favourite with her master, but she soon discovers that she cannot help but love him. Rochester, though the mere mention of Mr Mason had fallen on him like a thunderbolt on an oak, and though he has concluded that Jane will obey her conscience and reason, however furiously the passions may rage, persists in believing that she will regenerate him. Yet the dangers of uncontrolled fire, or passion, and of madness, or the breakdown of moral reason, are a continual threat.

When Jane returns from Gateshead, the sky is blue and the hedges are full of roses. On Midsummer Eve the garden is Eden-like, and the nightingale is heard. Here Rochester (the fallen seraph of the abyss) declares his love; he is confident that God approves. The chestnut tree writhes and groans in the wind. Lightning strikes and thunder crashes. God has spoken, and the next day, before Jane is up, Adèle reports that half the tree has been split away. The morning is brilliant, but nothing in nature exceeds the happiness of Jane; Rochester is becoming the whole world to her, and she cannot 'see God for his creature' (xxiv). Just before her wedding-day, she

experiences dreadful omens. Between the halves of the cloven chestnut tree she sees the moon, blood-red and half-overcast; it throws a
doleful glance before disappearing, and the wind wails in the distance. The previous evening, chilled by a fireless hearth (in Rochester's
absence), she had retired early; the rising gale with its 'mournful
under-sound' continued in her dreams as she followed an unknown
road, carrying a little child (to dream of which was 'a sure sign of
trouble', xxi).[1] She had also dreamt that Thornfield was a ruin, and,
waking up, had seen a candle burning on the dressing-table, and,
reflected in the mirror, the discoloured, savage face of a tall woman,
who proceeded to tear the wedding-veil in twain and trample it on
the floor. When, after the interruption of the wedding ceremony,
the horrible truth is disclosed,

> A Christmas frost had come at midsummer . . . ice glazed the ripe
> apples, drifts crushed the blowing roses; on hay-field and corn-field
> lay a frozen shroud. . . . I looked at my love . . . it shivered in my
> heart, like a suffering child in a cold cradle.

(The child she had carried in her dream shivered in her cold arms.)
She remembers God but is tempted to stay; Rochester revives her by
the warmth of his fire and the wine he puts to her lips. Yet she
remembers that he has almost made her his mistress, and resolves she
must be 'ice and rock' to him. Even reason and conscience betray
her, but, with her veins 'running fire', the 'law given by God' and
'sanctioned by man' reasserts itself.[2] The following night she is
warned in a dream to flee temptation; the moon is transformed into
a shining white human form which bends its glorious brow in the
azure sky and whispers in her heart. She obeys. God moves in a
mysterious way in *Jane Eyre*: 'signs, for aught we know, may be
but the sympathies of Nature with man' (xxi).

Whether Whitcross is emblematical or not, it leads Jane to St
John Rivers, a man who takes up his Cross, aspires to immortality
among the saints clothed in white round the throne of the Lamb, and
expects her to sacrifice earthly happiness for his sake. Reason, not
feeling, is his guide; his ambition is unlimited. He rejects the love he
felt for Miss Oliver, but in despising the world and the flesh he seems,
unlike Becket in *Murder in the Cathedral*, to be unaware of the

[1] Based on Charlotte's experience and belief. See G. vii, 3rd edition.
[2] There is a parallel to this in 'Captain Henry Hastings', but not in
'Mina Laury'; see pp. 81–3.

temptation of working for self-glory, and of doing 'the right deed' as a missionary 'for the wrong reason'. He has no heart; altruism is a means to an end. For this reason he chooses Jane to be his helpmeet; she realizes that the servitude he offers is that of being chained for life to one who disregards her personally and thinks of her only as a 'useful tool'. With Rivers we associate winter and stone. In looks as in nature he contrasts with Rochester: his face is Grecian, his forehead 'pale as a white stone'; he offers Jane a loveless marriage (Rochester had offered love without marriage, but he is not wholly selfish as St John is). The white-walled room of Jane's cottage at Morton may represent 'principle and law', which had saved her from Rochester; when St John enters, his cloak 'white as a glacier' from the freezing snowstorm, his face is like marble (xxxiii). He is twice seen as a column, not a black pillar like Brocklehurst. Both are Calvinistic, but while one is filled with missionary ambition, the other is obsessed with sin, punishment, and damnation. Jane found her frankness congealed by Rivers' frozen reserve, and the fire of her nature subdued in his presence. She knew how icy his questioning could be, and the prospect of his anger suggested an avalanche or the breaking-up of a frozen sea. Yet, just as in the end she was tempted by Rochester's pleading, so she nearly succumbed to St John, thinking that he spoke for God.

> I was a fool both times. To have yielded then would have been an error of principle; to have yielded now would have been an error of judgment. So I think at this hour, when I look back to the crisis through the quiet medium of time: I was unconscious of folly at the instant.

She prays to be shown the path to follow, and hears the call of Rochester, the working through Nature of a spirit mightier than St John's; there can be no doubt that he regards her as a 'castaway' for heeding it (xxxv).

This call is very strange, since it seems to imply that God's views coincide with the moral law of the period, and that a marriage which Nature condemned as improper in the sight of God while Rochester's mad wife remained alive is now sanctioned by natural (or supernatural) agency. Charlotte introduced a telepathic call in 'Albion and Marina', one of her earliest stories; she may have remembered one, Mrs Humphry Ward thought, from George Sand's *Jacques*. But Mrs Gaskell heard her say enigmatically that 'it really happened' (G. xix).

Rochester's account of how he received Jane's answer suggests that Charlotte found confirmation of her belief in Wordsworth's 'Yes, it was the mountain Echo':

> Such rebounds our inward ear
> Catches sometimes from afar –
> Listen, ponder, hold them dear;
> For of God, – of God they are.[1]

Jane finds Rochester at Ferndean, a house where he would have lodged his mad wife, had not 'a scruple about the unhealthiness of the situation, in the heart of a wood' made his conscience recoil from the scheme (xxvii). The wood is gloomy and insalubrious; the house is dank and decaying. 'Can there be life here?' Jane asks as she approaches on an evening marked by a sad sky, a cold gale, and small, penetrating rain. She finds Rochester, whose eyes once flamed with passion, sightless and maimed; the fire in the grate is low and neglected. She restores it, and her lively spirit brings smiles and joy to his countenance. The next morning is bright, and she takes him out of the wet wild wood into cheerful fields, where they talk under a sparkling blue sky. With their marriage, the unhealthy site of the house seems to be forgotten. Partial sight returns to the face which had looked like a quenched lamp, waiting to be relit; and the married couple are 'ever together . . . as free as in solitude, as gay as in company'. This is a true marriage of soul and body, such as would have earned the approval, one feels, of the author of 'Rabbi Ben Ezra'. George Eliot's condemnation of it is disconcertingly unsympathetic. 'All self-sacrifice is good,' she wrote, 'but one would like it to be in a somewhat nobler cause than that of a diabolical law which chains a man soul and body to a putrefying carcase.' The repugnance she felt is more appropriate to the marriage of Dorothea and Mr Casaubon in *Middlemarch*; Jane Eyre would have been spiritually chained had she married Rivers. She brings 'regeneration' to Rochester, as he always insisted she would; she had been in love with him, despite the law and her conscience, for a long period, and had she rejected him on physical grounds she would have forfeited the reader's sympathy, and probably that of George Eliot.

It is impossible to do justice to the imagery which invigorates Charlotte's style. Predominantly it is deliberate rather than casual,

[1] See Appendix 4, p. 381.

emphasizing theme and contrasting components. Loveless eyes are cold; Rochester's flame or flash. Fire may be regulated, as we have seen with reference to Miss Temple's kindness and the early friendship of Jane and Rochester; or it may rage, as in the vindictive temper of Jane at Gateshead, her fury against Miss Scatcherd, and the early sensual passion of Bertha Mason and Rochester. Her madness and his are seen in the fiery West Indian night and a moon 'broad and red, like a hot cannon ball', throwing its 'bloody glance over a world quivering with the ferment of tempest' (xxvii). His sensuality and dissipation are symbolized in the fire which destroys Thornfield and disfigures him for life. When Jane's marriage expectations are crushed, her desolation is expressed in terms of frost and ice. Her natural feelings are imaged in fire, notably when she finds herself in conflict with the icy Rivers, whose inexorable will stifles all feeling, and makes him as stony as Brocklehurst faced with 'sinfulness'. Storm and calm, rain and sunshine, are other common elements in settings with human overtones.

Two images of a different kind are important. One is the association of the garden at Thornfield with Eden (suggestions of Rochester as the tempter having already been sown in the 'bad eminence' and 'fallen seraph' of xiv), and of Ferndean with 'paradise lost', where God tempers judgment with mercy, and love and light succeed misery and darkness. Jane is Rochester's 'better self', his 'good angel' (xxvii); she gives him new life and hope; the lovers take their solitary way, not in Eden, but to a decaying house in a wild and unhealthy woodland, related by imagery, particularly of darkness and light, to Bunyan's 'wilderness of this world' (cf. the opening of *V*. xxxviii). There is a stronger link with Milton's *Samson Agonistes*: 'A little onward lend thy guiding hand'. The theme is heralded by Rochester in 'your sun at noon darkens in an eclipse' (xx). It recurs twice (xxiv, xxvii) before we see the 'sightless Samson' of Ferndean, dependent on 'foreign guidance' as Samson was among the Philistines. As he accepted blame for failure to resist Delilah's wiles, so Rochester had condemned himself for 'the prurience, the rashness, the blindness of youth' which made him marry a woman in whom he found nothing admirable beyond her physical attractions (xxvii).

There are four aspects of religion which Jane cannot accept. Two are represented by Brocklehurst and Rivers, and a third by Helen Burns, whose precocious New Testament idealism of fortitude and forgiveness is beyond Jane's impassioned nature. The return to

Gateshead presents a fourth. Mrs Read may have been religious in her own light; she is certainly unforgiving by nature, and her daughter Eliza seems to have inherited her heartlessness. If she and her sister were the only people left in the world, Eliza would leave her. She is a rigid formalist, who takes the veil, becomes superior of a convent, and endows it with her fortune. Here Charlotte Brontë's antipathy towards cold, self-centred natures has merged with her anti-Catholic bias. Jane Eyre, looking back over the years to her last impressions of Georgiana and Eliza Read, wrote (xxi):

> True, generous feeling is made small account of by some: but here were two natures rendered, the one intolerably acrid, the other despicably savourless for the want of it. Feeling without judgment is a washy draught indeed; but judgment untempered by feeling is too bitter and husky a morsel for human deglutition.

Her religion is more human; it does not deny the virtues of forgiveness (she wishes, in fact, to forgive Mrs Reed), but it is rooted in nature and feeling. She believes in presentiments, sympathies, and signs, and seems to think that they trace their origin to a unitary source (xxi); the evidence of the novel indicates that this is God. She loves Rochester, even to the extent of forgetting God in her idolization of him, but her nature rebels against the idea of being his mistress, just as it rebels against Rivers' suggestion that she should be his wife. On each occasion divine intervention saves her, but the second takes her back to Rochester. Hardy would have considered him a victim of circumstances, meriting pity and more charitable divorce laws. Charlotte indicts him indirectly; Rochester condemns himself. He has not recovered from his self-disgust when he meets Jane, and he shows it in his attitude to Blanche Ingram (that 'armful'), who, tall, dark, and majestic, recalls the Bertha Mason of former years (xxvii). *Jane Eyre* is a morality romance, and the judgment tempered with mercy which befalls him is consistent with the religious beliefs expressed by Charlotte in her letters.

Jane's inner conflicts are expressed in debates between Conscience or Reason and cherished hopes (xvi) or passion, notably just after the double shock on the morning of her intended wedding, and in the psychological drama played out between temptation and respectability before she resolves to leave Thornfield (xxvii). Ironically, Rochester had foreseen how she would act, how judgment would have the last word, however furiously the passions raged (xix). The conflict would be strong; as she comments with reference to Rivers, she knew no medium between 'absolute submission and determined revolt' (xxxiv). With Rochester the question would be even more difficult to resolve; he was insistent, and she was not repelled. Her conscience and reason turned traitors and clamoured wildly, 'Oh, comply! Think of his misery; think of his danger –'. Still indomitable was the reply, '*I care for myself.*' Here the device has a strong dramatic appeal, but the personification technique is essentially a generalizing, abstract method, which loses some immediacy of experience at best, becomes a rather tiresome mannerism with Charlotte Brontë, and (when, for example, conscience holds passion by the throat) is in danger of not being taken too seriously.

Frances Henri's engagement compact in *The Professor* should guard against reading a Miltonic view of marriage in Jane's readiness to serve. It was a change rather than servitude she sought when leaving Lowood. She would serve gladly where she was esteemed and wanted for her own sake, just as she had done with Miss Temple. Her first meeting with Rochester is proleptic; he will have to lean on her in the end, as he does physically when the news of Mason's arrival staggers him. Only the anxiety of love in this emotional crisis explains why she says she would give her life to serve him (xix). After Mason has been secreted away, and enough has been seen and said to make Jane puzzled, Rochester asks if he can rely on her, and she answers guardedly (again with proleptic intent on the part of the author) that she likes to serve him in all that is right. She has a mind of her own. She refuses to serve the despotic Rivers, and her relationship to Rochester is anything but servile; it is shockingly truthful at times. He is mastered by her when she seems to submit (xxiv). At Ferndean, where he has most need of service, the emphasis is on freedom and reciprocity. With true love, Charlotte seems to insist, there can be service which is perfect freedom.

The freedom which they enjoy almost from the outset to speak unflattering truths of each other, when the mood permits, saves the ending from the sentimentality into which it could easily have fallen. Jane used 'the needle of repartee' to save both from 'the bathos of sentiment' (xxiv). One has only to compare scenes in Dickens with the death of Helen Burns to see how the strength of true feeling imposes severe restraint.

Irony is neither as frequent nor as subtle as in Jane Austen. Three kinds may be observed. Rochester can make general forecasts without knowing their relevance to critical junctures in his future. One example (xix) has already been noticed; another occurs when, after getting rid of Mason, he says that his life is like being on a crater-crust which may spue fire any day (xx). The discernment in these forecasts places such examples of ironical statement in a different category from those born of blind elation. His assurance that he is right in contemplating marriage, and that he can defy public opinion (xxiii) must seem as blandly confident as the song he sings (xxiv), particularly when we remember his perspicacious assessment of Jane's behaviour in a moral crisis. Finally, we have a kind of dramatic irony where the intended reference has a connotation which is hidden from the agent or speaker, as when Rochester declares his love, and Jane, thinking of Blanche Ingram, says 'Your bride stands between us', or when she decides to write to her uncle about her forthcoming marriage, thinking that Rochester may benefit from her action.

How far Charlotte had moved from the sober rational world of Crimsworth and Frances Henri may be seen in the linking of the supernatural 'Gytrash' with Rochester's first appearance. Though not endowed with the handsome features of conventional heroes, he creates a romantic spell with his flashing glance, his dark powerful personality, and Satanic overtones. Visions, dreams, premonitions, ominous signs (of the moon, for example), portents (the cloven tree), and vocal telepathy, are linked with events in a mysterious way. Features of this peculiar heightening of experience are prefigured in some of the Bewick illustrations which create mystery, fear, and even terror in Jane at the opening of the story. The conjunction of a cold, ghastly moon with a wreck seems figuratively prophetic, as does the newly risen moon, attesting eventide, in association with a church-yard scene. Rochester sees destiny menacing him at Thornfield in the form of one of the witches in *Macbeth*. The episodes which he recalls from his period of dissipation have a direct Angrian-Byronic descent, though they may owe something to Gothic fiction. All the scenes relating to the maniac wife, from the 'shuddersome' to the frightening and horrible, belong to this tradition, though related to a world which is more real and human (including Grace Poole from Grimsby Retreat with her Dickensian weakness for gin). The candlelight revelation in a mirror of Mrs Rochester, with discoloured face and bloodshot eyes, like 'the foul German spectre – the Vampyre' before she tears Jane's wedding-veil and tramples it on the floor, however much it pandered to popular taste, is more convincing and less crude than the horror of seeing her in actuality by daylight, grovelling like a 'clothed hyena' before bellowing and springing at Rochester's throat.[1] Her death in the conflagration she had caused (xxxvi) has its parallel in that of the maniac Ulrica in Scott's *Ivanhoe* (xxxi).

One of the maniac scenes is of special interest (xx). After the lunatic's attack on her brother Richard Mason, Jane is left alone to tend the bleeding victim in an attic draped with antique tapestry. Apprehensively she waits for Rochester's return with a doctor, fearful lest the 'murderess' should break out of the adjacent room. The shadows darken, and the flickering candle casts its light on the cabinet opposite with its ebon crucifix and dying Christ, and the heads of the apostles in the twelve front panels.[2] The light hovers here and there, first picking out the bearded Luke, then making the long hair of John seem to wave, finally causing the devilish face of Judas to grow and gather life until it seems that Satan himself will emerge. In this harrowing scene the mobility of the chiaroscuro is so imaginatively presented that it creates vivid experience. Here the premonitory Satanic overtones reach a climax of intensity, though their significance is intended for the reader and entirely lost on Jane. For her all is obscure; the greatest terror is at hand. She has no inkling of Rochester's role; nor does she suspect that the greatest crisis in her life will be precipitated by his tempting her to abandon moral principle. This climactic struggle for her soul is anticipated here in an active antithesis (Luke-John: Judas-Satan) which harks back to the Christianity of the pre-Renaissance era, and the kind of expression it assumes in, for example, the Good Angel and the Evil Angel of Marlowe's *Doctor Faustus*.

Charlotte admitted that the only glimpses she had had of society[3] were observed when she was a governess, and it is from this viewpoint that they are presented in *Jane Eyre*. The unreality of their portrayal is evinced most in the dialogue, which is sometimes so

---

[1] Charlotte agreed that she had made *horror* too predominant, and felt that she ought to have created a greater sense of pity: 'Mrs Rochester indeed lived a sinful life before she was insane, but sin is itself a species of insanity: the truly good behold and compassionate it as such' (letter to W. S. Williams, 4.1.48).

[2] The original belonged to one of the Eyre families at Hathersage, and is now in the Brontë Parsonage Museum. It shows only the heads of the apostles, and they are painted, not carved, as the reader might imagine.

[3] See, for example, her letter of 30.6.39.

absurd that one begins to wonder whether she wrote it seriously or satirically:

'Oh, gracious, mamma! Spare us the enumeration! Au reste. . . .
Am I right, Baroness Ingram, of Ingram Park?'
'My lily-flower, you are right now as always.'

Blanche Ingram's concluding question is undoubtedly high-spirited, but the rest is serious. 'My queenly Blanche', 'my angel girl', Lady Ingram addresses her on another occasion. Rochester's reference to Jane as 'fairy', 'angel', and 'messenger from the eternal throne', are more meaningful, but equally unrealistic; in them we hear neither Rochester's voice nor Charlotte's. They are her fancies, characteristic of the non-dramatic, high-flown literary style which often got the better of her judgment, as in Rochester's comments when Jane is moved to hear his plight on discovering that his wife was mad (xxvii):

Your pity, my darling, is the suffering mother of love: its anguish is the very natal pang of the divine passion . . . let the daughter have free advent – my arms wait to receive her.

Since Jane Eyre had the advantage of being taught French by a French lady, we must be grateful that most of Adèle's conversation is reported in English.

Charlotte Brontë addresses the reader frequently, not in the stage-manager style of Fielding or Thackeray, but in a manner which is intimate and quite her own. It may be irritating, but it is often effective. A writer more expert in novel-design would have discarded it, nevertheless, as an amateurish device. In an autobiographical narration, it is as if the leading actor made a habit of stepping out of the play to address the audience briefly on particular points in the action. In the role of author-heroine, she tells the reader, in fact, that she is drawing up the curtain for one scene (xi), reminds him of important developments or facts (xviii, xxxvii), makes admissions (she was sorry for Rochester's plight, though he had intended to marry her bigamously), and enlists sympathy in a crisis (end of xxvii). The familiar 'Reader, I married him' may be bathetic, but it has the virtue of brevity, at a point when writer and reader do not wish to prolong the conclusion.

Charlotte does not use the novel to air her views as freely as she does in *Shirley*. On the haughty attitude of wealthy families to governesses she is explicit with reference to the excellences which they ignored in Diana and Mary Rivers (xxx), and fiercely satirical in the Ingrams' reminiscences on the subject (xvii). Charlotte's views on class and sex discrimination are fused with this issue in an impassioned protest at the very heart of the story (xxiii):

'Do you think, because I am poor, obscure, plain, and little, I am soulless and heartless? . . . I am not talking to you now through the medium of custom, conventionalities, or even of mortal flesh – it is my spirit that addresses your spirit; just as if . . . we stood at God's feet, equal, – as we are!'

'As we are!' repeated Mr Rochester – 'so', he added, enclosing me in his arms, gathering me to his breast, pressing his lips on my lips: 'so, Jane!'

It was this spirit and attitude which members of the Establishment found unforgivable. According to *The Christian Remembrancer*, the novel burned with 'moral Jacobinism'. The social structure, ordained by God –

> The rich man in his castle,
> The poor man at his gate,
> God made them, high or lowly,
> And order'd their estate

– was threatened. This is the key to *The Quarterly Review*'s condemnation (written by Miss Rigby, later Lady Eastlake): *Jane Eyre* was anti-Christian, 'a murmuring against God's appointment'; it breathed the kind of 'ungodly discontent' which had overthrown authority abroad and fostered Chartism and rebellion at home. 'Jane Eyre is proud. . . . It pleased God to make her an orphan . . .' The forwardness of a heroine who admits falling in love with the hero before she is aware that he is in love with her, their fondling, and expressions of physical as well as spiritual longing and union in marriage, disgusted some of the critics; the writer was repeatedly charged with 'coarseness'. Yet the early reviews were generally favourable, praising the novel's power, its successful mingling of reality and romance, its fresh and vigorous style, its heartfelt utterance, and its psychological penetration.

Charlotte had achieved a remarkable success, but *The Quarterly* criticism rankled. She answered it in *Shirley*.

'Shirley'

It is not surprising that Charlotte's publishers expressed interest before the end of 1847 in another work by Currer Bell. A serial was proposed, but she lacked the 'unflagging animal spirits' for the demands of such composition, and preferred 'another venture in the three-volume novel form'. After three starts, with all of which she was dissatisfied, she had made slow progress by the following February. Yet, according to Mrs Gaskell, she had almost finished the second volume when Branwell died in September 1848. She did not resume until June 1849, after Anne's death. Finding labour the only cure for a 'rooted sorrow', she wrote energetically. The work – resumed at 'The Valley of the Shadow of Death' (xxiv) – was, she thanked God, finished by the end of August, and ready for Mr Taylor to collect on his return to London from a holiday in Scotland.

The previous February she had sent the manuscript of the first volume to Mr Williams for comment; both he and Mr Taylor found a certain 'want of distinctness and impressiveness' in her 'heroes', and shared some Grundyish alarm over the satirical treatment of the curates (i) and the Briar Chapel scene (ix). Charlotte admitted that her limited experience made her surer in the delineation of women, but refused to withdraw the scenes relating to the Churches; she would not sacrifice 'truth', nor did she agree that the opening scene was irrelevant to the rest of the book. She was not afraid of *The Christian Remembrancer* and *The Quarterly*, 'those heavy Goliaths of the periodical press' (2.4.49). Unfortunately she was too sure of herself, too much, as Thackeray found, the 'austere little Joan of Arc' to be sufficiently self-critical on such questions as the relative priorities of art and truth: 'when once I have looked on [a work] as completed and submitted to the inspection of others, it becomes next to impossible to alter or amend. With the heavy suspicion on my mind that all may not be right, I yet feel forced to put up with the inevitable wrong' (13.9.49). In the end she was grateful to Williams and Taylor for sending favourable opinions on the book as a whole; such views were particularly welcome to one who no longer had the opportunity of discussing her work with anyone during its composition. How much her sisters could have influenced her is very doubtful, for she insisted that she 'must have [her] own way in the matter of writing'. Imagination had lifted her when she was sinking three months earlier, and its results now cheered her (21.9.49).

Charlotte seems to have set much store by G. H. Lewes's criticism of *Jane Eyre*. He advised her to beware of melodrama, and not to stray far from the bounds of real experience. She obviously hoped that she would be able to follow his advice, and observe 'the counsel which shines out of Miss Austen's "mild eyes", "to finish more and be more subdued"'; but she knew that when she wrote most fluently she was subject to an overmastering influence. 'Miss Austen' did not appeal to her, and nothing can be more ironical than Charlotte's wish, at this juncture, to follow her example. It would be difficult to find a novel by a major author which affords a greater contrast than *Shirley* to the disciplined proportion and design of Jane Austen's works. Is *Shirley* unified by a theme, or is it a social novel related to local history? Who is the central character, or who are the hero and heroine? One might think from their delayed entries that Shirley and Louis Moore were afterthoughts. Whether 'Hollow's Mill' was the first title is not clear, but by August 1849 the author did not favour it, fancied that Shirley was the most prominent character, and left her publishers to decide whether 'Fieldhead' or 'Shirley' was the more appropriate title. Louis Moore appears belatedly, just at the point (xxiii) where the novel was abandoned for nine months; but there is an early reference to him (v). Altogether there is nothing to indicate that the main design was radically changed, and that Robert Moore, for example, was intended to marry Shirley, as has been suggested.

Parts of the novel are largely and loosely assembled; a thread linking such scenes to the main action may be discerned, though its appearance may be brief and not always in the foreground. The term 'main action' must be considerably qualified, for there is no single action which dominates the plot. Whatever the minor links, they are soon forgotten; only major episodes, scenes, and characters are remembered.

In retrospect it may be asked whether there is any association, however tenuous and fleeting, between Robert Moore, Mr Donne, Miss Ainley, Mr Wynne, and others, and why so much time is spent on the Whitsuntide processions and Sunday school feast. Throughout her more ambitious Angrian fiction, and all her novels, one suspects that, compulsive writer as Charlotte Brontë was on certain subjects, she was more interested in scenes than plot, made the most of rather limited resources, and was not well endowed with the inventiveness required for a three-volume novel. In *Shirley* there are numerous irrelevances (such as portraits, asides to the reader, and the Briar Chapel scene) which suggest an unsophisticated but confident author anticipating the sheer problem of length. To some degree the novel became her 'Jew-basket', into which she tossed for good measure a miscellany of small articles to add to the principal contents. The latter relate to Robert Moore and the Luddites, Caroline Helstone and old maids, Shirley and the upper classes; and any of these parts of the story may be delayed or dropped for a long interval.

Many of Lewes's remarks on *Shirley* in *The Edinburgh Review* stung Charlotte: 'I can be on my guard against my enemies, but God deliver me from my friends!' she told him, in probably the shortest communication she ever wrote. She was annoyed by his complaints about coarseness of texture and 'over-masculine' vigour, flippancy, the disagreeableness of most of the characters, and the 'intolerable rudeness' of their manner. There is a certain justification for all these criticisms, though in the main they now appear exaggerated, class-conscious, prudish, and outmoded. He objected to vigorous colloquial expressions, but found Shirley 'a happy creation' despite her unmannerly way of addressing her guardian. The most valid complaint concerns plot:

In *Jane Eyre* life was viewed from the standing point of individual experience; in *Shirley* that standing point is frequently abandoned, and the artist paints only a panorama of which she, as well as you, are but spectators. Hence the unity of *Jane Eyre* in spite of its clumsy and improbable contrivances, was great and effective: the fire of one passion fused the discordant qualities into one mould. But in *Shirley* all unity, in consequence of defective art, is wanting. There is no passionate link; nor is there any artistic fusion, or intergrowth, by which one part evolves itself from another. Hence its falling-off in interest, coherent movement, and life. . . . Again we say that *Shirley* cannot be received as a work of art. It is not a picture; but a portfolio of random sketches for one or more pictures. The authoress never seems distinctly to have made up her mind as to what she was to do; whether to describe the habits and manners of Yorkshire and its social aspects in the days of King Lud, or to paint character, or to tell a love story. All are by turns attempted and abandoned; and the book consequently moves slowly, and by starts – leaving behind it no distinct or satisfactory impression. Power is stamped on various parts of it; power unmistakeable, but often misapplied. Currer Bell has much yet to learn, – and, especially, the discipline of her own tumultuous energies.

This is constructive criticism of a high order, and there can be little doubt that it was not overlooked when *Villette* was planned and written. *Shirley*, however, was the occasion for paying off an old score; Charlotte had not forgotten *The Quarterly Review* on *Jane Eyre*. Her first plan was to write a preface entitled 'A Word to the *Quarterly*', but, as her publishers were opposed to it, she cunningly inserted the gist of her satire in the novel itself. Fortunately she did not choose to have recourse to another appeal to the reader, but used fiction for her purpose. Mrs Pryor (*née* Agnes Grey), in order to dissuade Caroline Helstone from being a governess, recalled her experience in a family with considerable pretensions to good birth, mental superiority, and the usual endowment of 'Christian graces' (there was no *Christian grace*[1] in *Jane Eyre*). She was soon given to understand that as a governess *she was not their equal, and therefore could have no sympathy. She was a burden and restraint in society, and a tabooed woman to the gentlemen, who were interdicted from granting her the usual privileges of the sex, though she perpetually crossed their path.* The *ladies* found her a *bore*; the *servants detested* her; her *pupils could not be her friends*. Mrs Hardman, the lady of the house, told her to cease *murmuring against God's appointment.* Her eldest daughter said that governesses must be *kept in a sort of isolation: it was the only means for maintaining that distance which the reserve of English manners and the decorum of English families exacted.* She was afraid that Miss Grey had *inherited in fullest measure the worst sin of our fallen nature – the sin of pride*; she was *proud and therefore ungrateful too.* Miss Hardman went so far as to say, '*We*

[1] Here and in the sequel the words in italics are taken with as little change as possible from Miss Rigby's review. See *S*. xxi.

need the imprudences, extravagances, mistakes, and crimes of a certain number of fathers to sow the seed from which we reap the harvest of governesses. We shall ever prefer to place those immediately about our offspring who have been born and bred with somewhat of the same refinement as ourselves.' This almost incredible piece of Victorian self-indictment mirrors the common attitude of employers to governesses. It was to escape such degradation that Mrs Pryor made her disastrous marriage.

Mrs Pryor left her unsatisfactory husband, just as Frances Henri said she would have done a profligate, a prodigal, a drunkard, or tyrant. On this question also it is clear that Charlotte Brontë was not ready to accept what contemporary society might have termed 'God's appointment'. It was a subject on which Anne Brontë had written boldly in *The Tenant of Wildfell Hall*.

Shirley is the only novel in which Charlotte attempted a socio-economic and historical picture, and abandoned autobiographical narration by the hero or heroine for the more diverse role of omniscient author. It is evident from various scenes and links in the novel – the meeting of the curates, the expected attack on Hollow's Mill, Yorke's finding work for William Farren, Caroline Helstone's illness, the attempt to assassinate Robert Moore on Rushedge, and Shirley's rejection of wealthy suitors, for example – that no single character could have had the continuity of direct experience necessary to narrate the main historical incidents and the varied social contexts which are associated in the complex but somewhat rambling pattern of *Shirley*.

The principal Luddite scenes are charged with greater suspense than any other. They are graphically dramatized and often humorous in dialogue; so much so that Charlotte's ability to give greater prominence to this action had she wished can scarcely be in doubt. There are parts of *Shirley* one would willingly sacrifice for further appearances of Robert Moore – and, in a lighter mood, of his sister and her domestic trials. Nor need one look far beyond Malone and Helstone for the possibility of further comic relief. The story of Robert Moore and Caroline Helstone may be regarded as a legitimate complement of a historical novel in a realistic vein rather than in the romantic style of Sir Walter Scott. In this whole area alone, many authors would have had little difficulty in finding the main outlines of a full-length novel.

The sabotage and militancy of the Luddites had been a familiar subject to Charlotte from childhood (and interest in it had probably been reawakened in the Brontë household by recent Chartist agitation). At Hartshead in 1812 her father had been excellently placed to see and hear for himself a number of their movements before and after their attack on Rawfolds Mill. When she was at Roe Head, she had explored much of the country where their armed revolt had been organized; she may have heard more on the subject when she stayed at Gomersal with the Taylors, whose mill and cottage at Hunsworth suggested the setting at least of Robert Moore's;[1] and while on visits to Ellen Nussey she had become familiar with the Birstall district and Oakwell Hall, which she called 'Fieldhead' after the neighbouring hamlet.

When she informed her publisher's reader, Mr Williams, that *Shirley* was 'far less founded on the Real than perhaps appears', she was rather disingenuous. As an instance she referred to the original of Mr Helstone, without admitting unequivocally that he had one. He was Mr Roberson. Charlotte says that she saw him only once, when she was ten, and was 'struck with his appearance and stern, martial air' (21.9.49). This was not a typical example, for obviously, except from hearsay, she knew little of people who took part in the events of 1812. Many of the characters were based on people she knew very well: the Taylors became the Yorke family; Ellen Nussey and Anne Brontë each contributed to the portrait of Caroline Helstone; Shirley was an attempt to portray Emily Brontë as she might have been had she enjoyed health and prosperity; the three curates were well known in Haworth and its neighbourhood; Hortense Moore was immediately identified by one of the Wheelwright sisters as Mlle Haussé, a teacher at the Pensionnat Heger; and undoubtedly there were others who would have been readily recognizable. On this point *Shirley* (x) affords testimony more cogent than Charlotte's statement to Mr Williams:

> You must not think, reader, that in sketching Miss Ainley's character, I depict a figment of the imagination – no – we seek the originals of such portraits in real life only.

Lewes's remarks on melodrama in *Jane Eyre* had not been overlooked. In that novel Charlotte had recognized the appeal of 'the wild, wonderful, and thrilling', but perhaps *Vanity Fair* strengthened

[1] Charlotte stayed with Mary Taylor at the cottage for a week just before the latter emigrated to New Zealand early in 1845.

the conviction expressed in *The Professor* that novelists should make real life their study. Her admiration of Thackeray was great before she began *Shirley*, for when the last number of *Vanity Fair* appeared she regarded him as 'a Titan'. She was struck by his dedication to truth (29.3.48); later (14.8.48) she described him as its 'high priest'. Whatever the cause, her change of policy is made startlingly clear at the outset of *Shirley*:

> If you think, from this prelude, that anything like a romance is preparing for you, reader, you never were more mistaken. Do you anticipate sentiment, and poetry, and reverie? Do you expect passion, and stimulus, and melodrama? Calm your expectations; reduce them to a lowly standard. Something real, cool, and solid, lies before you; something unromantic as Monday morning, when all who have work wake with the consciousness that they must rise and betake themselves thereto.

Yet truth is sometimes stranger than fiction, and unacceptable to the reader. If she had told the truth about Malone, it would be regarded as impossible and inartistic (xxxvii):

> Note well! Whenever you present the actual, simple truth, it is, somehow, always denounced as a lie: they disown it, cast if off, throw it on the parish; whereas the product of your own imagination, the mere figment, the sheer fiction, is adopted, petted, termed pretty, proper, sweetly natural.

Charlotte believed that a novel should present life, and that romantic fiction was essentially inferior. If *Shirley* has excitement, suspense, surprise, and even mystery, they spring from historical events or related love stories, all strictly confined to the actual or probable. Caroline is unnecessarily alarmed one moonlight night at seeing Robert Moore and Shirley speaking in low tones outside Fieldhead; and Shirley is enigmatically depressed for some time before we learn the reason. The principal mystery, however, surrounds Mrs Pryor, and she is anything but a romantic figure. The mood in which Charlotte began the novel is challengingly expressed (iv):

> who cares for imagination? Who does not think it a rather dangerous, senseless attribute – akin to weakness – perhaps partaking of frenzy – a disease rather than a gift of the mind? . . . You would suppose that it imparted some glad hope to spring, some fine charm to

summer, some tranquil joy to autumn, some consolation to winter, which you do not feel. An illusion, of course; but the fanatics cling to their dream,[1] and would not give it for gold.

The author's inconsistency is seen in some of the rapidly written chapters of the third volume; *Shirley* is least convincing when Charlotte indulges her imagination in depicting the love that grows between the heroine and her tutor Louis Moore. She mistook, as Wordsworth had done,

> The light that never was, on sea or land,
> The consecration, and the Poet's dream

for the evocation of reality. This 'inspired', euphoric writing reveals more than anything in *Jane Eyre* why Charlotte Brontë had reason to distrust imaginative flights.

Though it is not inconsistent with her general attitude when Charlotte began *Shirley*, her aside on the imagination has an absoluteness which suggests improvisation or spontaneity rather than a considered statement. She tends to write too freely in this novel, airing her views at times, rather than resolving them artistically in her presentation of people, events, and their interaction (v):

> though I describe imperfect characters (every character in this book will be found to be more or less imperfect, my pen refusing to draw anything in the model line), I have not undertaken to handle degraded or utterly infamous ones. . . . Instead, then, of harrowing up my reader's soul, and delighting his organ of Wonder with effective descriptions of stripes and scourgings, I am happy to be able to inform him that neither Mr. Moore nor his overlooker ever struck a child in their mill.

On the political question of industrialists and labour during the period when exports and unemployment were disastrously curtailed by the Orders in Council, she did well, speaking reasonably from the workers' point of view through William Farren (viii, xviii), as Dickens did through Stephen Blackpool in *Hard Times*, and ultimately through Robert Moore, who came to learn, mainly through Shirley (rather than from the gentle hints of the 'little democrat' Caroline *vis-à-vis* this 'Coriolanus'), that there is more in life than 'a man's personal interest' (xxx):

[1] This recalls the opening of Keats's 'The Fall of Hyperion, A Dream'.

beyond the advancement of well-laid schemes; beyond even the discharge of dishonouring debts. To respect himself, a man must believe he renders justice to his fellow-men. Unless I am more considerate to ignorance, more forbearing to suffering, than I have hitherto been, I shall scorn myself as grossly unjust.

Chartism was not dead when Charlotte wrote *Shirley*. She understood the sufferings and rights of workers,[1] but had some mixed feelings about industrial development. After listing the victories of Lord Wellington in Spain which made it possible to repeal the Orders in Council in 1812, she could not resist reprimanding the Liberals and Radicals of Manchester who thought this hero (Shirley's also, xxxi) a political dotard (xxxvii). Robert Moore dreams that he and his brother can bring employment and prosperity to many, but his vision (though far removed from Blake's 'dark Satanic mills') is not utopian to Charlotte. The 'barren' hollow will be lined with cottages and cottage-gardens; its rough, pebbled track will become 'an even, firm, broad, black, sooty road, bedded with cinders from my mill'; 'the houseless, the starving, the unemployed shall come . . . from far and near'; and 'the waters of Pactolus' will 'pour' through the valley of Briarfield. There will be a day-school and a Sunday school. Caroline is horrified to think that the 'blue hill-country air' will be changed into the 'smoke atmosphere' of Stilbro'; and, after the partial realization of Moore's dreams, the author's housekeeper (we are back at Haworth with Tabitha Aykroyd) recalls how once the valley was 'bonnie', full of oaks and nut trees, and haunted by fairies (cf. xiii).

Charlotte's feelings were roused more strongly by the Churches. Though the story is set in 1812, her views stem largely from observation of very local representatives in her own contemporary world. Before getting under way, she makes a scathing reference to the Puseyites and 'tools of the Propaganda'. She cannot suppress her anti-Catholicism (x), and it is significant that one of the leading agitators for Luddite violence is a 'joined Methody' preacher. Her main concern, however, is for the Church of England. There is high-spirited farce in the presentation of the curates, which serves only to underline her criticism that, when they have time to discuss church matters, they spend most of it in arguments on 'minute points of ecclesiastical

---

[1] For her virulent attack on 'the mercantile classes', see the opening of *S.* x.

discipline, frivolities which [seem] empty as bubbles to all save themselves'.[1] Her views seem to coincide with Mr Helstone's and those of her Evangelical father. Faith should be seen in works; through lack of missionary zeal, parishioners were being lost to Nonconformist Churches (i). In contrast to the curates, who have little time for the poor and needy, Mr Hall is exemplary (xviii). Shirley voices the main weaknesses of the Church (xxi):

> When I hear Messrs. Malone and Donne chatter about the authority of the Church, the dignity and claims of the priest-hood, the deference due to them as clergymen; when I hear the outbreaks of their small spite against Dissenters; when I witness their silly narrow jealousies and assumptions; when their palaver about forms, and traditions, and superstitions, is sounding in my ear; when I behold their insolent carriage to the poor, their often base servility to the rich, I think the Establishment is indeed in a poor way, and both she and her sons in the utmost need of reformation.

It is left to Charlotte to say something in its defence in her summing up (xvi):

> Let England's priests have their due: they are a faulty set in some respects, being only of common flesh and blood, like us all; but the land would be badly off without them: Britain would miss her church, if that church fell. God save it! God also reform it!

Whatever unity *Shirley* may have, it is created as much by thematic links as by narrative. Attitudes of members of the Church, and of others such as Shirley, Coriolanian Robert Moore, and Mr Yorke, towards the upper and lower classes, workers, and unemployed, seep into many parts of the novel. Equally diffusive, but more sustained, is the note of disillusionment repeatedly struck on the rights of women, single and married, by an author whose experience had made her realize the plight of girls without interests or a regular occupation to save them from romantic daydreams, take their minds off the prospect of prolonged spinsterhood, or deter them from loveless marriages.[2] For a novel with the usual happy ending in double

---

[1] The origin of Charlotte's impatience with the curates may be seen in one of her letters (18.6.45).

[2] See letters to W. S. Williams, 15.6.48 and 3.7.49. Charlotte had protested in *Jane Eyre* (xii).

measure, *Shirley* focuses attention on the 'Monday morning' atmosphere of life to a remarkable degree. The world is indeed imperfect; it was so in *Jane Eyre*, but not to the exclusion of romantic love, despite moral retribution. Many readers, no doubt, have wished that Caroline Helstone could have lived in a more romantic world, but with Robert Moore business preoccupations override love. His opposition to the war (for selfish ends denounced by the author, x) leads to a quarrel with her Tory uncle, and meetings between them are banned. Moore's subsequent departure to track down the Luddite leaders responsible for the attack on his mill leads to long periods of loneliness for Caroline. Like her author, she is not convinced by the doctrine of self-abnegation; her unhappiness makes her think of old maids, and visit Miss Mann and Miss Ainley. Her love for Robert is too strong for her to attain the fortitude of the one or the serenity of the other. As she pines, she feels that life is intended to be prized and enjoyed, not to be blank and useless, as it is for large numbers of girls with brothers in business or the professions. Her lengthy reflections culminate in a plea (obviously the author's) that the problem should be faced nationally, even though it cannot be solved immediately (xxii):

> Men of England! look at your poor girls, many of them fading around you, dropping off in consumption or decline; or, what is worse, degenerating to sour old maids, – envious, backbiting, wretched, because life is a desert to them; or, what is worst of all, reduced to strive, by scarce modest coquetry and debasing artifice, to gain that position and consideration by marriage which to celibacy is denied.

When Robert's manner towards her changes, etiquette (which seems to have become second nature) forbids Caroline to ask questions (vii):

> A lover masculine . . . can speak and urge explanation; a lover feminine can say nothing. . . . Nature would brand such demonstration as a rebellion against her instincts, and would vindictively repay it afterwards by the thunderbolt of self-contempt smiting suddenly in secret. . . . You expected bread, and you have got a stone. . . . You held out your hand for an egg, and fate put into it a scorpion. Show no consternation . . .: in time . . . the squeezed scorpion will die, and you will have learned the great lesson how to endure without a sob.

The scales are weighted against young women. Furthermore, all men are more or less selfish (x). Despite this warning, Robert's disclosure late in the novel that he could not resist the temptation of proposing to Shirley in the hope of safeguarding his business comes as a shock. Here, as elsewhere, *Shirley* stresses true values, and Robert's goodness of heart is such that he never forgets the lesson (xxx). Marrying solely for financial advantage appeals to the curate Malone, and it is ironical that Robert Moore assents absent-mindedly to the principle when he is worrying about the safe arrival of his new machines (ii).

What we see and hear of marriage is not encouraging, but rather Crabbe-like in its realism. The marriage of Caroline's mother had been disastrous, and Mrs Pryor is permanently disillusioned. Mrs Yorke is an excellent mother, but nonetheless a cynic on marriage and children; she thinks Caroline's views on love absurdly romantic, 'better suited to a novel-heroine than to a woman who is to make her way in the real world, by dint of common sense'. Yorke's only romance remains in his memory of Mary Cave, yet he admits that it is an illusion, and that had his love been returned he would probably have left her; Robert Moore's idealized picture of her seems to spring unconsciously from his recollection of Caroline, whom he has just admitted he was prepared to sacrifice for commercial gain (xxx). Mary Cave married the self-centred, iron-willed Mr Helstone, who neglected her, just as he does his niece Caroline. She receives little comfort from him when she thinks of Robert; Helstone had come to the firm conclusion that marriage is folly, that husband and wife are fellow-sufferers, each likely to tire of the other in a month, and that it is wiser, especially for women, to remain single.

In the traditional novel it is customary to keep attention alive by, among other things, not holding up the action too long. In *Shirley* there are times when one must be prepared to forgo this amenity, as is illustrated by a full analysis of Mr Yorke or the portraiture of his family (iv, ix); yet some of Charlotte's most vigorous writing may be found in a sketch such as that of Miss Mann (x). *Shirley* is so much a novel of society that the plot is inevitably slowed down at times, and far less space is devoted to outdoor scenery than in *Jane Eyre*; the view from Nunnely Common has the value of a rarity (xii). Some members of the Yorke family are an irrelevance, and there is no reason for the recall of Jessie's grave (ix) except those feelings which overmastered Charlotte's artistic sense as she watched the rain beating down on the tower of Haworth church and recalled her visit to Martha Taylor's grave outside Brussels (xxiii).

Charlotte's addresses to the reader are sometimes more than mere irrelevances. The ingenuous lack of artistry in 'It is time, reader, that you should have some idea of the appearance of this same host: I must endeavour to sketch him as he sits at table' (ii) is breath-taking. In the next chapter the same abandon allows her to expand the opening twice, at a time when she probably felt she had space to spare in a three-volume novel. After a digression of a full page (iv), she continues candidly: 'These, however, are not Mr. Yorke's reflections: and it is with Mr. Yorke we have at present to do.' One does not have to look much further for parallels to these irritating intrusions. Yet they are often important to the tone and themes of the novel, as may be seen from extracts already quoted (including one put in the mouth of Caroline Helstone). Three other authorial 'asides' have a rather special interest: one clearly refers to Mme Heger (xiv); another underlines a Yorkshire pride which the author shares with Mr Yorke *vis-à-vis* the southerner (xx), and which is dramatically expressed by Shirley when she ejects Mr Donne; finally there is a taunting reply to some of the *Jane Eyre* reviewers in the Sympsons' 'young-ladies'-school-room code of laws' which makes 'Originality' an 'unutterable Thing', whether they hear it or read it in the 'fresh, vigorous style' of a book.

There is not as much French conversation as in *The Professor*. Charlotte remembers she is writing for English readers, but reverts to French immediately the conversation is continued (v). Her excuses for the use of French words in preference to English (xvii, xxxii, xxxiii) may be sound linguistically but show little practical sense.

Shirley is the only novel by Charlotte which has two heroines who play leading roles and are physically attractive. Neither, however, creates an impression as real and lasting as Jane Eyre or Lucy Snowe, who are both akin to their author. Shirley is a rather grand portrait of Emily Brontë; how far Ellen Nussey was the original of Caroline Helstone is conjectural (see p. 310), but Anne Brontë seems to have contributed to her character as the novel progressed, and this may explain why Caroline's eyes, which had been brown, changed to blue when the novel was resumed (*BST*. lxxi). The two are an obvious contrast in appearance and temperament. Caroline is fair, a 'Raffaelle in feature' according to Louis Moore, gentle, sensitive, but immature, lacking the equanimity which becomes the more wealthy and socially experienced Shirley, who, we are assured, is 'all right', not reading or sewing for hours, as Caroline does, 'like a love-lorn maiden, pale and pining for a neglectful swain' (xxii). Her loneliness at home makes Caroline more dependent; when she is not allowed to visit the Moores, her love-sickness makes her brood until at times she is a prey to Calvinism (xx), as Anne was in her adolescence at Roe Head. Shirley's views on love are akin to Charlotte's (see p. 178); she believes that passion is 'a mere fire of dry sticks, blazing up and vanishing', and far less trustworthy than compatibility and habitual kindness (xii).

In features and habits there is much in Shirley that recalls Emily. She has unflinching courage, but her masculine affectations reflect Charlotte's sense of humour. Whether this enigmatic sister was ever as communicative as Shirley seems very dubious. Charlotte may have recalled her views on Milton's Eve (xviii) and on men's illusions about women in life and literature, their 'good woman . . . half doll, half angel' (xx); the *devoir* on 'the bridal-hour of Genius and Humanity' (xxvii) could have been based on Charlotte's recollections of one written by Emily for M. Heger. Shirley's pagan anthropomorphic conceptions of nature (xviii), however, are often couched in grandiose pseudo-poetry more akin to Charlotte's pictorialism than to the expression and vision of Emily's poetry. The writer's overexcited imagination affects Shirley's speech at times just as it does Louis Moore's hyperbolical compositions. 'Lucifer – Star of the Morning! thou art fallen . . .', she begins her rebuke of Robert Moore in his hour of shame; she tells her guardian Mr Sympson that the World is his god; it rises before her as Bel, fish-tailed Dagon, a demon; raised to a throne and crowned, it busies itself with marriages, stretching out the arm of Mezentius and fettering the dead to the living (xxx, xxxi). Her most important role, from the literary point of view, is to express in words and action Charlotte's views on the Church, class divisions, party hatreds, and all forms of tyranny, injustice, and corruption (xxi, xxxi). She helps, in short, to give thematic cohesion to a novel which tends to sprawl.

Two happy endings had to be contrived. The main strands of the story are brought together in a conversation between Yorke and Robert Moore just before the latter is wounded on his way home from Stilbro', after a long absence during which he has learned to look at life in new proportions. Reconciliation between him and Caroline presents no personal problem. It takes place through an ingenious schoolboy ruse at Briarmains, where Moore is recuperating. Success depends on the Victorian nurse's weakness for strong drink, a device used in *Jane Eyre* for other ends. Outside, a wild Iceland blast is blowing, and the air is dark with snow; within there is a warm fire, and with this familiar omen we can be sure that all will end well. The episode is amusing but not highly probable, yet we are in a much more real world than that in which Shirley and Louis Moore reach an understanding. He is a shadowy figure, kept in the background until almost the end, and not convincingly portrayed.

Shirley has told her guardian that she will not marry until she esteems, admires, and loves: Mr Sympson (who represents the values of contemporary society) regards this attitude as indecorous for a woman. Louis Moore's love of Shirley (for which we are hardly prepared, though his love of birds and animals shows that he has the character she admires; see xii and xxvi) derives from an earlier period, but it had never been fed with hope. He is poor, but he must preserve his self-respect; now at times he feels 'a strange, secret ecstasy' steal through his veins, but he resolves like St Paul to 'speak forth the words of truth and soberness'. This is what Charlotte Brontë does not allow him to do, however. One evening, when the winds are high, the sky clears and 'the Moon reigns glorious'. 'No Endymion will watch for his goddess tonight . . . for . . . she welcomes Æolus.' Louis drops the curtains, shuts out 'Sovereign and Court and Starry Armies', and begins to write. We are invited not to be shy, but stoop over his shoulder fearlessly and read. We learn how his awareness of Shirley's love has grown, and how his strength (of which we are unaware) rejoices to serve her. He was not made to be mated with a lamb, but would find more congenial responsibility in charge of a young lioness or leopardess. Sir Philip Nunnely should beware; Louis never sees him with Shirley but he thinks of 'the fable of Semele reversed'. He continues with his version of the fable as it fits the doomed Sir Philip. After this Robert Moore and Rushedge bring us back to the real world which the author promised at the outset. For the sequel, the notebook technique is used once again. Louis begins with some of Charlotte's reminiscences of Emily:

Her hair was always dusk as night, and fine as silk; her neck was always fair, flexible, polished – but both have now a new charm: the tresses are soft as shadow, the shoulders they fall on wear a goddess-grace. Once I only *saw* her beauty, now I *feel* it.

Sir Philip has been rejected, and the lioness is tamed. We learn that Louis and Shirley have had a long conversation, during which he described her as 'sister of the spotted, bright, quick, fiery leopard'. He had refused to let her depart until he obtained his answer. He had 'flung off the tutor', begged to introduce her to the man, and asked her to remember that he was a gentleman. She trembled, and put her hand to his as if to remove it from the door lock. He felt neither crushed nor elated by her lands and gold. 'My pupil', he said; 'my master', was the low answer. He was no longer afraid of her, and they were equal at last. The world swam around him, and the sun was a dizzying scarlet blaze in a whirling violet sky. She reminded him that the leopardess is tameless, but she was glad to know her keeper at last. There must be no sordid talk of money and inequality between them in future. The masterly stance he had adopted with Shirley becomes masterly action when he seizes Mr Sympson by the throat, and compels him to leave the house.

The importance of a marriage which overrides divisions created by society (as in *Jane Eyre* and *Villette*)[1] is almost lost sight of in grandiose absurdity of scene and language. It seems almost a parody, suggesting that Charlotte never prepared her conclusion carefully, and never gave *Shirley* the revision and modifications it abundantly deserved. The last volume 'was composed in the eager, restless endeavour to combat mental sufferings that were scarcely tolerable' (5.9.50). One wishes she had been less eager, less confident, and more imbued with the spirit of 'Miss Austen', who, when the need for revision was far less great, rewrote the ending of *Persuasion* and made it a more deeply moving work of art than Charlotte ever approached, except perhaps in *Villette*. Some of the early reviews of *Shirley* were laudatory, but almost inevitably its realism, its critical and even revolutionary sentiments, and a further instalment of honesty on women in love, were condemned for coarseness and bad taste. The most important criticism came from G. H. Lewes, an admirer of Jane Austen, and even he seems to have savoured little of the delightful absurdity that she would have found in the journal of Louis Moore.

---

[1] The readiness of an heiress to marry a social inferior seems, to judge from some of George Sand's novels, to have been more acceptable in France than in England.

'Villette'

Villette was probably begun in the early autumn of 1851; by November, however, Charlotte's vitality and enthusiasm were declining. Towards the end of the month, possibly with *Shirley* in mind, she told her publisher that she would proceed with it as fast as her health allowed, consistent with its being done, if not well, as well as possible, but *not one whit faster*. For almost four months she was unable to add a word, and after her holiday at Filey found it impossible to settle down to the novel until August. She seems to have warmed up to her work with considerable success, for she sent the first two volumes to the publisher at the end of October, and the remainder on 20 November. She was anxious to have an outside opinion on the book, for she had had no one to consult, as she had for *Jane Eyre* and two-thirds of *Shirley*. To judge by results, her own critical and creative powers had improved since the latter was completed. *Villette* was published at the end of January 1853 and, despite the usual, though more subdued, comments on coarseness and vulgarity, was more favourably reviewed than either of her previous novels.

Charlotte's sense of loneliness and the long bouts of depression which interrupted the writing of her novel entered deeply into the mood and outlook of Lucy Snowe; the inner life of the heroine is more than a revival and adaptation of the author's experience in Brussels.

After failing to persuade her publisher to accept the proposed three-volume revision of *The Professor*, she very wisely decided to use the background recollections upon which it was based for a new novel, more directly related to her own experience. By reverting throughout to the heroine-narrator technique of *Jane Eyre* she could recall and re-create memories more vividly and successfully. The resulting singleness of vision, and the planning of a more integrated plot, enabled her to create a much greater unity of impression than she achieved in *Shirley*. It seems evident too that she rarely relaxed in her efforts to attain closer co-ordination and a more powerful impact by curbing the impulse to indulge in digression and by attempting a more consistent intensity of style.

The economy and gain are evident in the opening chapters. The prologue was undoubtedly written to ensure a novel of a certain length, but it is more thematically and artistically related to its sequel than that of *The Professor*. For the narrative, it has its disadvantages, since it leads to a series of improbabilities whereby Lucy Snowe meets the Brettons and their two mysterious visitors years later in Brussels, and all except the fond parents are involved in the main plot. The preliminary chapters include an interesting and amusing child-study (which, with those in *Jane Eyre* and the two fragments, 'Willie Ellin' and 'Emma', suggests that Charlotte Brontë might have revealed further genius in the delineation of children had she lived and written more novels), but their main importance is prefigurative.

Villette begins in calm and ends in storm; it passes from childhood to maturity. Its centre of interest is not in Villette but in the heroine-narrator Lucy Snowe; its settings, episodes, and plot-machinery are ancillary to her development. The major drama relates to her loneliness, her repressions and crises, and their final resolution. The result is at times a remarkable evocation of experience, inspired to such a pitch that *The Professor* seems laboured in comparison.

Polly is precocious, peremptory, and independent in manner, but her determination conceals unusually strong feelings (stronger than one would expect from the Paulina of the later scenes; like Graham, she is to be Fortune's spoiled darling). To Lucy it appears that her yearning for her father betrays a 'monomaniac tendency'; when he departs, she agonizes; later she displays keen jealousy for Graham's affection. When Polly leaves Bretton to join her father, the inexperienced Lucy wonders how such a dependent girl will endure the shocks and repulses which *books* and *reason* tell her are 'prepared for all flesh' (a philosophy of life which experience was to change radically). Lucy attributes self-possession to herself, and does not realize that it will be her role, not Paulina's, to 'battle with this life' and bear its 'desolations'. The 'calm' which she claims is superficial; at the outset we can see that she is anxious and excitable. The letter which

announces Polly's coming causes Mrs Bretton evident surp
Lucy's immediate reaction is to tremble; she fears that it
disastrous news from home. The meeting of Paulina and h
oppresses her with emotion; she longs for a vicarious outlet to her
feelings.

The Bretton scenes anticipate much of the sequel for Lucy.
Already she is outwardly composed, but suffers from loneliness and
lack of deep-rooted affection; she is jealous at times; and circumstances
reduce her to a role which is rather passively spectatorial.

After enjoying halcyon weather for eight years, Lucy's bark is
wrecked in a storm and all her crew are lost. We are left to guess
what circumstances, beyond bereavement, are concealed in the
elaboration of this image (iv); what had happened earlier to make her
dread disastrous news is equally obscure. There can be little doubt,
however, that some relationship exists between her early recollections
and her inhibited temperament. The moon at Villette makes her
recall this obscure past (xii):

> Oh! my childhood! I had feelings: passive as I lived, little as I spoke,
> cold as I looked, when I thought of past days, I *could* feel. About
> the present, it was better to be stoical; about the future – such a
> future as mine – to be dead. And in catalepsy and a dead trance,
> I studiously held the quick of my nature.

One of Charlotte's letters (7.8.41) shows that Lucy reflects tensions
peculiar to the author herself:

> I know my place is a favourable one for a Governess – what dismays
> and haunts me sometimes is a conviction that I have no natural
> knack for my vocation – if teaching only were requisite it would
> be smooth and easy – but it is the living in other people's houses –
> the estrangement from one's real character – the adoption of a
> cold frigid apathetic exterior that is painful.

This explains why Charlotte gave her heroine a 'cold name', and
then made it more frigid by calling her 'Lucy Frost'. Not until the
novel was on the verge of completion did she revert to 'Lucy Snowe'
(6.11.52):

> If it is not too late I should like the alteration to be made now
> throughout the MS. A *cold* name she must have; partly, perhaps,
> on the '*lucus a non lucendo*' principle – partly on that of the 'fitness
> of things', for she has about her an external coldness.

The principle here referred to, with its allusion to warm but restrained or inhibited feelings, is more appropriately symbolized in the snow image than in the frost.

In association with the shipwreck image, the Miss Marchmont episode (iv) gives hints of the conclusion. The artistic link between present and future is underlined in the sympathy which grows between Lucy and Miss Marchmont in her varying moods, and in the hint that Lucy, having formed this secluded attachment, had hoped to 'escape occasional great agonies'. After a calm winter, a wailing Banshee wind arose one February evening as the warm firelight reminded Miss Marchmont of the glorious year of her love and its fatal conclusion. More than thirty years had passed, yet she still thought of Frank more than of God, and wondered whether in 'thus loving the creature so much, so long, and so exclusively' she had not 'blasphemed the Creator'. (In retrospect, Jane Eyre had thought similarly, knowing that she had nearly lost Rochester.) The Banshee wail which upset Lucy, and the 'shipwreck', are a foretaste of the close, when love has swept aside all barriers, and helps her to attain calm even in storm. She had seen it in Miss Marchmont: 'a vein of reason ever ran through her passion: she was logical even when fierce'.

Charlotte's recollection of her journey to Brussels is more interwoven with the fiction than it is in *The Professor*, though it sometimes shows greater detail, as in the account of reaching the ship in the Thames estuary, which recalls her return to Brussels in January 1843. The description of the landscape is more subjective, Crimsworth being made of sterner stuff than Lucy Snowe, who is ceaselessly aware of 'anxiety lying in wait on enjoyment, like a tiger crouched in a jungle', as she approaches Villette.

Charlotte's tactlessness in allowing her dislike of her pupils (a 'swinish multitude') to vent itself in a general scorn for Belgium, referring to it as 'Labassecour' (farmyard),[1] calling its capital 'Villette' (small town), and then adding, with contemptuous irony more appropriate to Swift and Lilliput, 'the great capital of the great kingdom of Labassecour', shows the crass humour of an indrawn nature, a prey to long-pent-up feelings which have cankered judgment.

No one can write with more compact lucidity than Charlotte Brontë when she is in the mood. The chapter on Madame Beck

[1] Her name for one of its most distinguished citizens is the Duc de Dindonneau, i.e. 'young turkey' (xx, xxvii).

(viii) illustrates this as well as any other, in remarkable contrast to the figurative bombast which contributes to the unreality of a number of scenes in the latter part of *Shirley*. In *The Professor* Charlotte uses Mlle Reuter rather spitefully; she is less vindictive in *Villette*. She pays handsome tribute to the finer qualities of Mme Beck's original, and concentrates on creating her for a new role. Her constant surveillance is transformed into spying, as she glides ghostlike at any hour on her 'shoes of silence', adding to the sense of intrigue which gradually builds up through the visits of Dr John, the legend of the nun, and the casket mystery. She seems impassive, yet she is fascinated by the handsome young doctor; and her jealous suspicion adds to the suspense and early mystery created by the 'little ravelled plot', in which he, and Lucy, it seems, become involved.

At its face value, this plot as it develops is 'little', no better than the 'romantic rubbish' favoured by the Minerva Press. It serves to sustain mystery for the greater part of the novel, and it is not until the main plot reaches its final phase that its higher function is fully disclosed.

Until the end of the novel there are no love scenes. Mme Beck is attracted by Dr John, but he is over head and ears in love with the vain Ginevra Fanshawe. The engaging feature of this girl is her candour with Lucy Snowe, and her unresenting acceptance of the latter's criticisms and snubs. She is flattered by her conquest, but scorns Dr John for his bourgeois connections, and dotes on the little dandy, the Count de Hamal. Although she does not know with whom Dr John is in love, Lucy is jealous, and undoubtedly his kindness during her convalescence at La Terrasse makes her more fond of him. His letters excite unreasonable hope, and stir up jealousy in Paul Emanuel, who becomes another spy on Lucy at Mme Beck's. The directrice is still jealous; she reads all Lucy's letters from the doctor, but gradually recedes into the background of interest as M. Paul persists in claiming Lucy's attention. Their clashes spark off some of the most dramatic and amusing incidents before the novel reaches its climax. With the reappearance of Polly, now 'the little countess' Paulina, it soon becomes apparent that Dr John is not for Lucy, who promptly buries her letters and grief (xxvi).

Before this happens, certain episodes have occurred, the main importance of which is the light they throw on leading characters. The first is the school fête in honour of Mme Beck (xiv). Such is the force of M. Paul's personality that Lucy Snowe agrees to deputize at the last minute, despite her objections to acting and to the part she has to play. It is that of a fop vying with a sincere lover for a coquette. Such is Lucy's prudishness that she refuses to don a man's clothes; M. Paul has the intuitive sense not to oppose her, and she has time to calm down and think out a compromise. Ginevra plays the part of the coquette, and Lucy soon notices that the zealous partiality which she displays for her in the role of a fop is directed at Dr John in the audience. The effect is to make Lucy harden her heart against him, identify him with her rival, the sincere lover in the play, and resolve to outshine him. With Ginevra's ready co-operation, she does this so successfully from reawakened jealousy of Dr John that her role is transformed. The next morning she reverts to her normal self, having decided that the relish she has discovered for dramatic expression will not do for 'a mere looker-on at life'. Such she is at the ball which follows, where Ginevra points out her foppish beau, Colonel de Hamal, and her admirer, who is none other than Dr John. It was Lucy's knowledge that he was infatuated with some 'angel' at the pensionnat which got the better of her reserve in her stage performance, and enabled her to make the most of a situation which Ginevra played up at his expense. The discovery of Dr John's infatuation with Ginevra excites her strangely again; she begins to rally him on his illusions, but time passes before she dares to tell him what she really thinks (xviii).

The Cleopatra has been coupled with the Vashti scene as an indicator of Lucy Snowe's deeper feelings. The text does not support this interpretation. To describe the ludicrous proportions of this voluptuous 'commodity' as 'an enormous piece of claptrap' suggests not only a refreshing sense of humour but a healthy reaction against some traditional masculine values. The picture acts as a catalyst: it gratifies Colonel de Hamal's sensuality; it does not appeal to Dr John, who finds no beauty comparable to that of Ginevra; and it disgusts the despotic M. Paul, who makes Lucy sit elsewhere, facing a set of four pictures which present 'La vie d'une femme', all grim, cold, and moral, 'as bad in their way as the indolent gipsy-giantess, the Cleopatra, in hers', Lucy thinks. The concert is a great civic occasion; its main significance for the reader is that it enables Dr John to see the reality of the Ginevra he has idolized. It also marks another stage in the growth of M. Paul's jealous interest in Lucy Snowe. The effect of Vashti's acting on the latter is based on Charlotte Brontë's impressions of Rachel (see p. 336 and letters of 24 and 28 June 1851).

Horrible though the spectacle is, and the contemplation of 'Hate and Murder and Madness incarnate', it is 'a mighty revelation' of suffering and passions, in comparison with which the artistry of the Cleopatra is mere flesh-bound materialism. Lucy discovers that she has unsuspected sympathies with powerful forces; a nature that preferred to be temperate is carried away by passionate vehemence. She had never seen acting like this; it satisfied the imagination and 'disclosed power like a deep, swollen winter river, thundering in cataract, and bearing the soul, like a leaf, on the steep and steely sweep of its descent'. It also showed up some of Dr John's limitations:

> His natural attitude was not the meditative, nor his natural mood the sentimental; *impressionable* he was as dimpling water, but, almost as water, *unimpressible*: the breeze, the sun, moved him – metal could not grave, nor fire brand.

> Dr John *could* think and think well, but he was rather a man of action than of thought; he *could* feel, and feel vividly in his way, but his heart had no chord for enthusiasm. . . . [Vashti's] agony did not pain him, her wild moan – worse than a shriek – did not much move him; her fury revolted him somewhat, but not to the point of horror. Cool young Briton! the pale cliffs of his own England do not look down on the tides of the Channel more calmly than he watched the Pythian inspiration of that night.

Other shortcomings had been observed in Dr John; Lucy had found his self-love 'cruel'. In public he was oblivious of self, yet privately he loved to excite homage, and was vain when he received it (xix). Much later we learn that he is a man of the world: it was not enough for him to satisfy himself; the world must approve. In his 'victrix' he required all that he found in Paulina, 'the imprint of high cultivation, the consecration of a careful and authoritative protection, the adjuncts that Fashion decrees, Wealth purchases, and Taste adjusts'. She was a pearl of great price, but Dr John 'was not the man who, in appreciating the gem, could forget its setting' (xxxii). Had she not been protected by Providence, she would have suffered as Lucy had feared. For her and Graham Bretton, however, all is sunshine. 'Some lives *are* thus blessed: it is God's will: it is the attesting trace and lingering evidence of Eden.' 'Some real lives do . . . anticipate the happiness of heaven', and some are doomed to suffer, Lucy Snowe believes (xxxii, xxxvii). (Such were Charlotte's views, and in that conviction – not in the light of reason and books (iii) – she had resolved, as she told her publisher three days before requesting the alteration of her heroine's name to 'Snowe', never to be 'leniently disposed towards Miss *Frost*': 'from the beginning I never meant to appoint her lines in pleasant places'.) Lucy admired Paulina – her beauty, sweetness, and cultured reserve, which surrounded 'so much pure, fine flame' like 'gentle hoar-frost', before it was thawed by Graham's 'generous influence'. There seems to be a welcome *arrière-pensée* in one of her observations, however; she never saw M. Paul's Sylvie ('delicate, silky, loving, and lovable little doggie she was') without thinking of Paulina; 'forgive the association, reader, it *would* occur' (xxxvi). She and her doting father never seem to grow up, and it is generally a relief to get away from them. Charlotte Brontë was wise not to 'delay the happy truth' of Paulina's marriage. This enabled her to concentrate in the concluding chapters on the clouded fortunes of Lucy Snowe and the mystery surrounding M. Paul. A happy ending in the midst of all this would have been an artistic disaster.

Charlotte Brontë's reservations may be hinted at in the physical attributes of some of her more fortunate characters. Paulina is subject to no open criticism; she has 'a refined and tender charm', 'a subdued glow from the soul outward', not like 'an opaque vase' but 'a lamp chastely lucent'. Dr John's 'marble chin' and 'straight Grecian features' suggest a certain insensitiveness. The most severe disdain is reserved for Count de Hamal: 'as to his low, Grecian brow, and exquisite classic headpiece, I confessed I had no language to do such perfections justice'. St John Rivers is a familiar example of the association of art, especially Greek sculpture, with natural short-comings in Charlotte's characters. In *Villette* this characteristic may be seen best in her appraisal of some of the fine ladies at the great civic concert (xx).

Lucy Snowe is unfortunate. She inherits neither good looks (as Ginevra Fanshawe tells her in a frank exchange, xiv) nor 'sunshine'. She believes in submission to God's will, struggling valiantly on through 'the wilderness of this world' (xxxviii), trusting in his mercy (xxxii). She has always sought to penetrate to the truth, knowing that to face up to the worst is to reduce fear (xxxix). A white-haired old lady (v), looking back on her life, she knows how often she has been a prey to anxiety and excessive hope; the moral she has drawn is that 'day-dreams are the delusions of the demon' (vi). Three times events had told her that a wailing storm was unpropitious. The first heralded

Miss Marchmont's death and the sudden dissolution of an attachment which Lucy wished could last twenty years; the second occurred during the long vacation in Villette, when, after being left in the pensionnat with only a cretin for company, she became feverish, fell a prey to hypochondria and insomnia, and, feeling the dormitory oppressive as a tomb, and that Heaven offered hope for the loveless, went out and sought comfort through confession. The third marks the tragic ending of the novel.

There is a fourth period of storm which has some kinship with these, though it points to a gradual disappointment rather than to an immediate disaster. After her confession, Lucy collapsed and was providentially found by Dr John. She convalesced at La Terrasse. When she returned to the pensionnat, he was sorry for her and promised to write. What his letters meant to her may be seen from her over-wrought state when she thinks she has lost the first, and searches for it like a 'grovelling, groping monomaniac' in the dark attic (xxii). After taking her to see Vashti, he did not write for seven weeks (xxiv):

> Oh! – to speak truth, and drop that tone of a false calm which, long to sustain, outwears nature's endurance – I underwent in those seven weeks bitter fears and pains, strange inward trials, miserable defections of hope, intolerable encroachments of despair.

Then, one wintry day, when she had 'entered into that dreary fellow-ship with the winds and their changes, so little known, so incomprehensible to the healthy', a letter came from Mrs Bretton, inviting her to La Terrasse to meet old acquaintances. Who could understand what a relief it was, after going mad, as it were, from solitary confinement? In all the land of Israel there was but one David to soothe or comprehend Saul. The old acquaintances were Paulina and her father, now Count de Bassompierre. Looking back on his raillery, the writer wondered whether Graham's manner would have been the same had she been endowed with wealth and station, as Paulina was. 'No', she added (xxvii):

> you might sadden and trouble me sometimes; but then mine was a soon-depressed, an easily-deranged temperament – it fell if a cloud crossed the sun. Perhaps before the eye of severe equity I should stand more at fault than you.

Lucy's nature is repressed rather than morbid or masochistic. It is probable that loss of maternal affection created the same complex in

Charlotte Brontë. Had Lucy's childhood and adolescence been more normal, had she enjoyed home and friendships instead of enduring long periods of heart-loneliness and anxiety, her emotional life would have been far less exceptional. As it was, repression engendered tensions and feelings so importunate or depressing that she felt they should be subdued, and longed for a life of tranquillity. It is true that she felt strongly, for others as for herself (ii):

> On all occasions of vehement, unrestrained expression, a sense of disdain or ridicule comes to the weary spectator's relief; whereas I have ever felt most burdensome that sort of sensibility which bends of its own will, a giant slave under the sway of good sense.

There is little relief for the giant slave which oppresses her. Her first impulse when she realizes Mme Beck's suspicion that she is at the root of Dr John's mysterious appearance in the pensionnat garden is to laugh, but complicated thoughts and feelings wreck her composure, and she weeps 'hot tears'. It is a solace to be loved by little Georgette (xiii):

> Her clasp, and the nestling action with which she pressed her cheek to mine, made me almost cry with a tender pain. Feeling of no kind abounded in that house; this pure little drop from a pure little source was too sweet: it penetrated deep, and subdued the heart, and sent a gush to the eyes.

Affection from her old friends the Brettons, after her breakdown, rouses gratitude so strong that she wishes for moderation, and trusts that her life will be tranquil (as it had been at Miss Marchmont's), requiring only occasional, 'unengrossing' friendships to sustain it (xvi). Graham's letters give her a new belief in happiness; gratitude prompts her to write lengthy affectionate replies, but reason compels her to write tersely. In retrospect she is certain that she acted wisely, but can one be sure that she was right? His letters to her (like M. Heger's to Charlotte) had been like a goodly river; she loved her Rhine, her Nile, almost worshipped her Ganges, and, though stoical, grieved when it vanished like a mirage. Only after many trials and a crisis of hopelessness, did she find true love; a 'relieved heart' changed her life wonderfully; M. Paul's expressions of love during three years' absence sustained a 'genial flame', which (one feels) his tragic death subdued but could not quench.

The practical way in which Ginevra's agile lover makes use of the nun legend associated with the pensionnat would appear very cheap 'Gothic', with no imaginative appeal, if it were not curiously linked with Lucy's reactions to some of the crises in her life. To create a real interest, such a link is necessary when appearances, only ostensibly supernatural, occur in a setting which is ordinary and bourgeois compared with the battlemented Thornfield, where, in retrospect, even the vision of the hag, like one of the witches in *Macbeth*, writing in the air a warning which ran in lurid hieroglyphics along the house-front, does not seem out of place when Rochester is wrestling with destiny (*J.* xv).

There are four appearances of the nun, two related to Dr John and two to M. Paul. The first hint is the throwing of the casket into the garden. A new crescent moon is shining, and Lucy has just recovered from a period of longing; her Sisera lies quiet in his tent (xii). The nun is seen when Lucy ascends to the attic in order to savour Graham's first letter unmolested; her double excitement reduces her to a pathetic state until the letter is recovered. It is no wonder that Dr John concludes that the 'spectral illusion' is due to nervous excitement after her vacation illness (xxii). He witnesses the same excitement, and is much nearer the truth than he imagines, when he asks 'Ha! the nun again?' just before their theatre visit (xxiii). The second appearance finds Lucy more determined: she has buried Graham's letters and her delusive hopes at the foot of Methuselah, the pear tree associated with the legendary nun (xii). Again it is moonlight. Suddenly she sees the nun approaching; rather desperately, she stands her ground, and the nun flees. 'This time there was no Dr. John to whom to have recourse' (xxvi).

The nun appears a third time when Lucy has begun to find pleasure in M. Paul's presence. One spring Sunday afternoon, after watching Mlle Sauveur, his goddaughter, happy in his company, Lucy falls asleep. On waking, she thinks of taking a step towards independence (as she had done when she buried the letters) if the volatile Paul proves unkind. She does not assume that all will be easy. Pausing before Methuselah, she wonders what has happened to her 'curious, one-sided' friendship with Dr John, 'which was half marble and half life'.[1] She recalls her delight in his company, and then dismisses her fond memories. M. Paul appears; they talk; it grows dark and begins

---

[1] The hair 'still golden and living' at the root of the tree is Dr John's; Lucy Snowe has allowed her buried feelings to revive.

to rain. Suddenly he asks if Lucy believes in the supernatural; she admits that she has experienced 'impressions'. He is glad to hear this, for he feels a rapport between them. He reminds her of the nun legend, and says that he also has had impressions. Their attention is caught by a violent movement in the high tree adjacent to the first classe. The prayer-bell rings, and the nun sweeps swiftly past them (xxxi).

For the final confrontation with the nun we have to remember 'the night's drama' when Lucy wanders in a semi-trance through the moonlit park. The drug given her at Mme Beck's behest has excited her imagination, and what she sees has a dreamlike illusory quality: many people are in masks; the architecture is varied and exotic, and she recognizes that it is mere timber, pasteboard, and paint. The climax comes when the arrival of Justine Marie is announced. (She was named after her aunt, who became a nun when she was not allowed to marry Paul Emanuel. Lucy had seen her picture at Mme Walravens', and had associated it with the apparition.) So heightened is her imagination that she expects the 'dénouement' to disclose the spectre; instead she sees a comely girl join Mme Walravens and her group. She listens, and understands that Paul will be rewarded with a young bride and rich inheritance when he has made their fortunes in Guadaloupe. Justine Marie, she assumes, must be the bride. Although the 'play' she has witnessed that night is not over, Lucy has heard enough. She is torn by jealousy as never before, but she accepts the truth and, even though the iron has entered her soul, feels renovated and free. Returning to her dormitory, she sees the nun lying on her bed, rushes at it, and finds nothing but vestments, which she tears to shreds and tramples on. Relieved from all sense of the spectral, and overcome at last, perhaps by the narcotic, she sleeps soundly. The mystery of the nun is soon solved, but that of M. Paul remains. Lucy is still oppressed by 'the distorting and discolouring magic of jealousy'. When they meet, he makes it evident that he defies the 'junta', the 'basilisk with the three heads', which has conspired to part them. He takes her to the school and house he has prepared for her in his absence, and on the way back tells her that Justine Marie is engaged to a rich young German and will be one of her pupils. They walk home by moonlight, 'such moonlight as fell on Eden'.

Lucy had shown that her nature preferred 'to penetrate to the real truth' and that 'to see and know the worst is to take from Fear

her main advantage'. This is the theme counterpointed by the nun
scenes:

> Ah! when imagination once runs riot, where do we stop? What
> winter tree so bare and branchless . . . that Fancy, a passing cloud,
> and a struggling moonbeam, will not clothe it in spirituality, and
> make of it a phantom?

Once Lucy had seemed to 'hold' two lives, the life of thought and that
of reality; her needs for the latter were not great, she thought,
provided the former was 'nourished with a sufficiency of the strange
necromantic joys of fancy' (viii). She had now matured sufficiently
not to nurture illusions (as she had done with Dr John) but to face
life dauntlessly. This spirit undoubtedly prevailed at the end, when
she had to face the great sorrow of her life.

Although Charlotte Brontë relied on much from her own experience to provide the background for scenes in *Villette*, there is a danger
of underestimating her creative powers. Lucy's explanation of her
confession is more convincing than that of Charlotte to Emily (with
the caution, 'I think you had better not tell papa of this. He will not
understand that it was only a freak, and will perhaps think I am
going to turn Catholic', 2.9.43), but it does not follow that Paul
Emanuel, Mme Beck, and Dr John are faithful portraits of the
Hegers and Charlotte's publisher, George Smith. A person is reflected
in what he does, and when the actions of these characters are considered, we realize that inventive resources are used to reveal or
mould character for a highly imaginative theme. Despite his kindness
and excellent qualities, Dr John's foolish infatuation with Ginevra
Fanshawe and his serious shortcomings in the eyes of Lucy should
be sufficient to indicate that Charlotte's reproduction of traits was
mainly superficial, whatever its extent. So limited was her experience,
especially of men, that she was compelled more than most writers to
use individuals as originals. In *Villette* there is far more imaginative
re-creation than in *Shirley*, where some portraits were copied from
life without due regard for the needs of the plot. Mme Beck's im-
passivity and coldness, even to her children, were not true of Mme
Heger, whatever her reserve; Charlotte admitted that she was less
severe than one of Miss Wooler's sisters; the evidence of other pupils
shows that she was kind. Undoubtedly her jealousy of M. Heger's
interest in Charlotte was the origin of Mme Beck's elaborate scheming
to prevent the marriage of M. Paul and Lucy. M. Paul owes much to

M. Heger's character, as may be seen in the letter Charlotte wrote
to Ellen Nussey in May 1842:

> He is a professor of rhetoric, a man of power as to mind, but very
> choleric and irritable as to temperament; a little black ugly being,
> with a face that varies in expression. Sometimes he borrows the linea-
> ments of an insane tom-cat, sometimes those of a delirious hyena;
> occasionally, but very seldom, he discards these perilous attrac-
> tions and assumes an air not above 100 degrees removed from mild
> and gentleman-like. . . . When he is very ferocious with me I cry;
> that sets all things straight.

He was also very patriotic and anti-British (cf. xiv, xxix). He often
lent Charlotte books, and revealed beauties in the classics which she
had never perceived; she found his mind a library, and its tomes of
thought 'collyrium to the spirit's eyes' (cf. xxxiii). On this basis, by
emphasizing certain idiosyncrasies in imaginary scenes, she created the
most engaging and delightful of her characters. Paul Emanuel is
irascible; he loves to dramatize his emotions; yet, but for his great
humanity, he would be sheer caricature. Lucy enjoys seeing him
jealous. Despite his despotic tantrums and his exhibitionism, he is
good at heart and exceedingly charitable; on a minor scale, his nature
is seen at its best in the scene where, after accidentally breaking his
spectacles, Lucy becomes frightened (xxviii). Superficially he is a
comical little man, and this is how he first appears; as Lucy grows to
like him, his admirable qualities are increasingly shown. In the end
he exemplifies a love which admits no barriers of race or creed,
which overrules the power of Catholicism (its secular, material, and
spiritual aspects represented in Mme Beck, Mme Walravens, and
Père Silas), and is unquenchable in death. He belongs to a higher
order than M. Heger; he is the last and supreme manifestation of
Charlotte Brontë's belief that human love should transcend all worldly
distinctions (xxxvi).

Despite this triumph of spirit over form, Charlotte Brontë's anti-
Catholicism is not concealed; as Lucy Snowe, she couples some of its
excesses with those of Methodism (ii, xxxvi). The 'lecture pieuse'
with its 'tales of moral martyrdom inflicted by Rome' made her feel
like Mause Headrigg against Sergeant Bothwell (xiii); the Church
seemed to say, 'Look after your bodies; leave your souls to me' (xiv).
All Charlotte's antipathies seem to be embodied in Mme Walravens,
'Malevola', hunchbacked, dwarfish, doting, and bejewelled like a

barbarian queen. The thunder and lightning which accompanied Lucy's weird visit reinforce the 'Cunegonde' sorceress suggestion. Like Charlotte (letter to Ellen Nussey, July 1842), she thought that 'whatever Romanism may be, there are good Romanists' (xxxiv). Nevertheless she dared to say that God was not with Rome, though eventually He would pardon its 'mitred aspirants for this world's kingdoms' (xxxvi). One of these good Romanists came to see that formal differences are insignificant. He perished; but the 'junta', the representatives of Romanist power, prospered. The bitter personal irony at the end of *Villette* expresses the author's religious prejudice very sharply.

Villette lacks the variety of *Shirley*, especially in character, but it is a far more disciplined and powerful novel. In no other of Charlotte Brontë's characters is adult experience more keenly realized than in Lucy Snowe. The style is habitually charged and animated with imagery, which gives a glow to thought and intensifies feeling. Occasionally imagination gets the better of reason; G. H. Lewes noticed 'the fault of running metaphors to death sometimes'. This is evident in the Jael-Sisera passage, and the interpretative addition to the second paragraph, 'By which words I mean that the cool peace and dewy sweetness of the night filled me with a mood of hope' (xii). Personification, realistic or poetic in its imagery, is a dangerous medium for Charlotte, and the redundancy which it can precipitate may be illustrated from the passage on Reason and 'the divine Hope' which Lucy experiences at the prospect of letters from Dr John (xxi). It is an excellent example of what Coleridge called 'mental bombast', a fault, he added, of which only genius is capable. 'It is the awkwardness and strength of Hercules with the distaff of Omphale' (*Biographia Literaria*, xxii). Not surprisingly Charlotte illustrates this weakness when she writes on the Creative Impulse (xxx). In general, however, as is appropriate to a narrator who pleads 'guiltless of that curse, an overheated and discursive imagination', the style is controlled; and with this control it acquires intensity and power, nowhere more remarkably than in the concluding chapters.

Since Charlotte could not resist reverting to French frequently, and occasionally at length, in dialogue, it is rather egregious that she attempts to excuse its use on one occasion to 'veil' an uncomplimentary reference (xii). Addresses to the reader are less obtrusive than in previous works, and sufficiently relevant to be acceptable. Subjectivity in a heroine-narrator is to be expected; she is at pains, with reference to Dr John, to state that her feelings may change in the course of time (xviii), and that others did not think as highly of him as she did (xxii). One suspects some inconsistencies, however. Her claim always to have liked to penetrate to the truth (xxxix) seems to overlook the 'necromantic joys of fancy' on which she had once set store; she was frequently a prey to 'overheated imagination', and there is an excellent miniature example of this in her visit to Mme Walravens', when the picture of the nun 'fell away with the wall and let in phantoms'. The narrator's greatest flaw has been pointed out by E. M. Forster; if she delineates characters and events as she sees them at the time, there is little justification for concealment to create a 'good plot-thrill' later on. It is difficult to see any gain from the use of this trick (xvi: cf. x).

'Nearly all novels are feeble at the end', Forster goes on to say in *Aspects of the Novel*. *Villette* is one of the great exceptions to this generalization. It was a happy inspiration to make Lucy wander out on the night of the fête, her senses abnormally awakened by an opiate. The vivid scenes which Charlotte conjured up miraculously from the past, and which we follow with Lucy as if they were part of a motion-picture, hold the reader like a dream. By this device most of the principal characters reappear before the final curtain, and a climax of mystery is produced. The tempo is excellent. Much happens in the final chapters, and all is organized and lucidly presented. The prose reaches high levels; as the end approaches, economy and pace increase; and frequent short sentences are artfully introduced, without impairing rhythmical effects. If any criticism is to be raised, it is against a slight ambivalence at the end. Mr Brontë had requested a happy conclusion. All Charlotte could do, in the words of Mrs Gaskell, was 'so to veil the fate in oracular words as to leave it to the character and discernment of her readers to interpret her meaning'.

Assessments of *Villette* by contemporary writers are of interest. Matthew Arnold found it 'disagreeable' because 'the writer's mind contains nothing but hunger, rebellion, and rage'. Further light on this may be seen in the lines he omitted from his poem 'Haworth Churchyard':

> . . . younger passionate souls
> Plung'd in themselves, who demand
> Only to live by the heart,
> Only to love and be lov'd.

The view squares with Harriet Martineau's, that all the female characters are preoccupied with the need of being loved. The argument that 'it is not thus in life' undercuts this exaggerated criticism; a novelist or playwright can be expected to illustrate a theme, to select and concentrate, rather than present all aspects of a subject; Lucy Snowe is no ordinary person. G. H. Lewes found 'astonishing power and passion' in *Villette*, but thought that 'Currer Bell, in her next effort, should bestow more pains on her story'. George Eliot felt that it was 'a still more wonderful book than *Jane Eyre*', and discerned 'something almost preternatural in its power'.

Three Fragments

These, it may be claimed, belong to the period when Charlotte Brontë wrote with publication in mind. They are presented in chronological order. The first is a discarded opening, most of which was used in *The Professor*. The other two are more memorable, creating atmosphere and mystery around two young children.

*   *   *   *   *   *

'The Moores' (sometimes referred to as 'John Henry')[1] consists of three scenes. The first is between John Henry Moore, a mill-owner, and his wife, the daughter of an affluent nobleman's agent, at their home, Everintoyle, the name of which plainly indicates the husband's priorities. They have been married hardly six months, but they are already quarrelsome, and Moore's manner is blunt and hectoring. He has just received a letter from his brother William, who had been educated at Eton at the expense of Mr and Mrs Seacombe. They had found him a post as sub-editor, and would now like him to join the ministry, in the hope that he will marry the niece of a clergyman whom Mrs Seacombe thinks a model for William. To avoid this fate, he prefers his brother's counting-house. John Henry decides to make him clerk in charge of foreign correspondence.

Mrs Moore obtains her husband's permission to invite her friend Miss Whinn (later 'Wynne') to her home. Miss Wynne is snobbish but, finding life dull at De Walden Hall, thinks it will be diverting to air her superiority at Everintoyle and flirt with young millowners.

---

[1] Contained in *BST*. lxxvi, and in W. Robertson Nicoll's edition of *Jane Eyre*, London, 1902.

The third scene presents Mr Moore and his book-keeper Tim Steele, smoking and drinking in the back-parlour. Steele is a 'joined Wesleyan Methodist'.

As all the elements of the first and third scenes appear in *The Professor*, this fragment could have been written in 1845, but not later. The Wynnes of De Walden Hall appear in *Shirley*, though Miss Wynne does not play an important role. The Moores of *Shirley* do not resemble John and William very noticeably, but it is interesting to note that the name of J. H. Moore's mill was originally Helstone Mill, that Robert Moore was (with some justification) concerned to make profits, and that he had been expected to marry a Miss Wynne: first the dark, then the light (*S.* ii).

*   *   *   *   *   *

'The Story of Willie Ellin'[1] was written in the summer of 1853, and may have been the first creative writing Charlotte attempted after the publication of *Villette*. Two brief attempts at opening scenes survive, in addition to the one version which makes any headway with the story. Altogether they suggest a very unsettled plan compared with that of 'Emma'. The theme is the bullying elder brother in business; it first appeared in an Angrian story by Branwell Brontë (see p. 77), to be adopted in 'The Moores', and in *The Professor*.

Willie runs away to his ancestral home because his stepbrother threatens to make him a shop apprentice; he has been beaten because he is slow. He is terrified and asks that the doors be bolted. His red-whiskered brother follows, breaks into Willie's room, and is about to lash him with his gig-whip when prevented by his companion Mr Bosas, a merchant from a distant capital city. During the merchant's stay at Edward Ellin's, Willie is not harmed, but late one night, after the departure of Mr Bosas, he is whipped despite his pleas (which seem unnaturally cool and accommodating). He will not scream but, after a sleepless hour, he weeps; then, after kneeling in prayer, he falls asleep.

There is an alternative ending: a girl of seventeen (Edward's wife?) comes in, comforts Willie, and assures him that Edward will never hurt him again.

*   *   *   *   *   *

[1] *BST*. xlvi.

'Emma' was Charlotte's last work. One evening, at the close of 1854, according to Thackeray,[1] as she sat by the fire with her husband, Arthur Nicholls, she suddenly said, 'If you had not been with me, I must have been writing now.' She then ran upstairs and brought down, and read aloud, the beginning of a new tale. When she had finished, her husband remarked, 'The critics will accuse you of repetition.' The comment suggests an ill-qualified literary adviser, who, rather jealously, did not wish to encourage Charlotte in any independent avocation. There is a school, of course, in 'Emma', but nothing in narrative or situation that can be described as repetitive. The sureness and economy of style in this fragment make one wonder how much more Charlotte would have matured as a writer had she lived, and had her unimaginative husband encouraged her to write. Here, to return to the advice of Lewes after reading *Jane Eyre*, she achieves 'the nicest sense of means' to her ends. Its 'splendid economy' of means was 'charged with the most intense psychological suggestion' for May Sinclair, who found in Mr Ellin the proof that 'Charlotte Brontë could create a live man of the finer sort' with 'no earthly resemblance' to her previous heroes.

Two years before the narrator began her story, a gentleman had driven up to the school kept by her friend Miss Wilcox, and asked if she could take his daughter immediately. It was agreed that she should be allowed privileges, but favouritism did not make the heiress Matilda Fitzgibbon popular with the other pupils. She was by no means pretty, but had a wonderful wardrobe. She was taciturn, very dependent on the principal, and, according to Mr Ellin (a frequent visitor to the school), very unhappy. She began sleep-walking, moaning and holding out her hands as she passed through the bedrooms; once Miss Wilcox, going upstairs in the dark, trod upon her as she lay in a fit on the landing.

One winter morning a note arrived for Mr Ellin from Miss Wilcox (to whom he was devoted, according to rumour), requesting him to call. She was pretty, and dressed attractively, as did her sisters; but, though very proper, she lacked expression and feeling. She had written to make arrangements for her pupils during the Christmas holidays, but had received no reply from Matilda's father. That morning her letter had been returned with a note to say that no

[1] 'The Last Sketch', an introduction to 'Emma', both published in *BST*. x.

person of the name of Mr Fitzgibbon was known, or place such as had been given Miss Wilcox as his address.

Mr Ellin suggested that he should make some inquiries. He returned after about a week, and confirmed that it was impossible to trace Mr Fitzgibbon. Miss Wilcox could not afford to lose the fees, and said that, try as she might, she had never been able to like the child. She summoned Matilda, and told her she had a few questions to ask, and would endure no lies. The inquisition proceeded with increasing sternness, and Matilda gave no answer. Suddenly she cried, 'Oh, my head!' and staggered; then, as Miss Wilcox continued, harsh as ever, she appealed to Mr Ellin. In an unusual voice he asked Miss Wilcox to say no more; Matilda had fallen. He picked her up; as she rested beside him, she raised her eyes to him. He told her to have no fear, and gradually she became reassured. Then he insisted that she must be put to bed, and carried her upstairs himself. He returned to Miss Wilcox, told her to say nothing to the child, lest harm should be done, suggested that they should discuss the problem the next day, and that he should question the child . . .

The Fitzgibbons are not the only mystery; Mr Ellin is enigmatic. The narrator is Mrs Chalfont, a middle-aged widow and friend of the Wilcoxes. She begins the story by describing herself, after leaving the reader to expect some propitious event in her life. The reader feels that he has an unmistakable clue to Miss Wilcox's character, but to nothing else, and is anxious to continue the story. Of the openings to Charlotte Brontë's novels, that of *Jane Eyre* is the most arresting, but this is the most fascinating. It is a first draft in pencil; to her husband's laconic remark, she replied, 'Oh! I shall alter that. I always begin two or three times before I can please myself.'

In March 1858 Mrs Gaskell expressed the wish that George Smith would obtain Mr Nicholls' consent to the addition of this story as an appendix to *The Life of Charlotte Brontë*. She thought it 'a very good beginning' and added, 'it was begun a year or so before [Charlotte's] marriage & Mr Nicholls always *groaned literally* – when she talked of continuing it' (*Letters*, p. 496).

General Aspects

Image the whole, then execute the parts –
  Fancy the fabric
Quite, ere you build, ere steel strike fire from quartz,
  Ere mortar dab brick!

Such was Browning's advice in 'A Grammarian's Funeral'. Unlike her sisters, Charlotte Brontë seems to have suffered from over-confidence in the power of Delphic inspiration to order all things for the best; it was typical of her genius to assume that a capacity for taking critical pains was not required for the creation of a work of art in prose. For many years it had been her habit to write rapidly at the bidding of fancy or imagination;[1] she had never shown any great propensity or concern for coherence and proportion in plot, and her novels do not suggest that she was liberally endowed with plot inventiveness. It seems that, once a work was well under way, so little time did she give to revision that it could rarely have gone beyond stylistic improvements. When a novel was off her hands, she refused to reconsider it, whatever the consequences (13.9.49); she had to have her own way 'in the matter of writing' (21.9.49). *Jane Eyre* probably gave Charlotte little serious difficulty, but its success may have made her too confident. One gets the impression from their correspondence that, in the end, her publishers felt it wise to write favourably on *Shirley* and hope for the best; they would have been justified in being more critical. Charlotte became anxious after publication, and learnt from her mistakes. The evidence for this is in

---

[1] There was, she acknowledged at the opening of 'Julia', a 'sort of pleasure, in sitting down to write, wholly unprovided with a subject'.

Villette, and her refusal to hurry it. With greater experience in full-length novel-writing, she never advanced as far as Emily or Anne towards unity of plot – the best relationship of parts to the whole, and of due proportion within the parts. There is nothing in 'Emma' to suggest that she had not, but it is too brief to warrant any conclusion on its integral design.

'I believe language to have been given us to make our meaning clear', Charlotte wrote in the 'Biographical Notice of Ellis and Acton Bell'. Among her incidental weaknesses and irritants is an obstinate adherence to French. Its use in dialogue, particularly in *The Professor* and *Villette*, arises from self-indulgence rather than vanity. It shows an irrational disregard for most readers, though she might have defended it on the score that it was 'true', that it actually took place, as she illustrates before telling us that Yorke was a French-speaking gentleman (*S*. iii). How fatuous she can be may be seen at the opening of the novel, where, with Mrs Gale and the curates' heavy demands in mind, she writes, '"C'en est trop", she would say, if she could speak French.' 'Not a stiver, mon garçon – which means, my lad', Robert Moore answers Joe Scott. Hortense Moore's first words to Robert are in French, and then the author promises that, as this is an English book, the answer and the rest of the conversation will be in English; soon afterwards she reverts to French. Since much in *Shirley* could be reduced by intensification and dramatization, it is unfortunate that the lively and amusing Hortense does not have a larger role to give the novel relief; as it is, thanks to the author's obtuseness, many of her remarks are often unintelligible. Sometimes Charlotte Brontë defends the use of French words on the grounds that they give a more exact shade of meaning. So undoubtedly they did, to her; but what futility for the majority of readers, and what lack of practical sense in the author!

The less frequent and obtrusive addresses to the reader in *Villette* seem to mark a significant trend. It is arguable that when the central character is the narrator, as in all Charlotte's novels except *Shirley*, the technique is less objectionable. In fact, it is her habitual manner of establishing a cosy relationship of confidentiality with the reader. At times it is cunningly exploited for creating sympathy or reassurance; sometimes it is used to make convenient but not very artistic forms of presentation more acceptable. The free-and-easy style is found twice on the same page of *Shirley* as the rash promise to translate French into English for the sake of the English reader (v). First, in relation to Hortense, we have 'I must describe her before I go any further'; then, 'You will think I have depicted a remarkable slattern, reader; – not at all.' This is nothing but otiose, the expansion of a writer who leaves much to chance, and, at this early stage of her story, feels she has room to spare in a three-volume novel. A warlike parson (iii) occasions some chitchat but, in *Shirley*, the author airs her views more freely, whether she addresses the reader or not (see x, for example).

Some of the functional variation of Charlotte's addresses to the reader may be illustrated from *Jane Eyre*: the opening of xi, intimacy; xvii ('You are not to suppose, reader, that Adèle has all this time been sitting motionless'), the author's oversight and unreadiness to revise; and ('the reader knows I had wrought hard to extirpate from my soul the germs of love there detected'), the appeal for sympathy; xviii ('I have told you, reader'), a reminder of something important; xxxvi ('Hear an illustration, reader'), a plea for attention to an image which is apposite but wrongly placed, and would command more interest (without an appeal) had the reader's suspense not been unduly protracted; xxxvii ('And, reader, do you think I feared him in his blind ferocity?'), reassurance; and, near the end ('Reader, it was on Monday night'), a reminder for the unobservant. This brings us to the confessional 'Reader, I married him (xxxviii). Did Charlotte expect the reader to be surprised? Whether these well-known words are banal or an anticlimax, they illustrate the superfluity of addresses to the reader. A novelist can obtain his effects as well, or better, by other means; it is a facile device, even when it is effective, and sometimes no more than the shoring-up mechanism of a writer who is satisfied with the first form of presentation which springs to mind.

One of the minor peculiarities of Charlotte's style is her partiality for 'irid' and 'Peri'. She brought them into her novels from Angrian literature, and could never relinquish them. The use of the first for the 'iris' of the eye (from the plural, 'irides') is generally rare. 'Peri' suggests something above ordinary beauty in the female form, and is associated with an oriental heaven. Though the word was endowed with the charm of *The Arabian Nights*, Charlotte might not have used it in her novels without the romantic approval of Byron (see 'To Ianthe', prefixed to *Childe Harold*). Frances Henri is William Crimsworth's 'Alpine Peri'; Jane Eyre wonders what Rivers is thinking about 'this earthly angel', the 'Peri' Miss Oliver. 'Oh, my pupil!

Oh, Peri! too mutinous for heaven – too innocent for hell!' rhapsodizes Louis Moore. 'My angel', 'my Peri', Alfred de Hamal addresses
Ginevra Fanshawe.

In the assessment of people from appearances, the influences of
Lavater and Gall are seen. The former believed that physiognomy
was the key to character, and in this way Lucy Snowe was judged by
Paul Emanuel when she arrived at Mme Beck's; for testimony of the
rapport between them, he was to point out the similarity of their
eyes and foreheads (*V*. xxxi). Jane Eyre's most definite first impressions
of Rochester were drawn from his nose and nostrils (*J*. xiii); she
judged Rivers also by his facial features (xxix). Gall's phrenology is
responsible for descriptions and judgments which seem rather odd and
amusing. Juanna Trista had precisely the same shape of skull as
Pope Alexander VI; 'her organs of benevolence, veneration, conscien-
tiousness, adhesiveness, were singularly small, those of self-esteem,
firmness, destructiveness, combativeness, preposterously large' (*P*. xii).
Jane Eyre felt she must have a considerable organ of veneration, as her
admiration for Miss Temple showed; this same organ expanded as her
friend Helen read and construed Virgil. Mr Rochester lifted the sable
black hair which waved across his forehead, and revealed 'a solid
enough mass of intellectual organs, but an abrupt deficiency where the
suave sign of benevolence should have risen'; he assumed that Jane
had become attached to Thornfield because she had 'a good deal of the
organ of Adhesiveness'. Mr Yorke lacked the organs of Veneration
and Comparison, and was rather deficient in those of Benevolence and
Ideality (*S*. iv). Finally, the organ of philoprogenitiveness must have
been large in the Labassecouriens (*V*. xi): in its phrenological sense,
the term means no more than 'love of children', exactly as Charlotte
used it.

Not one of her plots is wholly satisfactory. Whatever links the
opening English scenes in *The Professor* and *Villette* have with the
main stories, they soon fade in retrospect. More than anything else
they suggest that Charlotte lacked confidence in her ability to develop
a full-length novel based on Brussels and the Pensionnat in particular.
With less dependence on her own experience and more courage to
invent plot and situation (and growing signs of this are evident in
Villette), she could have produced a more unified novel, with the
advantage of giving greater prominence to Paul Emanuel in the
main action. Her incapacity to develop the plot of *The Professor* is
remarkable. The foreground action of *Jane Eyre* consists of episodes,

the central one at Thornfield being the longest and most important; only an autobiographical presentation could give it coherence. Yet the linking of all the episodes except the first two is fortuitous, and the cry which snatches Jane from Rivers to Ferndean for the resolution of the plot is one of the greatest improbabilities in major fiction. Minor episodes at the expense of plot are more frequent in *Villette* than in *Jane Eyre*; the Cleopatra or gallery chapter, the concert, and the theatre visit have more solid interest than the rather trumpery scene in which Rochester acts the part of a gipsy fortune-teller, but they all illustrate the author's readiness to make ample expletive use of recollections; Lucy Snowe's spectatorial role is conveniently exploited. Despite all its improbabilities, *Jane Eyre* creates a greater unitary effect than any other of Charlotte's novels. At the other extreme is *Shirley*: some of its scenes are excessively long, and contribute little to the narrative; some of its inclusions (portraits and brief scenes of special interest to the author) are utterly irrelevant; and most of the main characters are kept off-stage too long at some time or other. The general impression it creates is that Charlotte never had a predetermined aim for the novel as a whole, or the courage to work more fully and dramatically within more restricted limits. The Hollow's Mill story had great possibilities for the weaving of fiction around local history, and Charlotte's creative resourcefulness was such that, with more direction, discipline, and daring, she could have made a success of it.

The plots of *Jane Eyre* and *Villette* depend on too much coincidence. That Jane's uncle in Madeira should know enough to prevent her bigamous marriage to Rochester is remarkable, but that she should find shelter, when at the point of exhaustion, at the remote moorland home of her unknown cousins, and then inherit a fortune which she can share with them, is too romantically incredible to be taken seriously. Whatever may be said in favour of the prelude to *Villette*, with its dramatic and narrative hints of the main theme, it is altogether amazing that Lucy Snowe should come into close contact with the Brettons and Homes again in Brussels, that Dr John should come to her rescue at Boue-Marine, be called in at the school where she is employed, rescue her when she faints in a poor quarter of the city, and be at the right place in the theatre to give assistance to the unrecognized Paulina, whom he has not met since she was a child. It seems strange that a writer who put so much emphasis on truth in the novel should resort to such improbabilities.

They occur in the two novels which blend personal suffering with romantic elements, and these include the 'Gothic'. In *Jane Eyre* these are associated with the first appearance of the hero, the tramp of his horse rousing 'Gytrash' premonitions before it appears in the moonlight; with a past which he alludes to in Byronic and even Satanic overtones; with maniac howls and scenes leading to the destruction of Thornfield by fire; and with the miraculous call which resolves the plot. In *Villette* the nun's successive appearances reduce terror to mystery, and there is more supernatural suggestion finally in the Banshee wind which twice heralds disaster.

The inclusion of 'romantic' elements in each of these novels was undoubtedly a reaction to the failure of, or sense of failure in, the previous novel. In *The Professor* and *Shirley* Charlotte had proclaimed her allegiance to Truth and Nature; and her moral preoccupation with this, after a long period of Angrian adolescent indulgence, tended to inhibit any impulse she may have felt to make lengthy excursions into wholly imaginary scenes. Her novels contain transcripts of actual scenes and people, and more that is imaginatively re-created from experience than is wholly imaginary. In her letters she repeatedly stresses the handicap she suffered as a novelist from the limitations of her life, nowhere more than in a letter to Mr Williams (4.10.47) just before the publication of *Jane Eyre*:

> I am, myself, sensible both of deficiencies of capacity and disadvantages of circumstance which will, I fear, render it somewhat difficult for me to attain popularity as an author. The eminent writers you mention – Mr Thackeray, Mr Dickens, Mrs Marsh, etc., doubtless enjoyed facilities for observation such as I have not; certainly they possess a knowledge of the world, whether intuitive or acquired, such as I can lay no claim to – and this gives their writings an importance and a variety greatly beyond what I can offer the public.

When the first chapter of *Shirley* was criticized, her defence was that it was *real*, 'as true as the Bible' (Williams, Lewes, 1.11.49). She did not mean an exact copy, but a re-creation (Williams, 5.4.49):

> I should say [that Alexander Harris] scarcely possesses the creative faculty in sufficient vigour to excel as a writer of fiction. He *creates* nothing – he only copies. His characters are portraits – servilely accurate.

Yet she had already included attempts at accurate portraits in *The Professor* (xii) and *Shirley* (ix). She had made good fictional use of her experience, especially as a teacher and governess. Perhaps this explains Mr Nicholls' unfortunate comment on 'Emma', though it is possible that by this time Charlotte was belatedly daring to use her imagination on a larger scale than ever before in her adult fiction, as she seemed to realize would be inevitable, when she answered Lewes's criticism of *Jane Eyre* (6.11.47):

> but, dear sir, is not the real experience of each individual very limited? And, if a writer dwells upon that solely or principally, is he not in danger of repeating himself, and also of becoming an egotist. Then, too, imagination is a strong, restless faculty, which claims to be heard and exercised . . .

Yet Charlotte's distrust of the imagination is voiced sharply in her novels (*S.* iv, *V.* ii, xxxix), and some of the later chapters of *Shirley* show that there was a realm of 'ideality' which, in her more mature years, constituted a greater threat than the 'romantic' or Angrian. Her reluctance to write outside her experience had unfortunate results, especially for her male characters. Paul Emanuel owes much initially, of course, to M. Heger, but he is largely imaginary, and at his greatest playing a part M. Heger never played. If Mr Rochester had any known origin, it was Angrian; he is a creature of Charlotte's imagination. Characters like Mr Hunsden and Dr John, who were drawn much more closely from real people, are comparative failures, however. In *Shirley* Charlotte seems to avoid giving men a leading role. The greatest loss comes from the neglect of Robert Moore. For him we could spare Louis, who remains unrealized, a pretentious writer, a voice, and ultimately a pose, a 'woman of genius' in 'very sadly fashioned and badly fitting breeches' to Swinburne. It is significant that at the end Robert plays a minor part to a schoolboy. That Charlotte had the power to project herself intensively into a created reality is clear from the opening scenes of *Jane Eyre* and the closing scenes of *Villette*. It was with reference to the latter that she told Mrs Gaskell 'the process she always adopted when she had to describe anything which had not fallen within her own experience' (G. xxvii):

> she had thought intently on it for many and many a night before falling to sleep – wondering what it was like, or how it would be – till at length, sometimes after the progress of her story had been

arrested at this one point for weeks, she wakened up in the morning with all clear before her, as if she had in reality gone through the experience, and then could describe it, word for word, as it had happened.

Charlotte's portraiture can be detailed and solid, as her 'portfolio' in *The Professor* shows, but it will be generally found to express character. Her sketch of Mme Beck (*V.* viii) seems to indicate that she never quite outgrew the style, though her touch has become swifter and more economical. After the Yorke sketches (*S.* ix), she did not hold up the story excessively for portrait descriptions. Appearances are given more incidentally as part of the action and, even where this does not happen, features are sometimes unforgettably portrayed in a few original strokes, as with Miss Mann (*S.* x). In presenting pictures of narrator characters, mirror reflections are used (*P.* ii, ix); in this way the reader can see the white face and glittering eyes of the terrified Jane Eyre in the red-room (*J.* ii) or the ghastly morning appearance of sleep-starved Lucy Snowe after her late-night clash with Mme Beck (*V.* xxxviii).

With the exception of Caroline and Shirley, Charlotte Brontë's heroines and heroes are not good-looking,[1] and this can be regarded as an important advance towards realism from the ideal portraits which excited Jane Austen's early amusement and persisted in the novels of Charlotte's contemporaries. The reviewer of *Villette* in *Putnam's Monthly Magazine*, May 1853, found the same 'fusion of elements usually considered repugnant to romance' in this novel as in *Jane Eyre*, the great success of which consisted, he thought,

> in its rejection of all the stage-appointments of novels – all the Adonis-Dukes and Lady Florimels in satin boudoirs, which puerile phantoms still haunt the pages of Bulwer (although he is rapidly laying them) and the remorseless James, and are, of course, the staple of the swarm of 'the last new novels' which monthly inundate the circulating libraries in England. The author takes the reader among a crowd of ordinary human beings, and declares proudly, 'Here you shall find as much romance and thrilling interest, as in the perfumed purlieus of palaces.'

Charlotte told Mr Williams that she could never believe in 'the standard heroes and heroines of novels' (September 1848), and that

[1] According to Harriet Martineau, she disagreed with her sisters on this issue; see G. xv.

she did not wish to have illustrations of her characters in her books: 'Bulwer and Byron heroes and heroines are very well, they are all of them handsome; but my personages are mostly unattractive in look, and therefore ill-adapted to figure in ideal portraits' (11.3.48). Had Rochester, when she met him, been 'handsome, heroic-looking', Jane Eyre would never have dared to talk to him as she did (xii):

> I had a theoretical reverence and homage for beauty, elegance, gallantry, fascination; but had I met those qualities incarnate in masculine shape, I should have known instinctively that they neither had nor could have sympathy with anything in me, and should have shunned them as one would fire, lightning, or anything else that is bright but antipathetic.

Nor are Charlotte's characters faultless. We think of Rochester and Robert Moore, and of M. Paul and Lucy Snowe:

> Warm, jealous, and haughty, I knew not till now that my nature had such a mood: he gathered me near his heart. I was full of faults; he took them and me all home.

Charlotte Brontë's experience as a governess accounts for her critical attitude towards the wealthier classes; it may be seen in the portrayal of Edward Crimsworth and Rochester's guests, and in Shirley's disregard for the Wynnes and the Nunnelys. Nor could the happy and prosperous (Dr John and Paulina, for example) enlist her creative sympathies greatly. Her own indrawn nature and a fretful inferiority complex which sprang from painful awareness of physical as well as social disadvantages made her respond almost instinctively to those who suffered in isolation; children such as Jane Eyre, Willie Ellin, and Matilda Fitzgibbon; Jane Eyre separated from the man she loved, Caroline Helstone pining for Robert Moore, and Lucy Snowe, in many ways the nearest figure to herself. Her central characters are lonely and parentless; there is no exception to this if we include Caroline Helstone, who has no companion until she gets to know Shirley, and no knowledge of her only surviving parent until Mrs Pryor discloses her identity to save her daughter from the grief and hopelessness which had endangered her life. All eventually find happiness in love; and all in marriage, except Lucy Snowe, the least confident of life, the most inhibited and subject to hypochondria, of all Charlotte's characters. The depth of her depression and longing undoubtedly owes something to the author's loneliness and gloom after the deaths of Branwell, Emily, and Anne. After suffering extremes of hope and disappointment, Lucy falls desperately in love with Paul Emanuel, thinks she has lost him, and finds his love is supreme against all obstacles; it sustains her through years of separation and is strong enough to endure the calamity of his death. In all vicissitudes, one spirit permeates all Charlotte's novels, and it stems from a philosophy which insisted that her first hero, as Adam's son, 'should share Adam's doom, and drain throughout life a mixed and moderate cup of enjoyment'.

In *Jane Eyre*, *Shirley*, and *Villette* love transcends barriers of class, race, and religion. There is nothing Miltonic in Charlotte's conception of it; her views are proclaimed through Jane Eyre, when she says that her spirit addresses Rochester's just as if they stood at God's feet, equal (xxiii). Marriage implied mutual respect; Shirley's problem was to find someone she admired and respected (xii), and, having found him, to remove his sense of social inferiority. The 'master-pupil' note at the climax of the most unconvincingly inspired love episode Charlotte ever wrote is unfortunate, marking the 'new spirit' which passed into Louis Moore. It is contradicted by Shirley's subsequent remarks:

'And are we equal then, sir? Are we equal at last?' . . .

'Sir!' she said, starting up, 'at your peril you ever again name such sordid things as money, or poverty, or inequality.' . . .

'Be my companion through life; be my guide where I am ignorant; be my master where I am faulty; be my friend always!'

She admits that she is 'feebler' and 'more ignorant' than Louis because she is younger; she wishes him to take charge in matters where he is better qualified than she. Charlotte's views on the question of mastery in love are given quite unequivocally in her letters (see p. 178).

Besides equality regardless of class, there is another aspect of love in Charlotte Brontë which ruffled contemporary readers and reviewers; it is her fearlessness in stressing its physical expression in courtship, especially in *Jane Eyre*. Criticism may have made her more circumspect in her later novels. She is saying what Browning could express more safely in verse years later:

> Let us not always say
> 'Spite of this flesh to-day
> I strove, made head, gained ground upon the whole!'

As the bird wings and sings,
Let us cry 'All good things
Are ours, nor soul helps flesh more, now, than flesh helps soul!'

In *The Professor* Charlotte's general outlook seems to be that the person who toils manfully up the Hill of Difficulty will be rewarded; in *Jane Eyre*, that one should retain faith in times of adversity, and that God tempers judgment with mercy. The pangs of unrequited love become the burden of her last two novels. One shows a more critical tone; the other, a more pessimistic. In *Shirley* she is sensible on the industrial labour problem, though she recognizes no easy solution; on the Church, she is satirical and outspoken. Her censoriousness is noticeably feminist: men are selfish; disappointed women in love must suffer in silence; single women are neglected, and should be found useful occupations. In *Villette* a religious change is noticeable, reflecting Charlotte's own view. Some people are born under 'benign planets' (xvi, xxxvii). For others, like Lucy Snowe, 'life is so constructed that the event does not, cannot, will not, match the expectation' (xxxvi); their way lies dark through the world's wilderness, but they endure in faith; their cross is their banner (xxxviii).

The cause of women is prominent in *Shirley*. That they could succeed professionally is illustrated by Frances Crimsworth in *The Professor*. Charlotte's fictional campaign undoubtedly owed something to the views of her friend Mary Taylor, who compared the lives of the Brontës at Haworth to potatoes growing in a dark cellar, encouraged Charlotte to work in Brussels, and set up business for herself in New Zealand. Charlotte was hardly a militant; her demands were moderate and long-term, but their influence has undoubtedly played a part in the progress of women towards equality of status with men in England.

The conflict between reason and excited emotions or passion continually arises. Crimsworth is less extreme; with him Love conquers Reason and Affection, and impels him to seek Frances (*P.* xxii). The heroines feel more strongly. Caroline pines passively, but she is presented less introspectively than the heroine-narrators of *Jane Eyre* and *Villette*, and reason is embodied in Shirley rather than personified as one of the contesting forces within Caroline's mind (xxii). Rochester judges Jane Eyre shrewdly: 'Reason sits firm and holds the reins. . . . The passions may rage . . . but judgment shall still have the last word' (xix). They do rage; Jane's equanimity comes and goes; only after crises and reflection does reason assert itself (xvi, xxvii). In the end a nice balance is established between Nature, which calls her back to Rochester, and reason, which finds her marriage consonant with 'laws and principles'. Loneliness and repression make Lucy Snowe the victim of irrational hope and hypochondria. The psychological drama is played out between personifications: Reason and Feeling (xvii), the hag Reason and divine Hope (xxi), Feeling and Reason (xxiii).

One early indulgence in psychological debate (*P.* v) is prosaic to such a degree that it verges at times on the comicality of Launcelot Gobbo. Generally the tensions are presented imaginatively, reflecting Charlotte's habitual mode of humanizing and visualizing abstract entities. An excellent example, though not from Charlotte's essay on the subject (*BST.* lxxii), is that of Human Justice in the exercise Lucy Snowe dashed off when M. Paul staged a trial of her genius before Messieurs Boissec and Rochemorte (xxxv). Charlotte's writings are strewn with personifications. After weeks of searching for Frances, Crimsworth was 'forced to loosen [his] grasp on expectation'; when he saw her sitting despondently in the cemetery, he put his hand on her shoulder, and she looked up: 'Amazement had hardly opened her eyes and raised them to mine, ere Recognition informed their irids with most speaking brightness' (xix). In *Jane Eyre* 'conscience, turned tyrant, held passion by the throat'; in *Shirley* the Disaffection of the workers was heard muttering, and swearing 'ominous oaths over the drugged beer of ale-houses'; in *Villette*, when Lucy Snowe wandered out at night after taking Madame's narcotic potion, the classrooms behind her seemed to be great dreary gaols 'filled with spectral and intolerable Memories, laid miserable amongst their straw and their manacles'. In the park she was certain that the unpleasant truth had been revealed, and 'invoked Conviction to nail upon [her] the certainty [and] fix it with the strongest spikes her strongest strokes could drive' until the iron entered her soul. In her infatuation she thought, 'While a Lie pressed me, how I suffered! Even when the Falsehood was still sweet . . . it wasted me with hourly torment. . . . Truth stripped away Falsehood, and Flattery, and Expectancy, and here I stand – free!'

The above examples, though not extreme, serve to show that Charlotte's personifications vary considerably. At their best, with vivid or vigorous imagery allied to appropriate rhythms, they can intensify the imaginative realization of thought and feeling. Her addiction to them, however, led on the one hand to pictorial over-elaboration, and on the other to the unexciting bareness of successive abstractions.

As late as *Villette*, the lure of imagery could lull Charlotte's critical powers. Reference has already been made to the two paragraphs on Jael and Sisera, joined by an angel of the author's devising, the whole purport of which (as she thought expedient to explain) was no more than that 'the cool peace and dewy sweetness of the night filled [Lucy Snowe] with a mood of hope'. Her capacity to express thoughts through one developing image is seen when St John Rivers talks on his love for Rosamond Oliver (*J*. xxxii); her revelry in a multiplicity of images expressing one idea, in the passage reflecting the end of Jane Eyre's marriage hopes (xxvi). More powerful is the simile describing the effect of Vashti's performance on Lucy Snowe: 'like a deep, swollen winter river thundering in cataract, and bearing the soul, like a leaf, on the steep and steely sweep of its descent'. In general the style of *Villette* is more disciplined and intensive than that of *Shirley*, whether it is plain or figurative. Mme Beck had lips like a thread; and Mlle St Pierre's petrifying influence kept her pupils in check 'as a breezeless frost-air might still a sprawling stream'. Paul Emanuel's intellectual wealth was a library to Lucy Snowe; his tomes of thought were 'collyrium to the spirit's eyes'; and what delight, she thought, to gather and store up those handfuls of gold-dust he flung so recklessly to heaven's winds. There is far more poetry in Charlotte's prose than in her verse. Leslie Stephen admired her 'flashes of vivid expression, where the material of language is the incarnation of keen intuitive thought'; at his worst, he found her style 'strangely contorted, crowded by rather awkward personifications', and degenerating towards 'a rather unpleasant Ossianesque'. 'More severity of style', he added, 'would increase the power by restraining the abuse.' There are, indeed, times when Charlotte's cluttered sentences make one sigh for the lucidity, intelligent control, and proportion of Anne's.

Charlotte's style varies considerably. It can be plain and compact, swift and strong. It tends to be energetic rather than delicate; yet it rarely fails to achieve an appropriate rhythm and emphasis, though some of the inversion caused by the latter may seem rather alien or artificial. May Sinclair distinguished between

her absolutely simple style, in which she is perfect; her didactic style, her fantastic style, which are temporary aberrations; and her inspired style, in which at her worst she is merely flamboyant and redundant, and at her best no less than perfect.

There is a development in her later works which seems significant in its consistency. Nothing surpasses some of the final scenes in *Villette* for swift imaginative narration; in 'Emma' a strong cumulative effect is created through language which is restrained and precise almost to the point of austerity.

Although there is a gaiety of tone and an almost Dickensian comic relish at times in *Shirley*, there is little humorous relief in Charlotte Brontë. Paul Emanuel and Hortense Moore are her most amusing characters; the curates are created in high spirits, and Mr Donne's ejection by Shirley is rather farcical; the ruse by which Martin Yorke brings Caroline Helstone and Robert Moore together has a delightful air of fictional unreality about it; but the Ingrams are handled too clumsily to create humour or satire. Especially is this true of the dialogue, which often strikes a false note in Charlotte Brontë. Blanche Ingram, her mother's lily-flower, lays her sovereign behest on Rochester to furbish up his lungs and other vocal organs in her service. 'Commands from Miss Ingram's lips would put spirit into a mug of milk and water', he answers. He asks Mrs Fairfax to act as 'auditress and interlocutrice' to Adèle, and informs Jane Eyre, when he is hardly acquainted with her, that he is 'disposed to be gregarious and communicative'. Soon he tells her that she is a pilgrim, a disguised deity, who has already done him good: 'my heart was a sort of charnel; it will now be a shrine'. The absurdity of the imagery here is negligible compared with that in the climactic dialogue between Shirley and Louis Moore, which confirms a suspicion that Charlotte Brontë's humour is sometimes unintentional.

Though strictly moral in outlook, Charlotte's views on love make her something more than Puritan. The Bible is the main source of her spiritual strength, and much of her imagery and language derive from it. Three examples must suffice; in every statement of the first there is a quotation from the Scriptures. Rochester reads Jane Eyre's forehead (xix): 'The passions may rage furiously, like true heathens, as they are; and the desires may imagine all sorts of vain things. . . . Strong wind, earthquake-shock, and fire may pass by; but I shall follow the guiding of that still small voice which interprets the dictates of the conscience.' The last chapter of *Shirley* contains a remarkable passage in which Napoleon's disastrous Russian campaign is alluded to in brief excerpts from Job (xxxvii. 4, xxxviii. 22–3) and Revelation (xvi. 1, 3, 8, 20). In the third example, Lucy Snowe reflects the more fatalistic outlook of Charlotte in her later years (xvii): 'Certainly, at some hour, though perhaps not *your* hour, the waiting waters will stir . . .' The sole visitant for many who seek healing in the pool of Bethesda is Azrael, the Muslim angel of death. Charlotte's faith remained, even though dimmed, and it influences all her work.

It was customary to emphasize passion more than anything else in her novels. Compared with Victorian writers such as Dickens, she must have appeared bold in *Jane Eyre*. Yet passion hardly glows in *The Professor*; it cannot be ascribed to the lonely love-sick Caroline Helstone, the only person in *Shirley* who seems genuinely to suffer for love; and, though she endures profound emotional crises, Lucy Snowe never experiences it until her story it almost at an end. Fiercer passion than love burns in the Jane Eyre who rebels at Gateshead; we remember it mainly through the vividness of the scenes associated with it. The intensity of Charlotte's imagination is her supreme quality. Its visualizing power is strong; it fuses emotion with setting; and it expresses itself in prose which often approaches or attains the power of poetry by virtue of its vitalizing imagery and controlled rhythms.

The Letters, and
Charlotte's Views

Had Ellen Nussey not preserved Charlotte's letters from 1831 onwards, we should know very little about the main lives of the Brontës; Mrs Gaskell's biography, if she had thought it worth pursuing, would have been relatively brief. Until *Jane Eyre* was accepted by her publishers, Charlotte had no correspondent of importance besides Ellen Nussey and Mary Taylor; the latter, less sentimental and discerning than Ellen in her friendship, destroyed all Charlotte's letters save one of great interest, on the sudden journey to London with Anne to attest the integrity of 'Currer Bell' (4.9.48). Charlotte desperately wished to correspond with M. Heger, but he was no letter-writer; his wife was jealous, and Charlotte's foolish pleading made her more so. The situation was so embarrassing that the admired 'master' invited her to address her letters to the Athénée, the school for boys where he taught. Charlotte scorned a clandestine correspondence, and her eager desire for a pen-friend of the opposite sex had to be stifled until her long correspondence with her publisher's reader, Mr Williams, began. After meeting him in London, she was able to discuss with him a number of subjects from literature to family affairs. Mrs Gaskell (*Letters*, p. 877) noted that Charlotte seemed 'heartily at her ease with him' in her letters. She corresponded with George Smith, the youthful head of the firm, and another representative, Mr Taylor, whose interest was to extend embarrassingly beyond literature to Charlotte herself.

Her letters comprise the bulk of the Brontë correspondence. Their first importance has undoubtedly been biographical, and such is their value that a generous selection would undoubtedly give a truer impression of her personality than any biography can do, and would be invaluable in curbing common autobiographical interpretations of her novels. The four-volume Shakespeare Head edition is the most complete and accurate, and is not likely to be very substantially wrong, though minor adjustments in personal and biographical dimensions will be necessary whenever a scholarly checking of texts and manuscripts is completed.

Few letters from Emily and Anne remain, and nearly all were preserved by Ellen Nussey. Emily's are brief and practical; she disclaims being a 'proper' letter-writer, and shows a sense of humour. Anne writes rather more freely, but always to the point. Compared with that of Branwell, who is often at the mercy of his feelings, her style is always sensible, clear, and controlled. Yet it is not false modesty which makes her say, at a time when she must have written much of her second novel (4.1.48), that there is 'a lamentable deficiency' in her 'organ of language' which makes her almost 'as bad a hand' at writing as at talking when she has nothing particular to say. She tells us briefly how severe the winter could be at Haworth parsonage; they are all 'cut up' by a cruel east wind. Her style is best seen in the letter on her proposed visit to Scarborough (which she made only to die and be buried there); it shows character in every line, unassuming but noble, dignified but sincere (5.4.49).

What a bizarre and pathetic figure Branwell cuts in his varying moods! His exuberance and undiplomatic conceit are amazingly exemplified in letters which the editor of *Blackwood's* refused to answer (7.12.35, 9.1.37); his long-windedness, flattery, and tactlessness, in a letter which disgusted Wordsworth (19.1.37), and his high-spirited, almost Falstaffian braggadocio, as he bids farewell to his 'old friend whisky', in a letter to John Brown, which was clearly intended for the entertainment of his old associates at the Black Bull (13.3.40). Typically, on completing his Horace translations, he sees 'the utter worthlessness of all former' ones (27.6.40). The 'querulous egotism' of some letters has a biographical interest, especially in his maudlin versions of the Mrs Robinson story. His later correspondence is often depressing; he still hopes for employment, or promises great literary achievements. There is a mournful veracity, however, in his letter to the sculptor J. B. Leyland (24.1.47):

Noble writings, works of art, music or poetry now instead of rousing my imagination, cause a whirlwind of blighting sorrow that sweeps

Sketches by Branwell Bronte in his letter to J. B. Leyland, *c.* January 1847. The first shows Leyland, with his mutilated statue of Theseus, and Branwell, the subject of the second and third.

over my mind with unspeakable dreariness, and if I sit down and try to write all ideas that used to come clothed in sunlight now press round me in funeral black; for nearly every pleasurable excitement that I used to know has changed to insipidity or pain.

Sometimes he includes improvised sketches, combining scenes of crapulence with hints of damnation and morbid portrayals of his dead self. One letter, possibly his last, is dated 'Sunday, Noon', and asks John Brown to 'contrive to get' him fivepennyworth of gin, assuring him that he will be paid *punctually* the next morning.

Whenever she is engrossed by her subject, Charlotte writes fluently, interestingly, and with the energy of conviction. The early letters to Miss Nussey show a regard for correctness of diction which makes them stiff and stilted at times. With growing maturity, they were written less studiously and with greater assurance; as friendship deepened, they were often hastily improvised, written in a more idiomatic style, in short sentences, phrases, and parentheses, mostly separated by dashes, and sometimes unpunctuated. To Mr Williams she writes very fully at times; ready, thoughtful adjectives add strength to sentences which are sustained by rhythm and balance. There is nothing facile or otiose in her composition; it reflects the sincerity and originality of a strong mind, and imaginative thought which is often the product of deep feeling.

Her friendship with Ellen Nussey was to a remarkable degree the attraction of opposites (3.1.50):

When I first saw Ellen I did not care for her – we were school-fellows – in the course of time we learnt each other's faults and good points – we were contrasts – still we suited – affection was first a germ, then a sapling – then a strong tree: now – no new friend, however lofty or profound in intellect – not even Miss Martineau herself could be to me what Ellen is, yet she is no more than a conscientious, observant, calm, well-bred Yorkshire girl. She is without romance – if she attempts to read poetry – or poetic prose aloud – I am irritated and deprive her of her book – if she talks of it I stop my ears – but she is good – she is true – she is faithful and I love her.

This love had gone through a highly emotional and religious phase in late adolescence. Both were puritanical. Charlotte's advice was sought on the question of dancing for parties of boys and girls; the reply came that it was harmless as exercise and amusement, but sinful in its usual consequences, 'namely, frivolity and waste of time'. At Roe Head in 1836 Charlotte's emotional thought (heated no doubt by the 'burning clime' of Angria) made her feel unworthy of Ellen; she knew the treasures of the Bible, but the pure waters of the Well of Life fled her lips as if she were Tantalus. 'You have cheered me, my darling. . . . If you love me, *do, do, do* come on Friday.' She abhors herself; 'if the Doctrine of Calvin be true I am already an outcast'. 'I have lavished the warmest affections of a very hot, tenacious heart upon you – if you grow cold – it's over.' Had they a cottage and a competency, they could live and love on together till Death. At the end of the year, her heart is 'a real hot bed for sinful thoughts', and Ellen must be kept from 'the contamination of too intimate society' with her. The following February they are still divided because they are in danger of loving each other too well, 'of losing sight of the *Creator* in idolatry of the *creature*' (a crucial thought in *Jane Eyre* and *Villette*). In this unsettled, depressed, pseudo-religious state, Charlotte could have been of little comfort to Anne during her crisis at Roe Head; she may even have contributed to it.

Charlotte's suggested reading (4.7.34) gives some idea of her own, since she does not seem to have discovered Ellen's limitations:

> If you like poetry let it be first rate, Milton, Shakespeare, Thomson, Goldsmith, Pope (if you will though I don't admire him) Scott, Byron, Campbell, Wordsworth and Southey. Now Ellen don't be startled at the names of Shakespeare and Byron. Both these were great men and their works are like themselves. You will know how to choose the good and avoid the evil. . . . Omit the Comedies of Shakespeare and the Don Juan, perhaps the Cain of Byron though the latter is a magnificent Poem and read the rest fearlessly. . . . Scott's sweet, wild, romantic Poetry can do you no harm. . . . For fiction – read Scott alone; all novels after his are worthless. For biography, read Johnson's Lives of the Poets, Boswell's Life of Johnson, Southey's Life of Nelson, Lockhart's Life of Burns, Moore's Life of Sheridan, Moore's Life of Byron, Wolfe's Remains. For Natural History, read Bewick, and Audubon, and Goldsmith and White – of Selborne. For divinity, but your brother Henry will advise you there.

Henry's offer of marriage was tempting; Charlotte thought that if she married him Ellen could live with her. However, she could not think that she and Henry were suitable. She was too wild and romantic for such a grave, quiet man, and she did not feel that 'intense attachment' which would have made her 'willing to die for him'; if ever she married, she would have to regard her husband 'in that light of adoration'. Her views on marriage became far less romantic. A year later she told Ellen that if 'you can respect a person before marriage, moderate love at least will come after; and as to intense *passion*, I am convinced that that is no desirable feeling'. It would prove to be temporary, certainly as far as the man was concerned. She had seen what had happened to Mary Taylor, who 'would *die* willingly for one she loved', and she reiterated her view that 'une grande passion' is '*une* grande *folie*' (20.11.40):

> Mediocrity in all things is wisdom – mediocrity in the sensations is superlative wisdom . . . no young lady should fall in love until the offer has been made, accepted – the marriage ceremony performed and the first half year of wedded life has passed away – a woman may then begin to love, but with great precaution – very coolly – very moderately – very rationally – if she ever loves so much that a harsh word or a cold look from her husband cuts her to the heart – she is a fool – if she ever loves so much that her husband's will is her law . . . she will soon be a neglected fool.

A woman of genius who had to stay at home, partly because she felt it incumbent on her to look after her father and take charge, the more so as Branwell proved incapable, partly because she could find no congenial employment, had good reason to feel strongly, as the author of *Shirley* did, on the question of professional opportunities and useful occupations or avocations for women. When she resigned her post as governess at Stonegappe, she was much happier doing menial tasks at home than 'living like a fine lady' anywhere. 'The bread earned by honourable toil is sweeter than the bread of idleness', she told Henry Nussey, on hearing that his future wife would bring him no fortune. There was no more respectable character, she wrote to her retired headmistress, Miss Wooler, than an unmarried woman 'who makes her own way through life quietly perseveringly' (30.1.46). She valued Mr Williams' correspondence because it made her reflect on 'new themes'. One of them was his daughters' careers. Louisa was interested in teaching, and the result was an interesting letter from Charlotte, speaking from experience on the qualifications (primarily personal) required by a governess. She thought that the time would come when, 'philosophers and legislators' having pondered over 'the better ordering of the social system', there would be 'room for female lawyers, female doctors, female engravers, for more female artists, more authoresses' (12.5.48). It was most desirable that men and women should have 'the power and the will to work for themselves – most advisable that both sons and daughters should early be inured to habits of independence and industry'; and this was particularly true of 'girls without a fortune', 'reared on speculation with a view to their making mercenary marriages' (15.6.48). Later, hearing that Louisa had the chance of a presentation at Queen's College, she stressed the 'priceless advantage' of education for girls. The girl who stayed at home doing nothing was 'worse off than the hardest-wrought and worst-paid drudge of a school'. Daughters waiting at home to be married were pitiable. If they married happily, they were fortunate; if they remained single and unemployed, 'the peevishness of disappointment and the listlessness of idleness' would 'infallibly degrade their nature'. 'Lonely as I am – how should I be if Providence had never given me courage to adopt a career?' she asked. 'I wish all your daughters – I wish every woman in England had also a hope and motive: Alas there are many old maids who have neither', she concluded (3.7.49).

Except for Calvinistic fears at Roe Head, the letters reveal nothing new on the subject of Charlotte's religion. The unlikelihood that the Brontë children were brought up in dread of damnation has already been stressed (pp. 16–17). They undoubtedly heard and read much on denominational matters as they grew up, and acquired some ineradicable sectarian prejudices; but there was, despite this, no rigid intolerance at the parsonage, and they developed their own views, as Emily on one notable occasion insisted was right. The novels show clearly the views of Anne and Charlotte; Emily's were less conventional and more fluid, but she does not appear to have differed radically, on the question of sin and salvation (see p. 215), from Anne and Charlotte and their evangelical father, who, though he did not consider death-bed repentance 'a safe criterion to judge of a man's character', thought it one of William Weightman's great merits that he had opened, 'through Christ, the door of salvation to all'. Whatever misfortunes she suffered in her later years, Charlotte never lost her faith in God: 'be the issue what it may, we are all aware that a wisdom superior to our own guides the course of events, and we should feel confidence that everything will in the end work together for good' (26.2.48). The death of Emily put her faith to the test, and there is no doubt that it assumed a more melancholy, rather fatalistic tinge. It was not the lot of all to have their lines fall in pleasant places, she concluded, but one had 'to be brave and submit faithfully':

> there was (G. xxvii) some good reason, which we should know in time, why sorrow and disappointment were to be the lot of some on earth. It was better to acknowledge this, and face out the truth in a religious faith.

She was glad to find Mr Taylor in agreement with her on the Comtist philosophy proclaimed by Miss Martineau and Henry Atkinson in their joint work on the social nature and development of man. Charlotte thought it presented a 'hopeless blank', and that it could do Miss Martineau irreparable harm: 'who can trust the word, or rely on the judgment, of an avowed atheist?' (11.2.51, 24.3.51).

Her sectarian prejudices remained strong, and were never more comprehensively expressed than when she was in Belgium in July 1842:

> my advice to all protestants who are tempted to anything so besotted as turn Catholic – is to walk over the sea on to the continent – to attend mass regularly for a time to note well the mummeries thereof – also the idiotic, mercenary, aspect of *all* the priests . . . – I consider Methodism, Dissenterism, Quakerism, and the extremes of high and low Churchism foolish but Roman Catholicism beats them all.

In her letter of 1840 to Hartley Coleridge (see p. 85), she stated that had she continued her Angrian story she would have included a Puseyite, and 'polished-off the High Church with the best of Warren's jet bleaching'. Ten years later, after enjoying a public letter by Lord John Russell, and thinking one of the best paragraphs was that in which he referred to the Bishop of London and the Puseyites, she wrote (9.11.50):

> Oh! I wish Dr Arnold were yet living or that a second Dr Arnold could be found. Were there but ten such men amongst the Hierarchs of the Church of England, she might bid defiance to all the scarlet hats and stockings in the Pope's gift. Her sanctuaries would be purified, her rites reformed, her withered veins would swell again with vital sap; but it is *not* so.

The following summer she heard Cardinal Wiseman speak in London 'in a smooth whining manner, just like a canting Methodist preacher', yet she could acknowledge that there were very good people among the Romanists. The same strong prejudices, and the same qualification, are found in *Villette*; the novel concludes with an affirmation that man is capable of overcoming religious differences along with others. This conviction is reflected in the letter which expressed Charlotte's longing for ten Dr Arnolds in the Church of England:

It is well that Truth is indestructible; that Ruin cannot crush nor Fire annihilate – her divine essence; while forms change and institutions perish *Truth* is great and shall prevail.

In the assessment of literature, her moral preoccupations come to the fore. After reading a biography of Mirabeau, she asks Mr Williams if his son could read it without forming the impression that there is 'a grandeur in vice committed on a colossal scale. . . . The fact is that this great Mirabeau was a mixture of divinity and dirt.' She admired Thackeray's genius, particularly his regard for truth. In *The Paris Sketch-Book* she found vinegar and gall, but no dregs; 'you never go and wash your hands when you put it down, nor rinse your mouth to take away the flavour of a degraded soul'. Yet his light-hearted remarks on 'his false god' Fielding shocked her. 'Had I a brother yet living, I should tremble to let him read Thackeray's lecture. . . . I should hide it away from him', she told Mr Williams. She grieved that nothing had been said to warn young men against following his example. 'You will think this far too serious . . . but the subject is serious, and one cannot help feeling upon it earnestly' (–.5.53).

Some of the most interesting views in Charlotte's letters are on novel-writing and art generally. She had resolved to follow Nature and Truth as her sole guides in her first novel, only to discover that the reading public wanted something more startling. This she provided in *Jane Eyre*, only to be warned against melodrama by G. H. Lewes. He recommended her to read Jane Austen, 'to finish more and be more subdued'. Charlotte read *Pride and Prejudice*, and found it cultivated but commonplace; she thought George Sand 'sagacious and profound' but Miss Austen 'only shrewd and observant' (12.1.48). In his next letter Lewes stressed Jane Austen's greatness as an artist; he was thinking of her skill as a 'painter' of human character. Charlotte was convinced that she was not 'great' because she lacked '*poetry*', the quality which 'elevates that masculine George Sand, and makes out of something coarse something godlike'. Charlotte Brontë had strong prepossessions, and read impatiently, one suspects, when her sympathies were imperfect. As yet she was too self-assured to realize the validity of Lewes's criticism; she went back to Truth and Nature in *Shirley*, and forgot his advice on discipline ('the nicest sense of means to an end'), though she recognized it in Jane Austen.

On receiving Mr Williams' comments on *The Tenant of Wildfell Hall*, she wrote as follows (14.8.48):

> The first duty of an author is, I conceive, a faithful allegiance to Truth and Nature; his second, such a conscientious study of Art as shall enable him to interpret eloquently and effectively the oracles delivered by those two great deities. The Bells are very sincere in their worship of Truth, and they hope to apply themselves to the consideration of Art, so as to attain one day the power of speaking the language of conviction in the accents of persuasion; though they rather apprehend that whatever pains they take to modify and soften, an abrupt word or vehement tone will now and then occur to startle ears polite, whenever the subject shall chance to be such as moves their spirits within them.

Mr Williams could not have felt very reassured by this reply. It did not hold out any strong hope of an early amendment, and its conclusion plainly hinted that the writer's sense of what was appropriate was likely to take precedence over what was acceptable to the reader. The passage is not concerned with the art of the novel as we understand it today, but with the art of writing, the problem of presenting life in persuasive or acceptable language rather than offending readers through 'coarseness' of expression and presentation. Charlotte was in the middle of *Shirley* when she wrote the above, and was giving less thought than ever to the question of artistic design.

She returned to the subject in September 1848, and said that neither she nor Anne could accept the view that their heroes and heroines should conform to standard types. 'Unless I can look beyond the greatest Masters, and study Nature herself, I have no right to paint. Unless I can have the courage to use the language of Truth in preference to the jargon of Conventionality, I ought to be silent.' In this she was fundamentally right; she was not prepared to sacrifice much of 'the language of conviction' in the cause of 'persuasion'.

The question of design, together with that of 'tone', was raised when Mr Williams read the first part of *Shirley*. She assured him that he would find the first chapter on the curates relevant to the rest of the book, and was reluctant to withdraw it because it was *true* (2.3.49). 'Truth is better than Art', she averred. 'Ignorant as I am, I dare to hold and maintain that doctrine' (2.4.49). She could hardly fail to realize that truth artistically presented is more satisfying in a novel than scenes which are disproportionate and a drag on the action; unfortunately she had too much confidence in the power of inspiration. To Lewes's excellent advice, she replied (and the weakness of her answer is evident as soon as she offers 'most fluently' as an alternative to 'best'):

> When authors write best, or, at least, when they write most fluently, an influence seems to waken in them, which becomes their master – which will have its own way – putting out of view all behests but its own, dictating certain words . . ., new-moulding characters, giving unthought-of turns to incidents. . . . Is it not so? And should we try to counteract this influence? Can we indeed counteract it?

This is how she expressed it in her preface to *Wuthering Heights*:

> the writer who possesses the creative gift owns something of which he is not always master – something that, at times, strangely wills and works for itself. He may lay down rules and devise principles, and to rules and principles it will perhaps for years lie in subjection; and then, haply without any warning of revolt, there comes a time when it will no longer consent to 'harrow the valleys, or be bound with a band in the furrow' – when it 'laughs at the multitude of the city, and regards not the crying of the driver' – when, refusing absolutely to make ropes out of sea-sand any longer, it sets to work on statue-hewing, and you have a Pluto or a Jove, a Tisiphone or a Psyche, a Mermaid or a Madonna, as Fate or Inspiration direct.

One cannot deny the truth of what she says with so much flourish, but it has no relevance to the inspirational excesses and weaknesses she refused to modify in *Shirley*. *Villette* suggests that, though she could probably never have disciplined herself to the careful plotting of *Wuthering Heights* and *The Tenant of Wildfell Hall*, she had, when she gave herself time to look at her work more circumspectly, the critical insight to learn from her graver mistakes. The progression towards a more ascetic style in 'Emma' reinforces the impression that she had realized the unwisdom of self-sacrifice to the tyrannical Creative Impulse she had formerly worshipped.

Branwell Brontë
Poems

Branwell's literary talent, unlike Charlotte's, is felt more often in his poetry than in his prose. Such was his posthumous reputation that inevitably someone had to act as counsel for his defence, and this was well done by John Drinkwater in his edition of Branwell's translations of Horace (1923). Assessing his life and work sympathetically and reasonably, he had no hesitation in claiming that 'Branwell Brontë was the second poet in his family, and a very good second at that.'

In his boyhood Branwell seemed to regard his birthday as a milestone in his literary progress, and commemorated it suitably. On his thirteenth he began the play 'Caractacus'; on his fifteenth he wrote his 'Ode to the Polar Star', which is remarkable for its sea imagery (a recurring feature of his poetry). As Young Soult, he had already composed much 'Glasstown' verse, showing a penchant for odes, all characterized by unusual fluency. On his fifteenth birthday he also wrote a lengthy 'Ode on the Celebration of the African Games', in which the four 'mighty Genii' appear:

> Here dim forms involved in gloom,
> Like spectres rising from a midnight tomb,
> With winds and tempest fill the air.
> I see, I see appear
>   Awful Brannii, gloomy giant,
> Shaking o'er earth his blazing air,
> Brooding on blood with drear and vengeful soul
> He sits enthroned in clouds to hear his thunders roll.
> Dread Tallii next like a dire eagle flies
> And on our mortal miseries feasts her bloody eyes.
>   Emii and Annii last with boding cry,
> Famine and war foretell and mortal misery.

In 'The Fate of Regina', inspired by Pope's translation of Homer, he had displayed his love of war and his narrative talent in heroic couplets:

> Regina's Kings while arms or strength remain
> Still nobly fight, but fight, alas! in vain.
> But when they heard the sad foreboding cry
> Which warned them from their native homes to fly,
> When they beheld the clouds of smoke and fire
> Borne by the wind to heaven's black arch aspire,
> Their own ancestral mansions wrapt in flame,
> And their high temples but an empty name,
> Then, then hope leaves them sinking on the ground
> All heedless of the battle roaring round,
> To heaven's tempestuous shriek they raise their eye,
> And mournful to their Guardian Genius cry . . .

On his seventeenth birthday Branwell began a prose story, 'The Wool is Rising'; one of its poems, 'The Rover', is written in a rousing metre perfectly attuned to the spirit of its piratical hero Percy:

> Where am I? – dashed into the hold upon a strangling foe;
> All men, and smoke, and shouts above, a writhing wretch below.
> He dies. I rise and grasp a rope, I'm on the deck once more,
> And Percy's arm, and Percy's sword, now bathe that deck with gore.

A little later his interest in battle led him to write the ambitious poem 'Thermopylae'.

In 'An Hour's Musings' the sea is an image of life; Alexander Percy is

> Doomed from life's first bitter breath
> To launch upon a sea of death,
> Without a hope, without a stay
> To guide him upon his weary way.

All his future seems threatened with 'storms of misery'. Branwell sent his poem 'Misery' for inclusion in *Blackwood's Magazine*: it was the second of a series of abortive efforts to find favour with its publishers. The poem, which seems to belong to the Angrian saga, opens impressively with night and tempest; a rider, all his followers slain in battle, comes to a sudden halt before a 'raging torrent', and pauses to reflect. He has only one hope. Then, plunging into the 'wild water', he crosses, and disappears among the trees. He reappears before his castle, only just in time to see his wife Maria die. The second part opens with another impressive scene, after defeat in battle. The chieftain is dying; his thoughts sometimes assume the form of sea imagery, and for a second time the dove and olive branch are associated with Maria. Yet he dies without hope: 'Thou art alone and Heaven is gone'. The poem opens with hurrying horse and rider; it concludes with the sudden arrival of a riderless steed, in a sensational culmination to the glimpses of carnage which preceded the dying chieftain's thoughts on death:

> See through the shadows of the night,
>   Burst hotly, hasting onward there,
> A wounded charger vast and white
>   All wild with pain and mad with fear.
> With hoofs of thunder on he flies
> Shaking his white mane to the skies,
> Till on his huge knees tumbling down,
> Across the fallen chieftain thrown,
> With a single plunge of dying force
> His vast limbs cover Albert's corse.

In January 1837, just after Charlotte wrote to Southey for advice on her poetry, Branwell sent 'Still and bright, in twilight shining' to Wordsworth. He calculated that its subject, intimations of immortality, would help to create a good impression, but his accompanying letter was so intemperate, hailing the recipient as 'a divinity of the mind' and dismissing contemporary poetry as worthless, that Wordsworth was disgusted and probably gave scant attention to the poem. It is rather prolonged and sentimental, designed as 'the prefatory scene of a much longer subject'. What is most amazing about the poem is not the style, which suffers from lack of restraint, but the disclosure that the imaginative 'Angel Child' became Percy of Northangerland. Branwell was so pleased with the opening lines that he repeated some of them in 'Caroline', a poem which, though (like 'Harriet') related to the Percy story, contains a picture undoubtedly based on the poet's recollections of his coffined sister Maria.

'Harriet' has passages which remind one technically of Scott, and even approximate 'Christabel', though the verse never attains its charm and magic. The narrative is arrested for soliloquies of troubled feeling. If only Branwell could have checked the flow, and concentrated on the music and nuance of words, he would have made greater poetic progress. 'Sir Henry Tunstall' (the first draft of which was called 'The Wanderer', and completed in the summer of 1838) is his most controlled and finished poem; it observes good proportion, and ends artistically. Its texture is finer than most of Crabbe's. Collateral to the Caroline and Harriet stories, it shows better than they the unmistakable perceptiveness of Branwell's psychological imagination. The narrative is interesting, but the real subject resides in the changes wrought by sixteen years' absence:

> The piece endeavours . . . to describe the harsh contrast between the mind changed by long absence from home and the feelings kept flourishing in the hearts of those who have never wandered, and who vainly expect to find the heart returning as fresh as when they had bidden it farewell.

This interest in the inner life was probably deepened by the accelerated changes in Branwell's habits away from home, and by periodic remorse and repeated resolve to overcome weaknesses. 'The Triumph of Mind over Body' was written at Luddenden Foot, and its theme was suggested by the inn he frequented and his continual failure to withstand temptation. Its subject is Nelson; it purports to be the work of Northangerland, but surely the cry is the writer's:

> Give me – Great God! – give all who own thy sway
> Soul to command, and body to obey: . . .
> We have our task set – Let us do it well;
> Nor barter ease on earth with pain in Hell.
> We have our Talents, from thy treasury given –
> Let us return thee good account in heaven.

The same thought is to be found in the sonnet on Samuel Johnson, 'Man thinks too often that his earth-born cares', and is repeated in 'The desolate earth, the wintry sky'.

Near the end of his life Branwell had two poems in hand: 'Morley Hall' (designed as an epic poem relating to the Leyland family of Leigh in Lancashire) and 'Percy Hall', a return to the life of his favourite character in Angrian fiction. He made little progress with either. The most important of his later poems are personal, none more poignant than the lines written at Luddenden Foot, 'Amid the world's wide din around', in which he recalls his boyhood 'world of wonders wild'. It is often assumed that the voice of the poem is that of his sister Maria, but she cannot be associated with the glorious world of fictional creation and the sea heroes of his imaginative youth. It is probably that of the 'angel child' in Branwell himself –

> Since to thy soul my light was given
> To give thy earth some glow of heaven,
> And, if my beams from thee be driven,
> Dark, dark, thy night will be!

– with recollections of the child in Wordsworth's 'Intimations of Immortality':

> Mighty Prophet! Seer blest!
> On whom those truths do rest
> Which we are toiling all our lives to find,
> In darkness lost . . .

What Branwell thought of death cannot be surely gauged from the narrative-dramatic poem 'Azrael, or Destruction's Eve'.[1] His true feelings are painfully apparent in 'Peaceful Death and Painful Life'. 'Why dost thou sorrow for the happy dead?' he asks:

> So, turn from such as these thy drooping head
> And mourn the 'Dead alive' whose spirit flies –
> Whose life departs before his death has come –
> Who finds no Heaven beyond Life's gloomy skies,
> Who sees no Hope to brighten up that gloom,
> 'Tis HE who feels the worm that never dies –
> The REAL death and darkness of the tomb.

It was with Mrs Robinson in mind that he wrote the closing lines of 'Juan Fernandez', where he imagines himself like Cowper's castaway –

> Tossed overboard, my perished crew
> Of Hopes and Joys sink, one by one

– and 'Penmaenmawr':

> Let me, like it, arise o'er mortal care,
> All woes sustain, yet never know despair;
> Unshrinking face the grief I now deplore,
> And stand, through storm and shine, like moveless
> PENMAENMAWR!

---

[1] Composed by 30 April 1838, according to Branwell's notebook (Daphne du Maurier, p. 83).

This tune goes manly, but the sentiments did not last long. Branwell was more than half in love with easeful death. 'Real Rest' and 'Epistle from a Father to a Child in her Grave' show that he had given up the will to live by 1846.

After the poems of 1837–8, when Branwell reached his peak, his Horace translations are hardly a major achievement, though they have considerable merit. They were finished in June 1840. Hartley Coleridge found their versification often masterly (*TLS.*, 14 May 1970); John Drinkwater thought more than half of them excellent, and a few 'decidedly the best' he had read. Branwell's own poetic output, however, was slight and fitful in the years of his majority. Both his resolution to write and his performance declined. By the time that he wrote 'The Triumph of Mind over Body' (the first draft belongs to 1841–2), he must have known that his talents were failing; the poem shows his willingness to derive defeatist consolation from the thought that God had made him what he was. In poetry, as in everything else, Branwell's remarkable early promise was never fulfilled in his later years.

Emily Brontë
Poems

Emily's poetry is very uneven; some of it is undistinguished or fragmentary, and, despite its poetic impact, much remains vague and puzzling from ignorance of Gondalian contexts (see pp. 371–3). Metrically it can have the conventional simplicity of a hymn, as in 'When days of Beauty deck the earth', where the imagery is general and commonplace, or it can be jejunely inappropriate, as in 'King Julius left the south country', which nevertheless contains some striking imagery and expression:

> Close by his side a daggered death
> With sheathless point stands sneering.

Yet Emily's greatest poetry has an individuality which makes it arresting by any standard; it possesses qualities which are scarcely noticed in that of Charlotte, or Anne, or even Branwell. Charlotte found its excellence 'startling'. When she read the poems 'alone and in secret', she heard the notes of 'genuine' poetry; they stirred her heart 'like the sound of a trumpet'. She tried to analyse their power, and found 'condensed energy, clearness, finish – strange, strong pathos' (letter to W. S. Williams, September 1848). In her 1850 biographical notice of Ellis and Acton Bell, she wrote: 'I thought them condensed and terse, vigorous and genuine. To my ear they had also a peculiar music – wild, melancholy, and elevating.'

It seems unlikely that Emily composed with the same rapidity as Charlotte or Branwell. Her poetry suggests that she was more aurally sensitive in the selection of words to create desired effects not only through sense but even more at times through stress, pitch, sound, and movement. She had 'an extraordinary power', Charles Morgan wrote,[1] 'when the secret virtue commanded her stresses and her open vowels, to change a commonplace metre into a winged charge of the squadrons of the spirit'. Emily's poetry is not often 'winged', as Shelley's is, but Morgan's general observation is profoundly true. If we restrict ourselves to some of the metrical patterns which do not seem unusual, we can see some of her characteristics. One of the least intricate is that of 'Gleneden's Dream' (H. 63):

> Over Death and Desolation,
> Fireless hearths and lifeless homes;
> Over orphans' heart-sick sorrows,
> Over fathers' bloody tombs.

Here, in the bold repetition of 'Over' and its open-vowelled assonance, the sound (strengthened in 'Desolation') indicates a sense of something sustained. The stresses at the opening of each line, and their more crowded incidence in the second and fourth lines, where they occupy the final place, are like hammer blows in the strength of their impact, and so effective that the weaker syllables at the end are hardly noticed. All this is most appropriate to the consequence:

> Over friends, that my arms never
> Might embrace in love again –
> Memory pondered, until madness
> Struck its poignard in my brain.

For more subdued effects, this verse from 'Alcona, in its changing mood' (H.117) may be taken:

> How sweet it is to watch the mist
> From that bright silent lake ascend,
> And high o'er wood and mountain crest
> With heaven's grey clouds as greyly blend.

Assonance and longer, rather than open, vowels lend attractiveness to the scene as it is conveyed, and the pitch of sound, slowly rising in 'ascend' to its maximum in 'high', levels out as the pace slows down in the last line, all in conformity with the changing view. Repetition with its prolonged sound is artistically used to give the colour tone which slowly prevails.

---

[1] *Reflections in a Mirror*, London, 1944, p. 146.

In the long poem 'The Death of A.G.A.' (H.143) one verse, which takes human overtones from its context, is specially interesting for its audio-visual effects:

> At last, the sunshine left the ground;
> The laden bee flew home;
> The deep down sea, with sadder sound,
> Impelled its waves to foam.

The light lift of 'left' contrasts with the steady, weighted movement of the next line; and a sense of the depth and sounds of the sea is conveyed by assonance ('down', 'sound'), the alliterative buffeting of the 'd's in the third line, and the more obvious onomatopoeia of 'its waves to foam'. In all this the aural appeal of the verse is increased by long open vowels. In the next verse, from 'Ah! why, because the dazzling sun' (H.184), sadness is associated not with the departing, but with the rising, sun:

> Blood-red he rose, and arrow-straight
> His fierce beams struck my brow:
> The soul of Nature sprang elate,
> But mine sank sad and low!

The assault on the spirit is couched in imagery of medieval warfare, its ferocity being reinforced in the alliteration of 'straight' and 'struck'. The hyperaesthetic contrast between the outer world and the inner world of feeling is strengthened by the swift stress, the rising pitch, and the open vowels which help to flash the brightness of the natural scene in the third line, and the sinking, almost stifled, sounds of the last.

With few exceptions, the poems which Emily preserved belong to the pre-*Wuthering Heights* period of 1836 to 1845.[1] Most of the verse is Gondalian, and the writing of poems on the same situation or episode at wide intervals of time shows that Emily and Anne had agreed on the main events of their saga at a relatively early stage in its composition. For example, 'Light up thy halls', a dramatic monologue recording Fernando De Samara's suicide for love of A.G.A., is

---

[1] Emily's last poems are: 'No coward soul is mine', completed 2 January 1846; 'Why ask to know the date – the clime?', 14 September 1846; and, after a long interval, a shorter version of this poem, dated 13 May 1848.

dated November 1838, and Emily returned to the subject in January 1840 ('Thy sun is near meridian height'). The birthday notes of 1841 and 1845 suggest periodic, but not rapid, progression in the course of subsequent events.

Biographers, ignoring Emily's Gondalian themes, have repeatedly made the mistake of extracting too many personal records from her poems. She was attracted imaginatively to tragic and hopeless situations, but can we believe that at the age of eighteen she was the gloomy, disillusioned creature of 'I am the only being whose doom'? Even if she continued teaching at Law Hill throughout 1838, she would hardly have been mourning absence from home in 'The blue bell is the sweetest flower' as late as 18 December, when she would have been at Haworth, or on the point of returning home, for Christmas.[1]

Undoubtedly Emily expressed her own feelings and experience in some of the Gondal poems; the problem is to gauge where, and to what extent. ''Twas yesterday, at early dawn' contrasts the climate and scenery of Gondal and Gaaldine but, inwoven at the end (as the Shakespeare Head edition suggests), there may have been thoughts of the return of Anne and Branwell and Charlotte at the end of 1843. The poem begins with what could have been an actual scene at Haworth, and ends:

> Home to our souls whose wearying sighs
> Lament their absence drear,
> And feel how bright even winter skies
> Would shine if they were here!

'A little while, a little while' (4.12.38), though its second line, 'The noisy crowd are barred away', has suggested Law Hill to some, has a clear Gondal link in 'my dungeon bars recoil'. The prisoner dreams of home, and, though the house is old, the scene is undoubtedly Haworth:

> There is a spot 'mid barren hills,
> Where winter howls and driving rain,
> But if the dreary tempest chills
> There is a light that warms again.

---

[1] In 1850 Charlotte Brontë assumed from what appeared to be their autobiographical evidence that this poem (H. 94), 'A little while' (H. 92), and H. 91 were composed at Law Hill. See p. 58, however.

The second scene presents a view from Haworth in summer:

> A little and a lone green lane
> That opened on a common wide;
> A distant, dreamy, dim blue chain
> Of mountains circling every side;
>
> A heaven so clear, an earth so calm,
> So sweet, so soft, so hushed an air
> And, deepening still the dream-like charm,
> Wild moor-sheep feeding everywhere.

In 'How still, how happy!', a poem written three days later, the Gondal link ('I loved the plashing of the surge . . . More than smooth seas') is equally slight. Emily notices the 'wintry light o'er flowerless moors' above Haworth, and thinks of 'Spring's budding wreaths':

> The violet's eye might shyly flash
> And young leaves shoot among the fern.
>
> It is but thought – full many a night
> The snow shall clothe those hills afar
> And storms shall add a drearier blight
> And winds shall wage a wilder war,
>
> Before the lark may herald in
> Fresh foliage twined with blossoms fair
> And summer days again begin
> Their glory-haloed crown to wear.
>
> Yet my heart loves December's smile
> As much as July's golden beam;
> Then let us sit and watch the while
> The blue ice curdling on the stream.

How far *Wuthering Heights* is anticipated in the poems is a hazardous field in which to speculate. One of the earliest poems in which Emily displayed the strength and terseness Charlotte admired is 'I am the only being whose doom'. It relates to the dark, inscrutable, fated child of Gondal, in whom Miss Ratchford saw the 'prototype' of Heathcliff:

> First melted off the hope of youth,
> Then fancy's rainbow fast withdrew;
> And then experience told me truth
> In mortal bosoms never grew.

> 'Twas grief enough to think mankind
> All hollow, servile, insincere;
> But worse to trust to my own mind
> And find the same corruption there.

Two companion poems 'A.E. and R.C.', written as late as 1845, introduce a childhood contrast and theme which has its parallel in Heathcliff and Catherine Earnshaw. The first of these, 'Heavy hangs the raindrop', reinforces through image and rhythmic stress the 'grim Fate' of one of the 'unblessed of Heaven'.

Lockwood's nightmare has its precursor in 'A sudden chasm of ghastly light':

> My couch lay in a ruined Hall,
> Whose windows looked on the minster-yard,
> Where chill, chill whiteness covered all —
> Both stone and urn and withered sward.
>
> The shattered glass let in the air,
> And with it came a wandering moan,
> A sound unutterably drear
> That made me shrink to be alone.
>
> One black yew-tree grew just below —
> I thought its boughs so sad might wail;
> Their ghostly fingers, flecked with snow,
> Rattled against an old vault's rail.
>
> I listened — no; 'twas life that still
> Lingered in some deserted heart:
> O God! what caused the shuddering shrill,
> That anguished, agonising start?
>
> An undefined, an awful dream,
> A dream of what had been before;
> A memory whose blighting beam
> Was flitting o'er me evermore.

The strange visitor with his basilisk look in 'And now the house-dog stretched once more' foreshadows Heathcliff; and his wish to die and be buried with Catherine is seen in 'A thousand sounds of happiness':

> Enough of storms have bowed his head:
> Grant him at least a quiet bed —

> Beside his early stricken dead –
> Even where he yearns to be!

The end of the novel has its parallel in 'The linnet in the rocky dells'.

Even more dangerous is it to make the expressed beliefs of characters in Gondal a basis for conclusions on whatever philosophy of life is inherent in *Wuthering Heights*. They are inconsistent and even contradictory; retribution overtakes crime sooner or later in the general Gondal plan, and one can hardly expect the unprincipled A.G.A. to utter Emily's religious views (H.137):

> I know our souls are all divine;
> I know that when we die,
> What seems the vilest, even like thine
> A part of God himself shall shine
> In perfect purity.

There is a mournful monotony of subject and tone in many of the poems and fragments; 'drear' and 'dreary' are variants of perhaps the commonest epithet:

> There are two trees in a lonely field;
> 　They breathe a spell to me;
> A dreary thought their dark boughs yield,
> 　All waving solemnly.

'Some natures become vocal at tragedy', Hardy wrote, and this was particularly true of Emily Brontë as a poet.

> Month after month, year after year,
> My harp has poured a dreary strain,

she wrote in June 1839. The Gondal characters seem made to suffer:

> Thy sun is near meridian height,
> And my sun sinks in endless night;
> But, if that night bring only sleep,
> Then I shall rest, while thou wilt weep.

The supernatural of the border ballad appears in 'The night was dark, yet winter breathed':

> It was about the middle night,
> And under such a starless dome
> When, gliding from the mountain's height,
> I saw a shadowy spirit come.

A Gothic relish for the horrible and ominous is evident in this brief dramatic poem:

> The starry night shall tidings bring:
> Go out upon the breezy moor,
> Watch for a bird with sable wing,
> And beak and talons dropping gore.
>
> Look not around, look not beneath,
> But mutely trace its airy way;
> Mark where it lights upon the heath,
> Then wanderer kneel thee down and pray.
>
> What fortune may await thee there
> I will not and I dare not tell,
> But Heaven is moved by fervent prayer
> And God is mercy – fare thee well!

How much of the substratum of sensational romantic literature, in English or from the German, influenced Emily Brontë has never been discovered. There is more than a Byronic element in 'And now the house-dog stretched once more', and the result is something akin to the supernatural emanating from Geraldine in Coleridge's 'Christabel':

> And something in his voice's tone
> Which turned their blood as chill as stone.
> . . . .
> No – lightning all unearthly shone
> Deep in that dark eye's circling zone,
> Such withering lightning as we deem
> None but a spectre's look may beam;
> And glad they were when he turned away
> And wrapt him in his mantle grey,
> Leant down his head upon his arm
> And veiled from view their [*sic*] basilisk charm.

In 'Written in Aspin Castle' (H.154) we hear an echo of Blake:

> And did he never smile to see
> Himself restored to infancy?

Whether Emily Brontë had read much of his poetry is not known, but occasionally there is an unmistakable resemblance between their thought, and the expression of it, as in this independent quatrain:

In dungeons dark I cannot sing,
In sorrow's thrall 'tis hard to smile:
What bird can soar with broken wing?
What heart can bleed and joy the while?

In succumbing to the 'Gondaland' spell, Emily ran the gravest danger of remaining within the confines of an unreal imaginative world. Wordsworth had experienced this adolescent phase, when

There came among those shapes of human life
A wilfulness of fancy and conceit
Which gave them new importance to the mind;
And Nature and her objects beautified
These fictions, as in some sort in their turn
They burnish'd her. . . . the Yew-tree had its Ghost,
That took its station there for ornament:
Then common death was none, common mishap,
But matter for this humour every where,
The tragic super-tragic, else left short.[1]

Emily's longest poem 'Were they shepherds, who sat all day?', on the death of A.G.A., reveals a sickening morbidity of subject. It is true that 'On the Fall of Zalona' and 'Why ask to know the date – the clime?' condemn the horrors and miseries consequent on war, yet, though Branwell delighted in descriptions of slaughter, his boyish interest is healthy compared with Emily's obsessive application to the tragic events which overtake her principal characters. His feelings were not involved; hers were, and she was overwhelmingly attracted by such melodramatic subjects as imprisonment and suffering, revenge and death.

She is less the narrative poet than Charlotte or Branwell, and more responsive to mood and feeling in dramatic situations. An early poem, the 'song' of 'Douglas's ride', shows remarkable narrative pace; the setting for the climax of this Gondalian pursuit may have derived (as John Hewish suggested) from Scott's *Old Mortality* (xliii). Emily's skill in ballad metre is seen again in 'On the Fall of Zalona'. When she changes to quicker measures, she is generally too enslaved by them to be wholly successful. 'Written in Aspin Castle' shows that she responded more effectively to the influence of 'Christabel' and Scott. In 'Light up thy halls' and 'Silent is the House', the

---

[1] *The Prelude*, viii, 519ff., 1805 edn.

verse assumes long six-stress lines of vigorous dramatic-narrative effect. The second was composed in October 1845, nearly six years after the first. Much of it is equally shackled by metrical regularity, yet it contains some of Emily's finest lyrical lines:

> He comes with western winds, with evening's wandering airs,
> With that clear dusk of heaven that brings the thickest stars;
> Winds take a pensive tone, and stars a tender fire,
> And visions rise and change which kill me with desire.

More than eight years earlier, she had experienced such feelings, and been unable to express them (H. 27):

> Because I could not speak the feeling,
> The solemn joy around me stealing
> In that divine, untroubled hour.
>
> I asked myself, 'O why has heaven
> Denied the precious gift to me,
> The glorious gift to many given
> To speak their thoughts in poetry?'

In March 1845 she wrote her Gondalian poem, 'Cold in the earth, and the deep snow piled above thee', perhaps her greatest achievement in dramatic lyricism. Emily's lyrical talent is more concentrated than Branwell's. In artistry and simplicity of diction, there is a reminder of some of the best lyrics of the late sixteenth and early seventeenth centuries in:

> If grief for grief can touch thee,
> If answering woe for woe,
> If any ruth can melt thee,
> Come to me now!
>
> I cannot be more lonely,
> More drear I cannot be!
> My worn heart throbs so wildly
> 'Twill break for thee.

'Fall, leaves, fall' suggests the disciplined poetry of the same period, but whether it is dramatic or personal (on the July–December theme already noted), it is impossible to say. 'The Night-Wind', a lyrical poem of greater length, seems to be wholly personal.

Perhaps Emily thought that her 'Gondaland' reflected the real world, for in two of her poems ('To Imagination' and 'O thy bright eyes must answer now') she regards the world of the imagination as a refuge from guile and hatred:

> So hopeless is the world without,
> The world within I deeply prize;
> Thy world where guile and hate and doubt
> And cold suspicion never rise;
> Where thou and I and Liberty
> Have undisputed sovereignty.
>
> . . . .
>
> I welcome thee, benignant power,
> Sole solacer of human cares
> And brighter hope when hope despairs.

If the subject of the two poems is the same, the new kind of imagination to which she wishes to become a slave is inseparable from the religious thought of some of her most personal poems. In one of these (H. 147) Earth wishes to recall her mind:

> Few hearts to mortals given
> On earth so wildly pine;
> Yet none would ask a Heaven
> More like this Earth than thine.
>
> Then let my winds caress thee;
> Thy comrade let me be –
> Since nought beside can bless thee,
> Return and dwell with me.

Transferred to Catherine Earnshaw, the same thought took a different form (*W*. ix). In her next poem, 'Aye, there it is! It wakes to-night', Emily's religious views (set in a Gondal context) are similar to Shelley's in *Adonais*:

> Dust to the dust! but the pure spirit shall flow
> Back to the burning fountain whence it came,
> A portion of the Eternal, which must glow
> Through time and change, unquenchably the same.

The two thoughts combine in 'I see around me tombstones grey'; despite her sorrows, Earth still holds her affections:

We would not leave our native home
For *any* world beyond the Tomb.
No – rather on thy kindly breast
Let us be laid in lasting rest;
Or waken but to share with thee
A mutual immortality.

Shelley's pantheism is at the heart of 'No coward soul is mine':

With wide-embracing love
Thy spirit animates eternal years,
Pervades and broods above,
Changes, sustains, dissolves, creates and rears.
. . . .
There is not room for Death
Nor atom that his might could render void
Since thou art Being and Breath
And what thou art may never be destroyed.

The thought is similar to that of *Adonais*: the spirit of Keats is not dead; he is made one with Nature; he is a presence

Spreading itself where'er that Power may move
Which has withdrawn his being to its own;
Which wields the world with never-wearied love,
Sustains it from beneath, and kindles it above.

He is a portion of the loveliness
Which once he made more lovely: he doth bear
His part, while the one Spirit's plastic stress
Sweeps through the dull dense world, compelling there,
All new successions to the forms they wear.

For the eloquent expression of metaphysical thought in English poetry, some would award the palm to Shelley; Sir Herbert Read thought that Emily Brontë's 'absorption in metaphysical problems has no parallel in the poetry of her age' and, in 'No coward soul is mine', 'rises to an intensity of emotional thought not surpassed in the whole range of English literature'.

The more closely one examines Emily's poetry from 1844 to 1846, the more impregnated it appears with Shelleyan thought. 'The Philosopher' is dominated by it. The conflict between 'power and will' and good and ill makes the poet wish for the repose of death, since no heaven could satisfy human desire. The 'warring gods' within man are symbolized by three rivers, one golden, one like blood, and one like sapphire, which join and tumble into an 'inky sea'. This is the darkness or obscurity of 'the clouds that 'wilder' the philosopher who has been dreaming,

> Unlightened, in this chamber drear
> While summer's sun is beaming.

A spirit 'bent his dazzling gaze' through the inky sea:

> Then – kindling all with sudden blaze,
> The glad deep sparkled wide and bright –
> White as the sun; far, far more fair
> Than the divided sources were!

Once again Emily's guiding light is *Adonais*:

> The One remains, the many change and pass;
> Heaven's light forever shines, Earth's shadows fly;
> Life, like a dome of many-coloured glass,
> Stains the white radiance of Eternity,
> Until Death tramples it to fragments.

The 'dome' of life creates a 'veil' between earth and heaven's splendour; it breaks up light into its component colours, the many, the imperfect, the 'broken arcs' in Browning's 'perfect round'. The link between 'The Philosopher' and 'No coward soul is mine' is evident in the conclusion of the latter poem:

> Had I but seen his glorious eye
> *Once* light the clouds that 'wilder me,
> I ne'er had raised this coward cry
> To cease to think and cease to be.

(The wish for oblivion in death contrasts strongly with the faith of 'I, Undying Life, have power in Thee' in 'No coward soul'.) After reflecting on the transience of life in 'A Day Dream', the poet takes comfort in Shelley's Platonism (with perhaps an allusion to his sonnet, 'Lift not the painted veil'):

> 'To thee the world is like a tomb,
> A desert's naked shore;
> To us, in unimagined bloom,
> It brightens more and more.

'And could we lift the veil and give
One brief glimpse to thine eye
Thou would'st rejoice for those that live,
Because they live to die.'

In moments of vision, the mystic can pierce the veil and become
one with the universal and eternal Spirit. Something approaching
this experience lay behind 'I'm happiest when most away'. This
early attempt to express the spirit's release into the 'infinite immensity'
of 'worlds of light' (with its echo of Henry Vaughan's 'They are all
gone into the world of light') is the subject of 'Ah! why, because the
dazzling sun', where the emphasis is on the shock when the ecstatic
spell is broken by daylight. The experience is more intensely communicated in 'Silent is the House – all are laid asleep', a Gondal
poem:

Mute music soothes my breast – unuttered harmony
That I could never dream till earth was lost to me.

Then dawns the Invisible, the unseen its truth reveals;
My outward sense is gone, my inward essence feels –
Its wings are almost free, its home, its harbour found;
Measuring the gulf it stoops and dares the final bound!

Oh, dreadful is the check – intense the agony
When the ear begins to hear and the eye begins to see;
When the pulse begins to throb, the brain to think again,
The soul to feel the flesh and the flesh to feel the chain!

The 'chain' is Shelley's chain of Time, but in this dramatic poem it is
a prisoner's fetters. To adopt Emily's symbolism, which could have
been suggested by the poem of Henry Vaughan referred to above,
the bird will not leave its cage, and earthly love is preferred to the
soul's release. In *Wuthering Heights* the unfulfilment of earthly
love creates a desire, first (in Catherine Linton) for release, then (in
Heathcliff) for reunion, through death.

'Wuthering Heights'

Few English novels have excited greater interest in recent years than *Wuthering Heights*; its intensity of vision and the challenging qualities of its uniqueness have elicited more critical essays than all the other Brontë novels. It has been the subject of psychological exegesis, and it has been described as a spiritual or religious novel. From the outset it has been condemned for the structural clumsiness of its plot; more frequently in modern times the artistry of the same plot has been the subject of panegyric or admiration. Heathcliff has been recognized as a Marxist hero who turns into a Marxist villain. Joseph has been seen as the villain of the piece; so too has Nelly Dean. Incest has entered into the reckoning.

Some of these questions will be referred to later. Broadly speaking, Heathcliff, like Macbeth, is a hero-villain; and Emily Brontë presents him fearlessly with the same 'delight' which, according to Keats, the 'chameleon poet' or true artist experiences in conceiving an Iago or Imogen. This does not mean that Shakespeare and Emily Brontë present their characters in such a way that they are removed from the world of moral assessment; the action which concludes the novel, for example, conveys an artistic and implicit commentary on the tragic shortcomings and errors of the two principal characters. Nor does it imply that Heathcliff is an Iago. His malignity is far from motiveless, and one can be sorry for him; yet he lacks the heroic virtues of a Macbeth, and his brutality shows human nature on one of its lowest levels.

The case against Joseph is stronger than that against Nelly Dean, whose occasional weakness or negligence is sometimes, one suspects, not a symptom of the fallibility which makes her human so much as the convenient device of an author not highly expert in plot inventiveness. The story which follows the death of Cathy,[1] and which leads to Catherine's marriage to Linton Heathcliff, fails to sustain the interest and cogency which characterize the direct presentation of the Heathcliff-Cathy theme in the first half of the novel and its concluding chapters. There is a lull; the imagination flags; and the plot has an unmistakable air of contrivance, of avoidable rather than ineluctable chance. *Wuthering Heights* is a work of astonishing genius, but it is not strong at all points.

In 1959 it was suggested that Heathcliff was Earnshaw's illegitimate son, and that fear of an incestuous relationship between him and Cathy was the reason for her marriage to Edgar Linton. If such was the author's implication, only her ineptitude can explain the oversight of readers for more than a century. No tangible evidence was given for the deduction, which is contrary to all the reasons provided for Cathy's marriage. The theory, which persists, hinges on Mr Earnshaw's declared intention to walk to Liverpool and back, 'sixty miles each way', and his return after three days with a foundling 'big enough both to walk and talk', whom he had picked up out of pity in the streets of Liverpool and brought home because he had neither the time nor the money to house him there. The story is regarded as impossible. It has, in fact, like other elements in the novel, the aura of a 'fairy tale'; yet the evidence, both internal and external, suggests that it was by no means improbable. Mrs Earnshaw, it should be noted, expected her husband to return a few hours before he did, and Emily Brontë knew that her father had thought nothing of walking forty miles a day.[2]

Liverpool, a foundling child, and some other features of *Wuthering Heights* may have been long connected in her memory by a story relating to her grandfather, Hugh Brunty.[3] Ellen Nussey remembered from her first visit to Haworth how Mr Brontë told strange stories he had heard from the oldest of his parishioners of grim events in the lives of people in outlying places, and she recognized some of these in *Wuthering Heights*. Some could have been substantiated by Tabitha

---

[1] 'Cathy' is used throughout this chapter for Catherine Earnshaw or Mrs Linton; 'Catherine', for her daughter, Catherine Linton.

[2] Mrs Gaskell recorded his complaint when he was seventy-six: 'Where is my strength gone? I used to walk 40 miles a day' (*Letters*, September 1853).

[3] See Appendix 5, pp. 383–5.

Aykroyd, who worked on a farm before coming to Haworth parsonage. The main action owes much, however, to the history of Law Hill, where Emily taught in 1837–8.[1] Architectural and topographical features were transferred from this neighbourhood when Wuthering Heights was set above Haworth Moor.

As John Hewish pointed out, an episode in Byron's life and its imagined sequel in 'The Dream' may have made an important contribution to the Heathcliff story. In his *Letters and Journals of Lord Byron*, Thomas Moore wrote:

> He either was told of, or overheard, Miss Chaworth saying to her maid, 'Do you think I could care anything for that lame boy?' This speech, as he himself described it, was like a shot through his heart. Though late at night when he heard it, he instantly darted out of the house, and scarcely knowing whither he ran, never stopped until he found himself at Newstead.

Moore then referred to 'The Dream', in which we are told that the boy grew up, went abroad, and became a changed man; the lady was stricken with madness; and both died in misery.

How much Emily read on the life of Byron is not known, but her familiarity with Moore's biography is beyond doubt. It seems likely that, whether she realized it or not, she drew a number of suggestions from it for her novel. They could include: the resentment kindled by violent punishment in boyhood; a thwarted affection which induced

---

[1] See Winifred Gérin, *Emily Brontë*, pp. 77–80. Mr Walker of Walter Clough Hall adopted his nephew Jack Sharp, an orphan, and brought him up to be his partner in the wool business instead of his own sons. Jack became so overbearing that he dominated the business and family. When his uncle retired, Jack stayed on and prospered. The heir, however, claimed the hall on his father's death. Jack Sharp built Law Hill, and took everything of value from Walter Clough Hall when he removed to make room for the second Mr Walker and his bride. To further his revenge, he apprenticed Mr Walker's cousin and encouraged him to drink and gamble. When his nephew's fortunes declined, Mr Walker impoverished himself by paying his debts. The cousin returned to Walter Clough Hall when Jack Sharp's business came to an end, taught Mr Walker's son foul language, and delighted in setting children and servants at variance.

The principal resemblances between fact and fiction are: the adoption of an orphan who is favoured; the return of a newly married son on the death of his father; the encouragement of gambling to ruin one of the despised family; and the attempt to degrade an heir.

thoughts of heartlessness and crime;[1] Byron's marrying with an eye to large estates; reports that he treated his wife cruelly to avenge his wounded pride; glimpses of 'the only *real* love of his whole life', for Countess Guiccioli, a girl of eighteen when she married not long before meeting him, their separation causing her frequent illnesses, with symptoms of consumption, and a serious relapse, which ended only when Byron came to see her at the Count's request; Byron's abandoning his return to England because 'farewell' to her would have been 'death' to his happiness; and scenes from the final act of *Manfred* which stress hell within the mind, and may have confirmed Emily Brontë's views on the individuality of religious belief (see p. 63):

> whate'er
> I may have been, or am, doth rest between
> Heaven and myself.

There are minor parallels: Heathcliff's way of dealing with a dangerous bull-dog (vi) is comparable to that employed with Byron's ferocious bull-dog Nelson; and Isabella's access of fury after leaving Heathcliff, which leads her to throw her gold wedding-ring to the floor, smash it with a poker, and burn it (xvii), recalls Byron's fit of rage, when he dashed his favourite watch upon the hearth, and 'ground it to pieces among the ashes with the poker'.

The influence of Scott is unmistakable. In her delirium, Cathy, seeing Nelly Dean pick up feathers she has scattered from her pillow, imagines her bed is the fairy cave beneath Penistone Crags, and that Nelly is an old witch 'gathering elf-bolts to hurt our heifers; pretending, while I am near, that they are only locks of wool'. This recalls

---

[1] See the poem ' "Oh! banish care" ' (generally entitled 'Lines to a Friend', and written at Newstead on 11 October 1811), which Moore includes, and from whose version the following lines are taken:

> I've seen my bride another's bride, –
> . . . .
> But if . . .
> Thou hear'st of one, whose deepening crimes
> Suit with the sablest of the times,
> Of one, whom Love nor Pity sways, . . .
> One rank'd in some recording page
> With the worst anarchs of the age,
> Him wilt thou *know* – and, knowing, pause,
> Nor with the *effect*, forget the cause.

the most memorable image in *The Black Dwarf*, that of Mucklestane, a huge granite column on a knoll in the middle of a heath. A witch who used to hold revels there caused ewes to miscarry, and kine to cast their calves, until the Devil transformed her and her geese to the stones which lay near the column. Scott's common use of dialect for dialogue exerted a general influence; but certain expressions ('despair which would have melted the heart of a whin stane', 'revenge is a hungry wolf'), names of characters (Isabella, Earnscliff < Earnshaw and Heathcliff), and a threatened forced marriage within doors, suggest a more particular indebtedness.

At one time it was customary to assume that Hoffmann's stories explained the violence of *Wuthering Heights*: more specifically that Lockwood's second dream derived from the opening of 'The Entail' (*Das Majorat*). There are technical similarities, but Emily Brontë's art is more subtle, and a poem she wrote at Law Hill (see p. 195) in October 1837 gives clear proof that the imaginative association of 'an awful dream' with the rattling of branches was in her mind at a time when she may already have become interested in the history of Law Hill and Jack Sharp. On the other hand, 'The Bridegroom of Barna', an excellently written Irish story published in *Blackwood's Magazine* in 1840, seems to have done much to transform the Jack Sharp story into a passionate romance.[1] In *Wuthering Heights* and 'The Bridegroom of Barna' we find the union of violence and an overmastering love which is almost spiritual. Ellen Nugent (whose golden hair and 'fairy-like' form recall Cathy) and Hugh Lawlor had been fond of each other from childhood, though severed for years by a family quarrel. Hugh murders an innocent man in order to deny his rival the fortune which would gain him Ellen's hand. One sentence referring to his thwarted love may have had special significance in the conception of Heathcliff:

> The long, and bitter, and hopeless opposition that attachment had to undergo, no doubt gave his spirit an inflexibility and sullenness that gradually hardened a heart not naturally ill-disposed, and imparted to it a selfishness by which it was finally corrupted.

Tom Bush, the villain responsible for the final tragedy of the lovers, also resembles Heathcliff; hell-fire glares in his eyes, and his looks

---

[1] See p. 359 (Leicester Bradner). For parallels with one of George Sand's novels, see Patricia Thomson, '*Wuthering Heights* and *Mauprat*', *The Review of English Studies*, 1973.

are like those of 'Angry demon sent / Red from his penal settlement'. He creates a quarrel among the sightseers gathered for the wedding of Hugh and Ellen: when Hugh drives him off, he rides away and plunges into the darkness of gathering night as peals of thunder announce an approaching storm. Similar ominous overtones mark Heathcliff's sudden departure from Wuthering Heights (ix). Bush betrays Lawlor, who becomes a fugitive. 'At the close of a sweet evening in July' he appears before the languid Ellen at her window. She is 'all of heaven' he ever hoped to gain (just before his death, Heathcliff says he has nearly reached his heaven, his spiritual union with Cathy, and desires no other, xxxiv); Ellen falls senseless in his arms; subsequently she raves in her delirium, though this is not dramatized. Here we have the seeds of the most moving dramatic episode in *Wuthering Heights* from the time of Heathcliff's return 'on a mellow evening in September' to Cathy's death. Ellen recovers, but dies of consumption the following spring. A few days after her burial her lover is betrayed by Tom Bush. In the moonlight the police see Lawlor embracing 'the form that had once comprised all earth's love and beauty for him, and which, like a miser, with mild and maniac affection, he had unburied once more to clasp and contemplate'. As soon as he heard his captors, he sprang to his feet, his eyes 'glaring with the fierceness of a roused tiger', and shot Bush. He was shot at the same time, and was buried beside Ellen, to be united in death as he had never been in life. In this grave scene and final union alone the resemblance to Emily's story is remarkable; even the incidental animal simile may have had its effect.

Emily's frequent concentration on the writing of poetry helped immeasurably to create the style of *Wuthering Heights* in all aspects of its intensity, vigorous or smooth-flowing, lucid, simple, figurative, dramatic, and lyrical. Yet the search in her poems for pointers to the theme of the novel is neither very productive nor conclusive. Most of them are dramatic, and express the views of characters of whom we know little. The punishment of sinners after death (H.111, H.133, H.192 – the last written after the novel) conflicts with their purification by woe on earth (H.133) and the idea of a God who is above vengeance (H.134). A.G.A.'s

> I know our souls are all divine;
> I know that when we die,
> What seems the vilest, even like thine

> A part of God himself shall shine
> In perfect purity (H.137)

and

> Thy soul was pure when it entered here,
> And pure it will go again to God (H. 61)

are contradicted by another speaker (H.143):

> The guiltless blood upon my hands
> Will shut me out from Heaven.

A significant relationship between religious views expressed in the Gondal poems and the theme of *Wuthering Heights* is often assumed, yet nothing in the novel, apart from a conventional remark by Nelly Dean (xxxiv), relates to the question of retribution after death. Cathy in her 'torment' (xv) wishes for death to escape from her 'shattered prison' into a 'glorious world', and remain there for ever, not 'seeing it dimly through tears, and yearning for it through the walls of an aching heart'. The thought and the expression are Shelleyan, and they have already been noticed in Emily's poetry (pp. 201–3). Ultimately Heathcliff wishes to escape his torment and die, in the certainty that his heaven will be attained in union with his soul's idol (xxxiv). This is the only after-life which is closely related to the main story of *Wuthering Heights*.[1] There is no reason to suppose that the 'heaven' of a love-crazed man, whose 'one universal idea' relates to an individual, can be identified in any way with the pantheism of Emily Brontë.

Heathcliff is superstitious; he cannot forget Cathy, and at times of anguish he is plagued by her. As he becomes more abnormal (and he changes very rapidly just before his death), he is haunted increasingly by her presence to the point of 'monomania'. Though exceptional in degree, this is a natural, psychic phenomenon, unrelated

---

[1] It is not to be found in the metaphysics of Cathy (quoted on p. 216), where she speaks of her posthumous existence in Heathcliff's mind. E. M. Forster's statement in *Aspects of the Novel* that 'Wuthering Heights has no mythology beyond what these two characters provide: no great book is more cut off from the universals of Heaven and Hell' is nearer the mark than J. Hillis Miller, who, after a brilliant opening on *Wuthering Heights*, uses a selection of Gondal views to form a 'divine law' which takes us further from the reality of the novel the more it progresses in support of his thesis.*

* *The Disappearance of God* (see p. 360 for further details).

to any metaphysical or religious beliefs. The novel therefore does not appear to support Lord David Cecil's claim that Emily Brontë believed in 'the immortality of the soul *in this world*'. In *Wuthering Heights* it is only the superstitious who believe in the continued existence of the spirits of the dead on earth; and, significantly, it is on this note that the novel ends. Here we have an echo of Emily Brontë's poem, 'The linnet in the rocky dells' (H.173). Though Heathcliff imagined he heard a sigh from Cathy's grave (xxix), the 'Dweller in the land of Death' is 'careless' of those who mourn her loss:

> And if their eyes should watch and weep
> Till sorrow's source were dry,
> She would not, in her tranquil sleep,
> Return a single sigh.
>
> Blow, west wind, by the lonely mound,
> And murmur, summer streams,
> There is no need of other sound
> To soothe my Lady's dreams.

This seems to be consistent with Cathy's most striking and explicit statement on the life after death: 'I shall be sorry for *you*. I shall be incomparably beyond and above you all' (xv).

The Gondal poems supply other minor anticipations of the novel: the girl with sunbright hair, an 'image of light and gladness', who pitied a mournful boy (H. 187); the black-haired stranger whose voice and basilisk look chilled the blood of his hosts (H. 107); and unbearable dreams associated with snow, a wailing wind, horror, and the rattling of branches below the room in which the sufferer tried to sleep (H. 29). The views in the following lines (which probably reflect Emily's; see H.149, 'I see around me tombstones grey') –

> No promised Heaven, these wild Desires
> Could all or half fulfil;
> No threatened Hell, with quenchless fires,
> Subdue this quenchless will (H.181)

– recall Cathy's dream of being in heaven, and weeping to return to earth (ix), and her rebellion with Heathcliff against the tyranny of Calvinistic Joseph. Catherine (who represents something positive in Emily Brontë's world) makes clear what she thinks of the latter, in language he will understand, when she calls him a 'castaway' (ii).

The novel opens with Lockwood's visits to Wuthering Heights near the end of 1801, and his two dreams when he is benighted there. His appetite to know the explanation of what he has seen and heard is appeased by his housekeeper, Nelly Dean, who tells her story in several sesssions[1] during his long convalescence. Her first item of information is that Cathy, her mistress, was married eighteen years earlier. The time scheme is not always given with quite the precision of *The Tenant of Wildfell Hall*, nor is Emily Brontë's attention to chronological detail for the sake of verisimilitude exceptional among novelists. It can be calculated from related facts and certain dates (e.g. at the end of vii) that the story began early in the 1770s. The sequel, including Heathcliff's death, is related when Lockwood revisits Thrushcross in September 1802, and ends with expectations of the wedding of Hareton and Catherine on New Year's Day, 1803. The plan of the novel (beginning towards the end of the action with the impressions of the visitor-narrator, who then hears the main story from Nelly Dean, leaving the sequel to be completed) was imitated less convincingly in *The Tenant of Wildfell Hall*. As the principal narrator necessarily depends on witnesses for parts of her story, e.g. Heathcliff (vi), Isabella (xiii, xvii), Catherine (xxiv), and Zillah (xxx), the reader is sometimes at three removes from events – without any mystification, however, since the fallibility of narrators was no part of the author's plan. On the contrary, this rather unsophisticated narrative technique enables the writer to give vivid, first-hand impressions. The evidence is there for the reader to assess; and it sometimes shows that the narrator's comments are human and biased.

Except for a number of heavy and facetious expressions (all in the opening chapters), to remind us that Lockwood is a member of the educated upper classes, alien to rural life, and somewhat affected, the style is 'dramatized' only in the dialogue;[2] it varies according to the subject, but is plainly the author's. Nelly Dean uses colloquialisms, but her style sometimes approaches Lockwood's in its Latinity ('and I tried to smooth away all disquietude on the subject by affirming, with frequent iteration, that the betrayal of trust, if it merited so

[1] After the first two, she told the remainder of the interim story (xv–xxxi) at 'different sittings'.

[2] Not always here; see the speech of Heathcliff quoted on p. 221.

harsh an appellation, should be the last'. She is here on her dignity, (xiv) Lockwood admits that he could not improve on her general style (xv); the explanation given for this excellence is that she has read and reflected a great deal (vii).

Lockwood's dreams provide the key to the moral theme of *Wuthering Heights*. Both arise from the events of the evening, and show the dreamer's nature. Before he falls asleep, much has happened. He would have kicked Joseph 'out of the door' from a sense of gallantry; Joseph unleashed the dogs on him as he tried to escape with the lantern; he was knocked down, and his anger and indignation induced copious nose-bleeding. When he retired to his bedroom, he felt sick and dizzy and faint. The window-ledge where he placed his candle had a few musty old books at one end, and was covered with writing scratched on the paint; 'Catherine Earnshaw' appeared many times, with 'Catherine Heathcliff' here and there, and 'Catherine Linton'. He could not help spelling the names over until his eyes closed. Soon 'a glare of white letters started from the dark, as vivid as spectres – the air swarmed with Catherines'. To dispel the name from his mind, he roused himself, attended to the candle, and looked into one of the books. He was amused to find an excellent caricature of Joseph, and then read one of Catherine Earnshaw's entries: Joseph had preached for three hours one Sunday, and insisted on the reading of pious books in the evening; she and Heathcliff had rebelled. Their previous master, Mr Earnshaw, had allowed them to play on Sunday evenings; the new master Hindley was a tyrant, and had forced them roughly into the kitchen.

The attack by the dogs and anger against Joseph account for the first dream; blood and the name 'Catherine Linton', for the second. In the first Lockwood set out for home with Joseph as his guide, found himself at the chapel, and listened to an interminable sermon on the four hundred and ninety sins rather than their forgiveness (see Matthew, xviii. 21–2). When the preacher finished the seventy-times-seven, and reached the first of the seventy-first, Lockwood rose and urged his fellow-martyrs to drag him down and crush him. In reply, the preacher ordered the assembly to punish Lockwood, who found that he was grappling with Joseph, his most ferocious assailant. Every man's hand was soon against his neighbour. The preacher's zealous tapping on the pulpit woke Lockwood, who found that the tumult of his dream was caused by a branch of a fir tree which rattled its cones against the window. The noise merged into his second dream. He thought that he rose to stop it and, finding the casement fixed, knocked his knuckle through the glass. Instead of seizing the branch, he grasped a little, icy-cold hand; he could not disengage, and was overcome with intense nightmarish horror. 'Who are you?' he asked, and the answer came, 'Catherine Linton'. A child's face looked through the window, and terror made Lockwood cruel. He pulled the wrist to the broken pane, and rubbed it to and fro until his bedclothes were soaked in blood. 'Let me in! . . . I've been a waif for twenty years!' the voice wailed. Lockwood yelled in his sleep, and woke Heathcliff, who came to see what was happening.

One might think from some commentaries that the spirit of Catherine Linton really did try to enter, but amid all the crowded details of this gruesome Gothic introduction to the strange story of Heathcliff there are clues as well as clear statements that this is no more than a dream; it is amazingly psychic and coincidental, but it does not conform to external facts. The variations in the scribbled names denote Catherine Earnshaw's girlish dreams, followed by her dilemma and its tragic resolution; but the 'Catherine' whom Heathcliff implored to enter as he wrenched open the lattice a little later was not a child. She was the Catherine Linton who had died less than *eighteen* years previously, after marrying Edgar and giving birth to a daughter. Heathcliff was possessed with the idea that she lived on the earth as a spirit; he had felt her presence but never seen her. Shortly before Lockwood's arrival at Thrushcross Grange, he had spoken to Nelly Dean of his anguished yearning to have but one glimpse of her (xxix):

I had not one. She showed herself, as she often was in life, a devil to me! And, since then, sometimes more and sometimes less, I've been the sport of that intolerable torture! Infernal! keeping my nerves at such a stretch that, if they had not resembled catgut, they would have long ago relaxed to the feebleness of Linton's . . . she must be somewhere at the Heights, I was certain! And when I slept in her chamber – I was beaten out of that. I couldn't lie there; for the moment I closed my eyes, she was either outside the window, or sliding back the panels, or entering the room, or even resting her darling head on the same pillow as she did when a child; and I must open my lids to see. And so I opened and closed them a hundred times a night – to be always disappointed! It racked me! . . . It was a strange way of killing: not by inches, but by fractions of hairbreadths, to beguile me with the spectre of a hope through eighteen years![1]

The dreams emphasize that deep down in man, despite the veneer of civilization (represented by the foppish Lockwwod), there is an instinct for cruelty and revenge. Perhaps Emily Brontë had discovered a streak of sadism in herself; it seems to find an outlet in many of her Gondal poems. It is very unlikely that she had seen 'The Gates of Paradise' by William Blake. Yet his first illustration to the poem has affinities with her caterpillar-butterfly analogy (see p. 59), and the thought of the opening lines has its parallel in *Wuthering Heights*. The corollary of

> Mutual Forgiveness of each Vice,
> Such are the Gates of Paradise

is that revenge leads to hell, and this is the Heathcliff theme. A few lines later Blake wrote, 'Jehovah's finger wrote the Law', and asked why Christians rear it high on their altars after Jehovah had buried it 'beneath his Mercy Seat'. The 'Law' is embodied in Joseph. 'In Hell all is Self Righteousness; there is no such thing there as Forgiveness of Sin', Blake wrote. Such is the havoc wrought in their natures by division that the lovers, even just before Cathy's death, are incapable of an atonement or mutual foregiveness which is lasting. The final conflict is greater in Heathcliff, and there is no appeasement for his wolfish spirit until his revenge is complete. Emily Brontë 'held that mercy and forgiveness are the divinest attributes of the Great Being who made both man and woman, and that what clothes the Godhead in glory, can disgrace no form of feeble humanity'.[2]

Retribution, brutality, and degradation, for the sake of revenge, occupy a large proportion of the narrative; and Joseph is never far away, rejoicing in the prospect of eternal punishment for the sinners. Mr Earnshaw's early indulgence of Heathcliff caused Hindley to bully the usurper of his father's affections mercilessly. When he became master, he degraded Heathcliff, and did his utmost to keep him from

---

[1] This illustrates Emily's chronological imprecision at certain points. Linton Heathcliff was still alive; he died in the autumn of 1801. Cathy, as the evidence of the novel shows, died on 20 March 1784.

[2] Charlotte Brontë, Preface to *Wuthering Heights*, 1850. Compare Catherine on the 'better nature' (xxix), and her sorrow that she had endeavoured to raise a bad spirit between Hareton and Heathcliff (xxxiii); also Nelly Dean to Heathcliff (vii).

Cathy, though punishment had the effect of making them wander further afield for the delight of each other's company. Her friendship with the Lintons deprived Heathcliff of hope and ambition, and it was his consequent self-neglect and moroseness which led to her engagement to Edgar Linton, though her heart was still with Heathcliff. Once she had dreamt of being in heaven, wept for earth again, and sobbed for joy to find herself on the heath near Wuthering Heights. When questioned on her love for Edgar, she ultimately tells Nelly Dean (ix):

> I've no more business to marry Edgar Linton than I have to be in heaven; and if the wicked man in there had not brought Heathcliff so low, I shouldn't have thought of it. It would degrade me to marry Heathcliff now; so he shall never know how I love him: and that, not because he is handsome, Nelly, but because he's more myself than I am.

(Heathcliff had overheard her, and like Byron he fled.) She thinks that she can help Heathcliff by this marriage, and that they are so much of one mind and spirit that he will understand her feelings:

> My great miseries in this world have been Heathcliff's miseries . . . my great thought in living is himself. If all else perished, and *he* remained, *I* should still continue to be; and if all else remained, and he were annihilated, the universe would turn to a mighty stranger: I should not seem a part of it. My love for Linton is like the foliage in the woods: time will change it . . . as winter changes the trees. My love for Heathcliff resembles the eternal rocks beneath: a source of little visible delight, but necessary. Nelly, I *am* Heathcliff. He's always, always in my mind: not as a pleasure . . . but as my own being.[1]

For this reason she cannot think of their separation. A violent thunderstorm sweeping over the Heights seems to signalize the fatefulness of her unnatural decision. Her illness is a consequence, the forerunner

---

[1] 'Annihilation' implies more than death. The thought of this dramatically impassioned passage is that the lover exists in the mind and soul of the beloved, and continues to live this subjective life after his death. If it were not so, the universe would become alien to the bereaved lover. As Mrs Ellis H. Chadwick pointed out (*In the Footsteps of the Brontës*, London, 1914, p. 340), Emily Brontë's views probably derived from the 'Love's rare Universe' of Shelley's 'Epipsychidion'; see, in particular, ll. 52, 573–89.

of the madness which assailed her, as it did the lady of Byron's 'The Dream'. Heathcliff's prolonged absence, Hindley's encouragement for the honour of his family, and Edgar's infatuation, ensured that this ill-omened marriage took place.

Not many months later, after an absence of three years, Heathcliff returned, telling Nelly Dean that he was 'in hell' until she took a message to her mistress. Their reunion was so rapturous that Cathy complained about his long absence. Her conflict of feeling is shown later when she finds that Isabella is attracted by him; jealousy makes her declare the worst she sees in Heathcliff; he is without cultivation, 'an arid wilderness of furze and whinstone', 'a fierce, pitiless, wolfish man', 'quite capable of marrying your fortune and expectations'. Subsequently this question provokes a quarrel, and Heathcliff announces his intention to be revenged on her for the 'infernal' treatment he has suffered at her hands. She sees that his bliss lies in inflicting misery. She then quarrels with Edgar for trying to evict him, and wishes Heathcliff would 'flog' her husband 'sick' for suspecting her. Heathcliff's feelings are more strongly expressed: Edgar is 'the slavering, shivering thing' preferred to him. The strain proves too much for Cathy. In her derangement, she also addresses Edgar as a thing, 'one of those things that are ever found when least wanted', an 'apathetic being', among his books while she is dying. She is burning; her blood rushes into 'a hell of tumult' at a few words. She is in exile, and wishes she were back at the Heights. After losing her, existence would be hell, Heathcliff tells Nelly. When he returns to Cathy, and she tells him he has killed her, he retorts, 'Is it not sufficient for your infernal selfishness, that while you are at peace I shall writhe in the torments of hell?' After a passionate reconciliation, he cries out, while caressing her frantically:

You deserve this. You have killed yourself. Yes, you may kiss me, and cry; and wring out my kisses and tears: they'll blight you – they'll damn you. You loved me – then what *right* had you to leave me? What right – answer me – for the poor fancy you felt for Linton? Because misery and degradation, and death, and nothing that God or Satan could inflict would have parted us, *you*, of your own will, did it. I have not broken your heart – *you* have broken it; and in breaking it, you have broken mine. . . . Do I want to live? . . . oh, God! would *you* like to live with your soul in the grave?

Here, in this frenzy, just before Cathy's death, we are near the truth. The division between the lovers has ended in madness for one, and life-in-hell, verging on madness, for the other.

Heathcliff marries Isabella because she is Edgar's heir. His cruelty to her is also part of his revenge. She soon wonders whether she has married man or devil (Byron said that his wife, Anna Isabella, would soon find she had married a devil); a tiger or venomous serpent could not rouse greater terror in her than he did (xiii). The first thing she saw him do was to hang her little dog; when she pleaded for it, he said he wished he could hang all connected with her except one person. Tormenting her gave him pleasure, but he sometimes ran short of ideas for discovering by experiment how much she could endure. His aim was to gain power over Edgar; but Isabella steeled herself to endure and frustrate his designs. 'I have no pity! I have no pity!' he muttered (xiv):

> The more the worms writhe, the more I yearn to crush out their entrails! It is a moral teething; and I grind with greater energy in proportion to the increase of pain.

After being struck with a knife beneath her ear and retaliating in kind, she was fortunate to escape. She would have rather been 'condemned to a perpetual dwelling in the infernal regions than, even for one night, abide beneath the roof of Wuthering Heights again'. From this loveless marriage the poor lymphatic creature, Linton Heathcliff, was born.

With Hindley, Heathcliff was murderously brutal. As soon as he returned, he told Cathy that he had intended to settle his score with Hindley, and 'prevent the law by doing execution' on himself (x). He changed his plans because he found Hindley was pleased to have him, partly because he paid liberally for his rooms, and partly because he was ready to gamble at cards; at Wuthering Heights he would have more opportunities of meeting Cathy, he thought, than if he were lodged at Gimmerton. The more money he lost to Heathcliff, the more Hindley wished to keep him, in the hope of winning back his gold for Hareton. Isabella described what happened when Heathcliff, after trying to wrest Cathy from her grave, came back confident that she was with him in spirit (xxix). Hindley was ready for him with knife and pistol, but Heathcliff flung himself upon him and, as he lay senseless from loss of blood, kicked him, trampled upon him, and dashed his head repeatedly against the stone floor. The next morning

Hindley sat by the fire 'deadly sick' while his 'evil genius' stood by
the chimney, his 'basilisk' eyes nearly 'quenched' with sleeplessness
and weeping for Cathy. Hindley died drunk as a lord, though there is
a broad hint that Heathcliff helped him to his death. He had gambled
away his money, which had been raised by mortgaging all his land
to Heathcliff (xvii).

Heathcliff had not finished; he intended to degrade Hareton as he
himself had been degraded by Hindley:

> Now, my bonny lad, you are *mine*! And we'll see if one tree won't
> grow as crooked as another, with the same wind to twist it!

He had already taught him to swear (xi), and there can be little
doubt that Hareton was following his example when he hanged a
litter of puppies from a chairback as Isabella made her escape. 'He
was never taught to read or write; never rebuked for any bad habit
which did not annoy his keeper; never led a single step towards virtue,
or guarded by a single precept against vice.' Joseph never interfered;
he took too much comfort in the thought of Heathcliff's damnation
for the youth's ruin (xviii).

After his mother's death, Linton was compelled to leave Thrushcross Grange, and live with his father at Wuthering Heights.
Heathcliff's final revenge was to acquire all the Linton property.
When Edgar was failing, Linton was terrified by Heathcliff into the
most abject ruses to ensure meetings with his cousin Catherine.
Ultimately – when there was no time to be lost, since Linton was
dying, and his father was afraid that he would predecease his uncle –
Nelly Dean allowed herself and Catherine to be decoyed into Wuthering Heights, where they were made prisoners until Catherine agreed
to marry Linton. As a result of the local lawyer's collusion with
Heathcliff, Edgar Linton was unable to change his will when he
realized Heathcliff's designs. While Catherine was with him, just
before his death, Linton was threatened or coaxed into making a will
bequeathing all the Linton estate to Heathcliff. No doctor was sent for,
and Linton was soon dead.

Catherine and Linton's ideas of heaven in this life (xxiv) indicate
the vitality of the one and the listlessness of the other. Neither is like
Cathy, in preferring Wuthering Heights to heaven itself (ix). She
associated happiness with Heathcliff and childhood, though an
essential part of the excitement of life for this gay, rather wild girl
came from their concerted defiance of the sanctions imposed by

Hindley and inflicted by Joseph. It is hardly surprising that she found
the gentility of Thrushcross Grange tame and uncongenial at times.

For the reader, however, Wuthering Heights has less pleasant
associations; and the question arises whether the title of the novel
has more than a topographical significance. The main story is that of
Heathcliff, and the successive warpings of his nature through
degradation and the consequent loss of Cathy. When their meetings
are resumed, thwarted love continually lapses into accusatory self-
pity, and they lacerate each other's feelings. Evil breeds evil; in
Heathcliff this is no less than a heartless mania for the widest
possible revenge. When he has achieved his material aims, he is
intent on making Hareton, Hindley's son, what he himself had been
when degraded and brutalized by Hindley; he would make one tree
grow as crooked as the other, 'with the same wind to twist it'. This
image seems to sum up the main aspect of the story, the distortions
in human nature caused by the gusts and gales of unpropitious
circumstance. It gives deeper meaning to the setting of Wuthering
Heights, as it is described at the opening of the novel, with reference
to the 'tumult' of the elements, the 'stunted' growth of the firs by
the house, and the way in which the cold northerly winds force the
branches of the 'gaunt thorns' in one direction 'as if craving alms
of the sun'. Heathcliff's pernicious influence is seen even more in the
vilifying effect he has on his son. Though weak, Linton is good-
natured, but Heathcliff makes him a repulsive, cruel, treacherous
creature, terrifying him to such an extent that Catherine is lured by
pity to her doom. It is significant that Nelly Dean wondered how he
would fare at Wuthering Heights, with Hareton and Heathcliff as
his playmates and instructors (xix). Whatever Cathy may have felt
about Wuthering Heights and her youth there, it is more or less
synonymous with hell while Heathcliff has power.[1] (His infernal role
is anticipated by Hindley, particularly after the loss of his wife.)

As Heathcliff's frustration diminishes, so his destructive passion
dies. Catherine is not cowed by him, and, without being disloyal to
him, Hareton comes to her defence. In both of them he now sees
Cathy's eyes, and with that he loses his taste for revenge on the

---

[1] There may be deliberate hints of hell or evil in the first interior
scenes at Wuthering Heights: fiend suggestions, even Catherine as a
guard and ministering angel, Grimalkin, Zillah urging flakes of fire up
the chimney with a colossal bellows ('Zillah' can mean 'which is roasted';
perhaps she was associated with Byron's *Cain*).

descendants of the two who had harmed him most. Everything he sees now recalls his beloved:

> I cannot look down to this floor, but her features are shaped in the flags! . . . The entire world is a dreadful collection of memoranda that she did exist, and that I have lost her! Well, Hareton's aspect was the ghost of my immortal love; of my wild endeavours to hold my right; my degradation, my pride, my happiness, and my anguish.

Such is his monomania that he never notices anything which is not associated with this 'one universal idea'; to take any action not prompted by it is like 'bending back a stiff spring' (xxxiii). Soon he seems to be aware of Cathy's presence, and follows it with his eyes wherever it moves. His soul's bliss kills his body. He has given up his ordinary bedroom for the panelled bed he had been forced to vacate, and it is there that he is found dead, the lattice opened, presumably in the hope that her spirit would enter.

For Joseph it was a welcome sign that the Devil had carried off his soul. There can be no doubt that the world of *Wuthering Heights* is a very superstitious one. The belief in witchcraft was widespread. It seems to Heathcliff that Isabella shrieks as if witches were running red-hot needles into her. Catherine frightens Joseph by threatening to make an image of him in wax and clay, and by dropping hints about her knowledge of the black art and its link with his rheumatism and the death of a cow. He thinks that Hareton is bewitched by her, and Heathcliff treats her as a witch when she dares to defy him. The superstition that heifers could be harmed by elf-bolts is referred to by Cathy in her delirium. Nelly Dean could not resist the thought that 'the little dark thing, harboured by a good man to his bane' was of more than human origin, and believed that her recollection of Hindley's childhood face was a warning of his death. She believed in goblins, and became familiar with other supernatural phenomena in books; hence her wonder whether Heathcliff was ghoul or vampire. He is frequently regarded as a fiend incarnate.[1] Ghosts were common. The local people swore that Heathcliff *walked* after his burial, and a shepherd boy cried and refused to go further along the road because he could see Heathcliff and a woman ahead. Nelly Dean's view was that 'he probably raised the phantoms from thinking', but it was fear

---

[1] Some of Emily's infernal tropes may have been caught from Branwell. His letter to John Brown (13.3.40) contains the expression, 'he whose eyes Satan looks out of, as from windows'; cf. *W.* xvii.

of Heathcliff's ghostly visitations which made her glad to leave Wuthering Heights for the Grange. In their youth Cathy and Heathcliff had often gone together to the churchyard to brave its ghosts. Heathcliff continued to believe in them; 'I have a strong faith in ghosts', he told Nelly towards the end of his life. In his anguish after hearing of Cathy's death, he prayed that she would haunt him (xvi):

> you said I killed you – haunt me, then! The murdered *do* haunt their murderers, I believe. I know that ghosts *have* wandered on earth. Be with me always – take any form – drive me mad! only *do* not leave me in this abyss, where I cannot find you! Oh, God! it is unutterable! I *cannot* live without my life! I *cannot* live without my soul!

He would have exhumed her the night after her burial, to hold her once again in his arms, but for the sudden realization that she was there with him in spirit, above the earth. She haunted him, gave him no rest, and drove him from her bedroom. It was torture, for he could never catch a glimpse of her. He was pacified a little on seeing her face, still preserved, when Edgar Linton's burial-place beside her was being prepared. Only when he began to fail just before his death did a change take place in his hallucinations; the eyes of Hareton and Catherine made him see Cathy, until her presence fixed his gaze, engrossed him, and made him serene. The note on which the novel ends, 'I . . . wondered how any one could ever imagine unquiet slumbers for the sleepers in that quiet earth', suggests that Cathy's phantom was indeed 'raised from' Heathcliff's 'thinking', and died with him, whatever the superstitious thought. Nor is this psychologically surprising; Heathcliff's thwarted love was of such extraordinary power that it preyed on his mind until it possessed him. His mental aberration has the same origin as his cruel pursuit of revenge. The one, springing from his better nature, and a monomaniac fixation, is torture to him; the other, unleashing the worst in him, gives him fiendish pleasure. Except in degree, there is no change in either manifestation of his crazed personality until the end, when he believes that Cathy is with him and he cannot lose her.

As Heathcliff's warped nature expresses itself in violence and sadism, Cathy's falsity to her own nature results in irrational outbursts and mental breakdowns. They first saw the Linton children in a drawing-room which looked like heaven, and despised them for their absurd behaviour. After a prolonged stay at the Grange, however, Cathy adopted double standards at home. She knew better than anyone the dilemma she was in as a result of Heathcliff's degradation, but deceived herself into thinking that she could turn her marriage to Edgar Linton into advantage for her soul-mate. She had 'no more business' to marry Edgar than to stay in the other heaven which made her homesick. Thrushcross Grange, the name of which suggests something more cultivated and Christian, less bleak and elemental, than 'Wuthering Heights', never gave her real happiness, despite all Edgar's loving attention and anxiety; it seemed a paradise for a few days after Heathcliff's return, but in reality he brought storm and tumult.

Cathy's excitability and self-division play havoc with her. Her temper is shown on the Lintons' first visit to the Heights; she breaks down after Heathcliff's departure, and is indulged, before and after her marriage, lest any vexation should over-excite her. Edgar and Isabella were very attentive. 'It was not the thorn bending to the honeysuckles, but the honeysuckles embracing the thorn.' For half a year 'the gunpowder lay as harmless as sand, because no fire came near to explode it'. So elated was she at Heathcliff's return that she was reconciled to God and humanity; she soon became 'an angel' in the heaven of her imagination, while her husband's unavailing protests against the intemperance of her joy reduced him in her eyes to a puling 'creature', guilty of never realizing the bitterness of her misery during Heathcliff's absence.

So much is Edgar Linton seen from the viewpoint of the two lovers, and so strong is their passion, that we are in danger of overlooking his merits and misfortune in falling in love with Cathy. Dispassionately viewed, there is no evidence to show that Nelly Dean was significantly prejudiced in preferring Edgar to his wife; she found him kind, trustful, and honourable. It is characteristic of Heathcliff and Cathy that their passion excludes all other considerations; it is so self-centred that they tend to blame each other for what has wrecked their lives. Thwarted passion maddens both, and the effect is seen in their behaviour to Edgar. Pride makes Heathcliff contemptuous, as his rodomontade demonstrates (xiv):

> he couldn't love as much in eighty years as I could in a day . . . the sea could be as readily contained in that horse-trough as her whole affection be monopolized by him. Tush! He is scarcely a degree dearer to her than her dog, or her horse.

The last remark is adapted from Tennyson's 'Locksley Hall', and the two situations have one thing in common: the woman in love declines to her lover's 'range of lower feelings' and behaviour, as we see in an earlier scene (xi). When Edgar, alarmed by Nelly's report that her mistress was in danger of losing self-control as a result of Heathcliff's quarrel with her, took steps to evict him, he probably spoke too strongly. Heathcliff's reply, 'Cathy, this lamb of yours threatens like a bull!', and the addition that he was sorry Edgar Linton was not worth knocking down, denote the bully who is aware of his physical superiority. Cathy's feelings are too strong for her to behave rationally, and she abets her lover immediately in deed and word, while her husband sits pale with anger. 'Cheer up! you shan't be hurt! Your type is not a lamb, it's a sucking leveret', she adds. An even worse insult from Heathcliff makes Edgar leap up and deliver a blow that would have felled a slighter man. When Heathcliff departs, Cathy's derangement is clearly developing; 'a thousand smiths' hammers are beating' in her head. Everyone, including Heathcliff, is to blame but herself, and she continues to express her contempt for Edgar. He is no weakling; some of the Linton spirit is also displayed by Isabella under Heathcliff's trial by torture. Detestation of Heathcliff stirs up the worst in Edgar's pride, and it is not until Isabella has left her husband and the neighbourhood that he relents towards her. His anxiety for Cathy's health, his forbearance, devotion, and loyalty to her memory, are remarkable. Her expressions of distaste for him are not a reflection of his character, but oblique hints of her own tormented spirit, thwarted, stunted, seeking a lost world to which there is no return, as the laments and recriminations of her final meeting with Heathcliff prove. Had their reconciliation been complete, and had Heathcliff really forgiven Cathy, he would not have been continually *tortured* by a sense of her spiritual presence after her death.

'What might have been in more favourable circumstances' is implied in the conclusion. Heathcliff blamed Cathy for their division, and said that she had done what neither God nor Satan could have done. 'Together, they would brave Satan and all his legions', Lockwood observed of the young lovers at the end. A new spirit had entered Wuthering Heights. As he returned to it in September 1802, he saw 'the mild glory of a rising moon' and 'a beamless amber light along the west'. He had neither to climb the gate nor to knock. How different from his wintry previous visit, when he had been churlishly received and entertained! From the garden came the fragrance of flowers, and through the open door he caught sight of 'a fine, red fire'. He heard Catherine teaching Hareton to read, and Nelly Dean singing (to Joseph's annoyance). Heathcliff was dead and buried. Catherine had sought reconciliation with Hareton, who had recovered from the resentment provoked by her teasing, and wished to be improved. Trouble had arisen when Joseph complained that some of his currant bushes had been dug up by Hareton to make room for flowers. Heathcliff's questioning on the subject had led Catherine to retort fearlessly that he had stolen all her land, and Hareton's. Hareton had come to her rescue; it was the last time Heathcliff attempted physical violence. Gardening continued in the spring, with fragrance around, and a blue sky. The young couple were radiantly happy. There had been difficulties,

> but both their minds tending to the same point – one loving and desiring to esteem, and the other desiring to be esteemed – they contrived in the end to reach it.

Cathy and Heathcliff could have behaved differently only if subject to other influences than those which prevailed at crucial junctures. Had she been more sympathetic, more honest, less ambitions, and less haughty and headstrong, she might have braved her tyrannical brother and helped Heathcliff in his degradation; had he been less stubbornly masochistic in his self-neglect and sullen pride, she might have been encouraged to take steps other than those which ruined both their lives.

After highly dramatic scenes in which speech rises often to the level of a hauntingly lyrical, almost disembodied cry, the concluding chapters of *Wuthering Heights* would be a relative anticlimax but for the graphic accounts of Heathcliff's strange transformation and death. Yet, though the symbolism of the final action is simple (especially in the device of reading as a sign of the will to achieve not just culture but the best in one's nature), it shows man's potentiality for good as the obverse of his great potentiality for evil. Nelly Dean had seen in Hareton 'good things lost amid a wilderness of weeds' and 'evidence of a wealthy soil, that might yield luxuriant crops under other and favourable circumstances'. It is significant that the lovers are to leave the barely cultivated Heights to Joseph, for the milder, more civilized atmosphere of Thrushcross Grange, the source of the books they enjoyed reading together.

Catherine and Hareton recall the endings of some of Shakespeare's last plays, Miranda and Ferdinand playing chess, for example, where the evil and divisions of a former generation have no place. Yet the means are rather slight, and the scenes of reconciliation fail to generate the imaginative power of the wild and violent drama, where Emily's creative genius seems more at home.

There is further poetic symbolism in the topography of the novel. Wuthering Heights suggests a tumult of winds and the warping of nature – Heathcliff's, and his vengeful, hellish policy of torturing and degrading others for his own ends; Hindley's also, and Cathy's too. She recalls it in her delirium, but it has overtones of meaning for the reader, as she asks why she is so changed and why her blood rushes into 'a hell of tumult' at a few words. Yet at this time and earlier, in the hour of rash decision, the Wuthering Heights of her pre-exilian youth was her 'home', her 'world', a real kind of paradise, preferable to the heaven of her dreams or the heaven she had associated with Thrushcross Grange (vi, ix, xii). Catherine is less rebellious; but the lure of Penistone Crags and its Fairy Cave (xviii), which cannot be dissociated from Cathy's madness (xii), leads to suffering after romance. Wuthering Heights becomes her prison. Unlike her mother, Catherine has the strength not only to endure but to adjust; she can pity even to the point of self-sacrifice (with Linton Heathcliff); she can be conciliatory (with Hareton). Less wayward and wild than her mother, she is kind and reasonable, a sweet civilizing influence (xxxii). It is significant that, in her most rebellious mood, she never loses sight of the values inherent in Thrushcross Grange and its surroundings. Her 'most perfect idea of heaven's happiness' (see xxi–xxii for the link between her first romantic love and her 'breeze-rocked cradle') is (xxiv):

> rocking in a rustling green tree, with a west wind blowing, and bright white clouds flitting rapidly above; and not only larks, but throstles, and blackbirds, and linnets, and cuckoos pouring out music on every side, and the moors seen at a distance, broken into cool dusky dells; but close by great swells of long grass undulating in waves to the breeze; and woods and sounding water, and the whole world awake and wild with joy.

Here, in the varied music of the birds and 'the evidence of a wealthy soil', the prospects for happiness and a more 'abundant' life are more certain.

The function of Lockwood, the outsider, is to give a sense of authenticity to a story full of extraordinary events. That he should be the witness of Heathcliff's uncontrollable passion and hear his anguished cry to an unresponsive spirit shows that his nightmare (the most startling event in the novel) is somehow related to the truth; it whets curiosity, and suspends imaginative disbelief in the psychic phenomena by which Heathcliff, we discover, has long been afflicted. Without Lockwood, these would have been regarded as romantic or supernatural absurdities. He sees enough to confirm a story which is extreme in passion, whether it manifests itself in violence or love. It would have a special interest for one who was afraid of love in reality, though he affected to be susceptible. Lockwood's affectations are reflected at various points in his style, and supply a kind of pedantic humour which contrasts with that of the gruff, damnation-minded, minatory or plaintive Joseph.

Emily Brontë's judgment is seen in the coherence and proportioning of her novel. She moves rapidly over less important intervals, does not hesitate to jump twelve years, and introduces nothing irrelevant. Such artistic discipline has been achieved by few famous English novelists. The intensity of her style is the product of strict control and imaginative power, a combination Charlotte often failed to achieve. Emily's imagination is extensively shown in dramatic scenes, which vary remarkably not just in tempo and pitch, but in levels of experience, from the uncouth and dialectal to the lyrical voice of passion. Nothing approaches it in her poetry, and there is little comparable to it elsewhere; in this context one thinks not so much of Shakespeare as of the last speech in Marlowe's *Doctor Faustus*. The general style (exceptions can be found in Nelly Dean's narrative as well as in Lockwood's) is the product of fully realized imaginative experience. Its precision and directness may give the impression of being 'natural'; if so, it has the qualities Keats had in mind when he made it one of his axioms in writing 'that if poetry comes not as naturally as the leaves to a tree, it had better not come at all'. If it came spontaneously, it was the result of imaginative familiarity with her subject, and this must have been the harvest of deep thought and critical control.

Effects are continually created through comparative imagery; it can give life and force to inanimate objects, as Miss Cooper Willis has illustrated from the use of active verbs and adjectives in the interior description of Wuthering Heights (i). Much of Emily's imagery, like Wordsworth's, is derived from nature:

> The outward shows of sky and earth,
> Of hill and valley, he has viewed.

Two of the most memorable scenes in the novel are conjured up and fixed in a few words by virtue of creative images: a snow-covered hill-back is seen as a billowy, white ocean, and a multitude of bluebells clouds the turf steps with a lilac mist (iii, xxii). This is direct description, but perhaps the incidental use of natural imagery is more significant: Zillah deals with the dogs so effectively that the storm subsides and she only remains, heaving like a sea after a high wind (i); the preacher pours forth his zeal in a shower of loud taps (iii); Heathcliff's story is that of a cuckoo, and Hareton is cast out like an unfledged dunnock (iv); Edgar Linton's soul is as different from Heathcliff's and Cathy's as the moonbeam from lightning or frost from fire (ix); Catherine rewards Edgar with a summer of sweetness and affection for several days, both master and servants profiting from her sunshine (x); Hareton's face blackens like a thunder cloud (xviii); no bird flying back to a plundered nest which it has left brimful of chirping young ones can express more complete despair in its anguished cries and flutterings than Catherine when she discovers that Linton Heathcliff's letters are missing (xxi); her face is like the landscape, shadows and sunshine passing over it in rapid succession (xxvii); and Hareton's honest, warm, and intelligent nature shakes off rapidly the clouds of ignorance and degradation (xxxiii). Animal images are important, especially those used to emphasize brutishness and cruelty in Heathcliff ('a fierce, pitiless, wolfish man', according to Cathy); perhaps they owe something to *King Lear* (ii). Others are drawn from the author's observation, generally to express character. They are not always used with detachment in direct description. Such is Cathy's attraction that Edgar, a 'soft thing', had no more power to depart than a cat to leave a mouse half-killed or a bird half-eaten. The description of Joseph when he discovers that his currant bushes have been wrenched up borders on the hilarious; his lip quivers with suppressed fury as he enters, and his jaws work so much like those of a cow chewing its cud that his speech suffers.

As may be expected, *Wuthering Heights* shocked contemporary readers; Charlotte had to base her defence of it on the more respectable secondary characters, though she did not apologize for the profanity of its language. Reviewers branded it for its brutality; it was improbable, wild and wicked, sickening, coarse, and disagreeable; its language was disgusting. The tenor of *The Atlas* review was damning, but it showed some discernment. The novel had 'rugged power' in every chapter, but was 'inexpressibly painful'. No other fiction had been met which presented 'such shocking pictures of the worst forms of humanity'. It 'exenterates'. 'The reality of unreality has never been so aptly illustrated as in the scenes of almost savage life . . . brought so vividly before us.' In all there is 'a touch of Salvator Rosa'. The characters harmonize with the scenery, but the book sprawls, and lacks both unity and relief. In 1850 a more discriminating review by Sydney Dobell appeared in *The Palladium*. He saw 'the chiaro-scuro of the whole' and found in it 'the triumph of description': its images live 'as a recollection of things *heard and seen*'. He found a 'nice provision of the possible even in the highest effects of the super-natural', admired its 'brave simplicity', but thought it 'the unformed writing of a giant's hand', so convinced was he that 'Currer Bell' had written, first, *Wuthering Heights*, then *The Tenant of Wildfell Hall*, *Jane Eyre*, and *Shirley*! In America one reviewer was spellbound by its 'strange magic', and could not choose but read what he disliked. *The North American Review* found Heathcliff a monster 'whom the Mephistopheles of Goethe would have nothing to say to, whom the Satan of Milton would consider as an object of simple disgust, and to whom Dante would hesitate in awarding the honour of a place among those whom he has consigned to the burning pitch'.

Leslie Stephen thought Emily Brontë's feeble grasp of external facts made her book a kind of baseless nightmare. Pater found romantic art ('the addition of strangeness to beauty') in it. Dante Gabriel Rossetti described it as a fiend of a book, an incredible monster, its action laid in hell. Frederic Harrison considered it 'a kind of prose "Kubla Khan"' (haunted, one must assume, by a woman wailing for her demon-lover). George Moore described it as 'the desperate efforts of a lyrical poet to construct a prose narrative'; C. Day-Lewis, as a great mad poem in prose. In *The Novelist's Responsibility* (1967) L. P. Hartley expressed the view that, had humanity progressed as was expected in the nineteenth century, Leslie Stephen's assessment might still be thought justifiable; he had no doubt, however, that events in the modern world underlined its fearful reality.

Anne Brontë
Poems

Nearly sixty of Anne's poems survive, and of these more than a third have links with Gondal. Most of the latter may be divided into two groups: her earliest poems, written when she was sixteen to eighteen, and those she wrote from September 1845, after resigning her post as governess at Thorp Green, to October 1846, before and after the adaptation of her recorded experiences to their fictional form in *Agnes Grey*. If Anne made no rapid technical advance in her poetry after her early period, it was almost certainly because she had little time to pursue it; she did not enjoy good health; and she was away from home, with little time or energy for creative writing.

Her poetry never suggests hasty or careless composition, or the fluency Charlotte and Branwell showed in their adolescence. From the dates of some of her earliest poems, it seems a fair inference that she did not experience great difficulty in writing competent verse, and that she gave it only intermittent attention. 'Parting' I and II were written on successive days, and would not discredit Emily, Branwell, or Charlotte, or any other poet of eighteen.

Though Anne's poetry lacks the fire and vision of Emily's best dramatic and personal poems, much of it is impressive. It genuinely reflects thoughts and feelings arising from her experience, and it has a personal appeal which is almost entirely lacking in Charlotte's verse. It steadily reveals a refusal to be swept away by emotional moods, and an insistence on philosophical judgment. Though often couched in general terms, it expresses felt personal experience more than most of the philosophical poetry of the eighteenth century, and is imaginatively nearer to that of Matthew Arnold. Her prevailing reason implies a regard for form and restraint; there are no excesses.

The lyrical note is relatively rare, and gentle rather than deep. 'Self-Communion' indicates that she was capable of sustaining thought in verse to an unusual degree.

In December 1836 Anne and Emily wrote poems which opened with the same subject, the storm on the mountain heath. Though both are Gondal, they are personal in tone. Emily's is set to a more exciting metre, and breathes the spirit of Borrow's gipsy, Jasper Petulengro –

> High waving heather, 'neath stormy blasts bending,
> Midnight and moonlight and bright shining stars;
> Darkness and glory rejoicingly blending . . .

The heroine of Anne's poem is filled with sadness when she hears the tempest; she has lost her parents, and all the former beauties of her native hill have vanished. The thought recalls Coleridge's 'Dejection' ode:

> For when the heart is free from care,
>   Whatever meets the eye
> Is bright, and every sound we hear
>   Is full of melody.

None the less, she leaves home happy in the expectation of activity. Perhaps this is how Anne remembered her transfer to school the previous October when she was sent to replace Emily at Roe Head. The poem shows endurance and determination.

Just before the end of her second holiday the following summer, she concluded a more sustained Gondal poem. It is silly sooth, and dallies with the innocence of love; but it is not without life. Like Emily, she became rather obsessed with dungeons and imprisonment. The influence of 'romantic' poets is felt. In the poem with the printed title, 'The Captain's Dream' (surely 'The Captive's Dream'?), where the blank verse lines are monotonously end-stopped, the diction is probably influenced less by Wordsworth than by Byron's 'The Prisoner of Chillon'. In 'The Parting' Scott is heard:

> He smiled again, and did not speak,
> But lightly kissed her rosy cheek,
> And fondly clasped her in his arms;
>   Then vaulted on his steed,

allied disconcertingly with Thomas Gray:

> And down the park's smooth, winding road,
>   He urged its flying speed.

Sometimes it is Wordsworth, as when the north wind recalls to an imprisoned girl the liberty of the mountains:

> When thou, a young enthusiast,
>   As wild and free as they,
> O'er rocks, and glens, and snowy heights,
>   Didst often love to stray.

In 'Verses to a Child' and 'Self-Congratulation', two dramatic lyrics which concentre stories of past and present with admirable artistry, the diction seems to confirm the Wordsworthian influence.

A Gondal poem of 1845, the song 'Come to the banquet', breaks the monotony of rather pedestrian metres, just as 'Lines Composed in a Wood on a Windy Day' does in the personal poems.

Some of these express Anne's admiration of William Weightman. They include 'A Reminiscence', where, in her wonted philosophical manner, she takes comfort in the thought that 'a soul so near divine' has 'gladdened' her life; 'Night', where she describes him as the darling of her heart; and 'Severed and gone', which concludes:

> Life seems more sweet that thou didst live,
>   And men more true that thou wert one;
> Nothing is lost that thou didst give,
>   Nothing destroyed that thou hast done.

Both 'Appeal' and 'Farewell to thee! but not farewell' could have been written with him in mind; if so, the latter was adapted for its inclusion in *The Tenant of Wildfell Hall* (xix).

Anne's longing for home, especially at Thorp Green, and her happy childhood recollections enter a number of poems. There are Wordsworthian echoes in 'The Bluebell', but we can see in 'Memory' that Anne's scrupulous honesty did not allow her sentimentally to accept any 'intimations of immortality' theory. Yet her views on the 'renovating virtue' of vividly recalled scenes from early years resemble those of Wordsworth; the present scene may be bright, but it has not the splendour of the opening primrose in the days of infancy:

Sweet Memory! ever smile on me;
Nature's chief beauties spring from thee;
   Oh, still thy tribute bring!
. . . .
Still in the wallflower's fragrance dwell;
And hover round the slight bluebell,
   My childhood's darling flower.
. . . .
For ever hang thy dreamy spell
Round golden star and heather-bell,
   And do not pass away
From sparkling frost, or wreathèd snow,
And whisper when the wild winds blow,
   Or rippling waters play.

These two poems recall the heroine of *Agnes Grey* (xiii), who delighted in primroses, bluebells, and heath-blossoms, by virtue of their association with the hills and valleys near her home.

Anne's maternal instinct is poignantly expressed in 'Dreams'. She imagines that her 'life of solitude' is over, and that she has a babe of her own; when the delusive dream is past, she returns to her 'dreary void':

   A heart whence warm affections flow,
     Creator, Thou hast given to me;
   And am I only thus to know
     How sweet the joys of love would be?

In three of her most successful poems, Anne's emotions are conveyed through parallel or symbol. 'The Captive Dove' expresses her loneliness and longing; in 'Fluctuations' the sun and moon are emblems of past happiness and reviving hope at a time of deep depression; 'The Arbour' is a complex of thought-imagery, relating to the past and the future but predominantly to the present:

   And winter's chill is on my heart –
   How can I dream of future bliss?

In her bouts of depression, Anne's hypercritical conscience made her feel that she had sinned greatly; yet to suggest, as Charlotte Brontë did, that she was like Cowper, even in a milder form, until her 'last moments', distorts the evidence of her poetry. In 'To Cowper' she rejects the Calvinistic doctrine which drove the poet to terror and madness. How could such a 'gentle soul' have lived without heavenly grace? If God is love, his soul must have assuredly found its place in heaven, she argues. In 'A Word to the "Elect"' she implies that the Calvinist God is inferior to man in passing over the *many* for the sake of the favoured *few*, and asserts (as in *The Tenant of Wildfell Hall*) that, with a 'God of justice and of love', there is redemption for all, eventually for 'even the wicked'. Hers was not an easy, unquestioning faith, but it prevailed over trials and despondency, recognizing God's glory not only in the universe but also in the 'moral world'.

Anne's philosophy of life, drawn from her own experience, is inseparable from her religion, yet a number of her poems, including her most ambitious, are philosophical rather than religious. In 'Views of Life' she strips away the veil of illusion and looks at 'naked truth', but realistically refuses to ignore the transforming power of hope:

> Because the road is rough and long,
> Shall we despise the skylark's song,
> That cheers the wanderer's way?
> Or trample down, with reckless feet,
> The smiling flowerets, bright and sweet,
> Because they soon decay?

She trusted in happiness after death. 'Vanitas Vanitatum, Omnia Vanitas' concludes that man should be:

> Thankful for all that God has given,
> Fixing his firmest hopes on Heaven;
> Knowing that earthly joys decay,
> But hoping through the darkest day.

In sustained passages of allegorical description, 'The Three Guides' presents a critical choice in Anne's 'pilgrim's progress'. She rejects short-sighted worldly reasoning and the pride of those who go their own way, confident in their own strength to surmount all life's challenges; to the worldly wisdom of earth and the sublime self-confidence of Pride, she prefers Faith, scorned by Pride for its meekness yet full of strength in times of affliction. In 'Self-Communion' the pilgrim reflects on life. Time or experience gives us 'help for that which lies before'; 'strength and wisdom spring from grief'. Regrettable though it is that youthful feelings and hopes should be subdued by fortitude and reason, one should be strong:

> Did I not tell thee, years before,
> Life was for labour, not for joy?

Rest is the reward after death for toil below:

> If Time indeed too swiftly flies,
> Gird on thy armour, haste arise,
> For thou hast much to do; –
> To lighten woe, to trample sin,
> And foes without and foes within
> To combat and subdue.

It was in that spirit that Anne wrote her second novel.

Anne's shorter lyrics create a more immediate and lasting impression; they have a delicate emotional appeal. Yet the moral poems are also personal. There is nothing conventional or facile in their thought. Life is faced courageously, and the philosophical reasoning is impressive; its logic is conceived in terms of experience. The quiet inner strength which can surmount pain and disappointment, and live by faith and hope, has its parallel in the poetry of the Wordsworth who wrote 'The Happy Warrior'. If Anne was influenced by it, the effect may be seen incidentally in some of her poems; her moral strength sprang from deeper, religious resources.

In 'The Narrow Way', as in 'Self-Communion', she stresses the rewards of resolution:

> And there, amid the sternest heights,
> The sweetest flowerets gleam.
> . . . .
> But he that dares not grasp the thorn
> Should never crave the rose.

She died, her aims unachieved:

> I hoped amid the brave and strong
> My portioned task might lie,
> To toil amid the labouring throng
> With purpose keen and high.

In *The Tenant of Wildfell Hall* she had shown that a novel could be imbued with high purpose without ever descending to the level of a religious tract.

'Agnes Grey'

'It remains clear as ever that her immortality is due to her sisters. Upon those bright twin-stars many telescopes are turned, and then there swims into the beholder's view this third, mild-shining star of the tenth magnitude, which otherwise would have remained invisible.'[1] Such was, and still is (if one makes due allowance for the style and its hyperbole) the common view of Anne Brontë as a writer. There has been some revival of interest in her in recent years, but she remains underestimated as a poet and novelist. Her works reflect her character, and there is much to admire in it. Though the youngest of the Brontës, she could set the example; she was the first to become a family governess, and the first to begin writing seriously. She faced death with amazing resolution, faith, and serenity. She wished to live in order 'to do some good in the world'; in that spirit she had written *Agnes Grey* and, more obviously, *The Tenant of Wildfell Hall*. Often it is because she wrote with a moral aim that readers are predisposed against her. Yet many novels besides *The Vicar of Wakefield* and *Moll Flanders*, for example, have had such a purpose and been popular. 'Critics follow a scent like hounds, and I am not certain that it wasn't Charlotte who first started them on the depreciation of Anne', George Moore wrote. There is greater truth in this than in his claim that Anne was 'the greatest of the Brontës',[2] yet some of the last scenes she wrote combine clarity and charm to a greater degree than is to be found elsewhere in the Brontë novels. She wrote perspicuously, and with more judgment, design, and control than

[1] Angus M. Mackay, *The Brontës, Fact and Fiction*, London, 1897, p. 21.
[2] See Virginia Woolf, *A Writer's Diary*, London, 1953, p. 87.

Charlotte; she had less passion and imagination, but more sense and sensibility. When she finished *The Tenant of Wildfell Hall* she was little more than twenty-eight, two years younger than Charlotte when she finished *The Professor*; the writers' main talents lie in different directions, yet there can be little doubt that Anne's novel is the greater accomplishment.

* * * * * *

Agnes Grey is almost certainly a fictionalized adaptation of *Passages in the Life of an Individual* (see p. 66). It is a slight and unpretentious work, based on Anne's experience as a governess at Blake Hall and Thorp Green. In her preface to the second edition of *The Tenant of Wildfell Hall*, we find that she was 'accused of extravagant over-colouring in those very parts' of *Agnes Grey* 'that were carefully copied from the life, with a most scrupulous avoidance of all exaggeration'. The parts which are wholly fictitious are easily per-ceived: the opening (very largely) and Agnes's return home after failure in her first post; the love story which develops during her second period as a governess; the marriage and disillusionment of Rosalie Murray; and, above all, the happy ending. As she wrote in the first paragraph, Anne Brontë, shielded by her obscurity (as 'Acton Bell'), by the lapse of years, 'and a few fictitious names', had little to fear from the publication of her true history.

This is the only Brontë novel in which the central character can think of home with unqualified affection, and has a mother to turn to for guidance. Agnes's mother sets a noble example, and is a source of strength and comfort to all her family. The contrast between Agnes's home and the society she encounters upon leaving it reinforces the 'instruction' implicit in the story.

'All true histories contain instruction', Anne believed. She dwelt on this conviction at greater length, and with more obvious implica-tions, in the preface to her second novel: 'truth always conveys its own moral to those who are able to receive it. . . . Let it not be imagined, however, that I consider myself competent to reform the errors and abuses of society, but only that I would fain contribute my humble quota towards so good an aim . . .' Reveal life as it is, she implies, and right and wrong will be clear to a discerning reader without sermonizing. She adheres to this principle. In *Agnes Grey* her main aim is to expose society through its exploitation of the governess. Had Dickens been able to present the subject, he would have given more sensational and colourful scenes, with caricature and satire, but nothing more faithful and convincing.

Governesses were untrained, and it must be admitted that the coercive methods dictated by the desperate determination of Agnes Grey to succeed were bound to fail. The gravamen of the case, however, lies in attitudes towards governesses; they were treated almost contemptuously by their employers (many of whom made them menial drudges), expected to treat their charges as social superiors, and continually let down by indulgent parents. Agnes Grey, who had set out with laudable ambitions ('Delightful task! To teach the young idea how to shoot'), soon found that her pupils had 'no more notion of obedience than a wild, unbroken colt', and that the term 'governess' was 'a mere mockery'. The viciousness of the Bloomfield children may seem incredible, but there is not the slightest reason to think that Anne Brontë exaggerated. Cruelty to birds and animals was overlooked by their parents and, together with the drinking of wine and spirits, encouraged in Tom by Mr Robson; such habits promoted manliness (v). The most memorable sketch of the Bloomfields is at lunch (iii). Mr Bloomfield is no gentleman, but one of the *nouveaux riches* whose critical bullying of his cringing wife gives a hint of his nagging ruthlessness in the acquisition of wealth as a tradesman before his very early retirement. By contrast with the Greys, the defects of these representatives of society are obvious.

With Agnes's move to Horton Lodge, the story advances from interest in young children to the adolescent Murray girls, Rosalie in particular, and eventually, with her, to marriage and beyond. This progression provides new scenes and subjects for critical presentation. Far more members of society are seen in Agnes's new milieu; and the new curate, Mr Weston (probably sketched with fond recollections of William Weightman, who died during Anne's second year at Thorp Green), is introduced, not just to supply the hero of a love story but also to show how the Church could be reformed.

The two Murray sisters form an interesting comparison. At seventeen, Rosalie, the elder, 'began to give way to the ruling passion, and soon was swallowed up in the all-absorbing ambition to attract and dazzle the other sex'. One of the first to be attracted to her was the rector, Mr Hatfield. Matilda was a hoyden, whose main interest was riding, and romping with her dogs, or with her brothers and sister. From her father she had learned to swear 'like a trooper'.

Like Emily Brontë (to judge by *Shirley*), Anne believed that a person's character could be judged from his behaviour to animals. Matilda allowed Miss Grey to take charge of her terrier Snap, but, when he showed gratitude to his new mistress, treated him with harsh words and many a spiteful kick and pinch. Mr Weston and Agnes rebuke her for taking delight in seeing her dog kill a leveret (xviii):

> ' . . . didn't you hear it scream?'
> 'I'm happy to say I did not.'
> 'It cried out just like a child.'

Anne probably knew the views on hunting (in connection with the passage on his tame hare) which Cowper expressed in *The Task* (iii, 326–36). Her heroine was so sad to leave her 'dear little friend, the kitten' that she kissed her, 'to the great scandal of Sally, the maid' (i). Reference has already been made to the horrible Tom Bloomfield and his uncle. Unlike Mr Hatfield, who on one occasion vented his annoyance by kicking Nancy Brown's cat across the floor, and later 'knocked' her off his knee (to appear in worse light than Chaucer's friar in 'The Summoner's Tale'), Mr Weston is kind (xi):

> and when th' cat, poor thing, jumped on to his knee, he only stroked her, and gave a bit of a smile: so I thought that was a good sign; for once, when she did so to th' Rector, he knocked her off, like as it might be in scorn and anger, poor thing. But you can't expect a cat to know manners like a Christian, you know, Miss Grey.

The rector had more to answer for; while he was seeking to engage Rosalie's attention, Snap caught hold of her dress, only to receive a resounding thwack on the skull from Mr Hatfield's cane (xiv).

Mr Hatfield is an interesting study of the socially superior rector. Like other country ladies and gentlemen, he did not speak to the governess after the Sunday morning service. How refreshing by comparison she found Mr Weston's simplicity of manner and evangelical truth! The rector was a foppish exhibitionist in church; his sermons were artificial compositions, usually on 'church discipline, rites and ceremonies, apostolical succession, the duty of reverence and obedience to the clergy', and 'the atrocious criminality of dissent'. He represented 'the Deity as a terrible taskmaster rather than a benevolent father' (x). He was a man after neither Mr Brontë's heart nor Cowper's. In *The Task* (ii, 372ff) hints for a model curate

like Mr Weston can be found, and a description of the type exemplified by Mr Hatfield. In church he displays the diamond on his lily
hand, holds his handkerchief to catch the eye, and pays attention to
his hair; he also is 'frequent in park with lady at his side' and

> Constant at routs, familiar with a round
> Of ladyships – a stranger to the poor.

The chapter on the cottagers supplements this antithetical criticism
of the Church. Mr Hatfield speaks of Nancy Brown as 'a canting old
fool', and holds out little hope of her salvation as long as she makes
rheumatism an excuse for not attending services. Mr Weston, like
Mr Brontë and his favourite curate Mr Weightman, is ready to
preach cottage-sermons (the author with moderate brevity gives the
reader the benefit of them); they renew Nancy's hope, and lead to
good works.

Further criticism is directed towards the education of young ladies.
In substance it is comparable to Jane Austen's in *Mansfield Park*.
Mrs Murray seemed anxious only to render her daughters 'as superficially attractive and showily accomplished' as possible. It was
because she found much to like in Rosalie that Agnes Grey regretted
the 'sad want of principle' in her more than she did in any other
member of the family. She preferred to visit the cottagers alone, for
the education of the Murrays had done nothing to make them
sympathetic towards the poor, whom they treated as stupid and
derisory, assuming that their own conduct was excused by condescend-
ing visits or gifts of money and clothing. Before she knew Mr Weston,
Agnes began to feel that association with the Murrays was gradually
petrifying her feelings and deadening her moral perceptions (xi).

When Rosalie hears that Miss Grey's sister is to be married to a
vicar, her questioning continues (viii):

> 'Is he rich?'
> 'No; only comfortable.'
> 'Is he handsome?'
> 'No; only decent.'
> 'Young?'
> 'No; only middling.'
> 'Oh, mercy! what a wretch! What sort of a house is it?'
> 'A quiet little vicarage, with an ivy-clad porch, and old-fashioned
> garden, and – '
> 'Oh, stop! – you'll make me sick. How *can* she bear it?'

It seems impossible to convey more social criticism than Anne Brontë does here, in the minimum of words, and without comment. Rosalie marries for rank and wealth, and soon regrets it. Mrs Grey's refusal, in agreement with her daughters, to humour her father (a squire), by pretending that she repented what he had chosen to regard as her unfortunate marriage to a clergyman, continues the process of under-lining a moral by the use of contrast (xix).

In Agnes Grey's love for Mr Weston, delicate touches, like the gathering of the primroses, hover on the brink of sentimentality. It does not follow a smooth course; Rosalie's attempt to 'fix' him creates jealousy. Like Jane Eyre and Lucy Snowe, Agnes suffers also from the reproaches of a conscience which tells her that she is 'mocking God with the service of a heart more bent upon the creature than the Creator' when she admires Mr Weston in church (xvi). Both Rosalie, after her engagement to Sir Thomas Ashby, and Matilda take pleasure in describing their meeting with Mr Weston until she is thoroughly depressed. Agnes does not write at length upon her feelings; she has a sense of proportion:

> I fear, by this time, the reader is well-nigh disgusted with the folly and weakness I have so freely laid before him. I never dis-closed it then, and would not have done so had my own sister or my mother been with me in the house.

She sought relief in poetry, and gives one short specimen, the poem 'Oh, they have robbed me of the hope', which may have been adapted from lines written in memory of Mr Weightman (xvii).

There is humour in *Agnes Grey*, and the best example is probably the letter from the unhappy Rosalie, inviting her former governess to stay with her at Ashby Hall (xxi). Her marriage, however, and Mr Robson's encouragement of Tom Bloomfield to drink wine and spirits foreshadow *The Tenant of Wildfell Hall*. As Agnes sits alone, apparently forgotten by her hostess, she thinks of Rosalie's past and present, and of Mr Weston whom she has missed ever since her departure from Horton. Her life is 'quiet, drab-colour', and seems 'to offer no alternative between positive rainy days, and days of dull grey clouds without downfall' (hence perhaps her name). Then she watches the lengthening shadows through the window, 'forcing the golden sunlight to retreat inch by inch' and at length take refuge in the tops of the rookery trees. That light vanishes; only birds soaring above catch the lustre, which imparts to their sable plumage the brilliance of deep red gold. That, too, at last departs. Twilight steals on, and she becomes more weary, and wishes she were going home on the morrow. The description has a wonderful definition and clarity, and it harmonizes with the thoughts and feelings of the beholder. She regrets to see the rookery, 'so lately bathed in glorious light, reduced to the sombre, work-a-day hue of the lower world, or of my world within'. It is one of those scenes which reveal a writer capable of combining feeling and imagination with high artistry.

The contrast between this and the final scene by the sea reflects the heroine's happiness when at last she encounters Mr Weston again and accepts his marriage proposal, while they watch a splendid sunset mirrored in the waters. Sentimentality is avoided in an unromantic postscript: we are all imperfect, even Mr Weston. The moral seems to be summed up in 'never attempting to imitate our richer neighbours'. 'And now I think I have said sufficient', the unpretentious writer concludes. In his *Conversations in Ebury Street* George Moore launched into superlatives in praise of *Agnes Grey*: 'the most perfect prose narrative in English literature', as 'simple and beautiful as a muslin dress', 'the one story in English literature in which style, characters and subject are in perfect keeping'. There is enough truth in this to make *Agnes Grey* worthy of careful reading, though most admirers would make less exalted claims. When Moore wrote that 'Anne's eyes were always on the story itself, and not upon her readers', he was grossly in error; preoccupation with style must have blinded him to the persistence of her moral purpose.

'The Tenant of Wildfell Hall'

This is a more sensational and ambitious novel than *Agnes Grey*; it has a relatively complex plot, and is exceptionally well organized in detail. One might think it less a transcript from life, and a revelation of considerable inventiveness and creative power. Though this supposition is undoubtedly warranted, it may be less true than is commonly assumed, as two letters from Charlotte Brontë to Ellen Nussey show. The first (12.11.40) contains this passage:

> You remember Mr and Mrs C——? Mrs C—— came here the other day, with a most melancholy tale of her wretched husband's drunken, extravagant, profligate habits. She asked papa's advice; there was nothing, she said, but ruin before them. They owed debts which they could never pay. She expected Mr C——'s instant dismissal from his curacy; she knew, from bitter experience, that his vices were utterly hopeless. He treated her and her child savagely; with much more to the same effect. Papa advised her to leave him for ever, and go home, if she had a home to go to. She said this was what she had long resolved to do; and she would leave him directly, as soon as Mr B. dismissed him.

The second (4.4.47) is less substantial but more relevant:

> Do you remember my telling you, or did I ever tell you, about that wretched and most criminal Mr C——, after running an infamous career of vice, both in England and France, abandoning his wife to disease and total destitution in Manchester, with two children and without a farthing, in a strange lodging-house? Yesterday evening Martha came upstairs to say that a woman 'rather ladylike', she said, wished to speak to me in the kitchen. . . .

I could almost have cried to see her, for I had pitied her with my whole soul when I had heard of her undeserved sufferings, agonies and physical degradation. She took tea with us, stayed about two hours, and frankly entered into the narrative of her appalling distresses. Her constitution has triumphed over her illness; and her excellent sense, her activity and perseverance, have enabled her to regain a decent position in society, and to procure a respectable maintenance for herself and her children.[1]

The question of what a wife should do in such circumstances was, as we have seen (p. 97), raised in *The Professor*.

Inevitably the subject had been kept alive in Anne's mind by Branwell's growing depravity. The allusion in Charlotte's 'Biographical Notice of Ellis and Acton Bell' is unmistakable:

She had, in the course of her life, been called on to contemplate, near at hand, and for a long time, the terrible effects of talents misused and faculties abused: hers was naturally a sensitive, reserved, and dejected nature; what she saw sank very deeply into her mind; it did her harm. She brooded over it till she believed it to be a duty to reproduce every detail (of course with fictitious characters, incidents, and situations), as a warning to others.

There was a sickening monotony about Branwell's life which made him a poor subject for a novel. It seems very likely that the story of Mr C——, revived by Mrs C——'s visit to the parsonage on 3 April 1847, made a deep impression on Anne, and supplied much detail for the behaviour of Huntingdon and his companions. From *Agnes Grey* it can be seen that she had been alarmed to find a young boy encouraged to take manly drinks. Branwell's account of the Mrs Robinson story may also have contributed to certain scenes, possibly (if we can judge from the similarity of an episode in 'And the Weary are at Rest') to the shrubbery assignation between Huntingdon and Lady Lowborough. Other incidents in the story may have been observed at Thorp Green; there is a hint in Anne's note, 'during my stay I have had some very unpleasant and undreamt-of experience of human nature'.

It was probably as a result of reading Thomas Moore's biography of Byron, with its hints of gambling and other forms of dissipation,

[1] A possible link between Mr C—— and Huntingdon was pointed out in the Shakespeare Head edition of the Brontë letters. It was first noted by F. A. Leyland in *The Brontë Family* (1886), reprinted 1973, Didsbury, Manchester.

that Anne chose for her novel a period immediately following that of the Regency. Some major features of her plot may have derived from Lady Byron's hopes of reforming her husband, from Moore's belief that she was 'too perfect' for him, and from Byron's reluctance to give up his child. Anne may have heard or read that one of the reasons for Lady Byron's refusal to return to her husband was her determination to protect her child against his influence.

Some Passages in the Life and Death of John Earl of Rochester may have strengthened Anne's resolve to write as she did in her second novel. The title of what is assumed to be the first version of *Agnes Grey* suggests that she was familiar with Bishop Burnet's work. 'Rochester', the name of a hero with a dissolute past in *Jane Eyre*, and 'Wilmot', the name of an old reprobate in *The Tenant of Wildfell Hall*, are fictional descendants of John Wilmot, Earl of Rochester, poet and debauchee of the Restoration period. Burnet's brief work contains no autobiographical scenes or impressions which could have helped Anne as a novelist, yet his aims in writing it were precisely hers, and he stresses more than once a point made by Huntingdon (xlix), who dies unconvinced of the efficacy of any death-bed repentance:

> and the repentance of most dying men, being like the howlings of condemned prisoners for pardon, which flowed from no sense of their crimes, but from the horror of approaching death; there was little reason to encourage any to hope much from such sorrowing.

Not surprisingly *The Tenant of Wildfell Hall* was attacked for its 'coarseness' and brutality; its scenes of debauchery were 'disgusting' and 'revolting'; and objections were raised against the profanity of its language. Moral attitudes were questioned by one reviewer, and the moral of the story praised by another. Charles Kingsley (Winnifrith, p. 120) found the book utterly unfit for girls, yet had the courage to say that 'whitewashed English society' owed thanks to those 'who dare to show her the image of her own ugly, hypocritical visage'. Before some of these reviews appeared, Anne was dead. Perhaps she was gratified that a second edition was soon called for. In the preface she wrote for it in July 1848, she acknowledged the praise of 'a few kind critics', and added that both her judgment and feelings assured her that the asperity with which she had been censured was 'more bitter than just'. She argued sensibly that

> when we have to do with vice and vicious characters, . . . it is better to depict them as they really are. . . . Oh, reader! if there were less

of this delicate concealment of facts – this whispering 'Peace, peace', when there is no peace, there would be less of sin and misery to the young of both sexes who are left to wring their bitter knowledge from experience.

She continued spiritedly:

when I feel it my duty to speak an unpalatable truth, with the help of God, I *will* speak it, though it be to the prejudice of my name and to the detriment of my reader's immediate pleasure as well as my own.

Unfortunately Charlotte Brontë did not possess her sister's courage and clear-sightedness. She did not agree to the publication of the novel by Smith, Elder & Co. (letter to Williams, 5.9.50), stating that Anne's mind was tinged with 'religious melancholy', and implying, as she did in her 'Biographical Notice of Ellis and Acton Bell', that this made her 'morbid' in pursuing a subject which was unsuitable for fiction. In arguing thus, she seems to have ended on the side of the reviewers who had labelled her own novels 'coarse'. If she was thinking of her sister's reputation rather than her own, she was utterly misguided; no intelligent and conscientious reader could have mistaken Anne's purpose, and the outcry against the novel, like that against *Jane Eyre*, was mainly a muddle-headed reaction of writers springing to attack in defence of upper-class society.

The construction is similar to that of *Wuthering Heights*, with preliminary chapters creating a mystery, the explanation of which is unfolded in the journal narrative of the main story; the conclusion continues the opening. Anne's story is more complicated; it relates to far more characters and families, and its general organization indicates considerable planning in detail before full-length composition could begin. She was busy at it in the summer of 1847, and this is the time when she imagines it to have been concluded by Gilbert Markham. The main story (xvi–xliv) relates principally to Arthur Huntingdon; it was recorded by Helen from June 1821 to October 1827, and ends with a reference to the parish 'gentleman and beau', whose growing attachment to the mysterious lady of Wildfell Hall is the subject of the opening chapters. The sequel includes the death of Huntingdon and some exciting suspense before Helen and Markham are married in August 1830.

There are two unrealistic features in the design which show that Anne Brontë was technically inferior to Emily. George Moore thought

the 'diary' form for the main story a mistake. The heroine, he submitted, should have narrated it to the hero in such a way, with
gestures, questions, and comments, that 'the atmosphere of a passionate
and original love story' could have been preserved. As it is, the diary
breaks the story in halves (*Conversations in Ebury Street*). To this it
may be answered that the story is not really broken, and that interest
in it has been given momentum by the mystery and attractiveness
which already surround the heroine. Though the use of the 'diary'
method for the transmission of a lengthy, dramatized narrative lacks
all credibility, it seems reasonable to assume that Anne Brontë would
not have wished any atmosphere of passionate love between Helen
and Markham to distract attention from her main story concerning
the dissolute Huntingdon. The dedication to J. Halford, Esq. has less
justification. We are expected to believe that Markham copied almost
the whole of Helen's manuscript for his perusal (see the end of xv);
yet Halford is forgotten. The epistolary intention is noticeable at the
beginning; we are reminded of it when the Markham story is resumed,
and again at the end, but a correspondent for a long story which
depends on no interchange of letters is an absurdity. Halford's
function initially was to reinforce the impression that the writer was a
man of the world, a tremendous task for Anne, and, however far she
succeeded, ultimately impossible for one who was known to be the
author of *Agnes Grey*. Charlotte Brontë employed the same technique
at the opening of *The Professor*; but it is equally redundant, and, as
soon as it had served her purpose, she abandoned it completely.

The opening of *The Tenant of Wildfell Hall* is leisurely compared
with that of *Wuthering Heights*. There is a tendency towards introducing characters through flat portraiture in the earlier Charlotte
Brontë style, but the scenes bring to life a small educated community.
Its limitations are such that the hero finds the parson's daughter,
Eliza Millward, bewitching until he sees Helen (Mrs Graham). Her
protective care over 'little Arthur' leads to a discussion on whether he
should be brought up in cloistered virtue (iii); when Markham says
that girls need more protection and guidance than boys, she argues
as the Brontë sisters must have done, and as Charlotte wrote to Miss
Wooler (30.1.46), with reference to Branwell:

the mode of bringing [men] up is strange, they are not half
sufficiently guarded from temptation – girls are protected as if they
were something very frail and silly indeed while boys are turned

loose on the world as if they – of all beings in existence, were the wisest and the least liable to be led astray.

The argument is resumed more pointedly when Mr Millward, who enjoys all the good gifts of nature, hears how Mrs Graham makes her son dislike tempting liquors; it is 'criminal', he exclaims, and 'contrary to Scripture and reason' to teach a child to despise 'the blessings of Providence'. Mr Lawrence observes that laudanum may be considered a blessing of Providence, and yet it is better to abstain from it, even in moderation.

Helen's reviving happiness and Markham's admiration as she gazes at the scene are reflected in a seascape (vii):

the blue sea burst upon our sight! – deep violet blue – not deadly calm, but covered with glinting breakers – diminutive white specks twinkling on its bosom, and scarcely to be distinguished, by the keenest vision, from the little seamews that sported above, their white wings glittering in the sunshine.

Her mysterious tragedy is associated with the gloom of Wildfell Hall, its setting and description undoubtedly influenced by those of Wuthering Heights (ii). It assumes almost a Gothic aspect by moonlight (vi):

Silent and grim it frowned before us. A faint, red light was gleaming from the lower windows of one wing, but all the other windows were in darkness, and many exhibited their black, cavernous gulfs, entirely destitute of glazing or framework.

Markham's love makes him an eavesdropper; the result is ungovernable jealousy of Mr Lawrence, and a savage, unprovoked assault on him with a horse-whip. It is no wonder *The North American Review* described the hero as a 'ruffian'; perhaps *Wuthering Heights* was responsible for Anne's error of judgment.

Helen's journal begins after her introduction to London society. Despite the warnings of her prudent aunt Mrs Maxwell, not to allow her judgment to be dazed by good looks and charming manners, but to put principle and good sense first, she has been fascinated by the 'very lively and entertaining' Mr Huntingdon, as she could hardly help being after encountering the dull Mr Boarham, who, though he had acknowledged his fear of imprudence, persisted in proposing to her. On another occasion, Huntingdon had rescued her from Mr Wilmot, whom Helen regarded as 'a worthless old reprobate'. Mrs Maxwell had watched her growing attachment with alarm, and dropped hints about Huntingdon's past. Helen was eighteen, and full of the confidence of youth. She was certain she could judge people's characters by their looks; she hated the sins but loved the sinner, and would consider her life well spent in recalling him to the path of virtue. The London visit was curtailed by Mr Maxwell's indisposition, and Mrs Maxwell hoped that Helen would soon forget Huntingdon. Helen now found life tedious at Staningley, turned to drawing for distraction, and was always trying to paint or sketch a face. 'As for the owner of that face, I cannot get him out of my mind – and, indeed, I never try.'

The shooting-season brought Mr Maxwell's friends to Staningley. Huntingdon is quick to take liberties, and threatens to turn his attentions to Annabella Wilmot when Helen shows her annoyance. The latter's infatuation masters her judgment, and she persists in thinking that she is chosen to redeem Huntingdon: 'he meant no harm – it was only his joyous, playful spirit'; Annabella does not love him; she is playing a double game between him and Lord Lowborough; she is selfish, and will not deplore his faults or 'attempt their amendment'. After dinner Annabella sings at Huntingdon's request (see p. 232), and Helen's jealousy is sufficiently kindled for her to declare her love almost for the asking (xix). The more she hears of his associates, the readier she is to make excuses (xx):

> the more I long to deliver him from his faults – to give him an opportunity of shaking off the adventitious evil got from contact with others worse than himself . . . – to do my utmost to help his better self against his worse, and make him what he would have been if he had not, from the beginning, had a bad, selfish, miserly father, who . . . disgusted him with every kind of restraint; – and a foolish mother who indulged him to the top of his bent . . .

Yet her alarm increases as Huntingdon, talking about Lowborough, incautiously betrays his 'orgies' and those of his club companions, as they plied Lord Lowborough with strong drinks to drown his misery after he had incurred huge gambling debts. Lowborough's way of entering, 'silent and grim as a ghost', his recourse to laudanum, falling into a kind of apoplectic fit after drinking madly, and thinking that Annabella's love will save him from eternal damnation (xxii), recall Branwell Brontë. Anne believed his story about Mrs Robinson, and probably had his final betrayal in mind in the passage where Helen's heart bleeds for Lord Lowborough, after he has discovered the infidelity of his wife and Huntingdon (xxxviii). (Lowborough had been deceived into thinking that Annabella had loved him genuinely and not for his title; in marrying her and her fortune, he thought he had solved all his personal problems, in this world and the next.) The 'castaway' references at these two points[1] in the story may therefore echo Branwell's hope and despair.

After her marriage Helen is soon disillusioned; she would not have married Huntingdon had she known as much about him previously. Now she is glad, however, to have the opportunity of loving and reforming him. She cherishes the belief, based on her Scriptural research, that no sinner is eternally damned. Huntingdon does not take her seriously; God had not given him the 'proper organ of veneration'. After hearing of his former amours, she is offended, and he shows his ill-nature; 'had there been a lady anywhere within reach, of any age between fifteen and forty-five, he would have sought revenge'. This sample of the 'coarseness' which contemporary readers found distasteful is more than matched when Huntingdon, after the breakdown of his marriage, says that any of his friends who fancied her could have his wife 'and welcome: you may, by Jove, and my blessing into the bargain!' This toning down of oaths is far from general among the roisterers, and reviewers complained about profanity of language such as that used by Hattersley when he swears to reform: 'I've been a cursed rascal, God knows, but you see if I don't make amends for it – G-d d---n me if I don't!'

The exposé of Huntingdon's weaknesses and vices is never monotonous. We see everything from Helen's point of view. There are intervals when Huntingdon leaves her to enjoy himself in London; she meets local friends or acquaintances in the meantime. Journal entries vary in length and frequency according to the relative importance of the developments which take place. Sometimes a year passes before the next entry is made (see xxviii and xxix; xxxvi, xxxvii, xxxviii). The shooting-season usually brings Huntingdon's guests, and some exciting scenes. As a whole the progression is designed to give adequate relief and variety to a gradual revelation of the worst.

Helen wishes that her husband had some useful occupation which would give him something to think about besides pleasure. She

[1] xxii and xxxviii. The latter is found in the Shakespeare Head edition, and in American texts. See p. 352.

attributes his inability to exert or restrain himself to parental negligence or indulgence, and determines that if ever she has a child she will avoid such a *crime*. (The link between 'little Arthur' and Branwell Brontë is evident.) When Arthur is born, she feels that God has sent 'a soul to educate for heaven'. Huntingdon is jealous, and speaks of the child in abominable terms; at length Arthur wins his father's heart, and Helen dreads that he will be the victim of indulgence. This ultimately happens when Huntingdon and his friends try to 'make a man of him', and Arthur begins to tipple wine like papa, swear like Mr Hattersley, and send mama to the devil when she tries to correct him (xxxix).

Members of the Hargrave family have an interesting function in the novel, particularly with reference to marriage. Mrs Hargrave is mean, principally to keep up appearances and enable her daughters to make wealthy marriages. (In this respect, to some extent at least, she reflects Mrs Robinson of Thorp Green Hall.) To please her, Milicent accepts Hattersley; he chooses her because, unlike Helen, she is the sort of person who will let her husband do as he pleases. Esther, the younger sister, refuses to be sacrificed in the same way, and is encouraged by Helen not to marry without love, but to keep both heart and hand until she sees reason to part with them. Walter Hargrave is a man of fashion with an eye to the main chance; he is moved to champion Helen but, despite his importunities and a final passionate protestation when she makes it known that she is intent on leaving Huntingdon, she withstands him firmly, not so much from honourable motives, impeccable though they are, as from a natural aversion to him. His hopes of marrying a rich widow are disappointed because his interest in her wealth is too evident, and he has to be content with someone neither as rich nor as handsome. Hattersley has a good heart, and loves his children, but it requires a special plea from Helen, on behalf of her friend Milicent, to get him to realize what sorrow he has caused his uncomplaining wife, and make amends before it is too late.

Lord Lowborough is another to reform. He is a curious mixture of weakness and strength, an object of ridicule to Huntingdon and his friends, and ultimately of pity to Helen and the reader. There is a remarkable scene when the inebriates join the ladies after a long drinking session. Mr Grimsby performs amusingly over his tea, and then a remark from Lowborough on his return prompts Hattersley to think what a good idea it would be to force him from the room and make him 'blind drunk'. To free himself from this 'powerful mad-man', Lowborough implores his wife to give him a candle; she refuses, but Helen complies, and the flame is applied to Hattersley's hands until he lets go, roaring like a wild beast. (It seems unlikely that Anne would have introduced this incident without evidence for it.)

One can admire Lord Lowborough's firm resolution in abstaining from gambling and strong drink, but it is his faith in Annabella which makes him pathetic. Two years earlier (in the first year of her marriage) Helen had caught her husband flirting with her; he had promptly begged forgiveness, affecting to sob aloud, making excess of wine his excuse, and quoting Shakespeare in extenuation. The chapter (xxvii) ends in a sharp verbal duel between the ladies. The story is resumed when Huntingdon appears to be so well-behaved that Grimsby and Hattersley are annoyed at his negligence as a host, and attribute it to his wife's self-assertion. She is so pleased with him that she hurries after him into the shrubbery, and clasps him in her arms. He returns the embrace with the fervour (as it appeared to her) of former times, before realizing the lady is his wife. She is very happy, until the observant Rachel warns her against Lady Low-borough. A disclosure from the suspicious Hargrave makes her rush out to the shrubbery the next evening to find out the truth for herself. She hears it. Huntingdon refuses to let her leave with her child; she declares she will stay therefore to be hated and despised, but a wife only in name. Lady Lowborough implores her not to tell her husband, and she agrees for his sake. Her rival is proud of her influence over Huntingdon, and coolly asks her not to drive him back to his old courses in her absence. Huntingdon spends some time at Lord Lowborough's, but it is not until the usual party meets at Grassdale in 1826 that Lowborough discovers his wife's infidelity. He is annoyed with Helen for concealing the truth, and mourns his two years of 'cursed credulity'. Then suddenly, as he thinks of her suffering, self-pity leaves him:

> 'I have noticed a change in your appearance since the first years of your marriage', pursued he: 'I observed it to – to that infernal demon', he muttered between his teeth; 'and he said it was your own sour temper that was eating away your bloom: it was making you old and ugly before your time, and had already made his fireside as comfortless as a convent cell. You smile, Mrs Hunting-don; nothing moves you. I wish my nature were as calm as yours.'

That night she hears him pacing up and down his dressing-room, and forgets her own afflictions in thinking of his 'ardent affection so miserably wasted' (xxxviii). When his wife elopes, he makes a wise second marriage (l):

> The lady was about his own age . . . remarkable neither for beauty, nor wealth, nor brilliant accomplishments; nor any other thing that I ever heard of, except genuine good sense, unswerving integrity, active piety, warm-hearted benevolence, and a fund of cheerful spirits.

Ancillary movements impinge on the main plot to create a variety of dramatically presented scenes, with the result that the climactic chapters of Helen's journal sustain excitement very effectively. Suspense is maintained at the end, as a result of Huntingdon's discovery of Helen's intention to escape. Later, his engagement of a governess for Arthur, and Rachel's shrewd summing-up of the situation, make her put into immediate effect the plans she has concerted with her brother, to seek asylum in a wing of Wildfell Hall. Everything is packed and labelled 'Mrs Graham' (her mother's name), and all in the end proceeds according to plan. The journal begins with reference to Helen's attempts to paint and sketch a face she could not forget after her first visit to London; ironically Rachel makes the mistake of packing a portrait of Huntingdon which Helen painted during the first year of her marriage, and it was this which caught Gilbert Markham's attention at Wildfell Hall (v).

If Catherine Earnshaw is the most bewitching of Brontë heroines, Helen, despite her piety, is the most attractive. She suffers a great deal, but has remarkable resolution; she recognizes her initial errors but insists on facing up to the truth. When Markham returns her journal, she is a realist; she will not dare to make promises contingent on Huntingdon's death. If the lovers are to remain faithful, they may have to await 'the joys of heaven'. Such a hope (supported by the caterpillar-butterfly analogy which Anne must have discussed with Emily Brontë) is born of stoical despair, and her pent-up feelings are soon released:

> there was a sudden impulse that neither could resist. One moment I stood and looked into her face, the next I held her to my heart, and we seemed to grow together in a close embrace from which no physical or mental force could rend us. A whispered 'God bless you!'

and 'Go – go!' was all she said; but while she spoke she held me so fast that, without violence, I could not have obeyed her. At length, however, by some heroic effort, we tore ourselves apart, and I rushed from the house.

The concluding chapters contain some of Anne Brontë's greatest writing. If, as her preface suggests, and Charlotte confirms, she wrote the journal more from a sense of duty than from pleasure in her subject, it shows admirable inventiveness, imagination, and dramatic skill. In the sequel, which, like the preliminary chapters, sets the main theme in relief, she had greater freedom.

The final decline and death of Huntingdon, however, penetrates the conclusion like a heavy tapering shadow. Helen returns to nurse him, and Huntingdon's attitude to her turns gradually from scorn to pitiful dependence, as he clings to her, his only comfort in life. With her usual artistic sense, Anne makes Helen's letters on the subject increasingly brief. The last ends with the faith that inspires the novel and Anne's poetry:

> And oh, there lives within my breast
> A hope long nursed by me . . .
> That even the wicked shall at last
> Be fitted for the skies . . .

Helen writes (xlix):

thank God, I have hope – not only from a vague dependence on the possibility that penitence and pardon might have reached him at the last, but from the blessed confidence that, through whatever purging fires the erring spirit may be doomed to pass – whatever fate awaits it – still it is not lost, and God, who hateth nothing that He hath made, will bless it in the end!

The calibre of Anne Brontë may be judged from her refusal to indulge in facile repentance and didactic effusions, in the style of Defoe or the 'sentimental' drama of the eighteenth century. Her Christianity is an integral part of Helen's character; it is formative, and never extrinsic or overloaded.

Helen finds Esther Hargrave charming, and so she emerges. She withstands her materialistic mother, and threatens to leave home. Anne Brontë had been in correspondence with the Robinson girls, and probably had one of them in mind in the story of Esther, to judge from subsequent revelations by Charlotte (28.1.48, 28.7.48). Esther makes the kind of marriage Helen ought to have made at eighteen, and its disclosure is a most delightful surprise; the most enchanting scene in all the Brontë novels, it is dramatically heightened by Markham's fears that the wedding is Helen's, and a vague hope that he will arrive in time to prevent it. At first the situation recalls a Hardy scene, though Gilbert is far from passive in his feelings, as he grasps the churchyard gate for support after his long hurried journey, to take his last look on his 'soul's delight' and his first on the 'detested mortal' who had 'torn her' from his heart, when they emerge from the church. He is so intent on the bride as she approaches, and the colours which he discerns beneath her veil, showing golden ringlets and 'a younger, slighter, rosier beauty' than Helen's, that he does not notice the bridegroom until he is fully reassured. He is astonished to find it is Helen's brother, Mr Lawrence.

The scenes before us as we hasten with Markham to find Helen have the reality of rural England. The rustic humour is refreshing. Ragged urchins, hanging like bees to the church windows, suddenly drop off and make for the porch, 'vociferating' that the wedded couple are coming out. The ostler who drives Markham in a gig to Grassdale is amusingly informative on Mr Hargrave's marriage disappointment and prospects. The style is assured, and every word tells. Anne's vernacular, livelier than in *Agnes Grey*, is nearer to that of Dickens than it is to George Eliot's. Grassdale Park in its garb of snow is sketched in a style that could hardly be bettered (lii):

> the majestic sweep, the undulating swell and fall, displayed to full advantage in that robe of dazzling purity, stainless and printless – save one long, winding track left by the trooping deer – the stately timber-trees with their heavy-laden branches gleaming white against the dull, grey sky; the deep, encircling woods; the broad expanse of water sleeping in frozen quiet; and the weeping ash and willow drooping their snow-clad boughs above it – all presented a picture, striking indeed, and pleasing to an unencumbered mind, but by no means encouraging to me.

Markham is beginning to feel that his social inferiority disqualifies him for Helen's hand, and this fear increases as he travels to find her at Staningley. The passengers are entertaining, but not to him, as he learns that 'old Maxwell', on his wife's advice, left all his property to his niece:

'Humph! She'll be a fine catch for somebody.'

'She will so. She's a widow, but quite young yet, and uncommon handsome: a fortune of her own, besides, and only one child, and she's nursing a fine estate for him in —. There'll be lots to speak for her! 'fraid there's no chance for uz' – (facetiously jogging me with his elbow, as well as his companion) – 'ha, ha, ha! No offence, sir, I hope?' – (to me). 'Ahem! I should think she'll marry none but a nobleman myself.'

Descriptive narration can be psychological, as we find in the humorous account of Markham's journey, when his progress is hampered by a heavy fall of snow (li):

the animals were consumedly lazy; the coachman most execrably cautious; the passengers confoundedly apathetic in their supine indifference to the rate of our progression. Instead of assisting me to bully the several coachmen and urge them forward, they merely stared and grinned at my impatience: one follow even ventured to rally me upon it – but I silenced him with a look that quelled him for the rest of the journey; and when, at the last stage, I would have taken the reins into my own hand, they all with one accord opposed it.

His impatience during the early part of his extended journey is markedly different from the paralysis which seems gradually to grip him on the way from Grassdale to Staningley Hall. Would he have ever arrived if 'little Arthur' had not spotted him?

He is a less convincing character than Huntingdon. All the Brontë sisters seemed to think that manliness implied strong physical impulses and unmannerly behaviour. Markham's violent jealousy and his savage attack on Helen's brother have already been noted. Was it manliness which made him brush past the astonished footman and enter Lawrence's room against the latter's wishes? He shows remarkably little compunction, although he expresses regret for his brutality in the end. The invalid presents a 'very interesting' picture, he writes. Markham begs his pardon, and adds hastily that, if it is not accepted, he has done *his* duty. Later, he is convinced that it is beneath his pride to ask questions about Helen, or send her messages, when they are clearly expected. He is a man of energy, whose passion for Helen is undoubted; we sympathize with him, but he often lacks perception, poise, and charm. When he is assailed by early doubts on the probability of Helen's willingness to marry him, he wonders whether Huntingdon has drawn up his will (as Branwell alleged Mr Robinson had done), to place restrictions on his wife if she married again. The root of his obstinate 'pride' is a sense of inferiority; he is quite sure that Lawrence opposes his marriage to Helen because it would be what 'the world calls a mésalliance' (1).

When he reaches Staningley Hall with Helen, Arthur, and Mrs Maxwell, his spirits are at their lowest ebb. Helen cannot understand him. She makes it clear that there could have been no misunderstanding if he had communicated with her through her brother, as was expected. He insists that Lawrence very justifiably did not wish to be questioned about her, and is about to depart. It is a mark of Helen's love and patience that she asks him to stay. Then she opens the window, plucks a Christmas rose, observes that it has braved many hardships but is still fresh and blooming, and offers it to him. Never was there a prettier love proposal. He was so slow to understand her meaning, or decide what to say or do, that she snatched the flower from his hand and threw it out of the window. Gilbert was 'electrified at this startling change in her demeanour'. He leaped out, brought back the rose, and implored her to give it to him once more. He would keep it for ever. At last he asks for her hand. He was a lucky man:

> 'If you loved as I do,' she earnestly replied, 'you would not have so nearly lost me – these scruples of false delicacy and pride would never thus have troubled you – you would have seen that the greatest worldly distinctions and discrepancies of rank, birth, and fortune are as dust in the balance compared with the unity of accordant thoughts and feelings, and truly loving, sympathising hearts and souls.'

Anne's ideas on love and class coincided with Charlotte's, and with Emily's (as expressed by Shirley); and the double standards of Victorian morality are impugned when the libertine Huntingdon, who has offered his wife to any of his friends, has the temerity to accuse her of being false to him (xxxix).

Anne's style attains great fluency at times, but it is always firmly controlled. It has a clarity and strength which indicate high intelligence. In the art of novel-writing she had probably learned much from *Wuthering Heights* and discussions with Emily. She was improving rapidly, and already showing a more sustained ability than Charlotte to create dramatic scenes outside her own experience. George Moore ventured to say that, had Anne Brontë lived another ten years, she would have 'taken a place beside' Jane Austen, 'perhaps even a higher place'. It is a daring claim, and there are too many imponderables to pursue it. Jane Austen would not have chosen to 'dwell on guilt and misery' as Anne did, and their aims and styles are very different. Even so, one cannot but wonder how the best work completed by Jane at the age of twenty-eight (when not one of her novels as we know them had been written) would have compared with *The Tenant of Wildfell Hall*. For one who was attempting her first major novel, it is no ordinary accomplishment. Its development shows Anne's increasing confidence and inventiveness; and its general ordonnance and sustained interest are such that its minor, external improbabilities in presentation are soon forgotten. Anne's power of directing a story of some complexity is remarkable; and there can be little doubt that, had *The Tenant of Wildfell Hall* received more critical attention, its merits would be more widely recognized.

PART III

People and Places in the Novels

Minor characters and places of least significance and interest have been omitted or referred to wherever most appropriate.

Abbreviations for the novels are set out on p. xi.

Although the motives for her statement were far from disinterested, and some of her portraits are more literal than she suggests, Charlotte Brontë's warning to Ellen Nussey (16.11.49) on identifications in one of her novels has a much wider reference: 'You are not to suppose any of the characters in "Shirley" intended as literal portraits. It would not suit the rules of art, nor my own feelings, to write in that style. We only suffer reality to *suggest*, never to *dictate*.'

A——, a fashionable seaside resort, where Agnes Grey and her mother started a school, *is a rather generalized picture of Scarborough. Anne Brontë knew it well from her visits with the Robinsons; she died there, and was buried outside the 'venerable old church' near the 'bold hill' overlooking the sea,* where her heroine accepted Edward Weston's marriage proposal. *A.* xx, xxi, xxiv, xxv

Martha ABBOT, Mrs Reed's maid, found Jane Eyre a tiresome child, and tried to frighten her by saying that God might strike her dead in the midst of her tantrums. *J.* i–iii, xxi

Miss Mary Ann AINLEY *was, by the author's admission, drawn from life. Ellen Nussey stated that she was one of Miss Wooler's guests at Roe Head, and that Charlotte Brontë was 'particularly impressed' by her 'goodness and saintliness'.* She and Miss Mann were the two old maids Caroline Helstone visited, when her loneliness and unhappiness made her think of being useful to others. Miss Ainley was fifty and very ugly, but her great benevolence made her widely respected, except by inconsiderate young men, 'who described her as hideous'. She advised on the distribution of Shirley's alms to the poor. Mr Hall was her only gentleman friend. *See* Miss MANN. *S.* x, xiv–xvii, xx, xxii, xxv, xxxvii

Mr ARMITAGE was a clothing-manufacturer, whose life, like Mr Pearson's, had been attempted. At one time it was said that Robert Moore would marry his red-haired eldest daughter; she had four sisters. *S.* i, ii, xvii, xix, xxii

Sir Thomas ASHBY of Ashby Park admired Rosalie, the elder daughter of Mr Murray of Horton Lodge. She was not in love with him; but rank, the attractiveness of Ashby Park, and the influence of her mother resulted in his marriage to this very beautiful girl, who had gloried in her numerous conquests. Her obvious preference for Harry Meltham in London led Sir Thomas to cut short their honeymoon, after a long period in continental capitals. At Ashby Park he lived with his mother, a haughty woman whom the new Lady Ashby thought a spy, as detestable as Sir Thomas. He had been dissipated himself, and his young wife did not forgive him for rusticating her. *A.* ix, xii, xiv–xvii, xxii, xxiii

Moses BARRACLOUGH, tailor and 'joined Methody' preacher, with 'cat-like, trustless eyes' and a wooden leg, was discovered to be the leader responsible for the wrecking of Robert Moore's new machines on Stilbro' Moor. He was arrested, gaoled, and transported.

S. i, iii, viii, ix, xiii

Mrs BARRETT, Lucy Snowe's nurse, was housekeeper at a grand mansion not far from Miss Marchmont's. In explaining why her lady (Mrs Leigh) and little boy spoke in French, she gave Lucy the idea of seeking a position abroad. She supplied the address of the 'respectable old-fashioned inn' where Lucy stayed in London, and it was from her that Mr Marchmont obtained Lucy's address in Villette, when his conscience reproached him after a dangerous illness. *V*. v, xlii

Mr BATES was the surgeon who visited Lowood School. Mary Ann Wilson told her friend Jane Eyre that he had been sent for. When he was departing, Jane heard him tell a nurse that Helen Burns had not long to live. *The name shows that Charlotte Brontë remembered the visits of Dr Batty of Kirkby Lonsdale to the Clergy Daughters' School at Cowan Bridge.* *J*. ix

Mme Modeste Maria BECK was a widow and *directrice* of the girls' school in the Rue Fossette where Lucy Snowe and Paul Emanuel taught. She had three children, Désirée, 'a vicious child' (viii, x, xxxviii, xxxix), Fifine, 'an honest, gleeful little soul' (viii, x, xxxv), and Georgette, 'a puny and delicate but engaging child' (x, xi, xiii, xiv, xix). Her school was both *pensionnat* and *externat*; she had twenty boarders and about a hundred day-pupils. Her organizing ability enabled her to cope with teachers (full-time, and visiting masters), pupils, servants, and her own children. She was calm and firm, watchful and inscrutable; she had her spies, and was an unrelenting spy herself when anything unusual was happening. Her rule was mild and charitable, yet she acted decisively at the appropriate time; and teachers and masters disappeared suddenly and quietly from her establishment. In all respects her arrangements for her pupils were liberal and excellent. Her policy was to please pupils and parents. Self-interest was the mainspring of her life, and her actions were calculated; her benevolence and sympathy were rational and general, not individual. A 'Minos in petticoats', she had no heart, not even with her own children.

Her appearance was motherly and bourgeoise. She was short and stout, with a fresh sanguine complexion, and blue serene eyes. Her features blended harmony with sternness; her lips were thin, and her mouth could be rather grim. She welcomed Dr Bretton's visits, and set out to attract him, her toilette becoming 'complete as a model, and fresh as a flower'. She was not satisfied until she found and read his letters to Lucy Snowe. 'Without beauty of feature or elegance of form, she pleased.' At the fête in her honour, she paraded 'like a little Bonaparte in a mouse-coloured silk gown'. Her jealousy was awakened when she saw that Paul Emanuel was falling in love with Lucy Snowe. For this reason and in the hope of ultimate financial benefit (for she was related to Mme Walravens, who had no family), she, Père Silas, and Mme Walravens persuaded him to take charge of the latter's estate in Guadaloupe, in the confident belief that he would make it very profitable again. Mme Beck 'took care . . . to season her existence with a relish of the world', often attending operas, plays, and balls when others at the *pensionnat* thought she was asleep. She prospered 'all the days of her life'. *Undoubtedly some of Charlotte's dislike of Mme Heger entered her portrayal of Mme Beck. Mme Heger was an excellent directrice and a devout Catholic, who missed very little and bore a physical resemblance to Mme Beck, but the latter's less pleasing attributes and unprincipled actions are either wholly fictitious or imaginary extensions of basic traits.*   *V*. viiff

BENSON was the butler at Grassdale Manor. He and Mrs Greaves and 'every decent servant' left soon after Mrs Huntingdon's departure.

T. xxx, xxxi, xl, xli, xliii, xliv, xlvii

BESSIE Lee was the nurse at Gateshead Hall. She showed sympathy to Jane Eyre, who remembered her stories vividly. She married Robert Leaven, the coachman, and lived at the Lodge. One of her children was named Jane. *Her story of the Gytrash (xii) suggests that one at least of her characteristics was drawn from Tabitha Aykroyd.*

J. i–v, x, xii, xxi

BIRMINGHAM (with Nottingham and Manchester) was one of the centres of Luddite unrest. Police intelligence took Robert Moore there in pursuit of the leaders responsible for the attack on his mill. From there he went on to London. *See* HUNSDEN.   *S*. xvi, xxii, xxiv, xxv, xxx

Mrs BIRTWHISTLE and one of her daughters attended the great Whitsuntide fête at Briarfield.   *S*. xvii, xix, xxii

BLANCHE de Melcy, proud and handsome (xi, xiv), Virginie, and Angélique (xi, xx) were the three titled belles in the front row who were determined to wreck Lucy Snowe's first lesson from the start. *They are vividly presented in* The Professor: *Blanche is Eulalie; the other two are Hortense and Caroline (q.v.).*   *V*. viii

Mr BLOOMFIELD, a retired tradesman, was very critical of his wife, and ready to listen to his mother-in-law's criticism of her as well as of his children's governess, Agnes Grey. He was very short-tempered, and continually blamed Agnes for his children's misbehaviour.

A. i–v

Mrs BLOOMFIELD of Wellwood thought highly of her children, and believed everything they said. She was tall, spare, and stately, with thick black hair, cold grey eyes, and a very sallow complexion. She had four children: Tom, aged seven; Mary Ann, aged six; Fanny, four years old and very pretty; and Harriet, 'a little broad, fat, merry, playful thing of scarcely two'. Tom was tall and wiry, very selfish, and intractable as a pupil, though not without ability; he could be violent and cruel, taking great delight in torturing and killing birds. Mary Ann was a particularly obstinate pupil. Fanny soon proved difficult; she showed her displeasure by bellowing or spitting at the person who offended her. Mrs Bloomfield's indulgence led to the dismissal of Betty, the nurse, and, later, of Agnes Grey, the governess. Mrs Bloomfield's mother played her share in this. She appeared to be sympathetic, but Agnes found she was hypocritical; if only she had flattered her, the story might have been different. The old lady told Mr Bloomfield that the children needed more attention from their mother, and were shamefully neglected by their governess. *It can be assumed that the general characteristics of the Bloomfield family are based on Anne Brontë's first experiences as a governess with the Inghams of Blake Hall, Mirfield. The ages of the children show a remarkable correspondence, and two have the same names. See* BST. *lxviii, and letters: 15.4.39, 24.1.40.* *A*. i–v

Mr BOARHAM was encouraged by Mrs Maxwell to think that her niece would marry him. Helen had suffered so much from his company in London and at Staningley that it was a great relief to meet Arthur Huntingdon. Mr Boarham's talk was as dull as it was interminable. He was over forty, and had worried about 'the seeming imprudence of the match'; yet he was satisfied with Helen, and saw no reason why she should object. *T*. xvi–xviii, xxi

Messieurs BOISSEC and ROCHEMORTE were two college professors to whom M. Emanuel showed Lucy Snowe's essays. They thought he had written them, and for this reason he invited them to interview her. She recognized them as the pair who had followed and frightened her when she was trying to find the inn to which she had been directed on her arrival in Villette. *V*. vii, xxxv

BOUE-MARINE, *described from Charlotte's recollections of Ostend,*

was the continental port for which Lucy Snowe embarked on 'The
Vivid' from a London wharf. After being excessively seasick for much
of the passage beyond Margate, she was glad to land and secure a
room for the night. Not until the following morning did she decide
to travel to Villette. *V*. vi, vii, xv

The Rev. Dr Thomas BOULTBY, vicar of Whinbury, was a stubborn,
hot, opinionated, and portly old Welshman, who did much good, 'not
without making some noise about it'. His wife thought that, when he
fell asleep after a good dinner, his face was angelic. *S*. i, ii, x,
xiv–xviii

The Rev. Jabez BRANDERHAM (*Zechariah, iii. 2*) was the author of
the sermon 'Seventy Times Seven, and the First of the Seventy-First'
(*Matthew, xviii. 21–2*) in four hundred and ninety-one parts, each
discussing a separate sin. The title caught Mr Lockwood's attention
just before he fell asleep at Wuthering Heights, and the result was a
dream of pandemonium in the chapel of Gimmerden Sough, where
the original sermon had been delivered. Branderham's loud taps on
his pulpit woke up the dreamer, and he realized that the tumult had
been caused by the gusty wind which caused the dry cones of a fir
to rattle against his window. Mr Lockwood dozed, and the sound of
the bough against the lattice resulted in a nightmare so horrible that
he cried out in his sleep and disturbed Mr Heathcliff. *The scene in the
chapel is based on the account Emily remembered from her father of
the opening of Woodhouse Grove Academy chapel by Jabez Bunting
who played an important part in the secession of the Methodists from
the Church of England.* *W*. iii

Fräulein Anna BRAUN lived in the Rue Crécy, and taught Lucy Snowe
and Paulina de Bassompierre German. She was a very hearty woman,
who habitually consumed beer and beef for her first and second
breakfasts. *Possibly Mlle Mühl, Charlotte's teacher in Brussels
(29.5.43).* *V*. xxvi

BRETTON was the 'ancient' town where Lucy Snowe stayed with her
godmother Mrs Bretton. When recovering at La Terrasse from her
breakdown in Villette, she recalled Bretton's clean, handsome
buildings, the grey pavement of St Ann's Street, and the towers of the
minster. Paulina Home remembered attending St Mary's with
Graham Bretton when she was a child, and how he found the places
for her in her prayer-book. *Bretton has been identified with Bridlington,
but it is referred to as a city, probably with York in mind. Charlotte
visited these places in 1839 and 1849. The picture she presents is simple*

and typical, and there is nothing to indicate a particular place. See the next note. The name may have been suggested by Bretton Hall, between Dewsbury and Barnsley. *V.* i–iv, xvi, xxiv, xxv, xxxvii

John Graham BRETTON (known as Dr John at Mme Beck's) enjoyed playing with tiny Polly Home during her brief stay at Bretton. He was trained in London for the medical profession, and practised in Villette. On her arrival, he came to Lucy Snowe's rescue when she was in difficulties over her trunk. He was tall and handsome, with locks of leonine hue. Mme Beck, whose children he attended, was attracted by him; so too was Lucy Snowe. It was Ginevra Fanshawe who fascinated him, until he discovered her feather-brained class superiority at the concert; it was directed against his mother and himself, and he never forgave her. He happened to be passing when Père Silas found Lucy Snowe unconscious in Basse-Ville, and took her to La Terrasse, where Mrs Bretton followed his instructions in nursing her. He and Lucy attended the theatre to see Vashti; near the end of the performance a fire alarm created a stampede during which a girl was knocked down. Dr Bretton came to the rescue. Some time elapsed before it was discovered that she was Polly; her father was now the Count de Bassompierre, and the Brettons soon became their close friends. The Count vehemently opposed the marriage of Paulina and Graham, partly for class reasons, principally because he could not bear to think of losing his 'little treasure'. To Graham she was indeed a pearl of great price, but he was a man of the world who sought the approval of society, and, in appreciating the gem, he could not forget the setting. Paulina's love for him was such that her father could not in the end oppose it. She called forth all that was best in Dr Bretton, and their marriage was blessed. His son inherited his looks and disposition, and, like him, his daughters were stately. *George Smith, Charlotte's publisher, was quick to recognize features of himself in Graham. Winifred Gérin suggests that Charlotte may have been attended by a Dr Brett of Bridlington (then called Burlington) in 1839.* *V.* ii–iv, vii, ix–xiv, xvi–xxvii, xxx–xxxii, xxxvii,

xxxviii

Mrs Louisa Lucy BRETTON, Graham's mother and Lucy Snowe's godmother, was a widow. Her old friend Mr Home recalled her at eighteen, when her carriage and stature were 'fit for a princess'. The 'old lady' to her son, she was youthful in spirit. After living at Bretton, she moved to London for the sake of her son's professional training. She returned to her house in Ann Street, Bretton, and was then persuaded by Graham to join him and live in the country for the sake of her health. It was for this reason that he acquired La Terrasse, outside Villette. She died in 'ripe old age'. *George Smith recognized his mother in Mrs Bretton; 'several of her expressions are given verbatim'.*   V. i–iv, xvi, xvii, xix–xxi, xxiv, xxv, xxvii, xxxvii, xxxviii

BRIARFIELD included Fieldhead. The rectory where Mr Helstone lived with his niece Caroline was close to the churchyard. Among the inhabitants of Briarfield were the Wynnes and the old maids, Miss Mann and Miss Ainley. The curate, Mr Malone, was a notable figure. The Whitsuntide fête which it shared with the parishes of Whinbury and Nunnely was a great event. So too was the double marriage of Shirley Keeldar and Caroline to Louis and Robert Moore. *Briarfield is Birstall, which was familiar to Charlotte Brontë from her visits to the Nusseys at Rydings. The name may indicate a natural feature of the neighbourhood; see* THORNFIELD HALL. *More probably it originated from Brier Hall, which stood on the western side of Birstall.*
      S. ii, vi, vii, x, xvi, xvii–xix, xxii, xxiv, xxv, xxxiv, xxxvii

BRIARMAINS, where the Yorkes lived for six generations, was hardly a mile from Briarfield. *It is The Red House at Gomersal, the home of the Taylors, whom Charlotte visited as a result of the friendship which sprang up between her and Mary Taylor at Roe Head. The coloured windows with their medallions are now at the Brontë Parsonage Museum. An ancestor of Joshua Taylor* (Hiram Yorke) *built a small chapel for Methodist secessionists who wished to increase lay control of their church. It is thought that the singing Charlotte describes was heard there, though Briar Chapel is presented as a large building.*
      S. iii, ix, xxi, xxx–xxxiii

Mr BRIGGS, a London solicitor, acted for John Eyre in preventing Rochester's bigamous marriage, and administered his will in favour of his niece Jane Eyre.   J. xxvi, xxxiii, xxxiv

Marie BROC was the poor deformed imbecile pupil with whom Lucy Snowe and a servant were left at Mme Beck's during the long vacation. Her stepmother in a distant province would not allow her to return home. Lucy had to attend Marie for several weeks until a kind aunt came and took her away.   V. xv, xix

BROCKLEBRIDGE CHURCH *is named after Mr Brocklehurst, who preached there.* During the first winter Jane Eyre was at Lowood School, the girls were paralysed with cold during the morning service. It was too far from school to return for dinner, and bread and meat were served between the services. At the end of the afternoon service, they walked back two miles along a hilly road, exposed to wintry blasts. Helen Burns was buried in the churchyard. *The church is at Tunstall, more than two miles from Cowan Bridge. Mr Carus Wilson, the school 'patron', was the preacher. The girls ate their meal in a chamber over the porch; some of those who died of 'low fever' were buried in the churchyard.*   *J.* vii, ix

The Rev. Robert BROCKLEHURST, whose mother Naomi had founded Lowood School, was a tall man of severe aspect, who, in his buttoned-up surtout, appeared like a black pillar when Jane Eyre first looked up at him. As the school manager, he was extremely mean; Miss Temple was reprimanded because Agnes and Catherine Johnstone had each been allowed a second clean tucker in a week, when they were invited to have tea with friends in Lowood. The girls had to be plainly dressed and eschew all forms of vanity; hair was not to be braided; if it curled naturally, like Julie Severn's, it had to be cut off. His pupils were to be children of Grace; he tried to inculcate good behaviour through fear of hell fire. He lived in a large hall two miles from the school, and his wife and daughters dressed splendidly. During the fever epidemic, he and his family never came near the school. *In all that concerns the school and its manager at the time when she was a pupil there, Charlotte Brontë exaggerated very little. Mr Brocklehurst and Lowood School were founded on unforgettable memories of the Calvinistic Rev. William Carus Wilson and the Clergy Daughters' School at Cowan Bridge. Mr Wilson lived in relative affluence at Casterton Hall near Kirkby Lonsdale.*

     J. iv, v, vii, ix, x, xiii

BROWN (like Williamson, ix) was a female servant at Horton Lodge.

     A. vii, ix, xiv

Mr BROWN lived in Rue Royale, Brussels. In response to his old friend Mr Hunsden's request, he helped William Crimsworth to secure his appointment as teacher at M. Pelet's.   *P.* vii, xxi, xxii, xxiv, xxv

Nancy BROWN was a poor widow who lived with her son William in a cottage at Horton. She was discouraged by Mr Hatfield's visits, but derived much solace from Mr Weston's. He and Agnes Grey comforted her with readings from the Bible when her eyes gave her trouble. His influence encouraged her to help neighbours such as Hannah Rogers and Thomas Jackson.   *A.* xi, xii, xiv, xvii, xviii, xx

BRUSSELS. Mr Hunsden thought William Crimsworth had sufficient command of French to find suitable employment in Brussels, and sent him with a letter of introduction to his friend Mr Brown. He became a teacher, and married Mlle Henri. Their subsequent success as professor and directress of a *pensionnat* was so rapid that they were able to retire to England at an early age.

Charlotte Brontë recalled her feelings and impressions as she travelled through the country from Ostend to Brussels. The names of the places in the city (unlike those in Villette) *are actual.* Crimsworth admired the Rue Royale, gazed at the statue of General Belliard by the Park, then walked to the great series of steps beyond, and looked down into a narrow back street, the Rue d'Isabelle. *M. Pelet's school is based on M. Lebel's boarding-school (attached to the Athénée) in the Rue Terarken off the Rue d'Isabelle; it overlooked the garden behind the Hegers' house. Beyond was the school owned by Mme Heger* (Mlle Reuter). *On the left of the garden, immediately behind M. Lebel's, ran 'l'allée défendue', so called because the girls were forbidden to enter it on account of its proximity to the boys' school (the Athénée).* Crimsworth remembered waiting to hear Ste Gudule's deep bell, slowly tolling two, when he was due to teach his first English lesson in Mlle Reuter's school. After Mlle Henri's dismissal by Mlle Reuter, he walked around the city, whenever he had the chance, in the hope of finding her – on the Boulevards, in the Allée Verte (*where the gentry rode in their carriages; see Charlotte's letter, 5.6.43*), Ste Gudule (*the cathedral*) and St Jacques, the two Protestant chapels (*the Chapel Royal – the Eglise du Musée not far from the Place Royale – and St George's*), thence to the Place Royale, and along the Rue Royale and the Rue de Louvain to the Porte. He found her in the country, by her aunt's grave in the Protestant Cemetery (*where Mary Taylor's sister Martha was buried in October 1842*). He discovered that she lived in the Rue Notre Dame aux Neiges (xix). On hearing of the imminent marriage of M. Pelet and Mlle Reuter, Crimsworth set out on a long walk outside the Porte de Flandre, to decide whether he could remain in his master's service; he resigned immediately on his return. M. Pelet and Mlle Reuter were married a week later at St Jacques (xxii). *See map, pp. 334–5, and* VILLETTE.   *P.* vi–xxv

Helen BURNS, the subject of continual criticism and punishment from Miss Scatcherd at Lowood School, was amazingly learned and stoical. Unlike her friend Jane Eyre, she bore no resentment. She read *Rasselas*. For her, life was 'too short to be spent in nursing animosity'. She had great faith in Eternity. Her home was at Deepden in Northumberland, and she often recalled the rippling brook that ran near it. When Helen was dying of consumption at school, Jane crept to her bed, and was found asleep at dawn, her arms around Helen's neck. Helen was dead. She was buried in Brocklebridge churchyard, where a grey marble tablet was erected many years later (*probably by Jane*), inscribed with her name and the word 'Resurgam'. *Helen, Mr Nicholls stated, was in every way a portrait of Maria Brontë, the eldest of the Brontë children; 'she was real enough. I have exaggerated nothing there. I abstained from recording much that I remember respecting her, lest the narrative should sound incredible', Charlotte wrote (28.10.47). When Maria was very ill with consumption, her father removed her from school; she died at Haworth. For 'Resurgam', see p. 83.*   J. v–ix, xxi

CAMBRIDGE. *See* St John RIVERS. He had many friends there.

                       J. xxxiv, xxxv, xxxviii

CAROLINE de Blémont sat with Eulalie and Hortense at the front of William Crimsworth's class. He though her 'beautiful as Pauline Borghese' but 'scarcely purer than Lucrèce de Borgia'. M. Pelet said of her, 'Ah, there is beauty! beauty in perfection. What a cloud of sable curls about the face of a houri! What fascinating lips! What glorious black eyes! Your Byron would have worshipped her.' She was small but full-grown, and her complexion was a colourless olive.

                               P. x, xi, xiii, xiv

Mr CARTER was Mr Rochester's surgeon. He and Grace Poole were the only two who knew that the mad inmate of Thornfield Hall was Rochester's wife.   J. xii, xx, xxvii, xxxvi

Mary CAVE was eagerly wooed by Mr Yorke in his youth, though he had previously shown a preference for sprightly, dashing women. She was 'a girl with the face of a Madonna . . . stillness personified'. She preferred Mr Helstone 'for his office's sake'. He assumed from her silence that all was well, neglected her, and did not notice her decline. She died about five years after their marriage. Looking back, Yorke had to admit the probability that he would have jilted her, even if she had remained loyal to him.   S. iv, xii, xxx

CHARLES —— was at Eton with William Crimsworth, who years later wrote him a letter, outlining the career he had followed and his reasons for seeking employment with his brother Edward Crimsworth. To this there was no reply, for Charles had left the country to take up a Government appointment.   P. i

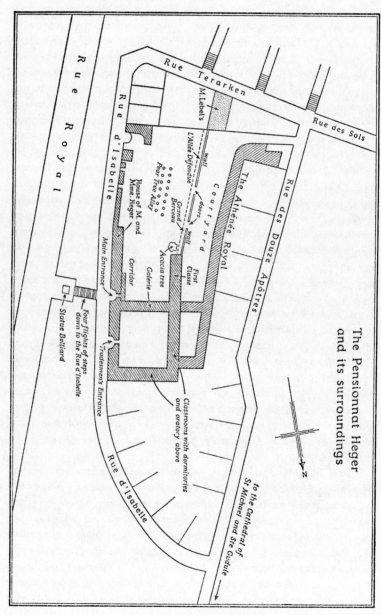

The Pensionnat Heger
and its surroundings

Rue Royal

Rue d'Isabelle

Rue Terarken

Rue des Sols

M.Lebel's

L'Allée Défendue

wall

Pear Tree Alley

Grand Berceau

Courtyard

wall

doors

The Athénée Royal

Rue des Douze Apôtres

House of M. and
Mme. Heger

Main Entrance

Corridor

Galerie

First Classe

Acacia tree

Statue Belliard

Four flights of steps
down to the Rue d'Isabelle

Tradesmen's Entrance

Classrooms with dormitories
and oratory above

Rue d'Isabelle

to the Cathedral of
St Michael and Ste Gudule

N

Mrs CHOLMONDELEY, Ginevra Fanshawe's chaperon, was 'a gay, fashionable lady'. Ginevra accompanied the Cholmondeleys on a tour in southern France.   *V.* ix, xiv, xvii, xviii, xx, xxvi, xxvii, xl

CLIFFBRIDGE, 'a fashionable watering-place', *is Scarborough. It is named after the bridge near the lodgings where Anne Brontë died at Scarborough; see plate no. 24 (lower).* When Caroline Helstone felt that Robert Moore had deserted her for Shirley, she said she would like to leave home and be a governess. Her uncle suggested a holiday at Cliffbridge. Shirley was introduced to Sir Philip Nunnely there.

S. xi, xxv, xxvii

CRIMSWORTH HALL, the home of Mr and Mrs Edward Crimsworth, stood four miles outside the industrial town of X——. It was sold with all its contents when Edward was declared bankrupt. *The name came from a hall at the lower end of Crimsworth Dean, a steep wooded valley north of Hebden Bridge. The Hall was suggested by Heaton Lodge, situated about two and a half miles north-east of Huddersfield, on the southern side of the Calder river. Charlotte had seen it when she was at Roe Head:* 'I looked in that direction – Huddersfield and the hills beyond it were all veiled in blue mist, the woods of Hopton and Heaton Lodge were clouding the water-edge and the Calder silent but bright was shooting among them like a silver arrow' (Roe Head Journal, *August 1836).*   *P.* i–iii, xxii

Edward CRIMSWORTH, ten years senior to his brother William, married a rich mill-owner's daughter, and acquired his father's mill and business. He was a handsome, powerful man, of athletic build; served no god but Mammon; and was most tyrannical, even to his brother. After becoming bankrupt, and paying tenpence in the £1, he started business again, and was soon flourishing. *See pp. 77, 154–5.*

P. i–vi, xxii, xxv

Mrs Edward CRIMSWORTH was young, tall, and shapely. She displayed vivacity, vanity, coquetry, but William Crimsworth could discern little intellect or soul, and wondered how she would fare without 'that Promethean spark' when youth and beauty had vanished, or in 'November seasons of disaster'. When her husband's business failed, his temper was such that she returned to her father's home; after being declared a bankrupt and setting up in business again, Edward coaxed her back.   *P.* i–iii, xxii

William CRIMSWORTH, after being educated at Eton, refused the living of Seacombe, and the hand of one of his Seacombe cousins in marriage, to become second clerk in his brother's business at X——, at a salary of £90 a year. His brother was a merciless taskmaster, but William served him faithfully. His antipathy grew until, after a scene in which he was falsely accused of calumny, he relinquished his post. On Mr Hunsden's recommendation he went to Brussels to seek employment. He was engaged to teach English and Latin at M. Pelet's school. Mlle Reuter, *directrice* of a neighbouring *pensionnat* for girls, hearing of his proficiency, secured his services as a part-time teacher of English. Crimsworth found her wily but, despite his toughness, proved susceptible to her attentions until he discovered that she and M. Pelet were virtually engaged. Steadily he was drawn to Mlle Henri, a young sewing-mistress who attended his class to improve her English. Mlle Reuter's jealousy led to her dismissal, whereupon Crimsworth resigned from her school. He met Mlle Henri at last in the Protestant Cemetery, by the grave of her aunt who had recently died. News of Mlle Reuter's imminent marriage to M. Pelet led to his further resignation and unemployment. Eventually, as a result of M. Vandenhuten's influence, he was appointed at a college in Brussels. He and Mlle Henri worked assiduously both before and after their marriage. She set up her own school, which was highly successful, and persuaded her husband to teach in it one hour each afternoon. So industrious and enterprising were they that they achieved financial independence after ten years, retiring to England, where they settled at Daisy Lane with their son Victor, a ready scholar, destined for Eton. *See pp. 93, 103.*   P.

DAISY LANE, the house to which Mr and Mrs William Crimsworth retired with their son Victor, after rapid success as teachers in Brussels, took its name from the lane above which it stood, in a smokeless hilly region, thirty miles from X——. *Despite this fictional location, it has long been identified with Nova Lane between Oakwell Hall and Birstall. There can be little doubt that the former suggested the 'very old mansion' near the end of the lane.*   P. xxv

Mrs Ellen (Nelly) DEAN, housekeeper at Thrushcross Grange, narrated the greater part of *Wuthering Heights* to the tenant, Mr Lockwood, during his illness. Though a poor man's daughter, she had read a great deal. While her mother nursed Hindley Earnshaw, Nelly spent most of her time at Wuthering Heights; she played with Hindley and Catherine when they were children, and helped in various jobs on the farm. When Catherine married Edgar Linton, she accompanied her mistress to Thrushcross Grange. *Directly or indirectly, she was able to give eye-witness accounts of the main*

episodes linking the lives of Heathcliff, the Earnshaws, and the Lintons.
When Mr Lockwood returned to Thrushcross Grange, he found that
Ellen had returned to Wuthering Heights. From her he heard an
account of the last days of Heathcliff's life. *See pp. 212–13.*

W. ii, ivff

M. DE BASSOMPIERRE. *See* Mr HOME. *The name was suggested by
that of a pupil at Mme Heger's. When an altercation broke out in the
first class on the subject of Napoleon, she came to Charlotte's rescue*
(BST. *xxiii*). *V.*

Mme la Baronne DE DORLODOT was Alfred de Hamal's aunt (and
possibly the mother of 'la petite de Dorlodot', *P.* xvii). *V.* xiv

Alfred DE HAMAL, a young count and colonel, with little but rank
to recommend him, but enough to captivate Ginevra Fanshawe, was
'a straight-nosed, very correct-featured little dandy', as 'trim as a
doll'. He had nephews, the sons of his eldest sister Mme de Melcy,
at the Athénée. The tradition that a nun in black and white haunted
Mme Beck's *pensionnat* suggested his disguise for assignations with
Ginevra. Pretending to visit his nephews, he scaled the wall between
the Athénée and *l'allée défendue*, and climbed a tree to a roof which
led to a higher one, where a half-open skylight gave access to the
attics. He eloped with Ginevra, and M. de Bassompierre had to give
the married couple financial aid more than once. *V.* ix, xii–xiv,
xviii–xx, xxii, xxiii, xxix, xl

Colonel DENT and his wife were guests at the Thornfield party.
'*Dent*' *is a well-known Yorkshire family name, associated with the
village of Dent, north of Whernside in the Pennines.*

J. xvi–xviii, xx

DOLORES, a Catalonian boarder at Mme Beck's, had to be disciplined
very summarily during Lucy Snowe's first lesson. This act pleased
not only Madame, who had been peeping through a spy-hole, but
the rest of the class, with whom Dolores was very unpopular. *See*
Juanna TRISTA, *a more graphic delineation of the same pupil.*

V. viii

Joseph DONNE, curate of Whinbury, lodged with Mr and Mrs Gale
on the outskirts of the town. (Mr Gale, a clothier and former church-
warden, was indulgent to clergymen, and especially to the noisy
curates who met in his house.) Mr Donne came from the south of
England, and his small talk consisted mainly of sweeping strictures
on people in Yorkshire. Arrogant remarks of this kind brought his
visit to Fieldhead, where Tartar had made him seek refuge upstairs

Originally this painting by Branwell included his own portrait
between Charlotte (right) and Emily. It may be discerned as
clearly as the 'great pillar' which once blotted it out. Mrs Gaskell
(G. vii) ascribed the picture to the 1835 period, when Anne was
fifteen, Emily about seventeen, and Charlotte nineteen

Ellen Nussey and Charlotte Brontë. If the portrait of Ellen is the work of Charlotte, it could have been sketched in 1833 when Ellen was at Haworth. She was then sixteen, exactly a year younger than Charlotte. The portrait of the latter, possibly in 1838, is a copy of an oil painting by J. H. Thompson of Bradford

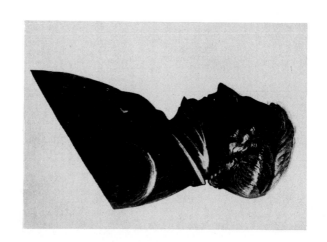

A silhouette of Branwell Brontë, and a portrait of Anne from a water-colour by Charlotte Brontë

Emily Brontë, a fragment of a canvas by Branwell Brontë

Law Hill above Halifax

Top Withins on the moors above Haworth (see p. 342)

High Sunderland Hall, an illustration published in 1835, with (below) detail of the side entrance leading to a paved yard, and of the main entrance. Suggestions may be seen for the 'wilderness of crumbling griffins and shameless little boys' above the 'principal door' of Wuthering Heights

[18]

A portrait of Elizabeth (Aunt) Branwell by an unknown artist

The Chapter Coffee
House, Paternoster
Row, London, where
Patrick Brontë and his
daughters stayed at
various times

The cathedral of Ste
Gudule, Brussels,
where Charlotte made
her confession

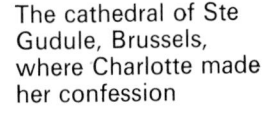

The Pensionnat Heger, Rue d'Isabelle, Brussels

The Galerie behind what remains of the pear-tree avenue. On the left is the 'allée défendue'; the 'berceau' and the 'first classe' are in line with it; beyond the latter, the second storey of the school building may be descried, with the attic roof above obscured by the branches of the tree in the foreground

(For the text of this facsimile, see below)

Part of Emily Brontë's Birthday Note of 30 July 1845

[The Gondals] still flourish bright as ever. I am at present writing a work on the First Wars. Anne has been writing some articles on this, and a book by Henry Sophona. We intend sticking firm by the rascals as long as they delight us, which I am glad to say they do at present. I should have mentioned that last summer the school scheme was revived in full vigour. We had prospectuses printed, despatched letters to all acquaintances imparting our plans, and did our little all; but it was found no go. Now I don't desire a school at all, and none of us have any great longing for it. We have cash enough for our present wants, with a prospect of accumulation. We are all in decent health, only that papa has a complaint in his eyes, and with the exception of B., who, I hope, will be better and do better hereafter. I am quite contented for myself: not as idle as formerly, altogether as hearty, and having learnt to make the most of the present and long for the future with the fidgetiness that I cannot do all I wish; seldom or ever troubled with nothing to do, and merely desiring that everybody could be as comfortable as myself and as undesponding, and then we should have a very tolerable world of it.

By mistake I find we have opened the paper on the 31st instead of the 30th. Yesterday was much such a day as this but the morning was divine.

Tabby, who was gone in our last paper, is come back, and has lived with us two years and a half, and is in good health. Martha, who also departed, is here too. We have got Flossy; got and lost Tiger; lost the hawk Hero, which, with the geese, was given away, and is doubtless dead, for when I came back from Brussels I enquired on all hands and could hear nothing of him. Tiger died early last year. Keeper and Flossy are well, also the canary acquired four years since. We are all now at home, and likely to be there some time. Branwell went to Liverpool on Tuesday to stay a week. Tabby has just been teasing me to turn as formerly to 'pilloputate'. Anne and I should have picked the black currants if it had been fine and sunshiny. I must hurry off now to my turning and ironing. I have plenty of work on hands, and writing, and am altogether full of business. With best wishes for the whole house till 1848, July 30th, and as much longer as may be — I conclude.

E. J. Brontë

A sketch by Anne Brontë in December 1836

Wood's Lodgings, Scarborough (near Cliff Bridge, 1843), as it was when visited by the Robinsons and Anne and Branwell. Anne died here

Norton Conyers, Charlotte Brontë's visit to which supplied the story of a mad woman immured in an attic and some features in the setting of 'Thornfield Hall'

Moorseats, the home of one of the Eyre families at Hathersage; it suggested 'Moor House' or 'Marsh End' in *Jane Eyre*

The hall of Oakwell Hall or 'Fieldhead'. The dog gates at the foot of the stairs suggested a scene in *Shirley*

Gawthorpe Hall, where Charlotte Brontë was the guest of Sir James and Lady Kay-Shuttleworth

George Richmond's portrait of Charlotte Brontë in 1850

Patrick Brontë, from a photograph

Arthur Bell Nicholls in 1854

on arrival, to an abrupt conclusion. This 'lisping cockney' made a sensible marriage, which domesticated and reformed him. He was as successful as he was bold in begging funds from rich and poor to build his church, school, and parsonage; people paid to get rid of him. The cash enabled him to be 'useful in his day and generation'. *In some ways prototype of the above, the Rev. Joseph Brett Grant, head of the Grammar School, Haworth, and Mr Brontë's curate in 1844, bore the author no ill-will. He became vicar of Oxenhope in 1845. See letters, 16.9.44, 28.1.50.* S. i, vii, xiv–xvi, xviii, xxxvii

Adèle DRONSART, one of the most disagreeable pupils at Mlle Reuter's, was a Belgian, not much more than fifteen but as fully grown as a stout English woman of twenty. She was like a Gorgon, sullen and vicious-looking. Even her fellow-pupils shunned her.

P. xii

Catherine EARNSHAW was wild and winsome in her girlhood, and her greatest happiness was in Heathcliff's company. When Hindley inherited Wuthering Heights, they were neglected and free to roam at will. Often they remained on the moors all day. One Sunday evening the lights of Thrushcross Grange beckoned; they ran all the way down to the park, made their way to the house, looked through the window, and laughed. A bull-dog was set loose, and seized Catherine by the ankle; Heathcliff wedged a stone between its jaws, but Catherine had to stay five weeks at Thrushcross until her wound was healed. So began her friendship with the Lintons, and Heathcliff's jealousy of Edgar. Heathcliff had responded to Catherine's influence, and had given up shooting lapwings at her request, but he had ceased for some time to make any effort to improve his mind, and she now realized that, despite her love, it would be a degradation to marry him. After overhearing these views expressed to Nelly Dean, Heathcliff vanished. Catherine looked for him until midnight, when she was caught in a thunderstorm and soaked; in consequence she became deliriously ill. After her convalescence, the doctor issued a warning that she might be subject to fits if contradicted or thwarted when she was bent on having her own way. Within three years she married Edgar Linton. When Heathcliff returned, she was inordinately pleased and excited to see him. She disapproved of his courting Edgar's sister Isabella, perhaps from jealousy as much as from awareness of his loveless policy of revenge. Angry words from Heathcliff and Edgar's plans to eject him roused her almost to frenzy. Her psychotic state was not realized, and soon she became mentally deranged. She was nursed tenderly by her husband during the two months following the elopement of Heathcliff and Isabella. On their return, Heathcliff insisted on seeing Catherine; their meeting was one of intense ecstasy mingled with agony and recrimination. That night, some hours after his departure, Catherine Linton was born and her mother died. She was buried in Gimmerton churchyard; later, in turn, her husband and Heathcliff were buried beside her. *The name Earnshaw may have been suggested by that of a servant at Law Hill when Emily Brontë was there; it may derive from Enshaw Knoll on the moors near Haworth. See pp. 207–8 on* The Black Dwarf.

W. ii–xvi, xxi, xxix, xxxiv

Frances EARNSHAW arrived with her husband Hindley at Wuthering Heights, when the latter returned from college for his father's funeral. Her origin was kept a secret. She was thin and very excitable, with bright sparkling eyes. After the birth of her son Hareton, the doctor announced that she had been consumptive for months. Hindley doted on both. The death of his gay wife completely broke him.

W. iii, vi–viii

Hareton EARNSHAW was the apple of his father's eye. When his wife died, however, Hindley's love for his only child was soon put to hazard, for intemperance made him behave alarmingly. Hareton ran the chance of 'being squeezed and kissed to death' or of 'being flung into the fire, or dashed against the wall'. He grew up wild and neglected, his brutality being encouraged by Heathcliff in a long-drawn-out attempt to settle scores with his father. Ironically, by developing the boy's viciousness and love of cruelty, Heathcliff made a friend of him. He and his cousin Catherine Heathcliff bore a great resemblance to Catherine Earnshaw, so much so that in the end Heathcliff could hardly bear to look at them. Their reconciliation through Catherine's encouragement of Hareton's reading and improvement created a new spirit at Wuthering Heights. Flowers brightened the garden, and the interior looked more cheerful when Mr Lockwood returned after Heathcliff's death. Hareton and Catherine were expected to marry and move to Thrushcross Grange on New Year's Day. *W*. ii–iv, viii, ix, xi, xiii, xvii, xviii, xx–xxiv, xxvii, xxx–xxxiii

Hindley EARNSHAW was like a foster-brother to Nelly Dean, since her mother had nursed him and they played together in childhood. Hindley regarded Heathcliff as an interloper, and bullied him. His father took the curate's advice, and sent him to college. He returned for his father's funeral with a young wife, and his hatred of Heathcliff was soon manifest. Heathcliff meditated revenge. The death of his wife Frances made Hindley execrate God and take to drink. At times he behaved like a madman, frightening his son Hareton, and threatening to murder others, Heathcliff especially. When the latter returned after three years' absence, Hindley invited him to gamble at cards, and then to stay at Wuthering Heights. After losing heavily, he kept him in the hope of winning back his money for the sake of Hareton. He was too drunk to attend his sister's funeral. In such a state he died at the age of twenty-seven, all his property mortgaged to Heathcliff, whom Joseph suspected of hastening his death.

W. iii–xi, xiii, xvi, xvii

Mr EARNSHAW, father of Hindley and Catherine, adopted, despite his wife's initial protest, a waif whom he brought to Wuthering Heights from Liverpool. He was called Heathcliff; Hindley's bullying of him made Mr Earnshaw sorry for the boy; when Mrs Earnshaw died, less than two years later, Heathcliff was the old master's favourite. Mr Earnshaw had always been strict and grave with his children. In the last stages of his decline, any suspected slight of his authority almost threw him into fits (*a trait inherited by Catherine*).

W. iii–v, vii

Josef EMANUEL was half-brother to Paul, and the finest ('first') music teacher in Villette. He gave lessons at Mme Beck's to pupils whose parents could afford them. Unlike Paul he was calm and taciturn. *His original was M. Chapelle, a pianist and brother-in-law of M. Heger's first wife. Charlotte taught him and M. Heger English, and he taught Emily the piano.* *V.* xx, xxvii, xxxviii, xxxix, xli

Paul Carlos David EMANUEL advised Mme Beck to accept Lucy Snowe as her nursery-governess. He was Mme Beck's kinsman, and taught part-time in her school. His main teaching was in the Athénée, the neighbouring boys' school. Generally he was to be seen in his *bonnet grec* and *paletôt*, with a cigar at his lips. Despotic and irascible, he 'fumed like a bottled storm' when he could not have his own way. 'A constant crusade against the "amour-propre" of every human being but himself, was the crotchet of this able, but fiery and grasping little man.' It was a mistake to fear him: 'nothing drove him so nearly frantic as the tremor of an apprehensive and distrustful spirit; nothing soothed him like confidence tempered with gentleness'. Meekness made him kind, as Lucy found when the question of presiding at the English examination arose. His love of authority and display was evident at the grand concert which the Royal Family attended. Dr Bretton's interest in Lucy aroused his jealousy, and her other friendships outside the *pensionnat* aggravated his anti-English, anti-Protestant feelings. In national politics his views were sensible and practical; injustice and oppression roused the best in him. Lucy Snowe learned to appreciate the 'library' of his intellectual wealth; 'his tomes of thought were collyrium to the spirit's eyes; over their contents, inward sight grew clear and strong'. Twenty years earlier he had loved Justine Marie Walravens, but the marriage had been opposed mainly by her rapacious grandmother, whom he now supported, together with her aged servant and Père Silas. The latter, Mme Walravens, and the jealous Mme Beck schemed to prevent the marriage they feared between Paul and Lucy. He had learned to respect her sincerity as a Protestant, and cast aside all barriers of prejudice. The 'junta' had persuaded him to direct Mme Walravens' estate in Guadaloupe for three years, in the hope of restoring its profitability, but he had prepared a school for Lucy to direct in his absence, intending to marry her on his return. *The ending was made rather ambiguous, not to distress some readers, especially Mr Brontë; but 'the idea of M. Paul Emanuel's death at sea was stamped on [Charlotte's] imagination, till it assumed the distinct force of reality' (G. xxv). He owes much, of course, to M. Heger. Both were highly gifted, dramatic, and volatile teachers; both were nationalists (M. Heger had fought for Belgian independence in September 1830), and apt to express their prejudices against the English. Readers of Charlotte's letters will be aware of minor similarities, but there is much in Paul Emanuel and his story which is highly imaginary. See pp. 149–50.*

V. vii, xiv, xv, xix–xxi, xxvi–xxxi, xxxiii–xxxvi, xxxviii, xxxix, xli, xlii

Mr and Mrs ESHTON lived at The Leas, ten miles on the other side of Millcote from Thornfield Hall. Mr Rochester attended a party there, and held one at Thornfield, which was attended by many, including the Eshtons and their daughters Amy and Louisa. Mr Eshton was a magistrate. *The name came from Eshton Hall, Gargrave-in-Craven, near Skipton. Here lived Miss Currer, a great bibliophile (from whom Charlotte took her nom-de-plume); she had been the patroness of William Morgan, a close friend of Mr Brontë and his family. She may have visited Stonegappe when Charlotte was governess there.*

J. xvi–xviii, xx, xxi

EULALIE was one of the pupils William Crimsworth soon had to discipline. She was 'the proud beauty, the Juno' of Mlle Reuter's school, tall and fair, with the features of a typical Dutch Madonna.

P. x, xi, xiii, xiv, xvi

Jane EYRE, *whose autobiographical story was written ten years after the marriage with which it concludes*, was the daughter of a poor curate and a lady disowned by her rich family on her marriage. In less than two years both had died of typhus, and Jane was adopted by her mother's brother, Mr Reed of Gateshead Hall. Shortly afterwards he also died, and Jane became 'a discord' in his family, receiving sympathy from none and being continually bullied by John, Mrs Reed's spoilt son. Jane was resentful and, after serious illness caused by harsh and unjust punishment, was sent to Lowood School, a charitable institution for clergymen's daughters. She was ten years old.

Conditions at the school were most unsatisfactory, and the endurance and faith of Helen Burns, a pupil friend who died of consumption there, astonished the indignant Jane. Improvements came after the outbreak of 'low fever'; Jane admired the superintendent, Miss Temple, and at the end of six years was top of the first class. She remained for two more years as a teacher but, with Miss Temple's marriage and departure, soon yearned for new experience. A newspaper advertisement led to her appointment as governess at Thornfield Hall. Her salary was doubled.

With Mrs Fairfax and her pupil, Adèle Varens, Jane found Thornfield rather dull, until the master of the Hall, Mr Rochester, returned. Small and plain though she was, he was attracted by her, and confided in her almost from the start. One night she was disturbed by a demoniac laugh, found smoke issuing from Mr Rochester's room, and promptly extinguished the flames arising from the bed where he slept. She could not help loving him, though the extended party he held indicated too clearly that Blanche Ingram was to be his wife. Jane lost hope, but was not jealous of a rival who was personally inferior though of higher rank. She soon learned, however, that he was in love with her. She was not afraid of him, enjoyed his company, and was ready to serve and obey in all that was right. She showed reason and restraint in their courtship, yet he was becoming all the world to her. The discovery of the horrible circumstances extenuating Rochester's bigamous intentions (which she had unwittingly foiled by writing to her uncle in Madeira) could not shake her principles, and she refused to live with him abroad. She had to leave him, without his knowledge.

On the brink of starvation, she was saved by St John Rivers and his sisters. She took charge of the school for girls which he had organized in his parish. By chance he discovered her identity, and revealed that she had inherited her uncle's fortune. They were her cousins, and she shared her inheritance with them. St John wished to be a missionary in India, and Jane would have shared his work out there, had he not insisted that they should marry. There was 'no medium' in her; she either submitted to hard characters or revolted against them. St John was inexorable. She knew he could not love her, and she rejected him. It was when he was making his final appeal that she heard the mysterious call for help from Rochester.

She returned to Thornfield, to find it a blackened ruin. Rochester's mad wife had set fire to the Hall, and jumped to her death from the roof. Part of the building had collapsed as he returned from an attempt to save her. Blinded and maimed, he was now living at Ferndean Manor. Jane hastened there. Their love for each other had not waned, and marriage was not long delayed.

The name 'Eyre' derives from Hathersage, the 'Morton' of the novel. The church contains an altar tomb and several brass memorials to the Eyres, and Charlotte must have examined them when she visited Ellen Nussey at the vicarage in the summer of 1845. See p. 160n. J. John EYRE, Jane's uncle, of Funchal, Madeira, called at Gateshead to see her when she was away at Lowood School. He wished to adopt her and make her his legatee. When Mrs Reed received a letter indicating this, she replied that Jane had died of typhus at Lowood School. The letter Jane wrote, after hearing her aunt's death-bed confession, served indirectly to prevent her marriage to Rochester. Uncle John left her £20,000, which she shared equally with St John Rivers and his two sisters (her cousins, she discovered), to whom he had left a mere thirty guineas.   J. x, xxi, xxiv, xxvi, xxx, xxxiii, xxxvii

F——— was the quiet seaside resort to which Helen Huntingdon took her widowed aunt Mrs Maxwell and Esther Hargrave. Mr Lawrence stayed with them nearly three months in the summer (*1829*).

T. l, li

Mrs Alice FAIRFAX was the rather deaf housekeeper at Thornfield Hall. She was a widow, whose husband had been incumbent of Hay and second cousin to Mr Rochester's mother. *Fairfax was the Parliamentary leader at the battle of Adwalton Moor (near Birstall) in 1643.* *See the note on* THORNFIELD HALL.   J. x–xiv, xvi–xviii, xxi–xxvi, xxxiii, xxxiv, xxxvi

FANNY and ELIZA were servants at Briarfield rectory. Fanny was often sent to escort Caroline Helstone home; Eliza was the cook.

S. vi, vii, x–xiii, xvi, xix, xx, xxiii–xxv, xxxv

Ginevra FANSHAWE was the niece of Mr Home's flirtatious wife. She was his goddaughter, and had been to a number of foreign schools at the expense of her uncle (now M. de Bassompierre). She was not interested in study; the only school pursuits she practised in earnest were music, singing, and dancing. Her parents were not at all wealthy; her father, Captain Fanshawe, was on half-pay, though well connected. She had three brothers and five sisters, one of whom (Augusta) had 'done perfectly well' by marrying a rich Mr Davies, who was 'the colour of a guinea' after having yellow fever in India. When Lucy Snowe met her, returning to school on 'The Vivid', she was seventeen. She was very pretty and talkative, neither intelligent nor learned, but very gay. With individuals she was not too proud to be sociable, but she was determined not to marry in the bourgeois class. It pleased her vanity, none the less, to find that she attracted Dr Bretton's attentions. Yet she found him too serious, and preferred a count and colonel, Alfred de Hamal. She liked fashionable company, as did her chaperon Mrs Cholmondeley; it was while she was with such friends, at the concert attended by the Royal Family, that Dr Bretton detected her quizzing himself and his mother. From that time he lost interest in her. The superstition associated with Mme Beck's pensionnat enabled Alfred to visit Ginevra in the disguise of a nun. Despite this, she was jealous and angry when Dr Bretton fell in love with her cousin Paulina, M. de Bassompierre's daughter. She eloped with Alfred, partly to spite them. She was to be married again when she came of age; her uncle provided her with 'a decent portion' fortunately, for Alfred had nothing but his nobility and pay. How delighted would her parents and the girls at home be to hear that she was a countess; better than 'Mrs John Bretton'! She wrote much to Lucy Snowe about the afflictions of young Alfred when he suffered the common ailments of children, as well as on the subject of his marvellous precocity. When Alfred the First ran into debt she succeeded in gaining sympathy and aid. She suffered little, obtaining her way, and 'fighting the battle of life by proxy'. *It was assumed that Maria Miller was Ginevra's prototype. However, it has recently come to light that Susanna Rodway Mills, another contemporary of Charlotte Brontë at Mme Heger's, eloped from the school* (BST. *lxxxi*). *V.* vi, vii, ix, xiii–xv, xvii–xxii, xxiv, xxvi, xxvii, xxxi–xxxiii, xxxviii–xl

William FARREN had been employed at Hollow's Mill. He did not believe in Luddism, but protested strongly against Robert Moore's policy of installing new machinery and creating unemployment. Moore's refusal to accept his advice made him think of emigrating. His master took pains, however, to find him a job as gardener to Mr Yorke; he often worked at Fieldhead, and found Shirley charming. She and Caroline Helstone gave him plants, lent him books, and found his conversation more interesting than that of others in higher positions. He tended Caroline's garden when she was ill, and wheeled her round the walks when she was convalescing. He thought highly of Mr Hall and Louis Moore; the former had helped his wife Grace to start 'a bit of a shop'.   *S*. viii, ix, xviii, xxiv–xxvi, xxxvi

FERNDEAN MANOR, 'a building of considerable antiquity' on one of Rochester's farms, about thirty miles from Thornfield Hall, was situated in the heart of a wood. Here Rochester retired after the disaster at Thornfield, suddenly to be given happiness with the arrival of Jane Eyre and their marriage. *The association of the Manor and Wycoller Hall (between Haworth and Colne) has become traditional. The Hall was damaged during the Civil War, but part of it was occupied until 1819. Its remains bear no resemblance to Ferndean Manor, a typical sixteenth-century Yorkshire house with 'two pointed gables in its front'. As ten years had passed when Jane Eyre wrote about her marriage, and references to Luddite rioting at S—— (xxxi) and Corsairs (xvii) point to a period not earlier than late Regency for the main story, the whole Ferndean period must extend well beyond 1819. The setting seems to be anticipated in 'Caroline Vernon'; see pp. 84 and 114.*   *J*. xxvi, xxvii, xxxvi–xxxviii

FIELDHEAD, Shirley's home, was situated near the Hollow, in the parish of Briarfield. *Its original, Oakwell Hall, remains relatively unchanged. It was built in 1583. Charlotte became acquainted with it when she stayed at Birstall with Ellen Nussey, some of whose relatives lived at Oakwell. The gates at the foot of the staircase to the open gallery above the hall with its large latticed window probably suggested the scene in which Malone prevented Tartar from pursuing Donne upstairs; see plate 26 (upper). 'Fieldhead' is the name of the neighbouring hamlet, where the scientist Joseph Priestley was born.*

        S. i, ii, xi, xiii–xvi, xviii, xx, xxii, xxvi–xxix, xxxvi, xxxvii

GATESHEAD HALL, the home of the Reeds, where Jane Eyre suffered in her childhood, *has been identified with Stonegappe, where Charlotte Brontë, acting as a governess for the first time (see p. 30), had some difficulty with the children. One of them threw a Bible at her, though this does not make him the original of John Reed! Gateshead Hall seems to be near hills and moorland, but its location remains concealed.* Mrs Reed's staff included Bessie Lee, the coachman, Robert Leaven, whom she married, Martha Abbott, and a housemaid called Sarah. *J.* i–v, xxi, xxii, xxvii,

Mrs GILL was Shirley's housekeeper and cook. *S.* xii, xiv, xviii, xx, xxvii, xxviii, xxxvi, xxxvii

GIMMERTON, the nearest village to Thrushcross Grange and Wuthering Heights, lay in a valley. It had a band which went the rounds of important houses at Christmas. Edgar Linton and Heathcliff were buried beside Catherine Linton in Gimmerton churchyard. *It seems certain that features of the country around Law Hill, near Halifax, were transferred to the moors above Haworth for* Wuthering Heights. *Gimmerton has the same etymological meaning as Shibden, north of Law Hill ('gimmer' = 'sheep'); it is significant that the name first appears as 'Gimmerden' (iii). The Sough in which the chapel or kirk stood could have been suggested by Chapel-le-Breer near the Sough Pastures, not far from Law Hill (Simpson, 59). In the Haworth district, Gimmerton would be Stanbury; the band, however, came from Haworth.* *W.* iii, v, vii, ix–xii, xv–xviii, xxi, xxiii, xxv, xxviii, xxix, xxxii, xxxiv

GOTON was Mme Beck's cuisinière. *V.* xii, xv, xvii, xxx, xxxiv, xxxviii

Mrs GRAHAM. *See* Helen HUNTINGDON. *T.*

GRASSDALE MANOR was the residence of Arthur and Helen Huntingdon. In retrospect, it was a scene of guilt and misery to her. She did not return after Huntingdon's death. It became the home of their son Arthur when he married. *T.* xxiii–xliv, xlvii–l, lii, liii

Mr GREEN was an easy conquest for Rosalie Murray, who described him as 'rich enough, but of no family, and a great stupid fellow, a mere country booby'. *A.* ix, x, xiii, xv, xvii, xxii

Mr GREEN, Heathcliff's lawyer, played a hireling's part in preventing Edgar Linton from altering his will before his death. Edgar had hoped to foil Heathcliff's plan of securing his property through the marriage of Catherine and Linton Heathcliff. *W.* xvii, xxviii, xxxiv

Agnes GREY, as a result of her father's misfortune, became a governess. She married Edward Weston, and undertook the early education of her children, Edward, Agnes, and Mary. *The autobiography of her disillusionment with the Bloomfield and Murray families is based*

*very largely on Anne Brontë's problems and observations when she was
a governess in 1839 with the Inghams of Blake Hall, Mirfield, and
with the Robinsons of Thorp Green Hall from 1841 to 1845. See*
HORTON, Mrs PRYOR, *and p. 241.*   *A.*

Mary G REY, Agnes's elder sister, stayed at home until she married
Mr Richardson, the vicar of a neighbouring parish. She was a gifted
water-colourist.   *A.* i, iii, vi, viii, xviii, xix, xxi

Mrs (Alice) G REY, a squire's daughter, was disinherited when she
married Richard. Of their six children, only Mary and Agnes survived
infancy or early childhood. She maintained her resolution and cheerfulness when her family had to face rigid economies. On her husband's
death, she spurned the legacy offered by her father with the proviso
that she acknowledged her mistake in marrying as she had done.
With Agnes's help, she started a school in A——. When Agnes
decided to marry, she could afford an assistant, and planned to continue
her school until she could purchase an adequate annuity.

A. i, iii, vi, xviii–xxi, xxiii, xxv

Richard G REY, father of Agnes, was a clergyman with a curacy
among the heath-clad hills of northern England. He sold a small
inheritance, and invested his money with a merchant, only to lose
all through shipwreck. The result was many economies, and Agnes's
departure to work as a governess. Mr Grey was not strong, and the
worry caused by his family's setback hastened his decline. He died a
few years later.   *A.* i–vi, xvii–xix

Mr G RIMSBY was one of the worst influences on Arthur Huntingdon.
He took particular pleasure in humiliating Lord Lowborough. He
was generally as lucky in gambling as the latter was unlucky, but
met his end, it was said, in a drunken brawl at the hands of a brother
scoundrel whom he had cheated.   *T.* xvii, xxi, xxii, xxv–xxvii,
xxxi, xxxiii, xxxv, xxxviii, xxxix, l

THE G ROVE, Grassdale, was the home of the Hargraves. Helen
Huntingdon often visited it to meet Milicent and Esther when she was
at Grassdale Manor.   *T.* xxv, xxvi, xxix, xxxii, xxxv–xxxviii, xli,
xlii, xlix, lii

G ROVETOWN (*probably Mirfield*) was the 'village of villas', about
five miles from X——, to which William Crimsworth walked by the
riverside road one January afternoon after his brother had dismissed
him.   *P.* v

Miss G RYCE, a 'heavy' Welshwoman who snored, taught with Jane
Eyre, and shared the same bedroom, at Lowood School.   *J.* x

J. HALFORD married Rose Markham. In response to his account of remarkable occurrences in his life, her brother Gilbert sent him the story of Helen Huntingdon, and of the events leading to their marriage and residence at Staningley Hall. *The opening, 'To J. Halford, Esq' is missing from most British editions of* The Tenant of Wildfell Hall.

T. To J. Halford, Esq., i, ii, xlv, liii

Cyril HALL, vicar of Nunnely, was a bachelor. He was dark and plain, forty-five years old, and already rather grey. He was charitable in disposition and deed, and much respected by all, whatever their class. Rather a bookworm, he was shy, and preferred Caroline Helstone's company to that of stylish young ladies. He had much in common with Louis Moore, and they went on a walking tour to the Lakes. Whether he or his relative, Pearson Hall of Stilbro', the solicitor Shirley consulted about her will, was left to make the best apportionment possible, for the benefit of 'the fatherless and widows', of £12,000 from her estate is not quite clear. Fittingly he officiated at the wedding of Caroline and Robert Moore. *This portrait, the most favourable among Charlotte Brontë's clergymen, reflects some of the characteristics of the Rev. W. M. Heald, vicar of Birstall.*

S. i, viii, x, xiv–xviii, xx, xxi, xxiv–xxviii, xxxv, xxxvii

Margaret HALL, bespectacled and learned like her brother Cyril, made him happy in his single state. *Mr Heald said his sister Margaret was in* Shirley. *She called* Jane Eyre *a 'wicked book'. See letters, 21.9.49, and (from W. M. Heald) 8.1.50.* *S.* viii, xiv–xvii, xxiv

HANNAH, the Rivers' old servant, had lived thirty years at Moor House. *In character and speech, she owes something to Tabitha Aykroyd.* *J.* xxviii, xxix, xxxiii, xxxiv

Mrs HARDEN, the housekeeper at Lowood School, was a woman after Mr Brocklehurst's heart. She refused Miss Temple extra food when the servant Barbara was sent to ask more for her guests, Helen Burns and Jane Eyre. Fear of 'low fever' made her leave, and her successor proved to be comparatively liberal. *Obviously appropriate though the name is, it occurred to Charlotte Brontë from her familiarity with Harden Grange (26.8.50) near Haworth.* *J.* viii, ix

Mrs HARDMAN and her eldest daughter *are introduced*, in Mrs Pryor's reminiscences, *to give Charlotte the opportunity to answer* The Quarterly Review; *see pp. 124–5.* *S.* xxi

Esther HARGRAVE was Milicent's younger sister. She had a mind of her own, and was a great favourite with Helen Huntingdon. She learnt from the advice and experiences of her sister and Helen, and refused to marry Mr Oldfield for mercenary reasons, despite persistent pressure from her mother and brother. Esther took charge of Helen's son Arthur, when his mother had to give all her time to her dying husband. She was happily married to Mr Lawrence. *See* F——, *and pp. 254–5.*   *T*. xxv, xxvi, xxix, xxxii, xxxv, xxxvii, xxxviii, xli–xliii, xlvii–xlix, li

Milicent HARGRAVE, though Annabella Wilmot's cousin, was gentle, and a great friend of Helen Huntingdon. She had hoped that Helen would marry her brother Walter. During her husband's long absences, Helen often visited The Grove to see her and Esther. To please her mother, Milicent married Ralph Hattersley. Unlike Helen, she did not oppose her husband, dissipated though he was. He reformed, for the sake of his wife and children, Helen and Ralph. Both he and Milicent gave welcome assistance to Helen when her husband was dying.   *T*. xvii, xviii, xxi, xxiv, xxv, xxx–xxxv, xli–xliii, xlix

Mrs HARGRAVE lived at The Grove, Grassdale. She was mean to others in order to keep up appearances which would enable her children, who had little fortune, to acquire wealth by marriage. Milicent married Mr Hattersley for this reason; her younger sister Esther was more independent. *Her marriage policy for her daughters recalls Mrs Robinson of Thorp Green Hall.*   *T*. xxv–xxvii, xxix, xxxii, xxxiii, xxxv, xxxvii, xxxviii, xli, lii

Walter HARGRAVE consorted with Huntingdon and his friends, more for gaining the reputation of being a man of fashion than for self-indulgence. His sister Milicent had hoped that he would marry her friend Helen, now Mrs Huntingdon. He admired her, and tried to win her favour by restraining her husband's excesses. When the breakdown of her marriage was evident, he persisted in declaring his love, and was rejected. After a period in Paris, he returned and championed Helen in her fight to save her boy from his father's pernicious influence. When he knew that she was intent on escaping, he wished to be her champion and lover. He was angry with his sister Esther when she refused to accede to her mother's wishes in marriage. He himself tried to marry a rich widow, but she was too perspicacious, and he had to be content with someone neither as rich nor as beautiful.
          T. xx–xxii, xxv–xxvii, xxix–xxxix, xli, xlviii, li, lii

Michael HARTLEY, an Antinomian and Jacobin leveller, was a visionary. One day, while working near Nunnely Priory, he saw thousands of soldiers drilling in the park; they moved towards Fieldhead and were enveloped in smoke; when it cleared they had vanished. This signified civil conflict, he said. He believed that Robert Moore should be chosen as an oblation and sacrifice, and it was he who wounded him as Moore was travelling home from Stilbro'. He died of delirium tremens, and Robert gave his widow a guinea for his burial. *The Luddites who attacked Mr Cartwright's mill in April 1812 assembled in a field between Roe Head and Kirklees Priory.*

S. i, xiii, xxx, xxxvii

Mr HATFIELD, rector of Horton, was captivated by Rosalie Murray. In church he was splendidly robed and rather dandyish; his addresses were primarily stylistic performances; he attached great importance to ritual, conformity, and the approval of the upper classes. Poor parishioners were afraid of him; he was apt to criticize and discourage them. Neither was he always humane to animals. After his rejection by Miss Murray, he was indifferent to her. He married an elderly spinster, for her wealth (according to Rosalie). *Mr Weston is his obvious foil.* *A.* ix–xi, xiv, xv, xvii, xxii

Helen HATTERSLEY, daughter of Helen Huntingdon's friend Milicent, married Helen's son Arthur. The two had known each other from early childhood. *T.* xxxi, xxxii, xxxv, xlii, liii

Ralph HATTERSLEY, one of Huntingdon's dissolute friends, and a baiter of Lord Lowborough, married Milicent Hargrave. She was the kind of wife who suited him: she let him do as he wished. He was the kind of husband Mrs Hargrave wanted her daughter to have: he was the son of a rich banker. He was fond of his children, and began to realize that he had to reform for their sake, as well as his wife's. Huntingdon's unhappy marriage and his early death brought him to his senses. He settled in the country as a gentleman farmer, inherited his father's wealth, and became famous for his noble breed of horses. *T.* xxi, xxii, xxv, xxx–xxxiii, xxxv, xxxviii, xxxix,
xlii, xlix, l

HAY was a village two miles from Thornfield Hall. It was along Hay Lane that Jane Eyre first saw Mr Rochester, and went to his assistance. A gipsy camp on Hay Common gave him the idea of appearing as 'one of the old Mother Bunches', in order to tell the fortunes of the young ladies who were staying at the Hall. *The village was imagined in hilly country near 'Millcote', probably not far from Birstall. There seems to be no justification for identifying it with Wath near Norton Conyers. See* Edward Fairfax ROCHESTER *and* THORNFIELD HALL. *J.* xi–xiii, xviii, xxiii, xxiv, xxvii

HEATHCLIFF (the only name given him by the Earnshaws, after a son who died in childhood; *see pp. 208 and 217 for its possible literary origin and its significance in the novel*) was brought to Wuthering Heights from Liverpool by old Mr Earnshaw, who had found him starving in the streets. He was a dirty, ragged, gipsy-looking child. Catherine Earnshaw and her father took to him, but Hindley hated and bullied him. He remained sullen and apparently insensible, as if he had been hardened to punishment. After his father's death, Hindley Earnshaw tyrannized and degraded him, but he was happy with Catherine, and they were free to roam as they pleased. He remained proud and resentful, and was soon very jealous of the friendship which sprang up between her and Edgar Linton. He made no effort to improve himself and, after overhearing Catherine say that she preferred him to Edgar but that it would degrade her to marry him, left suddenly.

More than three years elapsed before his return. He had a foreign accent and money to spare. Personally, he seemed much improved. His first thoughts turned to Catherine, now married to Edgar Linton. She was delighted to meet him but, realizing his avarice and his fierce thirst for revenge, warned her infatuated sister-in-law against him. For his own ends he paid liberally to stay at Wuthering Heights, much to the satisfaction of Hindley Earnshaw, who lost so much money in gambling with him that he wanted time to win it back for his son Hareton. When Hindley died, it was found that all his property was mortgaged to Heathcliff. The latter's visits to Thrushcross Grange had inflamed Edgar's anger and jealousy. Though he hated her, Heathcliff eloped with Isabella Linton; possibly, he thought, the marriage could lead to his acquisition of Linton's property. When he returned and heard of Catherine's illness, he continued to meet her not long before her death, and express the love which had devoured him for years. He prayed fervently for her recovery. His treatment of Isabella was brutal and pitiless, and she was fortunate to escape from him. After her death, her son Linton came to Thrushcross Grange, but Heathcliff claimed him immediately, found him a tutor, and took every opportunity to secure his engagement to Catherine Linton. Terrorized by his father, Linton decoyed her and Nelly Dean into Wuthering Heights. Mrs Dean was not freed until Catherine had given way and married Linton out of pity, when her father was within an inch of death. By ensuring that his dying son made his will in his favour, Heathcliff achieved his ambition. The property of his rival Edgar Linton became his. Thrushcross Grange was let, and Catherine Heathcliff continued to live at Wuthering Heights with Hareton, whom Heathcliff had deliberately brutalized. He behaved abominably to Catherine, and destroyed all her books. He believed firmly in ghosts; for eighteen years, he said, he had been continually disturbed by her mother's spirit, and tortured by his inability to see her. He had tried to sleep in her room, but she had driven him out. As his end approached, he was possessed with the thought and awareness of Catherine; he had nearly attained to heaven; his soul's bliss, he said, killed his body. When her husband was buried beside her, Heathcliff had persuaded the sexton to open her coffin; he had then struck the boards loose on the other side, and given instructions that, when he was buried in the same grave, his own should be slid out on her side. He died in the haunted bedroom, the rain driving in on the bedclothes, through the open window, his eyes fixed in a 'frightful, life-like gaze of exultation', and his parted lips and sharp white teeth set as it were in a sneer. *W*.

Catherine HEATHCLIFF. *See* Catherine LINTON. *W*.

Linton HEATHCLIFF was born in the south of England a few months after his mother's escape from Wuthering Heights. When she died, more than twelve years later, his uncle Edgar, anxious to be his guardian, as his mother had wished, took him to Thrushcross Grange. His father claimed him immediately, however. He was a fretful, ailing boy, the laughing-stock of Hareton. Heathcliff encouraged the friendship which developed between him and Catherine Linton, in the hope that he would acquire the Grange on Linton's death. When this seemed imminent, the youth was terrorized into acting as a decoy, and Ellen Dean was not allowed to return to Thrushcross Grange until the desired marriage between Linton and her protégée had taken place. So great was Catherine's anguish at being separated from her dying father that Linton was spurred to free her. Despite her insistence, Heathcliff allowed no medical help, and within a few days Linton was dead. *W*. xvii–xxviii, xxx

Caroline HELSTONE lived with her uncle, Mr Helstone, at Briarfield rectory. Loneliness made her seek the company of her friendly cousins, Robert and Hortense Moore. At the age of eighteen she loved Robert; but for his preoccupation with business worries and affairs, he could willingly have fallen in love with her. She wished that he would be less blunt, less of the proud inflexible Coriolanus, with his workmen. Caroline was very attractive; Jessie Yorke admired her, as

Martin did later. Her parents had separated soon after her birth; she had never seen her mother, and her father died when he was young.

When her uncle, after quarrelling with Robert on political issues, forbad Caroline's visits to Hollow's Cottage (where Hortense had taught her needlework and French), she spent her time in study, charitable missions, and exercise. She wished to be a governess. To cheer her, Mr Helstone introduced her to Miss Shirley Keeldar of Fieldhead. The growing certainty that Robert was courting Shirley made Caroline utterly miserable. Shirley's companionship helped her on social occasions such as the Whitsuntide fête. That evening Mr Helstone asked Shirley to stay at the rectory in his absence, and the two girls, full of anxiety for Robert, followed the Luddites, to see what action they took at Hollow's Mill. The next day Caroline's depression was almost Calvinistic; soon she was thinking seriously about society's lack of concern for single women without occupation. Her illness brought Mrs Pryor to nurse her. Caroline's joy at learning that Mrs Pryor was her long-lost mother accelerated her recovery. Louis Moore thought her virtues milder, more perfect than Shirley's, and exquisitely fitted to his brother's domestic habits and fastidiousness. Thanks to Martin Yorke's ingenuity, Caroline was able to see Robert at Briarmains when he was recovering from his gunshot wound. He had long realized his error in aspiring to Shirley's wealth to salvage his business, and resolved to marry for love. Caroline had not ceased to love him. When the repeal of the Orders in Council created prospects of security (he had thought of emigration), Robert did not delay his proposal, and they were soon married. *Ellen Nussey thought Caroline a portrait of herself. The change in the colour of the eyes from brown (xiii, xiv) to blue (xxiv, xxx) suggests that such an association (see p. 310) was overlooked, and that Caroline was identified with Anne Brontë after her death (see BST. lxxi). This inconsistency of detail illustrates both the tendency to improvise in Shirley and hasty revision.*   S. v–vii, ix–xxvi, xxix–xxxv, xxxvii

Matthewson HELSTONE, rector of Briarfield, ought to have been a soldier. He was short and erect, with broad shoulders, and 'a hawk's head, beak, and eye'. He generally wore a Rehoboam or shovel-hat. A widower, he had never had the qualities required of a good husband, especially by a quiet wife (*see* Mary CAVE); and he was a poor companion for his niece Caroline Helstone. In his lighter moods he enjoyed feminine society; occasionally he thought of marrying Hannah Sykes. Every penny of his inheritance was devoted to the building and endow-

ment of a church in his native Lancashire village. He was a high
Tory, and never flinched in coming to Robert Moore's aid when
Hollow's Mill was in danger from the Luddites. Moore's outspokenness
against the war with France led to a quarrel, and Helstone forbad
Caroline to meet him; in the end, when the repeal of the Orders in
Council ensured Robert's industrial future, he consented to their
marriage. *Charlotte Brontë drew Helstone to some extent from her
father, more from what he had told her of the Rev. Hammond
Roberson, one of his predecessors at Hartshead. Roberson's opposition
to the militancy of the mill-workers was strong, and his life was
threatened. From the profits of his boarding-school at Heald's Hall,
where he lived, he built Christ Church, Liversedge (1812–16). Charlotte
saw him at the consecration of a church when she was ten, and remembered his 'stern, martial air' (21.9.49). He was more estimable than
Mr Helstone; see W. M. Heald, 8.1.50.*   S. i, ii, iv, vi–xiv, xvi,
xvii, xix–xxii, xxiv, xxxiv, xxxvii

Frances Evans HENRI was born in Geneva. Her mother was English;
her father, a Swiss pastor. After the death of her parents, she lived
with her aunt Julienne in Brussels. In order to earn money for
continuing her education, she learnt lace-mending. At Mlle Reuter's
she taught needlework, though she had little control over her pupils;
she also attended William Crimsworth's English classes, her aim
being to teach French in England. She was an industrious, imaginative, and independent student. Her master's increasing interest in
her, and Mlle's jealousy, led to her dismissal. Shortly afterwards her
aunt died. Frances became a teacher of French in the first English
school for girls in Brussels. After marrying Crimsworth, she set up her
own school. Her increasing confidence, firmness, and enterprise made
it a great success; it attracted pupils from abroad and from families of
distinction. Both she and her husband worked long hours and had
little leisure. Victor was born in the third year of their marriage. To
increase their common interests, she persuaded William, who was
still a college professor, to devote one hour in the afternoon to teaching
in her school. In ten years they had earned their independence, and
were able to retire to England. *In her one feels that Charlotte portrayed
the kind of principal she had hoped to become. For the name 'Evans',
see* Miss TEMPLE.   P. xii–xix, xxi–xxv

HOLLOW'S COTTAGE was the home of Robert Moore and his sister
Hortense. He had converted it from a dingy house into a neat white
tasteful residence, 'a snug nest for content and contemplation'. It

stood in a rather secluded spot not far from Hollow's Mill, *and may have been suggested by the house near Rawfolds Mill or by a white cottage near Hunsworth Mill (see next note).*   S. ii, v–vii, x, xi, xiii, xx, xxiii, xxxv

HOLLOW'S MILL was situated below a copse in the Hollow, a valley near Fieldhead, in the parish of Briarfield. It belonged to Shirley, and was rented by the cloth-manufacturer Robert Moore, who courageously and successfully defended it against a Luddite attack. *The Hollow is the valley below Oakwell Hall. Hollow's Mill derived, however, from Joshua Taylor's mill at Hunsworth, two miles to the west. The Luddite story was based on local accounts of the attack on Rawfolds Mill, further south between Cleckheaton and Heckmondwike, on 11 April 1812.*   S. i, ii, v, viii, ix, xi, xvi, xviii, xix, xxii, xxxvii

Paulina Mary HOME was very tiny as a child. She was motherless, and always fretting for her father when with Mrs Bretton. She liked having her own way, and was precociously independent; only Graham Bretton pleased her. She soon joined her father in Europe. Unlike her cousin Ginevra Fanshawe's, her beauty, as she grew up, was not so much in complexion and features as in charm of personality and mind. Her eyes were eloquent, and the expression of her countenance winningly varied. Her French was faultless. Graham found her increasingly attractive. She was devoted and most dutiful to her father, but, though he could not part from her, and the thought of her marriage to Dr Bretton roused sharp animosity, her persistence and charm won the day. Her influence preserved the happiness of both, and she was blessed in her marriage and children. *Ellen Nussey thought that Fanny Whipp, the niece of the Hudsons with whom she and Charlotte stayed at Easton House near Bridlington in 1839, was the prototype of the child Paulina; Winifred Gérin thinks it was Julia, daughter of Mrs Gaskell.*   V. i–iii, xvi, xxiii–xxvii, xxxii, xxxvii, xxxviii

Mr HOME, afterwards Count de Bassompierre (*see p. 274*), was of Scottish and French descent. He spoke with a northern accent, was hard-featured but unusually sensitive, and spent much time experimenting in a laboratory. His butterfly wife (Ginevra Fanshawe's aunt) did not care for this; their marriage was uncongenial, and they separated by mutual consent, Mrs Home dying soon afterwards from a fever caused by over-exertion at a ball. Mr Home was not very practical; on medical advice he decided to travel. The result was that

his daughter Polly was left with the widow of his friend and distant
relative Dr Bretton. From his mother's family, Mr Home inherited
estates (and a title) on the Continent. According to Ginevra Fanshawe,
his home was in France. He and Paulina stayed for a long period at
the Hôtel Crécy in Villette. The Count was so attached to his 'little
treasure' that he could not part with her, even in marriage. His
opposition to Dr Bretton was unusually strong, but it was inevitable
that he had to accede to his daughter's wishes. He died 'in the fulness
of years'.   *V.* i–iii, vi, ix, xviii, xxiii–xxvii, xxxii, xxxvii,
                                                                    xxxviii, xl

Mrs Zillah HORSFALL was the most reliable nurse employed by the
elder Mr MacTurk. She was a dragon. Her weakness was gin, and
Martin Yorke took advantage of it for the sake of Caroline Helstone.
                                                         S. xxxii–xxxv

HORTENSE, a pupil at Mlle Reuter's, was stout and of middle size.
She had luxuriantly plaited and twisted rich chestnut locks, and a
roguish laughing eye.   *P.* x, xi, xiii, xiv

HORTON LODGE, near O——, was the home of the Murrays, where
Agnes Grey held her second appointment as governess. It was about
seventy miles from her home, and her main journey there was by
coach and train. The parish church, where the new curate Mr Weston
preached, was nearly two miles away. *This is the church at Little*
Ouseburn, which Anne Brontë attended with the Robinsons, when she
was governess at Thorp Green Hall from 1841 to 1845. The journey
from Haworth via Keighley, Leeds, and York, would be between sixty
and seventy miles. Thorp Green Hall, the original of 'Horton Lodge',
was destroyed by fire at the beginning of the twentieth century.
                                       A. vi–ix, xii, xiv–xviii, xx

Hunsden Yorke HUNSDEN, a manufacturer and mill-owner, was a
bachelor who lived in Grove Street in the suburbs of X——. He was
Radical in outlook, blunt and outspoken, widely read, particularly in
French and German literature, and partial to Scriptural reference.
He did not hesitate to stir up public criticism of Edward Crimsworth,
and advised his brother William Crimsworth to use his knowledge of
French to better advantage in Brussels. When Hunsden visited
Brussels the following autumn, bringing news of Edward's bank-
ruptcy, William found his conversation 'harsh, stringent, bitter', like
a draught of Peruvian bark. Yet Hunsden beneath his 'husk' was a
gentleman; he had not only bought the picture of William's mother
when Crimsworth Hall and its contents were sold but brought it over

for the sake of one who would treasure it. His actions belied his words; after abusing William later for his prosperity, he sent some of his cousins to Mrs Crimsworth's school in Brussels, and even gave Crimsworth advice on investments. After his father's death, he inherited Hunsden Wood, where he lived near the Crimsworths in their early retirement. Here he entertained free trade advocates from Birmingham and Manchester, and continental politicians with liberal sentiments akin to his own. He travelled abroad a great deal, spending part of each winter in London; whenever he was at home, he visited the Crimsworths two or three times a week. He gave their son Victor a dog, which was named Yorke after him; and once disclosed that he had been in love with a mysterious Lucia. *He is the precursor of Hiram Yorke in* Shirley, *and originated from Joshua Taylor of Gomersal, father of Charlotte's friend Mary. Mr Taylor was a practical man of Radical views, who travelled much and read widely; business took him to Brussels, and he lent Charlotte French novels (20.8.40). He owned a mill at Hunsworth, and after his death in 1840 his family moved from The Red House to live near it; hence his fictional name.*

P. iii–vi, xxi, xxii, xxiv, xxv

HUNSDEN WOOD was an Elizabethan mansion in a wooded valley below Daisy Lane. *See the previous note and* DAISY LANE.

P. iii, xxv

Arthur HUNTINGDON was the son of a rich old friend of Mr Maxwell, and 'a bit wildish'. He had not returned long from the Continent when he met Helen in London. She found him charming, particularly after being plagued by Mr Boarham. Blind to her aunt's warnings, she was ready to overlook Huntingdon's faults in the certainty that she could reform him. He was ready to leave his pleasure-seeking friends for her, he declared; soon they were married. Their honeymoon showed his selfishness; Helen was not allowed to stay long anywhere or make acquaintances, particularly in Paris and Rome. Huntingdon was afraid (as he confessed) that he might meet some of his lady friends, and was not happy until she was safely installed as mistress of Grassdale Manor. Helen was too religious for him. He admitted to an affair with Lady F—— (xxiv) when he was young. After quarrelling, the married couple went to London, but Helen was soon sent home. This was the first of a number of separations, usually prolonged, which enabled Huntingdon to be a man of the world again. In the shooting-season some of his closest friends came to Grassdale. Helen's devotion to her baby son roused his intense jealousy. He continually squandered his fortune in London, and used his wife's income to pay off his debts. More and more he had recourse to the bottle; his amours with Lady Lowborough came to light; and his absence at length brought relief to Helen. He and his friends found pleasure in encouraging his son Arthur to tipple and swear like a grown-up. It was this threat to her son which made Helen prepare for their escape. Huntingdon appointed a Miss Myers to be Arthur's governess, and the suspicions she aroused made Helen decide to leave without delay. Afterwards all the best servants left; even Miss Myers did not stay long. Huntingdon became seriously ill as a result of a fall while hunting, and Helen returned to nurse him. He recovered somewhat, but insistence on strong drink resulted in a relapse. The thought of death, and of judgment after death, filled him with horror before his final, painful collapse. *Branwell Brontë's intemperance undoubtedly caused Anne to write* The Tenant of Wildfell Hall, *but he was no Huntingdon, who undoubtedly originated from other sources, including Thomas Moore's biography of Lord Byron. See pp. 244–5.*　　　　　　　　　　T. v, xvi–xliii, xlvii–xlix

Arthur HUNTINGDON was about five when his mother brought him to Wildfell Hall to escape his father's evil influence. By the addition of tartaremetic, she had given him a complete distaste for all intoxicating liquors. He was very fond of Sancho, Gilbert Markham's black and white setter. Arthur lived up to his mother's hopes and expectations. After marrying Helen Hattersley, he resided at Grassdale Manor.　　　T. ii, iii, v–vii, ix, x, xiii, xv, xxviii–xxx, xxxii, xxxiii,
xxxv–xxxvii, xxxix–xli, xliii–xlv, xlvii, xlix, lii, liii

Helen HUNTINGDON, whose narrative began on 1 June 1821, after her first visit to London (xvi), lived before marriage with her aunt and uncle, the Maxwells, at Staningley Hall. Although her father was alive (xx, xxxi), they had been her guardians since her mother's death, when she was a small girl. All Mrs Maxwell's sage advice was lost on Helen after she met Arthur Huntingdon in London. She believed in his essential goodness, and that she had been providentially chosen to reform him. She was eighteen. After their marriage, she found increasingly, whatever his promises to amend, how dissolute he and his friends were, how false he was, and what a heavy drinker he had become. In Hattersley she could see grounds for hope; she could admire and feel sorry for Lord Lowborough (so much so that she refused to divulge his wife's infidelity); but in her husband she at last saw nothing but depravity and hypocrisy. She hated him. She was proof against Hargrave's advances. When her husband and his friends amused themselves by encouraging her little son Arthur to tipple and swear (to 'make a man' of him), she took steps which led ultimately to their escape with Rachel and to their asylum in Wildfell Hall; she had thought of emigrating. She adopted the name of Graham, her mother's before marriage, and hoped to maintain her separate ménage by the sale of her paintings. Gilbert Markham and she fell in love; his jealousy of Mr Lawrence (her brother, the owner of Wildfell Hall) made her give him the manuscript of her life history from 1821 to read. They agreed not to meet. Helen returned to nurse her husband during the last weeks of his life. Her inheritance of Staningley Hall from her uncle increased Markham's sense of his social inferiority, and but for chance and Helen's loyalty and initiative their marriage might not have taken place. It proved to be a happy one, and they were blessed with 'promising' children. *Helen owes something to Lady Byron; her faith reflects Anne Brontë's. See pp. 234, 245.*   T.

Mrs HURST, Paulina's nurse Harriet, was her servant and companion at the Hôtel Crécy.   *V.* i, xxiii, xxv

The Hon. Blanche INGRAM of Ingram Park, twenty miles from Thornfield Hall and on the border of another county, attended Mr Rochester's party with her brother, Lord Ingram, her sister, the Hon. Mary, and her mother, Lady Ingram. They were all tall. Miss Ingram had been considered the belle of the evening when she attended Mr Rochester's Christmas ball and party six or seven years earlier, at the age of eighteen. She had dark eyes and black glossy curls, and was altogether 'majestic'. Her French was excellent, and she was an accomplished pianist and singer. Unlike her brother and sister, she was vivacious; she was intent on capturing Mr Rochester. She knew that she did not love him; she was haughty and domineering, and he did not love her. To excite the jealousy of Jane Eyre, with whom he was in love, he talked of his forthcoming marriage to Miss Ingram. He severed connections with her family by making them believe that his fortune was much reduced. Then he proposed to Jane. *The Ingrams and their views on governesses owe much to Charlotte's observations at Stonegappe (8.6.39, 30.6.39).*   J. xvi–xviii, xx, xxi, xxiii, xxiv

ISABELLE was a boarder at Mme Beck's. She was an odd, blunt creature, who warned Lucy Snowe that she would burn in hell fire if she remained Protestant. Lucy had nursed her in sickness.

V. ix, xxxviii

JOHN was a servant at Thornfield Hall; his wife Mary was the cook. At Ferndean Manor Mr Rochester would have no one but old John and Mary to look after him. *J.* xi, xii, xv–xvii, xxv, xxvi, xxxvi–xxxviii

JOHN was one of Helen Huntingdon's servants at Grassdale Manor. *T.* xxiv, xxxiii, xliv

JOHN, Shirley's foreman, looked after the animals at Fieldhead, including Tartar and her horse Zoë (*named after Mme Heger!*).

S. xv, xx, xxii, xxviii

JOSEPH was a rough and tough lantern-jawed farmhand, who worked for the Earnshaws and Heathcliff many years, and lived at Wuthering Heights. According to Ellen Dean, he was the 'wearisomest self-righteous Pharisee that ever ransacked a Bible to rake the promises to himself and fling the curses to his neighbours'. His religion was Calvinistic: 'all warks togither for gooid to them as is chozzen, and piked out fro' th' rubbidge'. He loved to sermonize and hector tenants and labourers, frowned on fun and rejoicing, and believed in witch-craft. Isabella Linton, after her marriage to Heathcliff, found Joseph odious; Mr Lockwood thought he looked 'vinegar-faced'. In the assur-ance that Heathcliff would suffer eternal damnation for it, Joseph derived pleasure from the brutalization of Hareton Hindley. Heath-cliff's death gave him great satisfaction: the Devil had 'harried off his soul', and Wuthering Heights was restored to the Earnshaw family.

W. i–iii, v, vii–x, xii, xiii, xvii–xx, xxiii, xxiv, xxix–xxxiv

Shirley KEELDAR. *See* SHIRLEY.

Mr KENNETH, the doctor in attendance at Wuthering Heights and Thrushcross Grange, lived at Gimmerton. *W.* v, viii–x, xii–xiv, xvii, xxviii, xxxiv

Mrs KING was the landlady of William Crimsworth's lodgings in X——. *P.* iii–vi

M. KINT, a poor, hard-worked Belgian usher, was described by M. Pelet, his master, as a beast of burden (*bête de somme*). *P.* viii, xi

M. Victor KINT was Mme Beck's brother, and visited the school when their mother was staying with her for health reasons. *V.* xxii, xxxviii, xxxix, xli

Aurelia KOSLOW, a fräulein of German and Russian descent, was sent to Mlle Reuter's to 'finish her education'. She was deplorably ignorant and illiterate after twelve years' schooling, and had few compensatory features. She was physically unattractive, and rather dirty, but did her utmost to attract William Crimsworth's attention in objectionable ways when he was teaching. *Like Adèle Dronsart and Juanna Trista, she is drawn from life, and plays no part in the story. They represent three of the most disagreeable pupils Charlotte Brontë remembered at the Pensionnat Heger.*   *P.* xii

L—— was a large town between Gateshead Hall and Lowood School. Here the coach which was taking Jane Eyre to the school stopped to allow the passengers to dine.   *J.* v

L——, a market town, was seven miles from Wildfell Hall. Gilbert Markham was on his way there when he savagely attacked Mr Lawrence. Eliza Millward and Fergus Markham married two of its important citizens.   *T.* xiii, xiv, xliv, xlviii, li, liii

Mr LANGWEILIG, a German Moravian minister, *originated from Mr Lauten of the Moravian Church at Gomersal* (BST. *viii*).   *S.* vii

Frederick LAWRENCE, Helen Huntingdon's brother, lived at Woodford in Lindenhope. He was the owner of Wildfell Hall. There he prepared rooms for his sister's retreat when she escaped with her young son and Rachel from her husband at Grassdale Manor. Frederick's visits to Helen aroused Gilbert Markham to such a pitch of jealousy that he attacked him viciously with his whip, causing a severe head injury. After reading Helen's story, Gilbert was contrite, and Frederick forgave him more readily than he deserved. Gilbert warned him against Jane Wilson to some effect, for Lawrence married Esther Hargrave. He was puzzled by Gilbert's failure to make inquiries about Helen when she left Wildfell Hall. In his view, Gilbert's apparent calm justified his taking no action to promote a marriage which by worldly standards would be deemed a *mésalliance.*

   T. i, iv–vii, ix, x, xii, xiv, xv, xxxi, xxxix, xli, xliii–li, liii

LEAH was the housemaid at Thornfield Hall.   *J.* xi, xii, xvi, xvii,
                                                     xxii, xxvi, xxxvi

Léonie LEDRU was a pupil at Mlle Reuter's *pensionnat*. She was 'a diminutive, sharp-featured, and parchment-skinned creature of quick wits, frail conscience, and indurated feelings; a lawyer-like thing'.

                                                         P. xiv, xvi

M. LEDRU was the music master at Mlle Reuter's. She would rather trust William Crimsworth, young and single, with her girls than M. Ledru, who was married and nearly fifty.   *P.* ix

Mrs LEIGH lived in a grand mansion near Miss Marchmont's. Her housekeeper Mrs Barrett had been Lucy Snowe's nurse. When Lucy was visiting Mrs Barrett, Mrs Leigh did not recognize her, although they had been schoolfellows. Lucy saw that the unintellectual schoolgirl had grown into a good-natured and beautiful woman. It was her French (spoken with an incorrigibly bad accent as in her schooldays) and that of her little boy that led Mrs Barrett to talk about 'English-women in foreign families' and possibilities which Lucy had in mind when she decided to go abroad.   *V*. v

Mr and Mrs LINTON lived at Thrushcross Grange. During her five weeks' stay there, Catherine Earnshaw created such a good impression that she became their guest again, with disastrous results, when she was convalescing from the illness which developed rapidly as a result of her rejection of Heathcliff and his sudden departure. The aged couple caught the fever, and died within a few days of each other.   *W*. vi–ix, xvi

Catherine LINTON was born two hours before her mother's death. 'She was the most winning thing that ever brought sunshine into a desolate house: a real beauty in face, with the Earnshaws' handsome dark eyes, but the Lintons' fair skin and small features, and yellow curling hair.' She was more gentle than her mother. The view of Penistone Crags one evening attracted her, and this led to her first excursions outside Thrushcross Grange Park, and visits to Wuthering Heights. When Linton Heathcliff was taken there, his father did everything he could to strengthen their attachment; when he knew that Edgar Linton was dying, he used trickery to compel their marriage. Catherine managed to escape and see her father before his death. Linton died not many days later, and Heathcliff treated her harshly. He was not going to 'nurture her in luxury and idleness'; she had to work for her 'bread'. He destroyed her books, all except those which Hareton had taken in the hope of educating himself and win-ning her esteem. Hareton persuaded her not to arouse Heathcliff's wrath, as she had done, by plain speaking. Both had the eyes of Catherine Earnshaw, and Heathcliff found this disarming; he no longer had the will to afflict the last representatives of the two families he had sought to destroy. With Catherine's change of heart towards Hareton and an eagerness to help him read and improve, a new spirit prevailed at Wuthering Heights, the signs of which were visible both outside and within, as Mr Lockwood, who had previously been attracted by Catherine's beauty, was quick to notice when he returned after Heathcliff's death. She and Hareton, now eighteen and twenty-three, were to marry, he learned, and move to the Grange.

W. ii–iv, xiv, xvi–xix, xxi–xxxiv

Edgar LINTON was light-haired and fair, *and in most respects an obvious foil to Heathcliff*, who was soon jealous of him when he visited Catherine Earnshaw after her enforced stay at Thrushcross Grange. It was because marriage with Heathcliff would have been degrading that she preferred the young master of the Grange. Until Heathcliff returned, their marriage was happy. Then Catherine's ecstasy, Heathcliff's indignation, and finally Edgar's threat to have him removed were too much for her temper; frenzy led to delirium from which she never completely recovered. For weeks Edgar nursed her most devotedly. After her death, he did everything possible to avoid meeting Heathcliff; he gave up his magistracy, ceased to attend church, and hardly went beyond his park, except for solitary rambles on the moors when few people were about, or to visit Catherine's grave. He never forgave his sister Isabella for marrying Heathcliff, yet he responded to her wish that he would take care of her son Linton when she died, and was grieved when his father claimed him. The friendship between his daughter Catherine and Linton Heathcliff made him wish to change his will; he acted too late, however. Heathcliff had taken steps to balk him, and Edgar Linton died ignorant of his guile and of the treacherous means he had employed to enforce a marriage between Catherine and Linton.   *W*. v–xvii, xix–xxviii

Isabella LINTON at the age of eighteen fell in love with Heathcliff after his long absence. For reasons of avarice and revenge he was ready to court her, though he despised her. They eloped, and were absent for two months. He treated Isabella with cruelty and contempt. Edgar had been appalled at her infatuation, and never forgave her. She escaped from Wuthering Heights, but fear of Heathcliff drove her to the south of England, where her son Linton was born. She died a little more than twelve years later.   *W*. v–viii, x–xiv, xvi–xxi

Mr LLOYD was the apothecary called in by Mrs Reed to attend the servants when they were ailing. (For herself and her children she employed a physician.) He came to examine Jane Eyre after her fit, and advised that she be sent to school.   *J*. iii, viii

Mr LOCKWOOD was Heathcliff's tenant at Thrushcross Grange. He visited Heathcliff at Wuthering Heights, was snowbound there, suffered a nightmare, and encouraged his housekeeper, Ellen Dean, to tell him the story of Catherine Linton, or Earnshaw, and its consequences, while he was ill for several weeks at the end of 1801 and beginning of 1802. The following September, while on his way

north for the shooting-season, he called on Ellen and heard the story of Heathcliff's death. *See pp. 226–7.*   *W*. i–iv, vii, ix–x, xiv–xv,
xxx–xxxi, xxxii, xxxiv

LONDON. Rosalie Murray wished to live in London. She looked forward to its gaieties when she returned from her honeymoon abroad with Sir Thomas Ashby, but was so keen on meeting her old friend Harry Meltham there that Sir Thomas took offence and cut short their stay.   *A*. xv, xvii, xxii, xxiii

It was in London that Helen met Arthur Huntingdon and, despite her aunt's warnings, decided that he was the man of her choice and that she was the woman to save him from his errors and associates. He returned to them at intervals, and sometimes for prolonged periods; but so much did his character deteriorate, and such was his influence on his son that eventually she wished he would remain absent.

After incurring heavy debts through gambling and excessive drinking in town, Lord Lowborough resolved to reform; his salvation lay, he thought, in marrying someone rich enough to secure his future and endowed with sufficient sweetness and goodness to make him tolerable.

Despite her mother's schemes, Esther Hargrave returned from her first London season heart-whole and unengaged.   *T*. xvi, xvii,
xxii, xxiv, xxv, xxix, xxxi, xxxvi, xli

Isabella (Linton), Heathcliff's wife, escaped from the hatred and horrors of Wuthering Heights, and fled south, never to return. A few months later Linton Heathcliff was born. Their home was near London.

After his illness at Thrushcross Grange, Mr Lockwood planned to spend six months in London.   *W*. xvii, xxx, xxxi

Georgiana Reed was much admired in London, and would have eloped with Lord Edwin Vere, had not her sister informed against her. John Reed, unable to obtain money to pay his debts, died suddenly at his chambers; suicide was suspected. Mr Rochester planned to spend some time in London with Jane Eyre after their marriage. *See* Mr BRIGGS.   *J*. x, xi, xxi, xxv

Robert Moore was often in London for a week or two. Later, after the attack on his mill, he found time to reflect and meet people in town. The result was a change of heart. Self-interest was not enough; 'to respect himself, a man must believe he renders justice to his fellow-men'. He would still oppose mob violence, in the interest of the workers.   *S*. xii, xxv, xxvii, xxviii, xxx

On his way to Belgium, William Crimsworth spent a night or two at a respectable inn in London. Here for the first time he heard the great bell of St Paul's striking midnight in 'deep, deliberate tones'. From the small, narrow window of his room he first saw the dome, looming through the mist.   *P.* vii

Lucy Snowe stayed at the 'respectable old-fashioned inn' in London which had been recommended to her by her old nurse Mrs Barrett because Lucy's uncles Charles and Wilmot had often stayed there. *The inn in both novels is the Chapter Coffee House in Paternoster Row, which Mr Brontë knew in his younger days, and where he stayed with Charlotte and Emily and the Taylors, on their way to Brussels in February 1842. Once again Charlotte recalls* the 'deep, low, mighty tone' of St Paul's striking midnight, and the sight of the dome the next morning. *There are other recollections of this visit and of later ones.* Lucy entered St Paul's, mounted to the dome, and saw the city, its river and bridges, Westminster, and the Temple Gardens. She walked in the Strand, and up Cornhill, and dared the perils of crossings. (Since then she had seen the West End, the parks, and fine squares, but she preferred the city.) Late that evening she was rowed to the packet bound for Boue-Marine. *It was in 1848 that Charlotte and Anne Brontë made their memorable journey to London, to visit Charlotte's publishers, Smith, Elder and Co. at 65 Cornhill. See p. 37. On her return to Brussels in January 1843 she drove to London Bridge Wharf, after reaching Euston Station at 10 p.m., two hours late. A waterman rowed her in the darkness to the packet which was to leave the next morning for Ostend.*   *V.* v, vi

Lord LOWBOROUGH lost his fiancée Caroline when he dissipated a fortune in gambling. Two or three years later, after continued losses, he decided to marry someone who could repair his fortune and overcome his addiction to strong drink. He gave up gambling and drinking, but was completely duped when he married Annabella Wilmot. They separated. Annabella had no affection for her children; and he lived with them (a boy and a nominal daughter) in seclusion at his castle in the north of England. His second wife was very different from his first; she lacked wealth, beauty, and accomplishments, but was endowed with good sense, integrity, piety, benevolence, and cheerfulness.

         T. xviii–xxii, xxvi, xxvii, xxxi, xxxiii–xxxv, xxxvii, xxxviii, l

LOWOOD SCHOOL had been founded by Naomi Brocklehurst as a charity school for clergymen's daughters. Her son was the treasurer and manager; Miss Temple was the superintendent. Her staff included Miss Smith, Miss Scatcherd, and Mme Pierrot, with Miss Miller as under-teacher. *Its general conditions closely resembled those of the Clergy Daughters' School, Cowan Bridge, which Charlotte Brontë and three of her sisters attended soon after it was opened in 1824.* There were nearly eighty pupils, ranging in age from nine to twenty. All had to dress plainly and uniformly; meals were poor and inadequate. After a severe winter came fog and the 'low fever' epidemic. An inquiry into its causes resulted in a new school, better situated and more liberally run. *The new school at Casterton, near Kirkby Lonsdale, was not opened until 1833. See* BROCKLEHURST *and* BURNS. *Charlotte's description of the school situation, 'as unhealthy as it was picturesque – low, damp, beautiful with wood and water' (28.8.48), though rather inaccurately based on childhood recollections, indicates the source of the fictional name.*　　　　　　　*J.* iv–x, xiii, xxix

LOWTON (*Kirkby Lonsdale, Westmorland*) was the nearest town to Lowood School. Jane Eyre's visits to the post office and her farewell to Bessie (Mrs Leaven) at the door of the Brocklehurst Arms in Lowton are linked with her appointment as governess at Thornfield Hall.

J. vii, x

Sarah Martha LUPTON was 'a tall, well-made, full-formed, dashingly-dressed young woman', with whom Yorke Hunsden danced at Edward Crimsworth's birthday party, much to the delight of her mother (a stout person in a turban), though William Crimsworth 'soon saw that the grounds for maternal self-congratulation were slight indeed'. Hunsden had hastened to secure Sarah Martha for the dance when he saw Sam Waddy approaching her.　　　　　　　*P.* iii

Sir George LYNN (M.P. for Millcote) and Lady Lynn were guests at the Thornfield party. Their sons, Henry and Frederick, were 'very dashing sparks'.　　　　　　　*J.* xvi–xviii, xx

M—— was the coach-stop most convenient for Grassdale Manor.

T. xxxix, xliii, li, lii

Mr MACARTHEY succeeded Mr Malone at Briarfield, and did his country as much credit as his predecessor had done it discredit. Dissenters disturbed him unduly, but his parish work was thorough, and the schools flourished as a result of his exertions. *The Rev. A. B. Nicholls, who became Mr Brontë's curate at Haworth in May 1845, 'triumphed in his own character' (28.1.50). He and Charlotte were married in June 1854.*　　　　　　　*S.* xxxvii

Mr MACTURK was considered by Mr Helstone to be less of a humbug than Dr Rile. When Shirley was ill, she did not want either the young or old MacTurk to be called in. Both these surgeons attended Robert

Moore at Briarmains; their colleague was a Mr Graves or Greaves. *A distinguished medical practitioner at Bradford named Dr MacTurk was consulted during Charlotte Brontë's last illness.* S. xxiv, xxviii, xxxii, xxxiii

Peter Augustus MALONE, a tall strongly built Irishman, was the curate at Briarfield. Though besottedly arrogant like his father, he had little to say in the presence of ladies. Yet he attempted to charm Caroline Helstone, and presented a bouquet of roses to Shirley at the Whitsuntide fête. Fond of eating and drinking, he was apt to argue and vociferate. He carried pistols and a shillelagh, and needed no encouragement from Mr Helstone to help in the defence of Robert Moore's mill. His landlady was Mrs Hogg. Mr Malone disappeared suddenly from Briarfield, for reasons the author thought readers would find so incredible or unacceptable that she refused to disclose them. *The person who contributed to the creation of the above was the Rev. J. W. Smith, Mr Brontë's curate at Haworth, 1842–4. His interest in Ellen Nussey (who recognized herself in Caroline Helstone) was mercenary (16.7.44), and it is in this context that Charlotte calls him Lothario-Lovelace Smith (20.7.44). Nobody regretted his departure to Keighley, where he remained curate until 1846. It was said that he absconded in debt after misappropriating money which he obtained for charitable purposes (26.2.48). His shillelagh and pistols were suggested by Mr Brontë's; see p. 10.* S. i–iii, v, vii, x, xiv–xxi, xxxvii

Miss MANN was a grim-looking and apparently unamiable old maid; Robert Moore thought her look equal to Medusa's. Though censorious, she was no scandalmonger. Caroline's interest in her resulted in confidences. She had suffered greatly and needed friendship. Hortense Moore stayed with her twice at Wormwood Wells. *W. M. Heald, the vicar of Birstall, wrote to Ellen Nussey (8.1.50): 'Mary thinks she descries Cecilia Crowther and Miss Johnstone (afterwards Mrs Westerman) in two old maids [in Shirley]'.* S. x, xii, xvii, xx, xxv, xxvi, xxxiii, xxxv

Miss Maria MARCHMONT lived about fifty miles from London. She was a wealthy woman, who had been rheumatically crippled for twenty years when she persuaded Lucy Snowe to act as her companion. One February night just before she died, she recalled the death of her lover Frank, as he arrived one Christmas Eve thirty years previously, not long before their expected wedding. *The story, with its prelusive Banshee wind, reinforces the tragic ending of Villette.* V. iv, v

Mr MARCHMONT, second cousin of Miss Marchmont, inherited her

estate. She had wished to reward Lucy Snowe, but he was avaricious
and miserly, and it was not until she had started her school in Villette
that he sent her £100. With this conscience-money she was able to
buy the neighbouring house, and make her school a *pensionnat*.

V. v, xlii

Fergus MARKHAM, lively and red-haired, inherited the family farm
from his brother Gilbert, and married the vicar of L——'s eldest
daughter. Her superiority made him surprisingly industrious to
improve his position.   *T.* i, iv, vi, vii, ix, x, xiii, xiv, xlvi, xlvii, liii

Gilbert MARKHAM, despite his ambition, remained, in accordance
with his father's wishes, a farmer at Linden Grange (*or Linden-Car.
On the other hand, Linden-Car may have been part of the parish of
Lindenhope. 'Car' is found in place-names in the north of England; it
means 'pond' or 'bog'*). He was very friendly with Eliza Millward, but
soon fell in love with Mrs 'Graham', the new tenant of Wildfell Hall.
Jealousy of Mr Lawrence made him irrational in behaviour, and led
to a brutal attack on him. In order to prove the integrity of her love,
and remove his suspicions, Mrs 'Graham' gave Gilbert a manuscript
which told the story of her unhappy marriage, and why she had
sought refuge in Wildfell Hall, her brother Mr Lawrence's property.
Markham was gratified to learn that her affection for her husband
Arthur Huntingdon was dead. He apologized to Mr Lawrence, took
pleasure in warning him against Jane Wilson, and even more in
hearing of Huntingdon's death. Pride born of social inferiority
disinclined him to ask Lawrence about his sister after her departure
from Wildfell Hall, but the rumour of her marriage made him act.
When he saw Staningley Hall in its extensive grounds, his heart
sank. But for chance and Helen Huntingdon's initiative, they might
never have been married. As Grassdale Manor held most unhappy
memories for her, they made Staningley their home. *See pp. 256–7.*

T. To J. Halford, Esq., i–xv, xliv–liii

Mrs MARKHAM was left a widow at Linden Grange. She did everything possible to encourage her sons Gilbert and Fergus to make a
success of the farm and, with the help of Rose, to keep them happy
at home. She did not think Eliza Millward worthy of Gilbert, and
warned him against her designs. Like her neighbours, she was
suspicious of Mrs 'Graham', and upset to find that he had fallen in
love with her.   *T.* i–iv, vi, ix–xiv, xlvi, li–liii

Rose MARKHAM, Gilbert's sister, married J. Halford.   *T.* i–vii,
ix–xi, xiv, xlvi–xlviii, li, liii

MARSH END. *See* MOOR HOUSE. *J.*

MARTHA was Mrs Bretton's servant at La Terrasse.　　*V.* xvii, xx, xxv

Bertha Antoinetta MASON was the daughter of a wealthy West Indian planter and merchant, and Edward Rochester was married to her, by his father's connivance, for the sake of a fortune. He did not learn that her mother was insane until after his marriage. Bertha was tall, dark, and majestic; she had a violent temper, and gradually her behaviour became more vicious until, four years after her marriage, she was pronounced insane. By this time, his elder brother and father having died, Edward had inherited the family estate. He decided to take his wife to England, and confine her to the attics of Thornfield Hall while he went abroad. Grace Poole was paid liberally to be her keeper. Unfortunately gin got the better of her vigilance at times, and Bertha occasionally escaped. Once she tried to set fire to Rochester's bed; she attacked her brother Richard when he came to see her; she tore Jane's veil in twain the night before her intended wedding; and finally, after Jane's departure, set fire to Thornfield Hall. When Rochester tried to save her, she jumped from the roof and was killed. *See p. 118*, Jane EYRE, *and* THORNFIELD HALL. *At the Cowan Bridge school, Charlotte Brontë was friendly with one of the senior pupils, who came from the West Indies* (*W. Gérin*, Charlotte Brontë, *p. 9*).　　*J.* xi, xii, xv, xx, xxv–xxvii, xxxvi

Richard MASON was savagely attacked when he visited his mad sister at Thornfield Hall. On his way back to Jamaica, he called at Madeira, and met John Eyre, one of his business agents. They were together when Jane's letter on her forthcoming marriage arrived. Mr Eyre was ill, and implored Mr Mason to return to prevent the bigamous marriage. This he did, with the assistance of Mr Briggs, John Eyre's London solicitor.　　*J.* xviii–xx, xxvi

Mr and Mrs MAXWELL lived at Staningley Hall. Unlike her husband, Mrs Maxwell was very critical of Arthur Huntingdon, but her advice was wasted on her niece Helen, who lived with them. When Mr Maxwell was dying, she helped her aunt to nurse him; afterwards they spent a holiday at F——, a seaside resort. Helen inherited the estate from her uncle, but Mrs Maxwell remained there in her own apartments after her niece's second marriage.　　*T.* xvi–xx, xxx, xxxi, xxxiii, xliii, l–lii

Harry MELTHAM, Sir Hugh's younger son ('rather good-looking and a pleasant fellow to flirt with; but *being* a younger son, that is all he is good for'), was one of Rosalie Murray's conquests. She obviously liked him more than she did her husband, Sir Thomas Ashby.

A. ix, x, xiii–xv, xvii, xxii, xxiii

MICHAEL, a servant at Thrushcross Grange, was fond of reading. Catherine Linton gave him books when she wished to make her evening visits to her cousin Linton Heathcliff at Wuthering Heights. In return, he saddled Minny, and put her back in the stable.   *W.* xxiv

MILLCOTE, a large manufacturing town on the banks of the A——, was situated in a county seventy miles nearer London than Lowood. After travelling sixteen hours from Lowton, Jane Eyre waited at the George Inn for conveyance to Thornfield Hall. *Although details may be incorrect, Millcote is almost certainly Leeds on the Aire river and on the coach road from Kendal via 'Lowton' or Kirkby Lonsdale.*

J. x, xi, xiv, xvii, xviii, xxii, xxiv, xxxvi

Miss MILLER was an overworked under-teacher at Lowood School.

J. v, vii–ix

Eliza MILLWARD, the younger daughter of the vicar of Lindenhope, had enough charm and guile to attract Gilbert Markham. He found her 'a very engaging little creature', and her eyes 'irresistibly bewitching', until he met Mrs 'Graham'. Jealousy made Eliza indulge in mischievous and scandalous tattle about the latter. It pleased 'the little demon' to tell Gilbert that Mrs Graham had returned to her husband, and, later, to convey the rumour that she was marrying Mr Hargrave. Eliza married a wealthy tradesman at L——.   *T.* i, ii, iv, vi, vii, ix, xi, xiii, xlvi–xlviii, li

Mary MILLWARD, several years older than her sister Eliza, and of larger physique, was a plain, quiet, sensible person. She had nursed her mother during her long fatal illness, and had remained housekeeper ever since, valued by her father, loved by cats, dogs, children and the poor, and neglected by everyone else. She married her father's curate, Richard Wilson, and continued to live at the vicarage.

T. i, ii, iv, vi, vii, ix, xlviii

The Rev. Michael MILLWARD, vicar of Lindenhope, was tall, ponderous, elderly, and active. He wore a shovel hat over his square, massive-featured face, carried a stout walking-stick, and 'incased his still powerful limbs in knee-breeches and gaiters'. He was very partial to malt liquors, bacon and eggs, ham, hung beef, and other strong meat. He was intolerant of all forms of dissent, mighty in dogma, pompous in anecdote and oracular discourses, and sententious in jokes. In his declining years, his parish duties proved too much for

his vaunted energy. Richard Wilson became his curate, married his
daughter Mary, and succeeded him.   *T*. i, iii, iv, ix–xii, xliv,
                                                                         xlviii, li

M. MIRET was the bookseller and stationer for Mme Beck's establishment. At the *pensionnat* he had a reputation for being short-tempered,
but Lucy Snowe always found him civil and even kind. He found a
seat for her when she was listening to the late-night concert in the
park. He owned several houses in the Faubourg Clotilde, including the
one his friend Paul Emanuel (who was often to be seen reading and
smoking a cigar in his shop) furnished as a school for Lucy.

                                                                 V. xxxviii, xli

MOOR HOUSE or Marsh End was situated a few miles from Morton,
among marshes and ridges near the head of Marsh Glen. It was a
long, low, grey old building with latticed windows, and an avenue
of firs, all grown aslant under the stress of winds sweeping the moorland heights. There Jane Eyre received hospitality and shelter after
travelling as far as she could from Thornfield Hall. When Diana and
Mary Rivers left, St John returned to the parsonage, and Jane moved
into the school house, at Morton. After she had shared her legacy,
she returned to Moor House to prepare for the return of Diana and
Mary at Christmas. St John also returned, and Jane stayed until the
first of June, when she set off to find Rochester. *Whether Moor House
had an original is open to doubt. It has been identified with North Lees
and also with Moorseats, both above Hathersage. It bears no resemblance to the former, but there is evidence for associating it with the
latter. Moorseats is not dissimilar to Charlotte's general description
when viewed from the road above, and J. J. Stead* (BST. *iv*) *discovered
that, before enlargement, it resembled Moor House. It belonged to one
of the Eyre families, and Charlotte visited it with Ellen Nussey. It is
much nearer the parsonage than the novel indicates. Hints for the
setting were taken from the neighbourhood and the moors above.*

                                                     J. xxviii–xxx, xxxiv–xxxvi

Hortense Gérard MOORE was older than her brother Robert, for
whom she kept house at Hollow's Cottage. She was tall and stout, with
very black hair, which she kept twisted in paper curls in the mornings.
She preserved her Belgian habits, especially in dress and cooking,
was very industrious and orderly, thought a day well spent in the
invisible repair of a stocking, and did not underestimate her talents.
She played the guitar, sang, and helped her cousin Caroline to learn
French, making her grind away at grammar. She missed her greatly

when Mr Helstone forbad Caroline to meet her cousins. When Robert expected the attack on his mill, he arranged for Hortense to stay with Miss Mann; the two ladies enjoyed two holidays together at Wormwood Wells. She became a favourite with Mrs Yorke, and the two took great care of Robert when he was convalescing at Briarmains. *The Wheelwright girls recognized an 'absolute resemblance' in Hortense to Mlle Haussé, one of their teachers at the Pensionnat Heger.*

   S. ii, v, vi, xiii, xvii, xx, xxiii, xxiv, xxv, xxxii, xxxiii, xxxv
Louis Gérard M O O R E, Robert's younger brother, had been sent to England for his education. He became Henry Sympson's tutor. Henry's cousin Shirley had also been his pupil, and he had fallen in love with her. He came with the Sympsons to Fieldhead. Soon he was friendly with Mr Hall, whom he accompanied on a walking tour to the Lakes. When Shirley accepted him, Louis had loved her for years. She had a natural zest which appealed to him because it gave him something to be anxious about, something to alter. He assumed a protective role, and threatened Mr Sympson physically when he expressed his views on their intended marriage. Louis was virtually master of Fieldhead weeks before this took place; Shirley 'abdicated without a word or struggle'. *The final relationship between Louis Moore and Shirley is not as consistently or unequivocally expressed as it might have been, nor is Louis always presented in a favourable light. See pp. 135–6.*

   S. v, xxiii, xxv–xxix, xxxi, xxxii, xxxv, xxxvii
Robert Gérard M O O R E was a cloth-manufacturer who rented Hollow's Mill. His mother belonged to a family of merchants in Antwerp; his father was a Yorkshireman. He and his sister converted their cottage by the mill into a neat, tasteful residence. Robert was tall, thin, and dark, with fine features but a serious, rather anxious expression; his accent was rather outlandish. In the defence of his mill against Luddite wreckers and in the pursuit of their ringleaders, he showed immense courage, resolution, and pertinacity. He was a Whig, and bitterly opposed to the war with France, which ruined his business. He was in debt, and needed new machinery to remain competitive. He was not heartless on the subject of unemployment, and went out of his way to find work for an honest man like William Farren. Interest got the better of his love for Caroline Helstone. It made him wish that her uncle had not spent his inheritance on a church; and it was responsible for his gravest blunder in proposing to Shirley. He had sufficient integrity to realize it, and never make such a mistake again. His period of convalescence (after being wounded on his return to the

north) made him feel more than ever how much he and Caroline loved each other. He and Louis had thought of emigrating, but the repeal of the Orders in Council made him change his mind. Robert married Caroline, and his business flourished. He was able to do what he wished to do: 'take more workmen; give better wages; lay wiser and more liberal plans; do some good; be less selfish'. *The love story of Robert Moore and Caroline was suggested by one that seemed to be developing between Joseph (Joe) Taylor, who inherited his father's mill at Hunsworth, and Ellen Nussey (1.4.43, 15.11.43). Moore's fall from grace, the petrifaction of his feelings, and his Mammon worship, had their origin in Joe Taylor (24.4.45). His bold action against Luddite mob violence and his subsequent wounding were based on William Cartwright's defence of Rawfolds Mill, near Cleckheaton, and the attempt to assassinate him as he was returning from Huddersfield a week later in April 1812. Cartwright like Moore was tall and sallow; he also had lived abroad, and his French did nothing to reduce his unpopularity.*   S. i–iii, v–xiii, xvi, xvii, xix, xx, xxii, xxiv, xxviii, xxx, xxxi, xxxiii, xxxv, xxxvii

MORTON, which Jane Eyre reached penniless and hungry after her flight from Thornfield Hall, *is Hathersage in Derbyshire, near Sheffield. Its first school was opened about the time of Charlotte's visit (1845). She travelled from Sheffield to Hathersage with Ellen Nussey, who had come to meet her at the railway station. 'They alighted at the George Inn, a post station kept by James Morton' (BST. lxxiv). Whether the village was named after him or its proximity to the moors ('moor town') is uncertain. There had been metal-work on a small scale, including the manufacture of needles and pins, from the sixteenth century; a new business was established in 1811 (see Mr OLIVER). From the Eyre memorials in the church, Charlotte obtained her heroine's name. She might have been the vicar's wife, but Henry Nussey's marriage proposals had seemed to be based on nothing more than friendship and convenience. They were the germ of the relations which reached breaking-point between the heroine and St John Rivers. See pp. 36, 177–8, and* MOOR HOUSE.   J. xxviii, xxxi–xxxiv

Fred MURGATROYD, one of Robert Moore's workmen – with Pighills (ii, xxxiii) and Sykes – discovered Moses Barraclough's part in the Luddite conspiracy against his master's business. He and Barraclough met when each hoped to take Sarah out, and came to blows.
      S. ii, v, viii, ix, xxiii, xxxiii

John and Charles MURRAY had to be taught Latin by their governess

Agnes Grey as a preparation for school. The former was about eleven, strong and good-natured, but very rough and almost unteachable; he was sent to school within a year. Charles was his mother's darling, a little more than a year younger than John and much less robust; he could not read; everything had to be done for him, and he made no effort; he was fertile in falsehoods, which he invented ingeniously for the sake of making trouble. Seeing that his mother spoiled him and his governess could do little with him, Mr Murray sent him to school. When the two boys were at home in the holidays, it could be seen that they were still unruly and mischievous.

A. vii, xxii

Matilda MURRAY was about two and a half years younger than Rosalie, and a veritable hoyden. Her interest was in horses and dogs rather than in the usual accomplishments, and she swore like a trooper. She was too large to be pretty. As a pupil, she was ignorant and in-docile; she loved to be romping with the dogs or her brother John. After her sister's marriage, great efforts were made by her parents to improve her, and Agnes Grey suffered many a lecture on her lack of success. Under pressure, Matilda gradually changed her habits. When Agnes Grey left, she improved in manners under a fashionable governess; she was still wild and reckless, but more eligible for her début. *A*. vii, ix–xviii, xx, xxii

Mr MURRAY of Horton Lodge was a tall stout country squire with a rich ruddy complexion. Two of his main interests were farming and fox-hunting. He had a loud laugh, and was often heard swearing at any dependant who had annoyed him. In her language, and in other ways, his daughter Matilda resembled him. Too much choice wine and over-indulgence at the table resulted in gout, which did nothing to improve his temper. *Although he was a fox-hunting farmer, it is difficult to believe that the Rev. Edmund Robinson, Anne Brontë's employer at Thorp Green Hall, was quite like Mr Murray.*

A. vi, vii, ix, xii, xxii

Mrs MURRAY was a handsome lady of forty when Agnes Grey first met her. Her chief enjoyment appeared to be in frequenting parties or dressing at the height of fashion. She wanted her girls to be superfi-cially refined and accomplished, with the least exertion on their part. She was happy when Rosalie married; the remaining problem (which she expected Miss Grey to solve) was to make Matilda more polished. With that and another marriage of social distinction in mind, she engaged a fashionable governess when Agnes left. *Mrs Robinson was forty when Anne began her period as governess at Thorp Green Hall. She was very attractive, loved parties, and did all she could to secure advantageous marriages for her daughters.*   *A.* vi, vii, xiv, xvii, xviii, xxii

Rosalie MURRAY was sixteen when Agnes Grey first knew her. Within two years, she was strikingly beautiful. At first she had been cold and haughty, but gradually she became more agreeable. Her lack of principle was due to her faulty upbringing. At the age of fifteen she was moved by vanity to take an interest in the more showy accomplishments; she had a music master, and displayed great proficiency in music, singing, and dancing. At seventeen her interest turned to the opposite sex; her vanity, to making conquests. With Mr Hatfield, Mr Green, Harry Meltham, Sir Thomas Ashby, and others, she succeeded; on Mr Weston her artfulness was wasted. Mrs Murray's ambition was realized when her daughter became Lady Ashby, mistress of Ashby Park; Rosalie looked forward to her long honeymoon on the Continent and in London. Great was her chagrin when Sir Thomas cut short their stay in London because she displayed too much interest in Harry Meltham. The marriage proved to be hollow; Rosalie disliked Sir Thomas, had no love for her baby daughter, and wished she could be Miss Murray again. *In the quality of her 'accomplishments', Rosalie was rather like Lydia, the eldest of the Robinson daughters.*   *A.* vii–xviii, xx–xxiii

Alice MYERS was installed by Arthur Huntingdon, against his wife's wishes, as governess to his son at Grassdale Manor. Statements about her previous experience soon aroused suspicion: it was evident that she aimed at pleasing her master, and that she attracted him to the schoolroom. She left before his final illness; when his wife returned to nurse him he was delirious, and mistook her for Alice, his mistress.
T. xliii, xlvii

'NOAH O' TIM'S' was the second leader of the workers' deputation which met Robert Moore at Hollow's Mill just before the arrest of the leader, Moses Barraclough. His prepared speech was calculated to rouse the workers' prejudices against their foreign employer.
S. viii

NUNNELY was the parish of Mr Hall and his curate Mr Sweeting. Caroline Helstone walked over Nunnely Common with Shirley (xii). *The 'low-roofed Temple' is Hartshead Church, where Mr Brontë officiated from 1811 to 1815. To the east ran an extensive common. To the west, below Hartshead, is Kirklees Park, with its woodland ('Nunn-*

wood', *one of Robin Hood's haunts)*, *its priory (nunnery) ruins, and Kirklees Hall (Nunnely Hall, 'called the Priory')*.   *S.* i, vii, x, xii, xvi, xxvii, xxviii, xxix, xxxi

Sir Philip NUNNELY of Nunnely Priory hoped to marry Shirley but was rejected. They met at Cliffbridge. He was a rhymester who insisted on reading or reciting his poems to her; they made her wince. Old Lady Nunnely thought Shirley inferior to herself and her daughters, and opposed the marriage. Shirley thought him too immature, and looked for a husband she could respect.   *S.* i, xxvii–xxxi, xxxvi

O—— (*probably York*) was a large, non-industrial town not many miles from Horton Lodge. Mrs Murray was certain that it could supply masters to make up for any deficiency in a governess. She proposed to invite all the nobility and 'choice gentry' who lived there, and within a radius of twenty miles, to the ball which was to mark her eldest daughter's début.   *A.* vi–viii, xviii

Mrs Dionysius O'GALL of Bitternut Lodge, Connaught, Ireland, needed a governess for her five daughters, according to Lady Ingram. *One suspects she was invented by Rochester, to test Jane Eyre's feelings towards him, after he had deliberately created the false impression that he intended to marry Blanche Ingram.*   *J.* xxiii

Mr OLIVER, Rosamond's father, was the only rich man in Morton. He owned a needle factory and iron foundry, and lived at Vale Hall (*Brookfield Manor, once known as Brookfield Hall, at the upper end of a valley which runs through Hathersage; it was built in 1658 and enlarged in 1815*). He respected St John Rivers and his lineage, and would not have opposed his daughter's marriage to him. Both the Olivers were interested in Jane Eyre's school, and gave it financial support.   *J.* xxviii–xxxiii

Rosamond OLIVER was a beautiful and rich heiress whom St John Rivers might have married. She had been at school in S—— (*Sheffield*). She danced with officers stationed there after the riots, and suddenly became engaged to Mr Granby, grandson and heir to Sir Frederick Granby, and one of the most estimable citizens of S——.
          J. xxx–xxxiv, xxxvii

Mme PANACHE, a temporary teacher of history at Mme Beck's, had such unlimited confidence and volubility that Paul Emanuel clashed with her. She was 'bellicose as a Penthesilea', and he was not contented until she left. When he discovered that she was in distress as a result of unemployment, 'he moved heaven and earth till he found her a place'.   *V.* xxx

Louise PATH was the pupil with the happiest disposition at Mlle Reuter's. She was a country girl, neither well-taught nor well-mannered, and the very 'plague-spot of dissimulation'. *P.* xii

Mr PEARSON, Mr Sykes's partner, was shot at from behind a hedge, through the staircase window, as he was going to bed. He had three daughters; the eldest, Ann, had hoped to win Robert Moore when he first settled in Yorkshire; Kate and Susan were still at school. His business, like that of Mr Roakes (and Robert Moore's) suffered greatly as a result of the Orders in Council. *S.* i, ii, v, vii, ix, xii, xvi

M. François PELET, who engaged William Crimsworth to teach in his *pensionnat*, was a Frenchman of about forty who enjoyed a cigar and despised the Flemish people. Crimsworth found him intelligent, agreeable, and interested in Mlle Reuter. He was particularly keen to know what impression she had made on him, and ready to recommend any one of the trio of her more seductive pupils as a better matrimonial prospect. His jealousy prompted him to continue his jesting allusions to Mlle after Crimsworth had overheard him discussing marriage with her in the 'allée défendue'.

When Mlle hinted her partiality for Crimsworth, M. Pelet sought consolation in drink, and came home late at night, threatening his rival. He remained openly hostile until Crimsworth resigned his post at Mlle's *pensionnat*. Thereupon she turned to M. Pelet. Their marriage was not altogether harmonious, but their teaching business flourished. *Marion Spielmann (TLS., 13.4.16) identified M. Pelet as M. Lebel, the master in charge of a school-house for boys which overlooked the Hegers' garden. He was a Parisian, and readers of* The Professor *who remembered him thought no character had been recalled more faithfully in appearance and style. See* BRUSSELS. *P.* vii, viii, x–xiii, xx, xxi

Mme PELET managed her son's house and kitchen at his pensionnat. She said she had been handsome; now she was old, thin, and ugly, though on Sundays and fête days she dressed very colourfully. She talked incessantly, and was often indiscreet. *P.* viii, xx

PENISTONE CRAGS (*Ponden Kirk*) stood about a mile and a half beyond Wuthering Heights, and four miles further from Thrushcross Grange. In her delirium, Catherine Linton recalled scenes from her childhood. She thought her bed was the Fairy Cave under Penistone Crags, and Nelly Dean an old hag gathering elf-bolts to harm the Earnshaws' heifers. (*See pp. 207–8 for the origin of this superstition*).

Ponden Kirk, the 'Penistone Crags' of *Wuthering Heights*

Years later, the younger Catherine saw the crags glowing golden in the light of the setting sun; when she heard about the Fairy Cave, she determined to visit it. The secret excursion which followed led her to Wuthering Heights.   *W.* viii, xii, xviii, xxi

Mme PIERROT, who taught French at Lowood School, came from Lille.   *J.* v, viii, xi

Dr PILLULE's summons to see a rich old hypochondriac in the ancient university town of Bouquin-Moisi (*literally 'Musty Book', and probably Louvain*) led to the first of Dr Bretton's visits to Mme Beck's and to his infatuation with Ginevra Fanshawe. '*Pillule' in French means 'pill'*.   *V.* x, xi

Grace POOLE was hired from Grimsby Retreat (*Asylum*), and paid liberally to act as keeper to Mr Rochester's mad wife. She had one fault, a weakness for gin, and this enabled the dangerous Bertha Mason on more than one occasion to roam at night in Thornfield Hall, finally to destroy it by fire. Until their wedding was banned, Rochester was content to allow Jane Eyre to think that Grace Poole was the mysterious inmate of the attics.   *J.* xi, xii, xv–xvii, xix, xxvi,
                                                          xxvii, xxxvi

Mrs PRYOR was the name Mrs Helstone (Caroline's mother) adopted after separating from her husband. Previously, as Miss Agnes Grey, she had been unfortunate as a governess (*a reference to Anne Brontë's experiences and her novel*). Her unhappiness made her marry. James Helstone was handsome, but dissolute and cruel; she left him soon after Caroline's birth. As Shirley's governess she had been happy. A staunch Tory, she remained rather old-fashioned, especially in dress, but Shirley would not part with her. She had plans to live independently if Shirley married, and asked Caroline to join her, if that happened, rather than become a governess. Mrs Pryor's revelation, during her daughter's severe illness, that she was her mother brought Caroline immense happiness. She delighted in making Mrs Pryor more stylish dresses, and found her a charming conversationalist, rich in wisdom and knowledge. When she and Robert Moore married, they made provision for Mrs Pryor to have rooms and a servant with them. *She resembled Miss Wooler in some respects, particularly in sweetness of voice and conversational charm. Her name was probably suggested by Kirklees Priory near Miss Wooler's school at Roe Head. Charlotte may have known, however, that Miss Wooler seemed rather 'like a lady-abbess' to Ellen Nussey.*   *S.* xi–xiv, xvi, xix, xx–xxii, xxiv–xxvi,
                                                 xxxii, xxxiv, xxxv, xxxvii

RACHEL was Arthur Huntingdon's nurse and his mother's house-keeper at Wildfell Hall. She had been her maid before Helen's marriage, and was 'dear and faithful' to her.   *T.* vi, vii, x, xii, xv, xvii, xviii, xxii, xxv, xxix–xxxi, xxxiii, xxxv, xxxvii, xxxix, xl, xliii–xlv, xlvii, liii

Mrs RAMSDEN had ordered the children's socks which Caroline Helstone intended to knit for the Jew-basket (*see vii*). Her husband Timothy, a corn-factor, 'a stout, puffy gentleman, as large in person as he was in property', attended the Whitsuntide fête at Briarfield.
S. v, xvii

The RED HOUSE INN stood on the Fieldhead side of Briarfield church. Robert Moore and his brother Louis both had occasion to requisition its chaise. *See* BRIARMAINS.   *S.* ii, xxxv, xxxvi

Eliza REED, the elder daughter of Mrs Reed, was a headstrong, selfish, mercenary girl. She became a tall, sallow young woman, ascetic in appearance and dress, who preferred her own society. After her mother's death, she retired to a nunnery near Lille, where she became a Catholic and eventually mother superior; she left her fortune to the convent.   *J.* i, ii, iv, x, xxi, xxii

Georgiana REED, Eliza's sister, was slim and pretty, but spiteful, in her childhood. She retained her beauty and golden curls when she grew up, but became very plump. But for Eliza's informing, she might have eloped with Lord Edwin Vere. Finally she made an advantageous match with a wealthy 'worn-out man of fashion'.
J. i–iv, x, xxi, xxii

John REED, his mother's darling, was big, greedy, and vicious. He delighted in killing birds and doing much damage, but was never reproved. He hated school, and had little difficulty in getting his mother's permission to return home; his master, Mr Miles, said he would be healthier if she sent him fewer cakes and sweetmeats. Four years her senior, he continually bullied his orphan cousin Jane Eyre. At college he was 'plucked'. Then he tried law in London, where he took to gambling and dissipation. To keep him solvent, his mother kept mortgaging her property, but he was gaoled for debt; when she refused more money, he returned to London. The next news was that he was dead; according to report, he committed suicide.
J. i–iv, x, xxi

Mrs Sarah REED (*née* Gibson) was a widow; she lived at Gateshead Hall with her three children and her orphan niece Jane Eyre, whom her husband had adopted. Family dislike, and Mrs Reed's indulgence

of her children, especially John, caused unpleasant incidents, the
climax of which was Jane's incarceration, fright, and seizure, in the
red-room where Mr Reed had died. The outright antagonism between
Jane and her aunt led to her being sent to Lowood School, after Mrs
Reed had told Mr Brocklehurst that the girl was deceitful. Years
later, as she was dying, the news of John's suicide made her reflect
on the wrongs she had done Jane, and particularly the lie she had sent
Jane's uncle John (who had wished to adopt her and make her his
legatee) that she had died of typhus at Lowood School. Mrs Reed
refused her plea for reconciliation, and died hating her, as she had
always done.　　　　　　　　　　　　　*J.* i–v, vii, viii, x, xxi

Mme REUTER, mother of Zoraïde, was fat, rubicund, and jolly,
rather like a free-living Flemish farmer's wife. She had a twinkle and
a leer in her left eye, and habitually kept her right half-closed. She
managed the house and servants at her daughter's *pensionnat*.

P. viii, xx

Mlle Zoraïde REUTER was the *directrice* of the school for girls in the
Rue d'Isabelle, Brussels. She was 'little and roundly formed', with
expressive but not pretty features, and curled nut-brown hair. In
school she was grave, sagacious, and calm, 'profoundly aware of her
superiority', continually on the watch, and ready to act whenever
necessary. Though aware of her stealth and cunning, William
Crimsworth was succumbing to her allurements when he discovered
by chance that she and M. Pelet had already agreed on marriage. Her
jealousy of Crimsworth's pupil, Mlle Henri, was such that she dismissed her from her teaching-post at the *pensionnat*, and refused to
disclose where she lived. Her failure to win Crimsworth, and his
resignation from her staff, led to her reconciliation with M. Pelet, and
to their marriage not many weeks later. *Like Mme Beck, she is
modelled to a large extent on Mme Heger, one of whose forenames was
'Zoë', which recalled 'Zoraïde', the name of a heroine in one of
Charlotte's Angrian romances.*　　　　　　*P.* vii–xxii, xxv

Diana and Mary RIVERS, sisters of St John, were governesses in
B——, 'a large, fashionable, south-of-England city'. Although they
had travelled a great deal, they loved Moor House and Morton, and
the surrounding hills and moorland. Their father's death brought them
home for a few weeks. Diana was handsome; Mary's expression was
more reserved. Jane Eyre insisted that they and their brother should
share her £20,000 legacy equally with her. Diana married Captain
Fitzjames, a naval officer, and Mary, a clergyman, Mr Wharton, one

of her brother's college friends. *Resemblances between the two and Charlotte's sisters are so slight that they are probably accidental.*

J. xxviii–xxx, xxxiii–xxxv, xxxvi, xxxviii
St John Eyre RIVERS was one of a family who had lived at Morton for several generations, *like the Eyres of Hathersage; see* Jane EYRE. He was young (hardly thirty) and handsome, with very Grecian features. He would often go out on missions of love or duty (it was difficult to say which) with his father's old pointer Carlo. His preaching was Calvinistic and disturbing; it suggested a deep-rooted personal dissatisfaction. After establishing a school for boys, he opened another for girls, and persuaded Jane Eyre to take charge of it. He could no doubt have married the beautiful and rich Miss Oliver, but he regarded love as a temptation and lure from his calling. He admitted that he was cold and hard; he used Jane to help him to learn Hindustani, and soon decided that she was the kind of person who could be of invaluable help to him in the missionary work to which he was called in India. For this reason he proposed marriage; knowing that he valued her only as a helpmeet, Jane rejected him. He persisted, but she heard Rochester's call, and left him. She had shared her fortune with him and his sisters. St John went to India, and worked indefatigably in his Master's cause, hoping to join the Elect. *In all respects he is a contrast to Rochester. To some extent he reflects Henry Nussey, who had been affected by the strong influence of Charles Simeon at Cambridge, and had missionary yearnings in the early years of his ministry. His marriage proposal to Charlotte seemed to be merely rational; he also recommended that she should set up a school near Donnington, Sussex, where he was curate (5.3.39). St John's zeal and dedication seem to be on a higher level, however; and he owes much to the impressions Charlotte formed of the Wesleyan missionary Henry Martyn, of whom she heard much from her father, who met him at St John's, Cambridge, from which Rivers' forename may derive (could the whole name be linked with St John, vii. 38?). Henry Martyn had been in love with Lydia Grenfell, but she refused to go with him to India, where he died as a missionary.* J. xxviii–xxxvi, xxxviii
Mr ROBSON was Mrs Bloomfield's brother. He wore stays, drank heavily, and enjoyed coursing and shooting. He encouraged his young nephew Tom to drink, and did much to foster his cruelty to birds and animals. *A.* v
Edward Fairfax ROCHESTER was the victim of his father's avarice. While the elder son Rowland inherited the estate, Edward's fortune

was to be made by marrying the daughter of an old acquaintance. On leaving college, therefore, he was sent to Jamaica to be won by the tall, dark, majestic daughter of Mr Mason, merchant and planter. The trick worked; only after his marriage did he discover what his father and brother had known, that Bertha Mason's mother was in a lunatic asylum. Edward soon discovered that kindly conversation was impossible with his wife, and that she had a violent temper. She grew more vicious, and at the end of four years was pronounced insane. By this time, both his father and brother were dead.

He decided to take his wife to England and keep her confined under supervision at Thornfield Hall while he travelled on the Continent, hoping to find a good and intelligent woman whom he could love and in whom he could confide. He never met such a person. After living with three mistresses – Céline Varens (French), Giacinta (Italian), Clara (German) – and tiring of them all in turn, he loathed himself. In this state he returned to Thornfield and met Jane Eyre.

For nine years he had known that he was the husband of a mad woman with whom it was impossible to live. He was thirty-five; Jane was eighteen; and they soon fell in love. Mr Rochester was not handsome: his hair was dark, his features rather strong and grim; he was broad-chested and thin-flanked; neither tall nor graceful. He rode a black horse, Mesrour, and was generally accompanied by Pilot, a great black and white Newfoundland dog. Rochester had adopted a dictatorial tone, but as he talked to Jane he learned to respect her mind and principles, to become more considerate in manner, and talk without reserve about Céline Varens, Adèle's mother. At first it was his humour to mislead Jane into thinking that a match was being arranged between him and Blanche Ingram. The latter, however, reminded him of Bertha Mason when he first knew her, and her grand domineering manner did not impress him, despite her accomplishments, any more than it did Jane. He had come to feel that his real happiness and future depended on the latter, and was so much in love that he thought he could marry her. He had allowed Jane to think that the dangerous mad woman in the house was Grace Poole. When the wedding was banned, he revealed everything, and tried to persuade Jane to live abroad with him. Her sudden departure left him without hope.

The loss of Thornfield, and his own helplessness after being maimed and blinded as a result of ineffectually attempting to rescue his wife, who had set fire to the Hall, made him retire to his other home,

Ferndean Manor. His cry for Jane was mysteriously heard by her far away at Morton when she was wondering whether to go abroad with St John Rivers. He could not believe in his good fortune when he heard that she still loved him. They were married. Two years later he recovered the sight of his one eye. He could see that the eyes of his first-born, a boy, were large, black, and brilliant as his had been. Then, as before, Rochester firmly believed that God had tempered judgment with mercy. *In this Charlotte expressed her own religious belief; see her letter on the death of Branwell, 14.10.48. Rochester has an Angrian lineage, and cannot be dissociated from Lord Byron and his Newfoundland dog; Pilot recalls Zamorna's Roswal (see p. 80) and Mr Sidgwick's dog at Stonegappe (8.6.39). The Rochester link with Marston Moor (xxvi) was probably suggested by the legend which Charlotte must have heard at Norton Conyers of the horse which, after carrying Sir Richard Graham home from the battlefield, with Ironsides in pursuit, entered the hall, and mounted the staircase, leaving a hoof-mark on one of the lower steps.* J. xi–xxvii, xxxiii, xxxiv, xxxv–xxxviii

Mrs ROCHESTER. *See* Bertha MASON. *J.*

THE ROCHESTER ARMS was the wayside inn two miles from Thornfield Hall where Jane Eyre alighted from the coach which brought her from Whitcross in response to Rochester's call. After finding the Hall a blackened ruin, she returned to the inn, where she heard the story of the disaster which had overtaken it and Mr Rochester. *J.* xxxvi, xxxvii

ROSALIE, a smart French grisette, was the portress at Mlle Reuter's *pensionnat. See* ROSINE. *P.* ix, xvii, xviii

ROSINE Matou, the portress at Mme Beck's, was 'an unprincipled though pretty little French grisette, airy, fickle, dressy, vain, and mercenary'. *V.* viii, ix, xi–xiii, xxi, xxiii, xxiv, xxviii, xxx, xxxviii

ROYD LANE, between Briarfield and Nunnely Common, was so narrow that only two could walk abreast. '*Royd*', *common in Yorkshire place-names, means a clearing or open space, also 'road*'. At the Church of England Whitsuntide fête, twelve hundred children from three parishes were advancing along it when they were confronted by contingents from Nonconformist schools. Led by Mr Helstone, they kept firmly on until the Dissenters were forced back and turned tail. *This scene may be a tribute to Mr Brontë's fearlessness when he was a curate at Dewsbury; see p. 9. According to the Rev. J. C. Bradley*

(the original of Mr Sweeting), such an encounter took place in Haworth, when Mr Brontë cleared the way for his procession (BST. *Supplement, January 1905, p.78*). The corn-mill at Royd belonged to Mr Ramsden.
                                                                    S. xvii

RUSHEDGE was the top ridge of Stilbro' Moor. After a long absence, Robert Moore was riding home from Stilbro'; Mr Yorke accompanied him. They were descending the hill and within sight of home when Moore was shot at and severely wounded (by Michael Hartley) from behind the wall of Milldean plantation. '*Rushedge*' *is* '*Liversedge*' *(either from O.E. 'lēfer'=rush, reed, or from 'sedge'=rush, reed). It is Hartshead Moor to the west of Liversedge, where the Huddersfield road beyond Brighouse proceeds to Gomersal and Birstall. Mr Cartwright (see* Robert MOORE) *was on his way home from Huddersfield when he was fired on by two men, not far from Bradley Wood, south of Brighouse.*   *S*. xxii, xxviii, xxx, xxxi, xxxvii

Colonel RYDE of Stilbro' barracks provided military assistance for the defence of Hollow's Mill.   *S*. xiii

S——, twenty miles from Marsh End, *is Sheffield, probably the town ten miles from 'Whitcross'. See* Miss OLIVER. *Charlotte travelled by train from Leeds to Sheffield to stay with Ellen Nussey at Hathersage. The long ascent which Charlotte probably took along the Ringinglow road past Higger Tor would give a misleading impression of the distance. See* MORTON.   *J*. xxviii, xxxi, xxxii, xxxiv

Mlle Zélie ST PIERRE, senior mistress at Mme Beck's school, was a Parisienne, a callous epicure, thin, with lips like a thread, sallow complexion, prominent chin, and frozen eye. She hated work (and Lucy Snowe), but had one great asset in Mme Beck's eyes: she had not the slightest difficulty in obtaining discipline. She once aspired to be Mme Emanuel. Always in debt, she anticipated her salary in the purchase of confectionery, perfumes, cosmetics, and dress. *See* ZEPHYRINE. *Both may have been drawn from Mlle Blanche of the Pensionnat Heger. Of her Mlle Haussé said that when in a fury 'elle n'a pas de lèvres' (29.5.43).*   *V*. xiv, xv, xxviii, xxix, xxxi,
                                                          xxxiii, xxxviii

Lady SARA was Ginevra Fanshawe's companion at the concert. The two girls were addressed by the Queen of Labassecour as she left.
                                                                    V. xx, xxi

SARAH was the Millwards' servant; she was on friendly terms with Mr Lawrence's footman.   *T*. xlvii, li

SARAH had to serve under Hortense Moore at Hollow's Cottage.

Each had her standards of cooking, the one Yorkshire, the other Belgian; and each despised the other's. Fred Murgatroyd was in love with Sarah, and it was on the evidence that came to light through his jealousy of Barraclough that the latter was arrested. *S.* ii, v, vi, viii, xxiii, xxxiii, xxxv

Justine Marie SAUVEUR was related to the Becks and Walravens. She was named after her aunt, who became a nun when her parents refused to sanction her marriage to Paul Emanuel. She was young, rich, fair, and buxom, the bourgeois belle with the beauty indigenous to her country. M. Emanuel was her ward and godfather. She was to take lessons in English at Lucy Snowe's school. Heinrich Mühler, a wealthy young German merchant, was engaged to her.

V. xxxi, xxxix, xli

Miss SCATCHERD, teacher of history and grammar at Lowood School, was small, dark, fierce, and particularly harsh towards Helen Burns. *Her original was a Miss Andrews at the Clergy Daughters' School, Cowan Bridge.* *J.* v–vii

Joe SCOTT was Robert Moore's 'overlooker' or foreman at Hollow's Mill. He was an anti-feminist, and resented Shirley's 'petticoat government' or proprietorial interest in the mill. His son Henry (viii, xxiii, xxxv) usually hung about the premises, and proved to be a useful messenger for Robert and Hortense Moore. *S.* i–iii, v–vii, ix, xviii–xx, xxiii, xxxvii

The Hon. John SEACOMBE, Lord Tynedale's brother, shared the cost of William Crimsworth's education at Eton, and hinted that if he accepted the living of Seacombe he might marry one of his six daughters. *P.* i, vi

Mr SHIELDERS, the curate at Gimmerton, eked out his living by farming his land himself and teaching the Linton and Earnshaw children. After the death of Hindley Earnshaw's wife, such was the deterioration at Wuthering Heights that he ceased to call.

W. v, vi, viii, xi

SHIRLEY Keeldar (*for the origin of the surname, see p. 380*) had been brought up under the guardianship of her uncle Mr Sympson. Mrs Pryor had been her governess, and Louis Moore, her tutor. When Shirley came of age, she settled at Fieldhead with Mrs Pryor, then about forty. Shirley was slim and graceful, with a pale, intelligent countenance, and hair of the darkest brown. She was wealthy, but attached no great importance to money or position, though she was interested in the prosperity of Hollow's Mill, which she owned. She loved great poetry, but found few, besides Caroline Helstone, with whom she could share this enjoyment. Often she needed no other company but her own thoughts and the beauty of nature, provided Catherine were within call; after an active morning, she would spend a sunny afternoon lying motionless on the turf. She was annoyed that Robert Moore's friendship should spoil their relationship, and was troubled by the thought of her own wealth and the poverty of many families in the neighbourhood. With the help of the clergy, and of Miss Ainley and Miss Margaret Hall, she did much to alleviate the distress of the unemployed, and to reduce the chance of Luddite violence. When his trade was at an ebb, she gave Robert Moore financial aid, but her plan failed when the attack on Hollow's Mill (which she and Caroline witnessed) took place. She had admired Robert's resolution, but was distressed that a man of such worth should be tempted to propose to her from self-interest. Mr Sympson came with his family to Fieldhead, intent on promoting her marriage. She refused Mr Wynne's son and three other offers. She was in fact falling in love with Louis Moore, Henry Sympson's tutor. After being bitten by a mad dog, she cauterized the wound, but, fearing she would die, made a will bequeathing much of her property to charitable causes. She insisted that no surgeons should be allowed near her if she were seriously ill. Much to her guardian's annoyance, she rejected Sir Philip Nunnely because he was too young and immature to earn her respect. It was Louis Moore to whom she became engaged. She put off the marriage, but found she needed his society to compensate for her lost liberty, and decided that she must cease to reign in order that he should assume 'the powers of the premier'. *In her love of nature, poetry, and animals, her fearlessness, as illustrated in the rescue of Tartar (xx), the cauterization of her own wound (xxviii), and her refusal to accept medical assistance, she recalls Emily Brontë. Charlotte, according to Mrs Gaskell (xviii), tried to depict what Emily 'would have been, had she been placed in health and prosperity'. The rather irritating 'Captain' role assumed by Shirley arose from Emily's being called 'the Major'; see pp. 30 and 59. To some extent she is prefigured in Jane Moore; see p. 82.* S. xi–xxxi, xxxiii, xxxv–xxxvii

Père SILAS, Paul Emanuel's old tutor, and the priest to whom Lucy Snowe confessed, was anxious to convert her to the Catholic faith. He lived at 10 Rue des Mages, where he was supported by Paul Emanuel. *V.* xv, xvii, xviii, xxxiv–xxxvi, xxxviii, xxxix, xli, xliii

Miss SMITH was the needlework teacher at Lowood School. *J.* v–vii

Mr SMITH was the village draper, grocer, and tea-dealer, who, after
Agnes Grey had received the fond embraces of her parents and sister
(and had kissed the cat, 'to the great scandal' of Sally, the maid),
conveyed her in his gig over the hilly country to Wellwood.

A. i, ii

Lucy SNOWE *is a complex character, and in some respects very much
like her author. Villette is an autobiographical presentation, some of it
based on Charlotte Brontë's experience. Many of the actual scenes from
which the author drew are imaginatively re-created through the eyes
of Lucy Snowe in her varying moods. She may weep hot tears one day
and be her calm self the next. Beneath this appearance are frustrations,
jealousies, and intense prejudices. Charlotte changed her name to
'Frost'; she regretted this, and asked for the restoration of 'Snowe',
adding: 'A cold name she must have; partly, perhaps, on the* lucus a non
lucendo *principle – partly on that of the "fitness of things", for she has
about her an air of external coldness.' In her, reason and emotion,
judgment and imagination, are often in conflict. Charlotte thought her
'both morbid and weak at times'. 'It was no impetus of healthy feeling
which urged her to the confessional, for instance; it was the semi-
delirium of solitary grief and sickness' (6.11.52). A hint of Charlotte
Brontë in Lucy Snowe can be seen in a letter from Upperwood House,
Rawdon, where she admits that, though the situation is favourable for
a governess, she has to adopt 'a cold frigid apathetic exterior', and finds
it painful to be estranged in this way from her own character* (7.8.41).

The story begins at Bretton, where Lucy stayed with her godmother
Mrs Bretton, and met little Paulina and her father. Eight years after
her return home, undisclosed events made it necessary for her to
earn her living. She became Miss Marchmont's companion, and, on
her sudden death, decided to go to London and the Continent. It was
by chance that she thought of going to Villette, and even more
fortuitously that she obtained a post as nursery-governess and subsequently teacher of English at Mme Beck's. Almost against her will,
she acceded to M. Emanuel's appealing insistence that she should take
a part at short notice in the school play. During the long vacation she
became a prey to loneliness and melancholia, made her confession
(she was strongly anti-Catholic), and afterwards collapsed as she
wandered in the Basse-Ville. She was rescued by a doctor, Mrs Bretton's
son, who took her to their home outside Villette. Although he had
visited Mme Beck's, she had not at first recognized in him the Graham
she had known as a big schoolboy at Bretton; his infatuation with

Ginevra Fanshawe had pained her. During her convalescence Lucy visited various parts of the city with him; in the mornings he would sometimes leave her to study paintings in the principal galleries. They were present at the grand concert which the Royal Family attended, and they saw the play in which an actress of great renown performed the part of Vashti. As Graham became disenchanted with Ginevra Fanshawe, Lucy grew more devoted to him, only to find he was falling in love with Paulina, whose father, now Count de Bassompierre, was staying with her at the Hôtel Crécy. The climax of the story relates to Paul Emanuel, who, despite religious barriers, and the opposition of Père Silas and Mme Beck, fell in love with Lucy. Before leaving on his three years' mission in Guadaloupe, he prepared a school for her in the Faubourg Clotilde. Their intention to marry was never fulfilled; he was drowned on his return voyage. *The ambiguity at the end is deliberate, Charlotte hoping to satisfy those readers who cannot see, or accept, that Lucy's 'lines' were never appointed 'in pleasant places'.*   *V*.

STANINGLEY HALL, a stately mansion in extensive grounds, was Helen Huntingdon's home before her first marriage. It was bequeathed to her by her uncle, Mr Maxwell. She chose to live there, rather than at Grassdale Manor, after her marriage to Gilbert Markham.

T. xvi–xxii, xxx, xliv, l, lii, liii

Timothy STEIGHTON, Edward Crimsworth's confidential clerk, was almost thirty-five when his master's brother William worked in his office. His face was heavy and sly. He was a Methodist and 'at the same time an engrained rascal'. *See pp. 77, 79, 155. There is a village called Steeton, three miles from Keighley.*   *P*. ii, iii, v

STILBRO' was the market town from which Robert Moore expected the frames that were smashed on Stilbro' Moor. From the town barracks he obtained soldiers to help him guard Hollow's Mill. Moses Barraclough was gaoled in Stilbro' for organizing the destruction of Moore's machinery. After his long absence in Birmingham and London, Moore returned to Stilbro'; he was wounded on Rushedge, while riding home from 'The George'. Shirley rode to Stilbro' to consult her solicitor, Pearson Hall; and Samuel Fawthrop Wynne attended Stilbro' Grammar School. *If Stilbro' is any particular Yorkshire town, it must be Huddersfield, although Charlotte tried to conceal its identity in a number of ways. She says that it is east of Whinbury (ii), and makes Briarfield visible from the highest point of Stilbro' Moor. The attempt on the life of William Cartwright, the*

historical prototype of Robert Moore, took place while he was travelling
home from Huddersfield. See RUSHEDGE, *and note where* Michael
HARTLEY *worked.* '*The Stilbro' Courier' was suggested by* The Leeds
Mercury, *in which Charlotte read accounts of the Luddite outbreaks*
and trials. Huddersfield had its Cloth (*or Piece*) *Hall, and the George*
Inn was an important coach station.   S. i–iii, vi, viii, ix, xiii, xx,
                                      xxii, xxvii–xxx, xxxvi, xxxvii

SUGDEN was the constable called in by Robert Moore to arrest Moses
Barraclough and take him to Stilbro' gaol.   S. viii, ix

SUPPLEHOUGH, a Baptist, and Barraclough were Nonconformist
preachers whose activities were cited by Mr Helstone in a sharp
reprimand to the curates.   S. i, iii

Mrs SWEENY was an Irish woman, an impostor partial to liquor, who
had been accepted as nursery-governess to Mme Beck's three children.
She claimed to be an English lady in reduced circumstances, and her
wardrobe of rather ill-fitting splendour, especially a real Indian
shawl, enabled her to keep up the precarious deception and maintain
her post for a month. She was succeeded by Lucy Snowe.

                                              V. vii, viii, xxxv

David SWEETING, curate of Nunnely, was a 'little gentleman', a
flautist who sang hymns like a seraph (according to some young ladies
in his parish), and was dubbed 'the ladies' pet'. All the six Misses
Sykes enjoyed his company, but his favourite was Dora, 'the most
splendid and weightiest woman in Yorkshire'. On their marriage,
after David's induction to a comfortable living, she received a
handsome portion. 'They lived long and happily together, beloved
by their parishioners and by a numerous circle of friends.' *The Rev.*
J. C. Bradley, curate of Oakworth, one mile north of Haworth, was
one of the three curates who met weekly at each other's lodgings to read
Greek, and contributed to the fictional rôles of Mr Sweeting, Mr Donne
and Mr Malone. He was a well-known flautist in the neighbourhood.

                          S. i, ii, vii, xiv, xv, xxvi, xxxvii

Christopher SYKES, a rich cloth-manufacturer of Whinbury, was only
'*word*-valiant' when Luddism threatened his industry. He was a
tall, stout man of about fifty.   S. ii, v, vi, viii, ix, xvii, xxii,
                                                            xxxvii

Mrs SYKES had six daughters, with all of whom Mr Sweeting was on
good terms. He preferred Dora, the stoutest of them, and married
her. Mary was good-looking and well-meaning; Harriet was a beauty
but overbearing; Hannah, pushing and conceited, loved flattery, and

was Mr Helstone's favourite. Like their mother, they all assumed that they were infallible in standards of propriety. John Sykes (xiv, xvii), whom Caroline Helstone did not care for, was almost certainly one of this family. *It is generally assumed that the Sykes family were drawn from the Hallileys, whom Mr Brontë knew when he was in Dewsbury; one of them married the vicar.*　　　*S.* ii, vii, ix, xii, xvi, xvii, xix, xxii, xxxvii

Sylvie, the model pupil at Mlle Reuter's, was small and ugly. She was intelligent, but weak health dulled her spirits. She allowed herself no original views, but remained passive. Destined for the cloister, she had been 'early taught to make the dictates of her own reason and conscience quite subordinate to the will of her spiritual director'.

P. x, xii, xiv, xvi, xviii, xxiii

Henry SYMPSON, the youngest of the Sympson family, and an only son, was small, pale, and lame. He had an amiable and affectionate nature. His mother loved him; his tutor, Louis Moore, was devoted to him; and Shirley 'made him her pet'. When he came to Fieldhead, after a tour, he was fifteen. Shirley discussed the terms of her will with him when she thought she was going to die, and he was so grieved that he had to confide in Louis. He was 'bridesman' at their wedding.　　　*S.* xxii, xxiii, xxvi–xxviii, xxxi, xxxvi

Mr SYMPSON of Sympson Grove was Shirley Keeldar's uncle and guardian. She had passed two years of her youth in his family, her tutor being Louis Moore. Mr Sympson was a man of 'worrying temper, pious principles, and worldly views', very different in outlook from Shirley. His wife was 'a very good woman, patient, kind, well-bred'. Their daughters Isabella and Gertrude had been educated faultlessly; they recoiled from anything savouring of originality or heterodoxy. Mr Sympson's purpose in coming to Fieldhead with his family was to promote a suitable match for Shirley. When she rejected Sir Philip Nunnely, he was annoyed; when she announced that she intended to marry Louis Moore, he was furious, and so insulting that Louis laid hands on him and insisted on his immediate departure.

S. xxii, xxiii, xxvi–xxviii, xxxi, xxxvi

TARTAR, Shirley's dog, 'rather large, strong, and fierce-looking . . . being of a breed between mastiff and bull-dog', is remembered for the fright he caused the two curates, Donne and Malone, at Fieldhead. *Shirley and Tartar are Charlotte's memorial to Emily Brontë and her dog Keeper:* 'The tawny and lion-like bulk of Tartar is ever stretched beside her; his negro muzzle laid on his fore paws, straight, strong,

and shapely as the limbs of an Alpine wolf. One hand of the mistress generally reposes on the loving serf's rude head . . .' *S.* xi, xv,
xx, xxii, xxvi, xxviii, xxxi, xxxvi

Miss TEMPLE, superintendent of Lowood School, sympathized with the girls who suffered under Mr Brocklehurst's rigid rules. She was tall and stately. When she married the Rev. Mr Nasmyth and left, Lowood was never the same, and Jane Eyre, who admired her and had been a teacher for two years, soon chose to be a governess. *This favourable portrait is a tribute to Miss A. Evans, the superintendent Charlotte Brontë knew at the Clergy Daughters' School, Cowan Bridge. She married the Rev. James Connor, and lived for a time in the U.S.A. When controversy about the school arose after the publication of Mrs Gaskell's* The Life of Charlotte Brontë, *she wrote in its defence.* *J.* v–x, xvii

LA TERRASSE, rather a manor than a château, and built in the old style of Basse-Ville, was the Brettons' home outside Villette. A lane off the main road became an avenue which led to the house on a terrace. *It may have been the Château de Koekelberg which Charlotte visited when Mary and Martha Taylor were at school there; for its exact site, see Joan Stevens,* Mary Taylor, *Auckland, N.Z., 1972, p. 172.*
V. xvi–xxi, xxiii–xxv

THOMAS, parish clerk at Briarfield, joined his master and Mr Malone in helping Robert Moore against the Luddites. *S.* ii, xix, xx,
xxiv, xxxiv

THORNFIELD HALL, six miles from Millcote, was the home of Mr Rochester. Here Jane Eyre and her master fell in love. His first wife, Bertha Mason, mad and immured there for years in an attic, set fire to it after Jane's departure, and only a blackened ruin remained. *The name arises from the huge old thorns near the Hall (xi). These, the rookery, the tree cloven by lightning, and the battlements, as well as the distance from 'Millcote' (Leeds), derive from Rydings, Ellen Nussey's home at Birstall. The third-storey attics, and the field 'like a park' in front of the building, were suggested by Norton Conyers near Ripon, which Charlotte visited with the Sidgwicks when they were staying at Swarcliffe near Harrogate. There are no hills in the vicinity of Norton Conyers.* *J.* x–xxvii, xxxvi

THRUSHCROSS GRANGE, the home of the Lintons, became the property of Heathcliff as a result of a long-sustained strategy of cunning, cruelty, and revenge. Avarice made him let it. It stood among trees in a large park. Heathcliff met Isabella Linton in the plantation

at the back the night before her elopement. In their love, Catherine
Linton and Heathcliff were divided until a few hours before her death
at the Grange on 20 March 1784. *Although the Grange is situated
near moors like those above Haworth, and its park may have been
suggested by the avenue of trees which approached Ponden Hall, it is*

(Ponden Hall)

*largely imaginary. Its setting and surroundings may owe something to
Emily Brontë's knowledge of Shibden Hall (north of Law Hill, near
Halifax), with its trees and park above the river. Its rather secluded
position offered a sharp contrast to that of High Sunderland Hall; see*
WUTHERING HEIGHTS.   *W*. i–iii, vi, vii, ix–xxix, xxxii

Juanna TRISTA was a pupil at Mlle Reuter's. Her father was a
Catalonian merchant who lived in the —— Isles; her Flemish mother
was dead. She was fifteen. William Crimsworth, looking at her
countenance and head (shaped like that of Pope Alexander VI),

wondered how anyone could have accepted her. Her gaunt visage expressed hatred and mutiny. Her behaviour was so disgusting, and her influence so bad, that he turned her out of his class and locked her in a *cabinet*, much to Mlle's astonishment and alarm. Juanna joined her father, exulting in the prospect of having 'slaves' under her command whom she could 'kick and strike at will'. *See* DOLORES.

P. xii

Lord TYNEDALE was a maternal uncle of William Crimsworth. He and his brother shared the cost of William's education at Eton, and invited him to enter the Church, Lord Tynedale offering him the living of Seacombe. *P*. i, vi

M. VANDAM, like M. Kint, was a Belgian usher at M. Pelet's school. They were treated as drudges ('bêtes de somme') because they were Flemish. *P*. viii, xi

Victor VANDENHUTEN was a rich and influential Dutchman whose son, Jean Baptiste, when he was a pupil at M. Pelet's, had been saved from drowning by William Crimsworth (*probably in the grounds of the Palais Royal*). M. Vandenhuten promised that he would help his benefactor whenever he could, and Crimsworth turned to him after resigning his post at M. Pelet's. The eventual result was his appointment to teach English at a college in Brussels. When he and Mlle Henri were married, Victor gave the bride away. They named their son after him. The Vandenhutens hoped to visit them in England.

P. xxi, xxii, xxv

Jules VANDERKELKOV was a 'moon-faced' Flemish youth at M. Pelet's school. *P*. vii, x

Louise VANDERKELKOV's illness (feigned, M. Emanuel thought) led to Lucy Snowe's taking part at short notice in the vaudeville he was preparing for the fête in honour of Mme Beck. Despite herself, she dared not resist his appeal. *V*. xiv

Adèle VARENS was very much like her mother, Céline Varens, a French opera dancer (xi, xv, xxiv, xxvii), the first of three mistresses with whom Rochester lived after finding that his wife was mad. She was not his daughter but, not liking to leave her in poverty in Paris (with Mme Frederic and her husband, after her mother had left her, to accompany a musician or singer to Italy), he brought her to Thornfield with a French nurse, Sophie. Jane Eyre became her governess. When Jane left, Adèle was sent to school. *J*. xi–xviii, xxi–xxvii, xxxvi–xxxviii

VASHTI. *See* VILLETTE, *p. 336*. *V*. xxiii

VILLETTE, the capital of Labassecour (*see p. 140*), where the main story of Lucy Snowe's life is centred, *is Brussels as Charlotte Brontë knew it in 1842 and 1843. Since then many changes have taken place in and around the city. Most of it was surrounded by trees and boulevards; a canal flanked the trees on the north-western side.*

It was once assumed that Charlotte first called it 'Choseville', but the name occurs in a passage written at the expense of the rather unintelligent Ginevra Fanshawe (end of xxvii), whose habit of using 'chose' for anything which she could not exactly designate was first illustrated when she could not think of 'Villette' (vi).

Charlotte tried to conceal the actual by changing not only the names but often locations as well. There is no disguise in The Professor (*see* BRUSSELS). *Lucy Snowe would not have entered the city near the park from 'Boue-Marine', nor is it likely that she reached the Grande Place (in front of the Hôtel de Ville) on the night of public celebration (Charlotte wrote 'a Grande Place', which is more likely to be the Place Royale, if she had anything in mind but to put the reader off the scent). The fictional Porte de Crécy seems to be inappropriate for the road to 'La Terrasse'; it suggests the Porte de Namur near what had been the Place de Waterloo on the opposite side of the city.*

The upper part of the city, on the eastern side, was rebuilt after the great fire of 1731. Its main street, the Rue Royale, runs near the edge of the Haute-Ville by the park (where the struggle for national independence was soon brought to a conclusion in 1830), with the cathedral (Ste Gudule) prominent a short distance north-west. Much of the lower part of the city, the Basse-Ville, where Charlotte saw much poverty, is more central and ancient.

Mme Heger's school was in the Rue d'Isabelle, once called the Fossé-aux-Chiens; this and the narrowness of the street suggested 'Rue Fossette'. M. Heger taught at the Athénée Royal, a school which was transferred to the Rue des Douze Apôtres not long before the arrival of Charlotte and Emily Brontë in Brussels. Overlooking the end of the Hegers' garden was a boarding-house in the Rue Terarken; see BRUSSELS.

Travelling from Boue-Marine (*Ostend*) by diligence, Lucy Snowe reached Villette in darkness, and was escorted by Dr Bretton, whom she had not recognized, along the Boulevard and across the park. She was then directed across a broad street (*the Rue Royale*) to some steps, at the bottom of which she would find a narrow street with an inn where she might stay the night. Despite her diversion she made her way to this street, where she saw the pensionnat of Mme Beck (*Mme Heger's, 32 Rue d'Isabelle*), was tempted to call, and was given employment (vii).

Later she found it pleasant in the evening to listen to the bells of St Jean Baptiste (*Ste Gudule, the cathedral; see* BRUSSELS), the grey crown of which could be seen burnished at sunset from Mme Beck's garden (xii, xxxi, xxxvi, xli). From the long dormitory, she could hear bands playing in the park or in the Palace Square (*the Place Royale*).

During the long vacation, Lucy walked far into the country along the highways, beyond Catholic and Protestant cemeteries (*there are three near the Chaussée de Louvain*). Then, towards the end of a stormy period following an Indian summer, she entered in despair an old solemn church, where she sought confession (xv). *See Charlotte's letter of 2.9.43, where she describes her wanderings in the country, and then, after 'threading the streets in the neighbourhood of the Rue d'Isabelle' to avoid the house (Mme Heger's), how she found herself opposite Ste Gudule and, hearing the bell for* salut, *entered and, after* vespers, *'took a fancy' to confess for the sake of seeing what it was like. It would be a mistake to accept her explanation entirely at its face value, but perhaps an even greater one to assume that Lucy Snowe's experiences were hers.* It was dark when she left the church, and she lost her way; the storm and her illness were too much for her, and she collapsed. Dr Bretton rode up as a priest (her confessor, Père Silas, who had followed, probably to discover where she lived) was lifting her up outside 'an old church belonging to a community of Béguines' (*the Eglise de Béguinage*), and took her to La Terrasse, the small château which he had acquired in the country for the sake of his mother's health, about half a league from the Porte de Crécy. *See the note above and* LA TERRASSE; *the road to Koekelberg passed through the Porte de Flandre. The fictional Porte de Crécy must be associated with the Rue Crécy (is this the Boulevard of Crécy, xv?) and the Hôtel Crécy, where Paulina and her father were staying. If, as is probable, this is the Hôtel Cluysenaar (afterwards the Hôtel Mengelle) which Charlotte visited several times as a guest of the Wheelwrights, its location is thoroughly obscured, for this hotel was at the northern end of the Rue Royale, and the Rue Crécy suggests the Boulevard de Waterloo on the south-east perimeter of the city. From the Rue d'Isabelle*, the nearest route to it, which Lucy and Ginevra Fanshawe took (xxvii), *could not have been across a great square and through the park for either the Rue Royale or the Boulevard.*

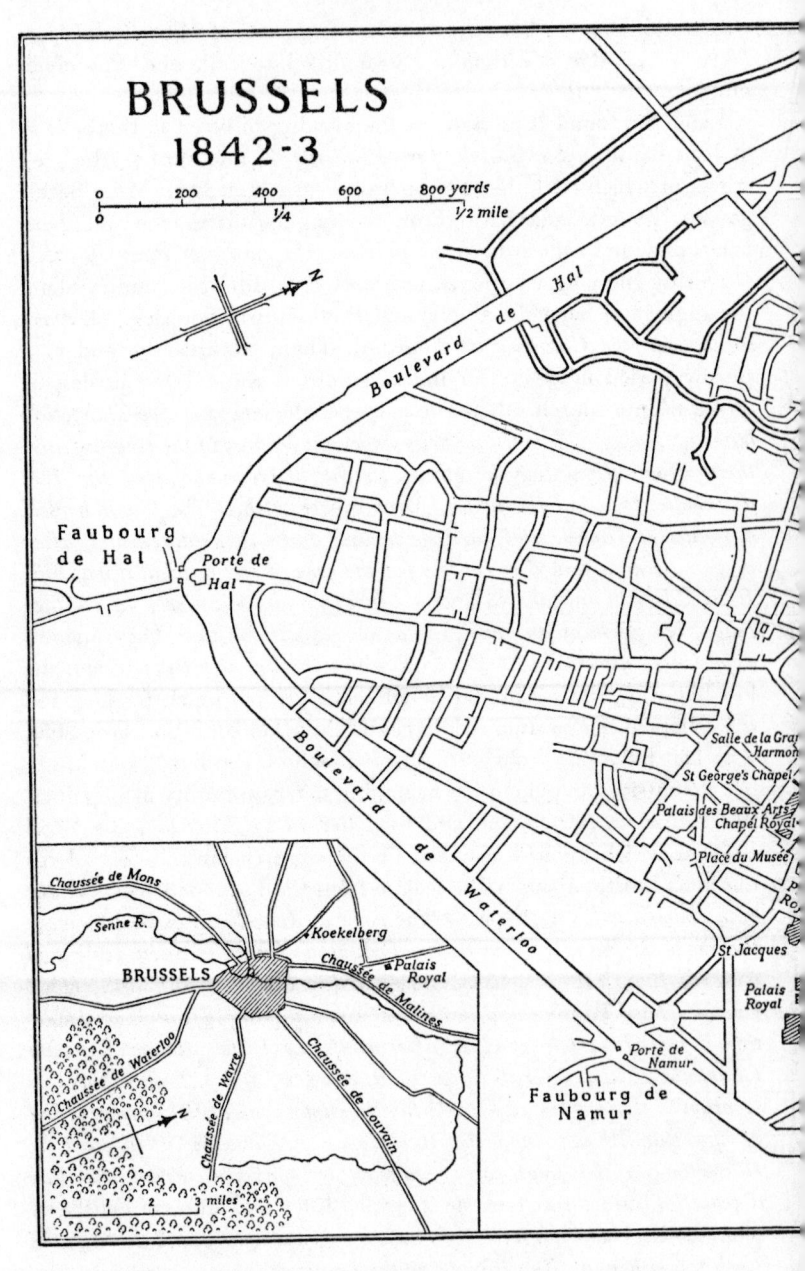

BRUSSELS
1842-3

0   200   400   600   800 yards
0   1/4   1/2 mile

Z

Faubourg
de Hal

Porte de
Hal

Boulevard   de   Hal

Boulevard   de   Waterloo

Salle de la Grae
Harmon
St George's Chapel
Palais des Beaux Arts
Chapel Royal
Place du Musée

St Jacques

Palais
Royal

Porte de
Namur

Faubourg de
Namur

Chaussée de Mons

Senne R.

BRUSSELS

Koekelberg
Chaussée de Malines
Palais
Royal

Chaussée de Waterloo

Chaussée de Wavre

Chaussée de Louvain

Z

0   1   2   3 miles

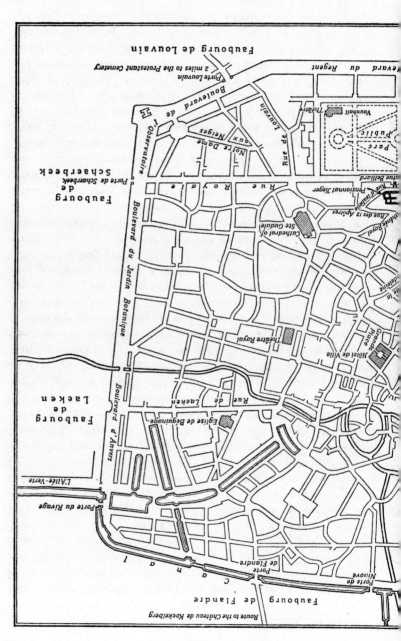

Map of Brussels

Towards the end of her convalescence at La Terrasse, Lucy accompanied Dr Bretton on missions to poor and crowded parts of the Basse-Ville. At other times he left her in the early morning to study pictures in the galleries before they were too crowded. *Charlotte's visit to the Brussels Salon is proved by her reference to pictures of 'La Vie d'une Femme', of which there were three, not four, in the actual exhibition. There was no picture entitled 'Cleopatra', but 'Une Almée' contained several of its characteristics, shocked some of the public, and was described as 'A Slave of the Harem'* (BST. *lxv*). He took Lucy to the concert attended by the royal party *at the Salle de la Grande Harmonie* (10.12.43, *ibid.*). Thus she learned more of Villette than ever before, its old and poor quarters, and its new and fashionable centres in the Haute-Ville. *Charlotte's description of the performance of 'a great actress' in the part of Vashti is based on her impressions of Rachel at St James's Theatre, London, in the summer of 1851. Charlotte thought her 'a snake', 'a demon'; see her letters, 11 June (to Amelia Taylor), 24 June, 28 June (Sydney Dobell), and 15 November, 1851. Rachel visited Brussels in the summer of 1843, but it is not known whether Charlotte Brontë saw her perform then. The idea of the fire-scare when the tragedy was reaching its end came from Charlotte's publisher George Smith, who (in a letter to her) suggested the danger when the scenery caught fire at Devonshire House, as Charles Dickens and other men of letters were giving a charity performance. Smith prevented his sister and a lady friend from rushing out, and the fire was quickly extinguished. He had taken Charlotte to the previous performance.* One mild October afternoon, Lucy rode through Bois l'Etang with Dr Bretton (xxii); the following summer (xxxvii) she saw him and Paulina, after their engagement, seated under a tree in the palace grounds at Bois l'Etang (*the park of the Palais Royal north of Brussels, with its 'lakelets or étangs'; see* V. *xxvi and* P. *xxi*).

Lucy made another incursion into the old and grim Basse-Ville when she visited Madame Walravens of 3 Rue des Mages. Père Silas lived in the same street (xv), which seemed part of a square overlooked by the dark, ruinous towers of a church, once the opulent shrine of the Magi (xxxiv). Père Silas, anxious for Lucy's conversion, had ascertained that she attended the three Protestant chapels, where French, German, and English services were held (xxxvi). *In* The Professor *we hear of 'the two Protestant chapels'; see* BRUSSELS.

Lucy's audio-visual impressions when she was drawn uncannily to the park form the most sustained imaginative episode in Villette. *It was a*

July night, yet the public festivities celebrated the successful struggle for Belgian independence at the end of September 1830, and Charlotte probably heard the grand concert, with a 'chant des montagnards' (the Jäger chorus) in September 1843 (BST. *lxv*). Instead of sleeping after taking Mme Beck's sedative, Lucy had such a potent vision of Villette at midnight, and of one scene in the park, that she was impelled to steal out. Lured by music, she proceeded towards 'the palatial and royal Haute-Ville', where she became one of a joyous throng. Villette seemed 'one blaze, one broad illumination'. She then followed the open carriage in which she saw the Brettons and the de Bassompierres. In the park she was diverted by music to the huge crowd which stood listening to a grand concert. There she recognized her friends but, obeying her feverish impulse and 'the push of every chance elbow', she found herself in an area where the crowd was split into groups by the trees. Here she saw 'the whole conjuration, the secret junta'. 'Fascinated as by a basilisk', she stayed and heard enough to feel that her final hope was shattered, though Paul Emanuel had not sailed. Nothing remained for her but to leave 'the radiant park and the well-lit Haute-Ville' for her bed in the 'dim lower quarter'.

Paul had not deserted her. He did not disclose his plans for the future until he took her, after they had walked in the boulevards, to the Faubourg Clotilde, to show her the school he had prepared for her direction during his absence. They walked back to the Rue Fossette in 'such moonlight as fell on Eden'. (*For Mme Heger's school, see the plan, p. 271 and Appendix 3, pp. 374–6.*) *V*.

Justine Marie WALRAVENS (*named after Marie Josephine, M. Heger's first wife*) was Mme Walraven's grand-daughter. Her parents had been wealthy, and opposed her marriage to Paul Emanuel because he was not rich enough for their needs. She became a nun, and died at an early age. *V*. xxxiv, xxxv

Mme Magliore WALRAVENS was very old, and as hideous as a Hindoo idol; she seemed to possess an idol's consequence in the estimation of her votaries. To Lucy Snowe she was the sorceress Cunegonde and the evil fairy Malevola. 'She might be three feet high, but she had no shape; her skinny hands rested upon each other, and pressed the gold knob of a wand-like ivory staff. Her face was large, set, not upon her shoulders, but before her breast; she seemed to have no neck.' She was hunchbacked, and heavily bejewelled like a barbarian queen. Her eyes were malign, 'with thick grey brows above, and livid lids all round'. She had been rich, and was likely to be so again. Mme Walravens had successfully opposed the marriage of her grand-daughter Justine Marie to Paul Emanuel because he was not wealthy. Yet during her poverty, he supported her and her old servant Agnes in the Rue des Mages. Mme Beck for personal reasons (she was a distant relative of Mme Walravens, who had no family of her own) and Père Silas, for the sake of religion and the Church, had decided that Paul was the man to go out to Guadaloupe for three years to make the Walravens estate highly profitable again. *In the figure of Mme Walravens, Charlotte Brontë embodied her antipathy to the worst in the Catholic Church.*　　*V*. xxxiv, xxxviii, xxxix, xlii

WARREN was Mrs Bretton's servant at Bretton.　　　　　　*V*. i–iii

The WATSONS were a rich family party on board 'The Vivid'. To the stewardess, who welcomed them boisterously, they were 'as good as a little fortune'. The group consisted of two men and two women; the men were short, fat, and vulgar, the women youthful. One of these was 'perfectly handsome', so young that one could only assume she had not long been married. Her husband was the elder of the two men, very plain, greasy, and broad. They were sick on the way to Boue-Marine, and the stewardess attended them with shameless partiality.　　　　　　*V*. vi

WELLWOOD, the home of the Bloomfields, where Agnes Grey had her first experience as a governess, was a stately mansion in its own grounds, separated by not more than twenty miles of hilly country from her home. *See* Mrs BLOOMFIELD.　　　　*A*. ii–vi, xvii

Edward WESTON, the curate who succeeded Mr Bligh at Horton, afforded a welcome contrast to his predecessor and to the rector, Mr Hatfield. He brought comfort and assistance to the homes of poor cottages, and his sermons were pleasingly evangelical to Agnes Grey. Miss Murray tried to 'fix' him, but his love for Miss Grey never faltered. He accepted the living of F——, a parish two miles from A——, where he met Agnes again and proposed to her. He had a 'respectable' house in a pleasant neighbourhood, and a stipend of £300 a year. They were happily married. He was devoted to his parochial duties, made some remarkable reforms, and was loved and esteemed by his parishioners. *This portrait was undoubtedly inspired to some extent by the more serious side of William Weightman.*
　　　　　　A. ix–xviii, xx–xxii, xxiv, xxv

Mrs WHARTON was the English lady in Brussels who engaged Mlle Henri (after she had lost her post at Mlle Reuter's) to repair some old lace for her eldest daughter's wedding. She and a Parisian lady were so impressed with Mlle Henri's general knowledge and her competence in both French and English that they helped her to obtain a teaching appointment at the 'first' English school in Brussels, where two of Mrs Wharton's younger daughters were pupils. The directress of the school was Mrs D——.   *P.* xxi

WHINBURY was a market town (*thought to be Dewsbury. Except for the first scene, it is peripheral and incidental to the novel*). It combined with Briarfield and Nunnely for the Whitsuntide fête. Its vicar was Dr Boultby; its curate, Mr Donne. Its leading industrial families included the Sykeses and the Pearsons.   *S.* i, ii, v–ix, xiv–xvi,
                                                                            xxiii

Mrs WHIPP was Mr Sweeting's landlady. *For the name, see the note on* Paulina HOME.   *S.* i

WHITCROSS stood at crossroads, ten miles from the nearest town. It was a stone pillar with four arms above it. Here Jane Eyre was set down after travelling by coach the greater part of two days from the neighbourhood of Thornfield Hall. All around her were moors, ridges, and 'waves of mountains'. From this point Jane made her way penniless to Morton, eventually to find a home at Moor House. *The claim that this is Moscar Cross, less than ten miles west of Sheffield, cannot be substantiated. It is a stone pillar with directions inscribed upon it. The 1809 map shows no crossroads near it, only a junction where a minor road from Penistone met the Sheffield–Manchester road. There is nothing to indicate that a road to Hathersage ('Morton') subsequently linked up with the Penistone Road at this point. The novel shows that Whitcross stood (or was imagined to stand) further south: Jane made her way from Whitcross to Morton with the sun 'fervent and high' behind her. See p. 111.*   *J.* xxviii, xxix, xxxiv, xxxvi

WILDFELL HALL was an Elizabethan house near the top of Wildfell, about two miles from Linden-Car and four miles from the sea. There was nothing to shield it from wind and storm but a group of Scotch firs, as gloomy as the Hall itself. Beyond it lay a few desolate fields and the heath-clad summit of the hill. It was owned by Mr Lawrence, whose family left it fifteen years earlier. Two or three rooms were prepared for the reception of his sister when she fled from her dissolute husband, Arthur Huntingdon, with her young son and his nurse Rachel. It was a dismal place, with the bleak wind moaning around and howling through the ruinous old chambers. While in refuge here, to save her son from his father's influence, she fell in love with Gilbert

Markham. Her sense of duty made her leave Wildfell Hall to return to her husband at Grassdale Manor, and nurse him during the last weeks of his life. *The name derives from its position. A 'fell' in the north of England is a high hill, ridge, or mountain.*   *T*. i, ii, v–viii,
x, xii, xv, xli, xliii-xlv

Annabella W ILMOT was an accomplished musician and flirt. Lord Lowborough was an easy prey; she married him for his title and family seat. Her main prize was Arthur Huntingdon, and she had little difficulty in winning him. Two years passed before Lord Lowborough discovered the affair. He and his wife separated; Lady Lowborough continued her dashing life, and went off with a gallant to the Continent, where she lived in gaiety and dissipation until they quarrelled and parted. She died at length (according to rumour) in penury and wretchedness.   *T*. xvii–xix, xxii, xxvi, xxvii, xxxi–
xxxv, xxxviii, l

Mr W ILMOT, Annabella's uncle, was (according to Helen Huntingdon) 'a worthless old reprobate' (*see p. 245*). It was at his party in London that Arthur Huntingdon declared his admiration of her. Wilmot was a friend of Mr Maxwell, and one of his guests at Staningley during the shooting-season.   *T*. xvi–xix, xxi

Jane W ILSON, Mrs Wilson's graceful and elegant daughter, had acquired accent and accomplishments at a boarding-school. She aspired to marry a gentleman, and had designs, it was said, on Mr Lawrence. She and her mother played their part in spreading slanderous reports about Mrs Huntingdon, and Gilbert Markham therefore had no hesitation in attempting to undermine Mr Lawrence's partiality for her; he could not bear to think that she might be Helen's sister-in-law. Mr Lawrence took note, it seems. Jane remained single, withdrew from Ryecote Farm when her mother died, and took rooms in the more genteel atmosphere of her county town, where she would remain (Markham imagined) 'a cold-hearted, supercilious, keenly, insidiously censorious old maid', spending her days in fancy-work and scandal.   *T*. i, iii, iv, vi, vii, ix, xi, xiii, xlvi, xlviii

Mr W ILSON had been English master at Mme Beck's. Lucy Snowe deputized in his absence so satisfactorily that she was promoted from nursery governess to his place. Her salary was raised, but Mme benefited, Lucy doing 'thrice the work . . . she had extracted from Mr Wilson, at half the expense'.   *V*. viii

Mrs W ILSON was the widow of a substantial farmer, and (according to Gilbert Markham) 'a narrow-minded, tattling old gossip', who made it her business to find out all she could about the mysterious tenant of Wildfell Hall. She lived with her sons and daughter at Ryecote Farm.   *T.* i, iii, iv, ix, xiii, xlviii

Richard WILSON of Ryecote Farm was a studious, retiring young man, who wished to enter the Church. The vicar, Mr Millward, helped him in classics. After graduating at Cambridge with hard-earned honours and an untarnished reputation, he became Mr Millward's curate, married his daughter Mary, and succeeded him.
                                                        T. i, iv, vii, xlviii

Robert WILSON, Richard's elder brother, was in charge of Ryecote Farm. He was thrifty, but too rough and unsophisticated for his sister Jane.   *T.* i, iv, xiii, xlviii

Alice WOOD was the little workhouse orphan for whom Miss Oliver provided a post as housemaid to Jane Eyre when Jane was mistress of the girls' school at Morton.   *J.* xxx–xxxii

Mark WOOD was the consumptive labourer whom Mr Weston and Agnes Grey used to visit.   *A.* xi, xiv, xv

Mr WOOD was the clergyman of the church between Thornfield Hall and Hay; John Green was the clerk. Both were officiating when the marriage of Rochester and Jane Eyre was banned.   *J.* xxvi

WOODFORD was Mr Lawrence's home. His family had left Wildfell Hall for this more modern and commodious mansion in Linden-thorpe.   *T.* i, xlv–xlvii, xlix, li

WORMWOOD WELLS. *Probably Harrogate. See* Hortense MOORE.
                                                        S. xx, xxiii, xxv

WUTHERING HEIGHTS, the property of the Earnshaws and subsequently of Heathcliff, stood very near the top of the bleak hill from which it was named. The eminence concealed it from Thrushcross Grange, four miles away (xviii). Its name derived from the local word describing 'the atmospheric tumult to which its station is exposed in stormy weather . . . one may guess the power of the north wind blowing over the edge by the excessive slant of a few stunted firs at the end of the house; and by a range of gaunt thorns all stretching their limbs one way, as if craving alms of the sun'. The architect showed foresight; its narrow windows were deeply inset, and the corners of the house were reinforced with large jutting stones. *The 'grotesque carving' over the front and the 'wilderness of crumbling griffins and shameless little boys' were suggested by the sculptural ornament of High Sunderland Hall (demolished in 1950), which Emily Brontë had seen in her walks on one of the heights overlooking*

Halifax, during her stay at Law Hill in the autumn and winter of 1837–8. Law Hill is situated on a high hill exposed to all the winds that blow, and is more of a 'wuthering height' than the simple farmstead of Top Withins above Haworth, which is usually assumed to mark the approximate location of Wuthering Heights. The history of Law Hill undoubtedly contributed to the story of the novel; see p. 206. Other features of the country around Law Hill were transferred to the country west of Haworth for the Wuthering Heights *setting. See* GIMMERTON *and* THRUSHCROSS GRANGE. *W.* i–xiv, xvii, xviii, xx, xxi, xxiii, xxiv, xxvii–xxxiv

Mr WYNNE and his family were members of the Briarfield gentry. He hoped that his son Samuel Fawthrop Wynne would marry Shirley, declared that his De Walden estate and hers were 'delightfully *contagious*', and actually proposed for him. Shirley scorned the offer; Sam was barely literate; he had been the booby of Stilbro' Grammar School. He was cruel to his pointers; and Phoebe, one of them, in a state of dangerous madness, bit Shirley. There had been a rumour that Robert Moore would marry first the dark Miss Wynne; then, the light one. *See p. 155.* *S.* ii, xii, xiv, xvi, xvii, xix, xxiv, xxvi– xxviii

X—— *Its description undoubtedly suggests Huddersfield as seen from the Roe Head district Charlotte Brontë knew so well:* 'At a distance of five miles, a valley, opening between the low hills, held in its cups the great town of X——. A dense, permanent vapour brooded over this locality', and here, in Bigben Close, stood Edward Crimsworth's mill and warehouse, where William worked as a clerk for three months before being dismissed by his tyrannical taskmaster. *P.* i–vii, xxii

Hesther YORKE, Hiram's wife, *was based on Charlotte's impressions of Mrs Taylor. She is 'a personage whom I might describe minutely. . . . I see her . . . very plainly before me' (ix). Of Mme Heger Charlotte wrote (15.11.43), 'as to warm-heartedness she has as much of that article as Mrs Taylor'.* She was large, very grave, and disapproved of cheerfulness, especially in female company. She was a most conscientious wife and mother, preferred that her husband should have no friends but herself, and attended to her six children unceasingly. They were Matthew (ix, xxxii, xxxiii), Mark (ix, xxxiii), Martin, Rose, Jessie, and the baby; as they grew up, they tended to rebel against their strong-minded mother. She held stern, democratic views, was always right in her own eyes, and suspected all men,

creeds, and parties. She had few friends, but liked the Moores. When she visited Hortense she was seen in a large cap (carefully transported in a vast bag of black silk like a balloon), the frill a quarter of a yard broad around her face, with ribbon flourishing in puffs and bows about her head. Her anti-matrimonial innuendo provoked Caroline Helstone, but Miss Keeldar was proof against her shafts. When she nursed Robert Moore at Briarmains, she was 'a mother' to him and very sorry to see him go.   *S.* ix, xii, xx, xxiii–xxvi, xxviii, xxxii–
xxxv

Hiram YORKE was a manufacturer who lived at Briarmains. He often spoke broad Yorkshire, was proud of being a Yorkshireman (*hence his name*), and could be blunt and rough in manner. His rather Radical views often brought him into conflict with Mr Helstone. To his workmen he was friendly and considerate; at Robert Moore's request, he found a job for William Farren. He was proud of his children. His home showed excellent taste and a genuine interest in art. He had travelled a great deal in Europe, and was adept in French and Italian. He had loved Mary Cave and lost her to Mr Helstone. Despite his political views he was haughty, lacking in human warmth and benevolence. He was independent and had few friends, though Robert Moore and he had much in common. He encouraged Robert to think of marrying Shirley; she had been his ward, and he gave her away when she married Louis Moore. Yorke accompanied Robert from Stilbro' when the latter was wounded by an assassin. *See* Yorke HUNSDEN. *Mary Taylor did not think Yorke was quite like her father: 'He hates well enough and perhaps loves too, but he is not honest enough.'*   *S.* iii, iv–vi, ix, xi, xviii, xx, xxi, xxvii, xxx–xxxv,
xxxvii

Jessie YORKE *is sketched from Martha, the younger sister of Mary Taylor, one of Charlotte's closest friends. Martha died at the Château de Koekelberg while Charlotte was in Brussels (more than 'twenty' years after the events of Shirley), and was buried in the Protestant Cemetery outside the city; see pp. 34, 95.* She was a gay, affectionate prattler, who was apt to repeat her father's Radical views in northern Doric.
S. ix, xxiii, xxxii, xxxv

Martin YORKE, a Briarfield Grammar School pupil, contrived the meeting between Caroline Helstone and Robert Moore at Briarmains. He was 'bridesman' at their wedding.   *S.* ix, xxiii, xxxii–xxxiv,
xxxvii

Rose YORKE resembled her father. She was sometimes stubborn, and longed to travel. *Mary Taylor emigrated to New Zealand in 1845, years after the time indicated in* Shirley.　　*S*. ix, xxiii, xxxii, xxxiv, xxxv

Mlles ZEPHYRINE, PELAGIE, and SUZETTE taught at Mlle Reuter's. They were all French, the last two commonplace. Zéphyrine was more distinguished-looking, but 'in character a genuine Parisian coquette, perfidious, mercenary, and dry-hearted'. *See* Zélie ST PIERRE.　　*P*. xii, xvi

ZILLAH was a stout and energetic housekeeper at Wuthering Heights during Heathcliff's latter years. She saw much that she disliked, but dared not disobey him for fear of losing her place. She left before his death, and was succeeded by Ellen Dean. *See the footnote on p. 220.*

　　W. i–iii, xxi, xxiii, xxiv, xxvii–xxx, xxxii

Glossary

(Only the more important of the French words are included.)

aboon, above
afore, before
agait, *agate*, afoot, astir
have agait, be up to, do
aght, *aht*, out
ahr, our
allus, always
alow, ablaze
an, if
anent, about, concerning; against, opposite, near
armoire, cupboard
arn, earn
'at, that
Aw, I
ax, ask
ayont, beyond

bahn, born
'baht, without
bairn, *barn*, child
ball, clog with snow
ban, curse, swear
barthen, burden
bas-bleu, blue-stocking
be, by
bend-leather, hard as the stoutest leather

bésicles, spectacles
biggin, building
blackaviced, dark-complexioned
blanc-bec, simpleton
blonde, silk lace
bogard, *boggard*, ghost, hobgoblin
bonne, housemaid
bonnet-grec, smoking-cap
bougie, candle
'bout, without
bravely, fine, well
brust, burst
bud, but

cabas, work-bag
cabinet, small room
'cahnt, mak noa, account, take no
callant, lad, young man
cannie, preternaturally wise
cannily, in secret, slyly
cant, talk humbug
canting, hypocritical
cantlet, portion, segment
canty, *cant*, cheerful, lively, hale and hearty
cap the globe, surpass everything
capped, at a loss to understand
castor, a kind of hat

chaussée, highway

cheeney, china

childer, children

chimney, chimney-place, fireplace

chitty-faced, baby-faced

classe, classroom

clomp, tread noisily

Cloth-hall, hall or exchange where dealers in woollen cloths transact business; cf. 'piece-hall', where cloth is sold by the piece

codger, fellow, chap

convive, table-companion

coquelicot, corn-poppy

cotch, catch

courroucée, displeased, incensed

crack, a sudden outburst of noise

crahnr, coroner

crânerie, boldness, bluster

crater, creature

crock, metal pot *or* pot black with soot *or* polished black pot

croisée, window, casement

croquant, crunching

currently, fluently (*a gallicism*)

custen dahn, cast down, depressed

cyphering, arithmetic

dahn, down

daht, doubt

dead-thraw, throes of death

deave, break

debarassed, disembarrassed (*a gallicism*)

device, motto

doddered, with decaying branches

don, dress, dress smartly

doubt, fear

Douglas larder, disorder, shambles

down (*of*), distrustful, suspicious (of)

dreary, doleful, **dismal**

dree, long, tedious

dunnock, hedge-sparrow

dunnut, do not

E, I've

ea, eea, yes

ébats, revels

een, eyes

eft, (like a) newt or lizard

eht, out

eld, old age

enah, enough

estrade, dais

externat, externe, day-pupil

faâl, fahl, ugly, bad

fand, found

faquin, scoundrel

fashion, contrive, manage

feard, for fear that, lest

feck, quantity

fell, fierce

fellies, followers, sweethearts

fettle, set in order, tidy; 'finish off', kill

fit, feet

fix, attach, win the heart of

flay, fley, scare, frighten

flaysome, frightful

flighted, scared

fly up, lose one's temper

(*what a*) *fooil* (*of a*), (how) idiotic

foreigners, strangers, non-local people

forrard(s), forward, on

frame, 'clear off', betake oneself

fresh, slightly the worse for drink

froo, frough, from

fry, bustle

gait, gate, way, path, road

(*get a*) *gate*, go on

gambado, surprising, sudden, or fantastic action

gang, go

gaufre, wafer, waffle (thin cake)

gaumless, stupid

gentleman, the old, the devil

gig-mill, machine, or mill, for raising nap on cloth

gird, spasm of pain

girn, grin, grin, show the teeth in laughing, snarl

girt, great

gleg, sharp, keen

gnarl, snarl

grat, cried, wept

greasehorn, flatterer

gros-bonnet, bigwig

guéridon, round table

(*another*) *guess sort*, (a) different kind

guilp, iron vessel for making porridge

habit, garment, coat

hagh, hah, how

hahs, house

hahsiver, however, none the less

happen, perhaps

happen to, might

harried, carried off

hauf, half

(*by the haulf*, much)

hearty, in good health, strong

hend, hand

hetman, captain, military commander

history, story

hit, reach, chance upon

hoile, hoyle, room, house

holm, meadow

hotel, town mansion

howe, depth, middle (of the night)

ideal, imaginary

ill, evil, naughty

imp, child, little devil, evil spirit

ing, meadow

intuh, into

jocks, food, provisions

joined Methody, a seceder who becomes a Methodist

juron, oath

keen, wail (for the dead)

kennel, gutter

kirk, church

kirstened, christened

kittle, difficult, 'ticklish'

laced, beaten, flogged

laiking, playing, having fun

laith, barn

lameter, cripple

lath of a crater, thin feeble creature

lick, beat

lig, lie

lig hold on't, grasp it

likely, proper, convenient

locataire, tenant, lodger

loon, scamp, rogue

lounder, thrash, beat

low, flame

lug, ear

madling, fool, simpleton

maigre-day, meatless or fish day

mark, embroider

marmot, little monkey, urchin

marred, spoilt, peevish

(*exactly one*) *mask*, (a perfect) likeness

maun, must

maw, my

meeterly, tolerably

mells, meddles

mensful, proper

mess, portion of food

mich, mitch, much; a marvel

mim, demure

mincing and munching, mincing and mumbling one's words

mither, mother

mony, many

mools, grave

moue, grimace

mud, mught, might

muh, may

mun, must

munnut, must not

nab, end of a hill or range of hills

nah, now

nave, neive, fist

nerves, sinews

nervous, sinewy, vigorous

nicher, snigger

noan, not

nobbut, nothing but, only

nor, nur, than

nor nuh me, not I (none o' me)

norther, neither

nought, worthless, good-for-nothing

nowt, blockhead

o'ered, over

offald, vile

on-goings, goings-on, proceedings (generally with implied censure)

onding on snaw, heavy with snow

onst, once

or iver, before

orther, either

orthering, order, command

ot', of the

owd, old

ower, owered, overed, over

owt ee knaw, anything I know

pale, knock

paletôt, overcoat

pared, reduced, deprived

parrain, godfather

parure, set of ornaments

pas de géant, giant's stride (*for recreation or physical education*)

pawsed, kicked

pensionnaire, boarder

pensionnat, boarding-school

pent, enclosed

person, physique

pikes, turnpike gates

pinched, in the grip of hunger or cold

(*in the*) *pip,* sick

pistolet, breakfast roll

plisky, rage

plotter, mud; wade through mud

plucked, failed, 'ploughed'

porte cochère, carriage or courtyard entrance

pose, puzzle, nonplus

pragmatical, self-important

prig, fop, self-indulgent or conceited person

quiz, odd person; make fun of

raight dahn, right down, not half, very

ranny, sharp, keen

ratton, rat

receipt, recipe

redd up, tidied up

régal, entertainment, treat

remarked, noticed (*a gallicism*)

retreat, asylum

rig, strip or ridge of growing corn

road, way, manner

roast, make a jest of

(*rule the*) *roast,* to be master

rout, fuss, to-do

rubbidge, rubbish

rusty, rancid (of meat)

sackless, feeble

sall, shall

salut, service of evening prayer

sap, blockhead

sartin, certain

savon, scolding

say, see

sconce, head

scout, dismiss with scorn

scrag, neck (*slang*)

scroop, back of a bookcover

seed, saw

seeght, sight, spectacle

sheltie, small pony (originally, Shetland pony)

shog, walk, jog along

shoo, she

shoon, shoes

shopping, being employed and told what to do

(*get*) *shut* (*of*), (get) rid (of)

sick, ill

side out, clear off, clear out

siding stuff, putting things away

sin', since, ago

sine as, when

skift, shift, move quickly away

snook, pry

sough, swamp

sponsers, responses

spoon, *spoonie*, fool

stale, steal

stalled, sick and tired of

stark, rigid (in death)

starved, chilled, frozen

sud, *suld*, should

summat, something

sup, drop (of rain)

surtout, overcoat

syne, since

t', the

taan, taken

tabouret, stool

tached, taught

taking, condition

teed, tied

tent, care

tenter, one who tends (sheep, for example)

thible, wooden porridge-stirrer

thrang, busy

threap, quarrel

thur, there

tinkler, tinker, gipsy

tisane, slightly medicinal drink (orig. barley-water)

tuh, *tull*, to

twal, twelve (o'clock)

tyne, lose

ud, *uld*, would

uf, of

uh, of; have

ull, will

un, one; and

underdrawn, covered with boards

unlikely, inappropriate

ut, that, at, of

ut', of the

wake, sit up with a sick person at night

wald, would

war, was; worse

went, want

wer, our

werseln, ourselves

whudder, *wuther*, (of the wind) bluster, rage

wick, *wik*, week(s)

win, reach

wink at, pretend not to notice

wisht, whist!, hush, be quiet, peace!

wollsome, wholesome, healthy

wor, wur, were

worriting, continually worrying

yah, you

yah'd as good, you might as well

yate, gate

yill, ale

Select Bibliography

Works

Early Writings

(ed.) Fannie E. Ratchford and W. C. DeVane, *Legends of Angria*, New Haven, 1933. Contains 'The Green Dwarf', the poem 'Zamorna's Exile', 'Mina Laury', and 'Caroline Vernon', with introduction and notes.

(Shakespeare Head Brontë) *The Miscellaneous and Unpublished Writings of Charlotte and Patrick Branwell Brontë*, Oxford, 1936 (vol. I), 1938 (vol. II).

(ed.) Winifred Gérin, *Charlotte Brontë, Five Novelettes*, London, 1971. Contains 'Passing Events', 'Julia', 'Mina Laury', 'Captain Henry Hastings', and 'Caroline Vernon', with an introduction.

Poetry

(ed.) Clement Shorter, *The Complete Poems of Anne Brontë*, London, 1920.

(Shakespeare Head Brontë) *The Poems of Charlotte Brontë and Patrick Branwell Brontë*, Oxford, 1934.

(Shakespeare Head Brontë) *The Poems of Emily Jane Brontë and Anne Brontë*, Oxford, 1934. Anne's poetry is more complete than in Shorter's edition.

(ed.) C. W. Hatfield, *The Complete Poems of Emily Brontë*, New York and London, 1941. The most reliable edition of Brontë poems.

Novels

There are many editions but relatively few standard texts.

Wuthering Heights presents a special problem, most editions retaining

Charlotte Brontë's simplifications of the dialect. The 1847 text is preserved in the World's Classics edition (Oxford University Press), the Norton critical edition, and the Rinehart edition (New York).

Except in the United States (see G. D. Hargreaves, *BST.* lxxxii), *The Tenant of Wildfell Hall* is usually printed without the introductory letter, chapter headings, and two paragraphs of chapter xxxviii. All are included in the rare Shakespeare Head edition (Blackwell, Oxford).

The Haworth edition has been reprinted a number of times, and is attractive, but it has the drawbacks referred to above concerning *Wuthering Heights* and *The Tenant of Wildfell Hall*. Its introductions by Mrs Humphry Ward are rather outdated, and its illustrations are introduced haphazardly.

The Clarendon edition supplies standard texts, with introductions, variants, and notes. So far two novels have appeared:

1. *Jane Eyre*, ed. Jane Jack and Margaret Smith, London, 1969; also ed. Margaret Smith, London, 1973.

2. *Wuthering Heights*, ed. Ian Jack and Hilda Marsden, London, 1974.

Letters

Clement Shorter, *Charlotte Brontë and Her Circle*, London, 1896, published as *The Brontës and Their Circle*, 1914; *The Brontës, Life and Letters*, London, 1908.

Both consist mainly of letters. In the first they are grouped according to subjects such as the Pensionnat Heger, Emily Brontë, literary ambitions, and Thackeray; it therefore lacks the advantage of continuous chronological arrangement such as we find in the second, a larger collection. The text is often less reliable, and altogether far less complete, than that of the Shakespeare Head edition.

(ed.) T. J. Wise and J. A. Symington, *The Brontës: Their Lives, Friendships and Correspondence in Four Volumes*, Oxford (published for the Shakespeare Head Press), 1932.

Though this is the best and most complete edition available, it is far from accurate, especially where it relies on earlier editions. For an example of the inaccuracy arising from Shorter's omissions and alterations, see Joan Stevens, 'Woozles in Brontëland', *Studies in Bibliography*, 1971.

Muriel Spark, *The Brontë Letters*, London, 1954 and 1966. The introduction and selection comprise a useful book for reading and reference. The principal aim is biographical. Correspondence from Maria Branwell, Patrick Brontë, and Mary Burder is included, together with Branwell's most important letters, the 'birthday' notes of 1841 and 1845, and two letters from Southey to Charlotte. Among over a hundred of Charlotte's letters are the four extant ones to M. Heger and some to G. H. Lewes.

Bibliography

(ed.) Lionel Stevenson, *Victorian Fiction*, Cambridge, Mass., 1964, pp. 214–44 (by Mildred G. Christian).
(ed.) A. E. Dyson, *The English Novel: Select Bibliographical Guides*, London, 1974 (by Miriam Allott).

Biography

(General)

G. F. Bradby, *The Brontës and Other Essays*, London, 1932.
The author may not be right in every detail, but his first three essays constitute a wholesome warning against romantic Brontë biography, and provide some enjoyable reading.

Irene Cooper Willis, *The Brontës*, London, 1933.
Despite certain weaknesses, this is an excellent brief introduction, often extremely well written, and characterized by sound incisive judgments. Mr Brontë may deserve a little more sympathy, and Branwell's decline probably began earlier than we are led to believe. The chronology contains a few inaccuracies. The author's interest in Emily results in disproportion towards the end, virtually to the exclusion of *Jane Eyre*.

G. Elsie Harrison, *The Clue to the Brontës*, London, 1948.
The clue is Wesleyanism, and the first five chapters on the religious background of the Brontës are of great importance. Nobody familiar

with Patrick Brontë's religious outlook could accept the common modern view that Aunt Branwell was responsible for the Calvinism which depressed three at least of the youthful Brontës. The author gives Patrick 'his undoubted due', and lays the blame for scandalous stories about him at Mrs Gaskell's door. Unfortunately she includes some of them in her biography, in addition to the allegation that the opening of *Jane Eyre* originated in punishment by Aunt Branwell. The author gives rein to her imagination, which is rather obsessional. The great Wesleyan figures keep cropping up, and we are told that the Brontës heard about them continually. Emily grew to admire the horrible Shirley, Lord Ferrers (of the same house as Lady Huntingdon, who was connected with the Hastings – hence the names of three Brontë characters), and re-created him, in combination with the renowned William Grimshaw, as Heathcliff. Maria Brontë continually walks; 'it is positively eerie the way that child haunts all Brontë literature'. 'Cold in the earth' is a recollection of her; she haunted the casement of the parsonage at Haworth, and appears as the child Cathy in Lockwood's dream. Rochester is M. Heger with his 'shadowy separating wife' in the background. When Charlotte was dying, she kept company with Maria and visited Brussels. The book has style and wit, especially at Patrick's expense. It is excellent on Wesleyanism, but often erroneous as biography.

Laurence and E. M. Hanson, *The Four Brontës*, London, 1949; revised edition, Hamden, Conn., 1967.
This comprehensive biography is a model of lucid compression and documentation. It provides a most valuable background, although some of its views are arbitrary or rather outdated. Mr Brontë and Miss Branwell are presented unsympathetically; Anne is tortured by Calvinism; Emily, unlike Charlotte, is very sympathetic towards Branwell. The latter occupies the centre of the stage too often perhaps. His affair with Mrs Robinson (or his account of it) was translated into the love story of *Wuthering Heights*. The legend of his dying on his feet is carried one stage further; he became an example to Emily in her last days. Biographical interpretations of some of the poems are sometimes open to question. Yet these reservations apply to only a small portion of this scholarly work. The advantage for the reader of a composite study (the avoidance of repeated contextual family events in single biographies of Branwell and his sisters) is enormous.

Margaret Lane, *The Brontë Story*, London, 1953.
Attractively illustrated by Joan Hassell, this study corrects Mrs
Gaskell, but includes some of her finest passages, and provides an
excellent introduction to the Brontës. Good judgment is evinced
everywhere in the writing. One slight misrepresentation arises from
the inclusion of what was later discovered to be a false (satirical)
prospectus for the Clergy Daughters' School.

Charlotte Maurat, *The Brontës' Secret* (tr. Margaret Meldrum),
London, 1969.
Though largely a scholarly pastiche of quotations, this is a very useful
biographical introduction. More attention is given to the earlier
Brontë writings than to the later. There are a few minor inaccuracies.
Does any evidence exist that Emily read *The Tales of Hoffmann*
avidly at the Pensionnat Heger, or elsewhere?

Phyllis Bentley, *The Brontës and their world*, London, 1969.
It would be difficult to find a more informative and attractive shorter
biographical introduction than this liberally illustrated book.

* * * * * *

(Patrick Brontë)
Annette B. Hopkins, *The Father of the Brontës*, Baltimore, 1958.
Although not factually complete, this is one of the most scholarly and
important books on the Brontës. It evades nothing in the evidence,
and the result is a convincing portrait of a man whose toleration, and
disregard of self in the face of misrepresentation, are eminently
worthy of respect and sympathy. A human figure emerges, not a
picture of perfection. Patrick Brontë's treatment of Mr Nicholls is
regarded as intelligible but inexcusable. This lucid, compact, and
artistically organized study pays welcome attention to Mr Brontë's
writings.

J. Lock and W. T. Dixon, *A Man of Sorrow*, London, 1965.
This massive and erudite volume is particularly interesting in the
early chapters. It suffers at times from over-documentation in church
matters and disregard for chronological continuity. Ample evidence
is provided to make amends for the misrepresentations of Mrs Gaskell.

As a reference book, this is a work of great value; the index is unusually helpful.

* * * * * *

(Charlotte Brontë)
Mrs Gaskell, *The Life of Charlotte Brontë.*
Although commonly described as a classic and, by Clement Shorter, as the *ne plus ultra*, this biography seems now to have only a secondary value. The first edition (1857) has a special historical interest, but there are modern studies which are more complete and accurate than the revised edition. Mrs Gaskell had made up her mind about Mr Brontë before she met him; she had noted all Lady Kay-Shuttleworth's tittle-tattle in 1850. As her work progressed, she included more and more of Charlotte's correspondence. The old-fashioned style of eking out biography with numerous letters constitutes a trial for the reader. Today one can read the Brontë story and the letters separately to great advantage (although it must be acknowledged that no selection of the Brontë letters yet exists which is adequate for those who are closely interested in biography). Mrs Gaskell's correspondence provides a living and more intensive impression of her views of the Brontës, her industry, mistakes, travail, and regrets. See J. A. V. Chapple and A. E. Pollard, *The Letters of Mrs Gaskell*, Manchester, 1966.

E. F. Benson, *Charlotte Brontë*, London, 1932.
This biography is based largely on the letters, and reveals Charlotte's character, rather unsympathetically perhaps. The author writes with vigour and eloquence, and has little difficulty in disposing of Mrs Gaskell's misrepresentations. Much of the delineation is excellent, but it contains minor errors and shows fictional tendencies. The history of Charlotte's letters to M. Heger is told fully; the author is convinced that she was in love with him, and that Mrs Gaskell deliberately concealed what she thought would never be divulged. Charlotte never forgave Branwell for his weakness in face of a hopeless passion parallel to her own. The result was antagonism between her and Emily, who 'stormed at' Anne for depicting Branwell's decline in *The Tenant of Wildfell Hall*. Undoubtedly the most intriguing legend in this book is that of Emily and Branwell's secret collaboration late at night over *Wuthering Heights*. Here, and in criticisms of Mrs Gaskell, the

influence of F. A. Leyland's *The Brontë Family* (see footnote, p. 244) is strong. The criticism of *Shirley* is admirable.

Margaret Crompton, *Passionate Search*, London, 1955.
Despite some minor inaccuracies and inconsistencies (the extent to which Mr Nicholls was 'pilloried' in *Shirley*, for example), and a dangerous reading of fact for fiction in *Villette* (there is some ambivalence, it seems, in the way in which the climax of Charlotte and M. Heger's relations is presented), this biography has very much to recommend it. It is judicious at critical points where other writers have accepted legend; it shows an excellent sense of proportion; and it is eminently lucid and readable.

Winifred Gérin, *Charlotte Brontë*, London, 1967.
This is indisputably the most important biography of Charlotte, the result of the most detailed research, with particularly interesting results for the Cowan Bridge and Brussels periods, Charlotte's visits to London, and her relationships with the Kay-Shuttleworths, Harriet Martineau, and Mrs Gaskell. Much space is devoted to early reading, to the influences at work in the early juvenilia, and to the Angrian writings. Extracts from the Roe Head journal are welcome, and the letters provide valuable reinforcement throughout. Perhaps a clearer statement on Aunt Branwell's religion and teaching is required; she appears to be too closely associated with Calvinism. Less attention is given to the novels directly than to the earlier writings collectively, and some incidental conclusions are rather surprising. Perhaps Charlotte could emerge more clearly if the remainder of the Brontë story were given less detailed attention. A more adequate index is required to make the most of this invaluable work.

* * * * * *

(Branwell Brontë)
Daphne du Maurier, *The Infernal World of Branwell Brontë*, London, 1960.
This is a shrewd and penetrating study, based on considerable research into the life and personality of Branwell. There is a large element of conjecture on the local originals of characters in the infernal world of Angrian fiction, but the conclusions drawn on Aunt Branwell, Charlotte's depression at Roe Head, and Emily at Law Hill, are

eminently sensible. Branwell lived too much in a world of fantasy, and failed in life because it differed from his 'infernal world'.

Winifred Gérin, *Branwell Brontë*, London, 1961.
A product of thorough and sustained research, this biography is of exceptional value for the background to Branwell's life. Throughout the greater part of its course it keeps close to the central character. His prose writings are presented in considerable detail, and the Robinson mystery contains interesting evidence, not found elsewhere, particularly on the large amount of money received by the servant Ann Marshall. One wonders whether too much autobiography is extracted from Branwell's writings, and whether his version of the Robinson story deserves as much credence as is given to it. The fact that Charlotte and her father believed it does not strengthen the evidence. A few incidental interpretations are dubious: Aunt Branwell drove her nephew down the path to hell very early, it appears; his orgy at Kendal was caused by the painful associations roused by the sight of the school buildings at Cowan Bridge; Emily was loyal to him at the end, but Charlotte held him in contempt. On Branwell and *Wuthering Heights* there is an interesting appendix, but can the subject of the novel be the portrait of the universal soul? If the poem 'Azrael' was written in 1838 (as Branwell's notebook indicates, according to Daphne du Maurier), William Dearden's story could appear even more apocryphal.

* * * * * *

(Emily Brontë)
Charles Simpson, *Emily Brontë*, London, 1929.
There may be a few biographical inaccuracies in this book, but it has evidence and characteristics which make it still worth careful study. Its illustrations are of great interest. Two of its strongest features are impressions of the country near Haworth which Emily knew so well and links between Southowram and *Wuthering Heights*. It closes with the problem of the Brontë portraits (*cf.* BST. *xlii, lxviii*).

Winifred Gérin, *Emily Brontë, A Biography*, London, 1971.
The author has done more research than any other writer on her subject, misses nothing, and gives thought to many possibilities. She is particularly interesting on Emily's stay at Law Hill. Not much is

definitely known about Emily's life. Much of her poetry enters this biography, and, for obvious contextual reasons, a great deal on the other Brontës. Some of the poetry is dubiously interpreted as biographical evidence, which includes a number of Heathcliff previsions. There is an interesting suggestion that the sight of starving Irish immigrants in Liverpool by Branwell explains Heathcliff's origin. The story of Branwell, which takes up a considerable part of the narrative, leads to *Wuthering Heights*. 'The outcast man succoured' by Emily, he 'invades' the novel; until she saw how much he suffered for Mrs Robinson, she did not know what passion was. Here, and in the explanation of Emily's silence and intractability near the end of her life, we seem to be in a world of conjecture. Emily remains an enigma.

* * * * * *

(Anne Brontë)

Winifred Gérin, *Anne Brontë*, London, 1959.

This work is the result of wide research; it is very readable and attractively illustrated. All the facts of Anne's life are here, and much has been added from the poems and novels. This method has dangers, creating sometimes a high degree of probability at best. There is an admixture of tradition and conjectural interpretation. Aunt Branwell plays a rather sinister role, and Charlotte (we are told) did not speak to Branwell for over two years at the end of his life. Most of his Robinson story is accepted. The second half of *Agnes Grey* reflects Anne's sadness after the death of Weightman. Such debatable questions, however, do not occupy a large portion of this valuable biography.

Critical Essays and Extracts

Virginia Woolf, 'Jane Eyre' and 'Wuthering Heights', *The Common Reader*, London, 1925.

J. A. Falconer, '*The Professor* and *Villette*', *English Studies*, 1927.

Leicester Bradner, 'The Growth of *Wuthering Heights*', *PMLA.*, 1933.

Lord David Cecil, 'Emily Brontë and "Wuthering Heights"', *Early Victorian Novelists*, London, 1934.

Melvin R. Watson, 'Tempest in the Soul: The Theme and Structure of *Wuthering Heights*', *Nineteenth-Century Fiction* (*NCF*), September 1949.

M. H. Scargill, 'All Passion Spent, A Revaluation of *Jane Eyre*', *University of Toronto Quarterly*, 1950.

Miriam Allott, '*Wuthering Heights*: The Rejection of Heathcliff', *Essays in Criticism*, 1958.

Robert B. Heilman, 'Charlotte Brontë's "New Gothic"', *From Jane Austen to Joseph Conrad* (ed. R. B. Heilman and M. Steinmann), Minneapolis, 1958.

Derek Traversi, 'The Brontë Sisters and "Wuthering Heights"', *The Pelican Guide to English Literature*, vol. 6, 1958.

Edgar F. Shannon, 'Lockwood's Dreams and the Exegesis of *Wuthering Heights*', *NCF*, September 1959.

Robert A. Colby, '*Villette* and the Life of the Mind', *PMLA.*, 1960.

Robert C. McKibben, 'The Image of the Book in *Wuthering Heights*', *NCF*, September 1960.

J. Hillis Miller, 'Emily Brontë', *The Disappearance of God*, New York and London, 1963.

Philip Drew, 'Charlotte Brontë as a Critic of *Wuthering Heights*', *NCF*, March 1964.

Barbara Hardy, *The Appropriate Form* (pp. 61–70 on *Jane Eyre*), London, 1964.

F. H. Langman, '*Wuthering Heights*', *Essays in Criticism*, 1965.

Philip Momberger, 'Self and World in the Works of Charlotte Brontë', *Journal of English Literary History*, 1965.

David Lodge, 'Fire and Eyre', *The Language of Fiction*, London and New York, 1966.

John Hagan, 'Control of Sympathy in *Wuthering Heights*', *NCF*, March 1967.

Q. D. Leavis, 'A Fresh Approach to *Wuthering Heights*', *Lectures in America* (F. R. and Q. D. Leavis), London and Toronto, 1969.

Andrew D. Hook, 'Charlotte Brontë, the Imagination, and *Villette*'. See Ian Gregor, below.*

Mark Kinkead-Weekes, 'The Place of Love in *Jane Eyre* and *Wuthering Heights*', *ibid.*

David Sonstroem, '*Wuthering Heights* and the Limits of Vision', *PMLA.*, 1971.

William A. Madden, '*Wuthering Heights*: The Binding of Passion', *NCF*, September 1972.

(Selections)

(ed.) Alistair Everitt, *Wuthering Heights: An Anthology of Criticism*, London, 1967.
Among the contents are essays by Drew, Langman, Sanger, Wade Thompson, and the first part of Irene Cooper Willis's study.

(ed.) Judith O'Neill, *Critics on Charlotte and Emily Brontë*, London, 1968.
A useful collection of extracts and essays, mainly on *Wuthering Heights*.

(ed.) Ian Gregor, *The Brontës, A Collection of Critical Essays*,* Englewood Cliffs, N.J., 1970.
The writers include Drew, Heilman, Hook, Lodge, Kinkead-Weekes, McKibben, Sanger.

(ed.) Miriam Allott, *Emily Brontë: 'Wuthering Heights'*, London, 1970.
Contains numerous entries, edited with notes, from early reviews (English and American) to modern essays, including Allott, Drew, Traversi. Jacques Blondel is valuable on origins. Other inclusions of note are Dobell, Swinburne, Irene Cooper Willis, and Mark Schorer.

(ed.) Miriam Allott, *Charlotte Brontë: 'Jane Eyre' and 'Villette'*, London, 1973.
A companion volume to the above. Contains early reviews, later Victorian assessments, and a number of twentieth-century views, including Lord David Cecil, Colby, Heilman, Scargill, and R. B. Martin.

(ed.) Miriam Allott, *The Brontës, The Critical Heritage*, London and New York, 1974.
The criticism extends from the earliest reviews to Mrs Humphry Ward's introductions; some French and American reviews are included. G. H. Lewes is prominent. Among the other writers are Thackeray, Matthew Arnold, D. G. Rossetti, Kingsley, Emile Montégut, W. C. Roscoe, E. S. Dallas, Mrs Oliphant, T. W. Reid, Swinburne, Leslie Stephen, Mary Robinson, Trollope, and Pater. The selection shows that the early reviewers were more perceptive and favourable to the Brontës than is usually thought.

Critical Works

(Juvenilia)

Fannie E. Ratchford, *The Brontës' Web of Childhood*, New York, 1941.

Some of its conclusions may not be acceptable, but the value of this remarkable book, the outcome of years of patient research, remains very high. It provides a clear and scholarly survey of the Glasstown-Angrian writings of Charlotte and Branwell, and records important discoveries relating to Gondal. The literary influences at work on these young writers are touched in lightly, and all is related to their lives and background. Appreciation of this work grows with knowledge of the whole of the Brontë writings. Perhaps the most interesting section ultimately is that where Charlotte's novels and *Wuthering Heights* are 'analyzed in light of Brontë juvenilia'. Angrian anticipations of characters and scenes are convincingly shown in *The Professor* and *Jane Eyre*. In *Shirley* the proof is more shadowy; in *Villette*, more protracted and forced, so that, by analogy, John Graham Bretton is proved to be the hero 'in Charlotte's mind . . ., for Zamorna could have no rival'. Several resemblances are found between Emily's Gondal poems and *Wuthering Heights*, but they are incidental and, with a few exceptions, very slight.

(General)

May Sinclair, *The Three Brontës*, London, 1912.

There are some excellent critical insights in this book. On Charlotte and M. Heger, and misleading biographies, many sensible judgments are made; errors and indiscretions are admitted even in Mrs Gaskell's *Life*. Owing to faulty editions, the author is unreliable on Emily's poetry (Percy and Zamorna appear). She exaggerates the links between it and *Wuthering Heights* (which she thinks probably the worst-constructed tale ever written), makes Heathcliff appear too passive, and Emily sublimely indifferent to evil and the physical world. Little space is devoted to Anne; almost every comment on her suggests she was feeble. The author's style is spirited, but rhetorical at times; it is significant that she rhapsodizes over the 'Titan Shirley' and 'Titanic' Emily. Nevertheless there is much to admire in this study, especially on Charlotte and her works, her triumphs and weaknesses.

Laura L. Hinkley, *The Brontës: Charlotte and Emily*, New York, 1945; London, 1947.
Arrangements and comments imply that Anne Brontë is hardly worthy of serious study; yet her novels and a survey of her life enter the book, making the sub-title rather a misnomer. The chapters on the remaining five novels are of less importance than other sections. The author has an unusual flair for drawing resemblances between characters and tracing ancestries; Rochester and Heathcliff are found to be cousins, originating, like Hunsden and Yorke, in Joshua Taylor of Gomersal. There is much for the reader who is interested in the earlier Brontë writings, but it is in some of the biographical interpretations that the book excels. Charlotte's relations with M. Heger are carefully assessed, and the whole chapter on Branwell is outstandingly shrewd. The question of his collaboration in *Wuthering Heights* is discussed. It is argued that Charlotte's first three novels owe more to 'the Brussels contretemps' than *Villette*. The author is well-informed, writes pungently, and shows a refreshing independence of judgment.

Phyllis Bentley, *The Brontës*, London, 1947.
There is much that is lucidly compressed in this brief introduction. It shows a just sense of proportion, and contains much that is excellent. Certain speculations, statements, and critical evaluations are open to question. Much is made of Yorkshire elements.

Inga-Stina Ewbank, *Their Proper Sphere, A Study of the Brontë Sisters as Early Victorian Novelists*, London, 1966.
Fortunately this work is not confined to the Brontës in the role of women writers. It includes a great deal of valuable criticism on all their novels; that on *Wuthering Heights* is the most sustained and important. The early Victorian attitude to female novelists is given special emphasis. This is an important study, characterized by careful research and sound judgment.

W. A. Craik, *The Brontë Novels*, London, 1968.
This work is remarkable for its concentration on the literature, with the minimum of biographical reference. Studies tend to be analytical, with attention to narrative points of view, themes, and characters in particular. Many minor points of comparison between the novels are made. Anne's novels are treated as worthy of serious attention. All the characters in *Wuthering Heights* are seen as facets of their author, and

perhaps the brutality of Heathcliff is over-extenuated. The complex pattern of *Shirley* is interestingly analysed; *Villette* is judged to be less well constructed, though it derives greater unity from its mood.

Tom Winnifrith, *The Brontës and their Background*, London and New York, 1973.
This work is the result of extensive research. The author indicates the textual unreliability of the letters, uncertainty of authorship in the Angrian writings, and the recurrence of traditions and fiction in Brontë biographies. The discussion of the religious views of the Brontës is important; they were subject to modifications, which are not always reflected in their verse and prose fiction. The prudery of the age, and its effect on reviews of the novels, are of particular interest. The study concludes with the question of contemporary snobbery, class attitudes of the Brontës, and a lengthy sociological survey of their novels.

* * * * * *

(Charlotte Brontë)
R. B. Martin, *The Accents of Persuasion*, New York and London, 1966.
Rather than stress the chronological alternation usually noted in Charlotte's novels, the author distinguishes between the first two and the last. Charlotte's growing doubt and pessimism casts its shadow first over *Shirley*. More detailed criticism might be expected on *The Professor*. The chapter on *Jane Eyre* is an excellent piece of sustained criticism; that on *Villette* is very enlightening. Caroline Helstone is deemed to suffer from 'shrinking femininity', and to be unsuitable for Robert Moore; but for love, Shirley might have become another Mrs Yorke. This is a lucid, well-documented, and very readable study.

Earl A. Knies, *The Art of Charlotte Brontë*, Athens, Ohio, 1969.
This work continually provides a salutary warning against the danger of reading much in Charlotte Brontë as autobiographical transcript. There are useful references to the views she expressed on novel-writing in her letters, but the study of the novels, with the exception of *Villette*, does not reveal much that is very striking in her art.

Margot Peters, *Charlotte Brontë, Style in the Novel*, Madison, Wisc., 1973.
The key is found in Charlotte's tensions. Predominance of feeling, brusqueness in characters at odds with themselves or others, self-discovery, and inner conflict are illustrated from adverbial frequency and stress, inversion, and various forms of antithesis. Aspects of figurative language are strikingly presented, though some sexual interpretations are doubtful. Examples of the language of the law-courts in *Jane Eyre* are rather over-inclusive, though the novel reflects a theme linked with punishments and moral choice; the author finds evidence in it of Charlotte's sense of guilt in reverting to Angrian passion *vis-à-vis* Victorian conventions. This intensive study is welcome for the close links it establishes between linguistics and literary assessment.

* * * * * *

(Emily Brontë)
Irene Cooper Willis, *The Authorship of Wuthering Heights*, London, 1936.
Anyone who is attracted by the idea that Branwell had a hand in the writing of *Wuthering Heights* should read this short study, which contrasts passages from the novel with extracts from Branwell's last prose work, 'And the Weary are at Rest'. The art, economy, and dramatic intensity of the one, its 'swift, direct, "spot-light" telling', and the flashy, uncontrolled improvisations of the latter, speak for themselves. Miss Willis's general comments and conclusions seem to be incontestable.

Muriel Spark and Derek Stanford, *Emily Brontë, Her Life and Work*, London, 1953.
It is as well, probably, that the picture of Emily which emerges from the biographical section is inconclusive and enigmatic. The poems are discounted for biographical purposes. Aunt Branwell and Emily's life at Law Hill are sensibly viewed, but one feels less certain of the presentation of Emily in her last years. She may have been 'unbalanced' but did she believe herself 'superhuman'; and did Anne condemn her? In this book of rather mixed elements, Derek Stanford's contribution is the more substantial. He discusses the poetry as poetry, irrespective of its Gondal associations, which often result, he maintains,

in inferior Byronic verse. There is much on poetry in general and from other poets. Close analyses of passages of Emily's poetry with distinctive tones, and of the natural background it evokes, are impressive. Illustrations of her stoicism, pantheism, non-Christian outlook (which seems rather debatable), and quietism, follow. Finally we have a rather technical, critical appreciation of her six 'major' poems. The best of the *Wuthering Heights* chapters is an analysis of the character of Catherine Earnshaw; much of Lord David Cecil's argument that this is a 'spiritual drama' relating to 'cosmic harmony' is accepted.

John Hewish, *Emily Brontë, A Critical and Biographical Study*, London and New York, 1969.
This very close scrutiny is compactly presented, and deserves very careful reading. The biographical section is devoted largely to the inner life reflected in the poems; the collocation of the imaginative and the factual results inevitably at times in a brief sense of incongruity. There is probably a tendency to read too much of the personal in Emily's poems, and to see in them too many foreshadowings of *Wuthering Heights*. Many questions are raised on the novel, and a final chapter discusses the changes in its critical reception from 1847 to 1968. The work shows wide research and temperate judgment; its detailed observation is sometimes remarkable, as when an echo of *Wuthering Heights* is found in an article on Shelley in *Fraser's Magazine*.

*   *   *   *   *   *

(Anne Brontë)
Ada Harrison and Derek Stanford, *Anne Brontë, Her Life and Work*, London, 1959.
This study aims at rolling away the stone which has virtually sealed Anne's tomb for over a hundred years, in deference to Charlotte's appraisal of her sister's work. Anne is rather lost for much of the time in the Brontë story, and her personality does not emerge strongly. Mr Brontë is treated scathingly at times. Anne's poems are given careful and judicious attention, but more could be expected on her novels, especially *The Tenant of Wildfell Hall*.

Appendixes

1. Mrs Gaskell's revision of The Life of Charlotte Brontë

A second edition followed close on the heels of the first in 1857. Then Mrs Gaskell found herself in a 'hornets' nest'. There were threats of legal proceedings on behalf of Mr Carus Wilson and Mrs Robinson. Mr Brontë complained; and other considerations made Mrs Gaskell more circumspect. Her omissions in the third edition are listed chapter by chapter:

III. The charge that the Brontë children had meatless meals, with nothing but potatoes for dinner.

Mr Brontë's Spartan principles: burning his children's gay boots, to discourage vanity in dress; cutting his wife's silk dress to shreds.

His volcanic wrath: worked off by firing his pistols rapidly out of the back door; shown also when he burnt the hearth rug, and sawed off the backs of chairs.

(These stories came from a servant who had been dismissed after very short service at the parsonage; they were refuted by other servants.)

A story about a seduction in a family near Haworth who were friendly with the Brontës when Mrs Brontë was alive. This scandal brought to an end, Mrs Gaskell believed, the only visits the young Brontës made to a friendly family in the Haworth district.

IV. Food at the Clergy Daughters' School. Mr Wilson lecturing the pupils 'on the sin of caring over-much for carnal things'.

His shaken self-confidence when, sickening for 'the fever', they did not respond to his spiritual exhortations.

His irritating habits and failure to understand people; the resentment felt by his pupils, and by Charlotte in particular; her faithful presentation of his 'unfavourable side'.

VIII. The story of the governess near Leeds who found that she was bigamously married. (Charlotte heard this while she was a teacher at Roe Head. It was omitted to spare the victim's feelings.)

XI. 'But, in the sixteenth century . . .': 'seventeenth' for 'sixteenth'.

XIII. Mrs Robinson and Branwell: she made the first advances, and 'made love' to him in the presence of her children. The story of his beguilement 'must be told'; perhaps it will awaken repentance in the flourishing, vivacious widow who frequents the gay circles of London society.

The story of this 'profligate woman' told at the parsonage when Branwell heard he was dismissed. Some months later they met clandestinely at Harrogate, but he refused to elope with her.

Branwell's expectations maintained by letters and sums of money. Mr Robinson's will made it impossible for his wife to inherit his property if she saw Branwell again. Messenger sent to Haworth to prevent his visiting her on hearing of Mr Robinson's death. He meets Branwell at the Black Bull; an hour after his departure, Branwell found in a fit.

He died, his pockets full of Mrs Robinson's letters.

In parenthesis, at the end, after Branwell's comment on a 'terrible night' he and his father had had: 'whimpering, "It's *her* fault, *her* fault"'.

XVI. The letters again, as Branwell stands up to die. 'He died! she lives still, – in May Fair. The Eumenides, I suppose, went out of existence at the time when the wail was heard, "Great Pan is dead". I think we could better have spared him than those awful Sisters who sting dead conscience into life.'

XXVIII. As a result of protests from friends of the 'village girl' whom Charlotte had comforted, 'seduced' was changed to 'betrayed'.

*   *   *   *   *   *

The following passages were added in the third edition:

II. Information from a Yorkshire gentleman on the presentation of the Haworth incumbency to Mr Brontë.

A long letter from the same gentleman confirming to some extent the 'foregoing account' of Mr Redhead's eviction.

III. The testimony of one of the former Brontë servants to the admirable likeness of the portrait of Charlotte (by Richmond) 'prefixed to this volume'.

IV. 'In some of the notices . . . on the subject from her' (two paragraphs).

'No doubt whatever can be entertained of the deep interest which [Mr Wilson] felt in the success of the school.'

From 'This original house was an old dwelling of the Picard family' to the starting of the bobbin-mill industry *after* the removal of the school (not before it was opened, as in the first edition).

Much in praise of Mr Wilson in the paragraph, 'All this occurred during the first two years of the establishment . . .'

VI. Two paragraphs: 'Some one at school said . . . as if it were gold.'

VII. Most of the first paragraph, which originally was no more than a sentence, ending with 'E' (Ellen Nussey), 'who has kindly entrusted me with as much of the correspondence as she has preserved'.

Two paragraphs from Mary Taylor's letter.

'Charlotte was certainly afraid of death . . . some feeling more, some less' (end of paragraph on Haworth churchyard).

VIII. Paragraph, 'She told me that one night . . .'

Paragraph, 'Mary' says, 'Cowper's poem . . .'

XI. Paragraph, 'Mary's account of the journey' (to Brussels).

Quotation of two paragraphs from Mary's letter.

XIII. Paragraph, 'Whatever may have been the nature and depth of Branwell's sins'.

Penultimate paragraph, 'In fact, all their latter days . . .'

XVII. Paragraph, '"A lady from the same neighbourhood . . ."'

Charlotte's letter to Martha Brown on Anne's death.

XVIII. Mary Taylor's reply to Mrs Gaskell on the subject of Charlotte and her fame.

XX. Charlotte's letter to Martha Brown (12 June 1853).

XXIII. 'Miss Martineau sends me . . . "Is my son dead?"'

XXVI. Charlotte's letter to Martha Brown (28 January 1853).
Letter to Miss Martineau (21 January 1853).

XXVII. Second paragraph, Charlotte's letter to Mrs Gaskell.
Another letter from Charlotte after Mrs Gaskell's return from Normandy.

2. The Gondal Story

The great pioneer in Gondal research is Miss Fannie Ratchford, who recorded her first conclusions in *The Brontës' Web of Childhood* (1941). Renewed investigations convinced her that almost all Emily's poems could be fitted into a deducible Gondal narrative, which she presented in her *Gondal's Queen, A Novel in Verse*, Austin and Edinburgh, 1955. The principal question left in the reader's mind concerns the evidence for the triune identification of the heroine, and the assumption that she could have appeared as Augusta Geraldine Almeda (A.G.A.), Geraldine S., and Rosina of Alcona.

In 1947 Laura Hinkley (see p. 363) put forward some alternative proposals, but the main dissent came from W. D. Paden in 1958. Inevitably his attempt at reconstructing the Gondal story from its remains provoked criticism, and such seems likely to be the doom of any proposed solution.

Briefly Miss Ratchford's reconstruction is as follows:

Augusta (who appears under different names at different stages) married Alexander, Lord of Elbë (designated sometimes as Elbë or A.E.), who was killed in a battle near Lake Elnor. She then fell in love with Lord Alfred S. of Aspin Castle, but sacrificed him for Julius, Lord Alfred committing suicide in England. In his student days Prince Julius of Angora had been imprisoned for falling in love with Princess Augusta; now he won her for revenge. After taking part in the conquest of Gaaldine, he had become King of Almedore; subsequently he overcame all rivals in both islands, including Gerald, with whom he had shared the rule of Gondal.

Angelica, the daughter of Lord Alfred, fell in love with a dark youth named Amedeus. He was seduced by Augusta, and then exiled. Angelica joined him and, to wreak revenge upon A.G.A., played a leading part with other outlaws and patriots in plotting the death of Julius. Amedeus was slain as he assassinated the Emperor. Augusta was eventually restored to the throne, but was murdered on Elmor Hill by Douglas, an outlaw loyal to Angelica.

As W. D. Paden's work (*An Investigation of Gonlad*, Bookman

Associates, New York, 1958) is less accessible to most readers, a longer summary of his conclusions is given:

> Gondal may have had five provinces, with Angora in the mountainous north and Exina in the south; the other three could have been Alcona, Almeda, and Elbë. There is no evidence that Regina, the capital, was situated on the shore of Lake Elderno.
>
> At the opening of the nineteenth century, Gondal was ruled by the father of Geraldine, Gerald, and Alfred.
>
> About 1820 Alexander (A.E.) sailed to Gaaldine, leaving his wife Augusta (A.G.A.) in Elbë. Years passed without news of him, and she fell in love with Alfred, who had recently lost his wife in childbirth. In 1824 they were married. The following spring Alexander returned, to be murdered by Alfred near Lake Elnore, where he was discovered dying by Augusta.
>
> A period of turmoil followed. Rosina, Queen of Alcona, came under suspicion, and her lover, Julius Brenzaida, was imprisoned in the Southern College (H. 178). Alfred fled to England; Augusta wandered among the mountains, and gave birth to a girl; the babe was abandoned but rescued by Blanche, who took it to Gaaldine. Augusta was apprehended and imprisoned in the Northern College (H. 180).
>
> By this time (1826) Julius had been released. Geraldine accompanied him to Gaaldine, where their son was born. Julius obtained rule over Almedore, and conquered Zalona. In 1828 he sailed with his army to invade Gondal (possibly on hearing of the death of Geraldine's father). Joint rule was set up with Gerald. In 1829 he had Gerald imprisoned and assassinated. In turn he was assassinated in his palace in Angora. Fifteen years later Rosina mourned his death (H. 182).
>
> Civil war broke out between Angora and Exina in 1830. Augusta fled to England, only to witness Alfred's death (H. 61). In Almedore Geraldine died of grief; her young son was hidden from the enemies of Julius. After the defeat of Angora, Augusta was recalled from exile, and took charge of Angelica, Alfred's daughter by his first wife. Under Augusta's sovereignty, there was peace in Gondal for a long period. She had a number of lovers, two of whom, Amedeus and Fernando, were exiled. Angelica too was exiled.
>
> In 1842 Lord Eldred (E.W.) was reminded of the youthful Alfred and Augusta by the sight of a black-haired boy and golden-

haired girl. They were Geraldine's son and Alexandria (H. 153).

In 1844 Augusta was murdered on Elmor Hill (H. 143), and Angelica was executed for complicity. Blanche appeared to claim the throne for Alexandria, who married Henry Angora – or Henry Almedore (H.A.) – the son of Julius and Geraldine.

3. The Carré of the Pensionnat in The Professor and Villette

Biographers generally show little interest in the pensionnat of the novels. Charlotte did not think it necessary to give the precise location of all its quarters, and was often, it seems, deliberately vague or confusing. Mrs Gaskell, who visited the Pensionnat Heger, provides little to solve the question which inevitably arises on how far the actual buildings were reproduced in fiction.

A plan of the Pensionnat Heger and its setting was made by a descendant of the Hegers, and is now to be seen in the Brontë Parsonage Museum. In a more professional form it appeared with an article on the Pensionnat and Charlotte's 'Villette' in *The Times Literary Supplement* of 13 April 1916. The plan suffices to show that the garden and the surrounding buildings were not altered in Charlotte's two novels (though the pear-tree Methuselah may have been moved), but the carré is not to be seen, nor is it mentioned in the article. (A modification of this plan is provided on p. 271.)

In the novels we find that the main entrance admitted one to 'a passage paved alternately with black and white marble'; in *Villette* this is the 'vestibule'. Beyond, through a glass door (in the corridor, one suspects from the next chapter), the garden could be seen. The house was on the left of the passage (*P.* ix).

Along the corridor (to the right) one came to a 'large, lofty, and square' hall; this is the carré of *Villette*. It formed one side of a quadrangle, the remaining sides of which were occupied by old buildings. At the far end of the hall were the folding-doors which led to the classrooms at the back of the premises. The refectory (of the novels) must have been on the street side, for the other two sides of the hall are opposite each other (*P.* x). On the right, at the far end, was a spiral staircase leading to the dormitories; on the left was the front of the hall, with glass doors opening on the playground and garden. In *Villette* this playground is the 'court', a term which may lead to confusion since it is not the quadrangle formed by the hall and the main school buildings. In *The Secret of Charlotte Brontë* (London, 1914) Frederika Macdonald, a former pupil of the school, tells us that the latter was the playground for the 'daily boarders' (the pupils who stayed for school dinners).

The first classe, the most important room in the novels, was a single-storey extension to the main buildings. It stood on the far side of the 'court' or playground at the front of the carré, and it could be entered from 'the large berceau'. It became Charlotte's classroom in 1843 (G. xii): 'She ruled over a new schoolroom, which had been built on the space in the playground adjoining the house. Over that First Class she was *surveillante* at all hours.'

The order of the rooms from the first classe and on three sides of the quadrangle to the refectory is neither consistently nor completely stated. A stove 'let into the wall between the refectory and the carré' sufficed to heat 'both apartments. Piercing the same wall, and close beside the stove, was a window, looking also into the carré' (*V*. xxi). From the carré one could look into the refectory, and see its tables, armoire, and two lamps (*P*. ix).

The dormitories (and the oratory) were on the first floor of the main buildings, the principal one being over the classrooms at the back. There were attics on all three sides of the quadrangle occupied by the older buildings. The hall was a single-storey structure. Frederika Macdonald refers to the 'large central hall, or *Galerie* as it was called, that flanked the square, enclosing the court or playground of daily boarders, whilst the *Galerie* divided the court from the garden'.

The plates in her book and in the Haworth edition of Mrs Gaskell's *The Life of Charlotte Brontë* do not show the high main school buildings clearly; too much is obscured by trees. However, the 1924 John Grant edition of Mrs Gaskell's biography contains interesting photographs of these buildings when local demolition had begun. The relatively high attic buildings are clear, but they suggest that the quadrangle behind the *Galerie* was rather small. One illustration gives a full view of the *Galerie* from a point near the playground on the garden side. It is elegant, with four high round-arched windows and a central double door taking up the greater part of the 'front'. This suggests that it was not very long. Nor could it have had much width, for the windows on the far side are clear. The corridor leading to the hall adjoins the house; *see plate 21* (*lower*). The photograph of the Rue d'Isabelle and the Pensionnat Heger in Victor Tahon, *La Rue d'Isabelle et le Jardin des Arbalétriers*, suggests that this was a substantial extension to the house of one storey only, and that the first classe and the *Galerie* had been removed by 1909.

The original *Galerie* was clearly wider than was indicated on the plan transmitted to Marion Spielmann, but not nearly as extensive as the hall or carré of *The Professor* and *Villette*. In the former, it is used by the heroine's classes. It has a variety of functions in *Villette*. Since Charlotte's description of the garden and its surroundings bears an unmistakable resemblance to those of the Pensionnat Heger, and the location of the school remains undisguised in *The Professor*, any changes in the buildings must have been made for fictional reasons.

4. Evidence, in her Novels, of Charlotte Brontë's Reading

First and foremost comes the Bible. Her novels show abundantly that, to quote M. Heger (G. xi), 'elle était nourrie de la Bible'. Sometimes it is mediated and reinforced by *The Pilgrim's Progress*. The manner in which Biblical quotation and reference enter Charlotte's style has already been briefly illustrated (pp. 171–2). Further examples follow in two sections:

(1)

P.   xxi, know neither the day nor hour when your —— cometh; xxii, flourishing like a green bay tree; xxiii, clothing it, as God does the lilies of the field.

J.   vii, outside of the cup and platter (Mat. xxiii. 25); end xxvi (Psalm lxix. 1–2); beginning xxvii, pluck out your right eye, one little ewe lamb (II Sam. xii. 1–14), tent of Achan (Josh. vii), Samson; xxviii, require my soul of me; xxxiv, Mat. viii. 9; xxxvi, kept these things . . . and pondered them in my heart; xxxvii, bone of his bone, and flesh of his flesh.

S.   i, Gospel for law, Acts for Genesis, the city of Jerusalem for the plain of Shinar (Gen. xi); xiv, the crackling of thorns under a pot; xx, Whom He loveth, He chasteneth; xxiii, buried his talent in a napkin; xxiv, The Valley of the Shadow of Death; xxv, sweat of agony (Luke xxii. 44); xxvii, pleasant pastures . . . by the still waters; xxxi, Your thoughts are not my thoughts; xxxv, with what measure we mete it shall be measured to us.

V.   iii, live, move, and have her being (Acts xvii. 28); xiii, pearl of great price (also xxxii and xxxvii: Mat. xiii. 46); xxi, dew-white harvest (later referred to as 'manna'), cloud and pillar, sepulchral summit of a Nebo (Deut. xxxiv. 1–6); xxvi, Ichabod was written on their covers; xxix, the dayspring on high, the mortal will have put on immortality; xxxii, sowed in tears . . . reaped in joy; xxxv, cared for none of these things (Acts xviii. 17), sufficient for the day is always the evil; xxxvii, God saw that it was good; xxxviii, Let us run that we may obtain, Let us hear the conclusion of the whole matter, the south wind quieting the earth (Job xxxvii. 17); xxxix, through a glass darkly . . . face to face; xli, faithful steward; xlii, imagines a vain thing, stone . . . scorpion (Mat. vii. 9–10), living water (John iv. 10–14).

(2)

tent of Achan, *J.* xxvii (above); *S.* viii, xvii. Agar, *S.* v. Ahasuerus, *J.* xxiv. Anak, *S.* xii. Baal, *V.* xxx. Belshazzar, *S.* xxxi. Bethel, *S.* xxii. Bethlehem, *V.* xxxviii. brand snatched from burning, *J.* xxxv; *V.* xxviii. Cain, *S.* xxx; *V.* xiv. the Crucifixion, *S.* xxv (above); *V.* iii, viii. rivers of Damascus (and Jordan), *S.* xxvi (II Kings v). vice of Demas, *J.* xxxiv (II Tim. iv. 10). Dives, *J.* xxxv. Eden, *J.* xxiii; *V.* xli. witch of Endor, *V.* xxxix. Esau, *V.* xx, xxi. Eutychus (Acts xx. 9), *J.* vii; *V.* xxx. ewe lamb, *J.* xxvii (above); *V.* xxxii. Felix (Acts xxiv. 25), *J.* vi. balm in Gilead, *P.* xiii. Hagar, *S.* xxxv. dew of Hermon, *P.* xxiii. Israelites in Egypt, *P.* v, xxi; *J.* xxvi. Jacob (at Peniel), *S.* xxiv; *V.* xx, xxxvii. Job, *P.* xxiii; *J.* xv; *V.* vi. Jonah's gourd, *V.* vi. Lazarus, *S.* xxiv. Lot, *P.* iv; *J.* xxxi. Lucifer, *S.* xxx (Isaiah xiv. 12); *V.* xiv. Macedonia (Acts xvi. 9), *J.* xxxiv. Methuselah, *V.* xii. Moses, (Meribah's waters) *V.* xiii (Exod. xvii. 5–7), (crossing of the Red Sea) *V.* xxiii. Nebuchadnezzar, *J.* xxxvii; *V.* x, xix, xxiv. Noah (dove and olive leaf), *V.* xxxviii. Paul and Silas, *J.* xxxvi. phylactery, *J.* viii. Rachel weeping for her children, *V.* xxxvii. Rebecca, *P.* iv; *J.* xviii. Revelation, *J.* xxxv. house of Rimmon, *V.* xxiii. Samson, *J.* xxiv, xxvii, xxxvii. Samuel, *S.* xxvi. Saul, *J.* xxxvii; *S.* xii, xxxiii; *V.* xxiv, xxxv. Sisera, *S.* xxxi; *V.* xii. Solomon, *J.* viii (Prov. xv. 17). Tadmor, *V.* xxxiv (II Chron. viii. 4). Tophet, *V.* xxiii.

* * * * * *

Two books which meant much to Charlotte are:

1. *The Arabian Nights*

J. viii, Barmecide supper; xvii, Mesrour (named after the chief of Haroun al Raschid's eunuchs).

S. xii, Prince Ali's tube.

V. xvi, Bedriddin Hassan, Genii; xix, 'Open! Sesame' (cf. xxxix, sesame-charm); xx, eastern genii, and the Slave of the Lamp; xxiv, Barmecide's loaf; xxvi, valley of Sindbad; xxxviii, Alnaschar dream, tent of Peri-Banou.

See 'Peri' (p. 160), and note 'Afreet' in Charlotte's preface to *Wuthering Heights*.

2. Bunyan, *The Pilgrim's Progress*

P.   preface, Hill of Difficulty (same image, vii), 'He that is low need fear no fall'.

J.   xv (end), sweet as the hills of Beulah; xxxi, the silken snare; xxxviii, Greatheart and Apollyon. See pp. 108, 109.

S.   iv (end), Ignorance and Vain-Confidence.

V.   i, Christian and Hopeful; xi (end), Apollyon; xxx, thorns and briars, flints . . . the pain-pressed pilgrim; xxxviii (opening), on pilgrimage through the wilderness of this world, Apollyon and Greatheart, Vanity Fair.

* * * * * *

In the selection of authors listed below, the most important are Milton, Scott, and Shakespeare:

Matthew Arnold.   S. vii, to look on life steadily.

Robert Burns.   J. xxiv, from 'Bonnie Wee Thing'; S. xii, lords of the creation, xiii, wee sma' hours ayont the twal, xxvii, Pleasures, like poppies; V. xvi, 'Auld Lang Syne' (quoted xxv), xx, 'giftie' of seeing myself, xxiv, 'John Anderson, my jo, John'.

Lord Byron.   P. xxv; J. vi, 'stony street' (*Childe Harold*, III. xxii), xxvii, upas-tree (*ibid.*, IV. cxxvi). See pp. 160–1 for 'Peri'.

S. T. Coleridge.   J. xxxii, 'burst' . . . 'the silent sea', xxxiii, gush of pity . . . heart.

Fenimore Cooper.   (His novels are in the 1840 list of books available at the Mechanics' Institute, Keighley.) J. xxvii, the Indian . . . canoe; S. x, tomahawk tongues, xxi (end), xxxvi.

William Cowper.   J. vii and xxxv, castaway; S. xii, 'The Castaway' quoted.

John Dryden.   J. xxiv, the world for love . . . well lost.

Oliver Goldsmith.   P. vii, *The Vicar of Wakefield* (cf. V. xx); J. i, *The History of Rome*, xiv, pride in his port ('The Traveller'); S. xi,

Tony Lumpkin, xv, 'concatenation accordingly' (*She Stoops to Conquer*).

Thomas Gray.   P. xxiii, 'the purple light of love'.

John Keats.   J. xix, Did I wake or sleep ('Ode to a Nightingale'); S. iv, fanatics cling to their dream ('The Fall of Hyperion').

Richard Lovelace.   V. vi, 'Stone walls do not a prison make . . . cage'.

John Milton.   P. xix, xxiv, Abdiel the faithful; J. xiii, likeness of a Kingly Crown, shape which shape had none (Death, born of Sin, *Paradise Lost*, ii. 666–73), xiv, bad eminence (Satan, *ibid.*, ii. 6), fallen seraph, xvii, 'Some natural tears she shed', xx, noon darkens in an eclipse, *Samson Agonistes*; cf. xxiv, xxvii, xxxvii, sightless Samson, foreign guidance, prop and guide; S. xxxvi, mountain nymph, Liberty; V. xx, confusion worse confounded, xxiii, neat-handed Phillis.

Mrs Radcliffe.   J. General influence of the 'terror' story; S. xxiii, *The Italian*.

Samuel Richardson.   P. xxiv, Sir Charles Grandison and Harriet Byron; J. i, *Pamela*.

Sir Walter Scott.   P. xxiii, xxv; J. iv, 'onding on snaw' (*The Heart of Midlothian*, viii), xxv, 'with a sullen, moaning sound' (*The Lay of the Last Minstrel*, I. xiii), xxxi, 'The air was mild . . . balm' (*ibid.*, III. xxiv), xxxii–iii, *Marmion*, xxxiv, 'Looked to river . . . hill' (*The Lay of the Last Minstrel*, V. xxvi), xxxvi, death of Mrs Rochester (see p. 118); S. Shirley's family name, Keeldar, was remembered from note li of *The Lady of the Lake* (the link with Emily Brontë seems to be confirmed by the quotation from note xlix in *W*. ix), xvii, the Covenanters; V. xiii, Mause Headrigg and Sergeant Bothwell (*Old Mortality*, viii), xvii, Azrael, and xxiii, scimitar of Saladin (*The Talisman*, xxvii).

Shakespeare.   P. xxiv, Othello smothered Desdemona; J. xi, 'after life's fitful fever they sleep well', xiii, head and front of his offending (*Othello*, I. iii; note also, from the same scene, xv, passing strange,

xvi, plain unvarnished tale), xv, a hag like one of those who appeared
to Macbeth on the heath of Forres, xix, 'Off, ye lendings' (*King Lear*),
xxiv, Mustard-seed, gild refined gold, unction to my soul, xxviii, if I
were a . . . dog . . . you would not turn me from your hearth (*King
Lear*), xxix, a night when you should not have shut out a dog, xxxii,
delicious poison (*Antony and Cleopatra*); *S.* vi, Coriolanus, xxvii,
prophetic soul (*Hamlet*), there is a tide in the affairs of men . . . fortune,
xxx, 'Patience on a monument', 'Et tu, Brute!'; *V.* viii, head and front
of her offending, xi, never to grow old, never to wither (*Antony and
Cleopatra*), hag . . . 'All-hail', xiv, to the top of your bent (*Hamlet*),
xvii, Titania and Bottom, green and yellow melancholy, xxv, too, too
solid flesh, xxx, sound and fury, signifying nothing, xxxiii, course . . .
had never run so smooth.

P. B. Shelley.   *S.* xx, wind . . . the dirge of departing winter.

R. B. Sheridan.   *S.* xvii, *contagious* – a malapropism.

Christopher Smart.   *S.* xiii.

Jonathan Swift.   *P.* xix and *J.* iii, *Gulliver's Travels*, Lilliput and
Brobdingnag (cf. iv, Jane's view of Mr Brocklehurst).

William Wordsworth.   *P.* vii, 'The boy is father to the man', xxiii, a
mountain echo, xxv; *J.* xxxvi, My heart leapt up, xxxvii, The rain is
over and gone ('Written in March'), a hill-sent echo, mountain echo
(see 'Yes, it was the mountain Echo'); *S.* xix, 'earth's first blood' ('It
is not to be thought of that the Flood'), xxxvii, The winter is over and
gone.

Charles Wolfe.   *V.* viii, left . . . alone . . . glory.

* * * * * *

Cervantes, *Don Quixote* (unstabled Rosinante), end *V.* xxxix. Rousseau,
'sentimentalising and wire-drawing', *V.* xxxiv, Jean-Jacques sensibility, *V.* xxxviii; Béranger, *P.* xi; Chénier, *S.* v, vi; Bernardin de
Saint-Pierre (whose works had been presented to Charlotte by M.
Heger in August 1843), mentioned in *S.* xxvi, and thought to have
influenced the description in the last paragraph of *P.* xix and at the

very end of *Villette* (J. N. Ware, *Modern Language Notes*, June 1925);
French writers in *P.* iv, almost certainly the authors of works Charlotte
borrowed from Mary Taylor's father at Gomersal; Schiller, *Die
Räuber* quoted, *J.* xxviii, and one of his ballads, *V.* xxvi. The 'iron
shroud' of *J.* xxxiv has been traced by J. M. S. Tompkins (*The
Modern Language Review*, 1927) to a story in *Blackwood's Magazine*,
August 1830.

5. Wuthering Heights *and the Story of Hugh Brunty*

After a devastating attack on its historical accuracy by Angus M. Mackay and J. Horsfall Turner at the end of the last century, the story has remained discreetly buried, though Jack Loudan dared to unearth it in 1952.[1]

The critical question is not whether the tale is based on fact, but whether it could have been a highly romanticized family story told by Hugh Brunty for the entertainment of his eldest children when they were very young; he was, according to tradition, a great raconteur, and he wrote verse.[2] The fact that the story attributed to him is full of chronological inexactitudes does not rule out the possibility that it was told. If so, it was probably one of the tales which his eldest son Patrick narrated to his own children.

The author of the extraordinary book[3] which brought this story to light was taught by the Rev. William McAllister of Finard, Newry. In his boyhood, we are told, the latter knew Patrick Brunty, and heard his father tell a story which shows links with *Wuthering Heights*. Hugh Brunty's stories were so thrilling that William Wright's teacher used them as subjects for composition exercises. This particular tale has romantic elements, and they are very evident in the account of the wedding which concludes it.

Hugh's grandfather had a farm near the banks of the Boyne. He was a cattle-dealer, and often crossed the Irish Sea from Drogheda to sell cattle in Liverpool. On one of his return voyages a strange child was found in the hold. It proved to be a very young boy, dark, dirty, and almost naked. There was no doctor on the vessel, and only one woman, Mrs Brunty. As nobody would take care of him, and there was no foundling hospital nearer than Dublin, she decided to adopt him. From his gipsyish complexion, the boy was thought to be Welsh, and called 'Welsh' by the Bruntys. He grew up to be sullen, envious,

[1] See *The Listener*, 18 December 1952.

[2] Jane Eyre's reply, 'To the finest fibre of my nature, sir', to Rochester's 'Jane suits me: do I suit her?' (xxxvii) may be traced to one of his poems. Charlotte probably inherited the expression from her father.

[3] William Wright, *The Brontës in Ireland*, London, 1893.

and cunning, and attached himself to Mr Brunty, who took him, instead of his own sons, to fairs and markets, to listen to farmers' conversations and gain the information he needed to drive hard bargains. Welsh was taken to Liverpool for the same reason, and in time Mr Brunty became prosperous; the more attached he became to Welsh, however, the more his children disliked the interloper. Ultimately Welsh gained almost complete management in business matters. When his master died suddenly on board ship, after selling the largest consignment of cattle that ever crossed the Irish Sea, he professed to know nothing of the proceeds or the documents relating to the sale.

The Bruntys were well educated, knew very little about farming or dealing, and were unable to support themselves. Welsh arranged a meeting at which he proposed to tell them how they could be re-habilitated. He appeared dressed as he had never been seen before, in black broadcloth and fine linen, white as his prominent teeth. He would continue dealing and supply the family needs, provided Mary, the youngest sister, married him. The proposal was indignantly rejected. As he left, Welsh shouted, 'Mary shall be my wife, and I'll scatter the rest of you like chaff from this house, which shall be my home!' The Bruntys had friends, and three of the brothers obtained good positions, two in England. They were able to send home enough money to pay the rent of the farm and maintain their mother and sisters.

Welsh did not return to cattle-dealing; he became a sub-agent for an absentee landlord, with responsibility for collecting rents, including the Bruntys'. He could exploit his cunning to the satisfaction of his master and overlord, but, as he could never get the better of the Bruntys, who continued to pay their rent regularly even when it had increased, he decided to change his tactics, and employed an un-principled woman to impress on Mary how much he had done and spent to save her family from eviction. Forged receipts were shown. Finally Mary was induced to meet Welsh one night in a plantation, in company with the go-between, in order that she might express her gratitude. Her fate was sealed. Marriage to Welsh was preferable to scandal. He had no difficulty in bribing his agent into making him the tenant of a farm.

Years later the agent was assassinated after a bout of heartless evictions, and Welsh's house was burnt to the ground. He was so poor that he could no longer retain the favour of the new agent, and soon

lost his sub-agency. As he and Mary were childless, they offered to
adopt one of his nephews. So it was that Hugh Brunty, whose father
lived in the south of Ireland, was allowed to be taken by the pair from
his comfortable home on the condition that his father should never
visit or communicate with him, and that he should never be told
where his parents lived. Hugh was five or six at the time. Four nights
were spent on the road, partly to save the cost of lodgings, more
particularly (so the story goes) that the boy should be unable to recall
his way home. From the outset he was treated harshly, and even
brutally. He received none of the education Welsh had promised his
parents, but had to work on the farm. Welsh's right-hand man was a
tall, gaunt, rather primitive, and hypocritical peasant (rather like Joseph
in *Wuthering Heights*); he had a habit of invoking 'the Blessed Virgin
and all the saints'. Hugh's best friend was the farm dog Keeper (the
name of Emily's favourite dog). Aunt Mary was sorry for him,[1] and
told him the story of her husband's villainies. The discovery that his
uncle was not a Brunty afforded Hugh great relief.

The story of his escape, at the age of fifteen, and how he swam
naked down the Boyne to a rendezvous with an enemy of Welsh, a
neighbouring farmer, who was waiting with a suit of clothes to assist
him, is romantic. He settled in northern Ireland, eventually becoming
overseer of some lime kilns. One of his friends was a red-haired youth
named McClory. During a Christmas holiday he stayed at McClory's
home, and soon fell in love with his beautiful sister Alice. Their
marriage was opposed by her family on religious grounds, and prepara-
tions were made for her wedding to a Catholic farmer. All was ready
for the ceremony when it was discovered that the bride was missing.
Soon it was heard that she had been seen galloping with a tall gentleman towards Banbridge; later a boy rode up on her horse to say that
she had just been married to Hugh Brunty at the Protestant Church of
Magherally. (This was in 1776.) The clergyman who took the service
thought the bride the most beautiful woman he had ever seen. Their
first home was the cottage at Emdale in the parish of Drumballyroney.

[1] There is a parallel situation in Charlotte's story of Willie Ellin (see
p. 155).

6. Brontë Films

Background

Devotion. Warner Brothers, 1944 (released 1946). A biographical film on the four Brontës. Ida Lupino, Olivia de Havilland, Nancy Coleman, Arthur Kennedy.

The Brontë Sisters. Attico Films, 1970. Locations and buildings of Brontë interest in Yorkshire.

The Brontës Lived Here. BBC, 12.7.73. Margaret Drabble visits Haworth and the Yorkshire moors.

The Brontës of Haworth. Yorkshire Television, 30.9.73, 4-part serial. Scripts by Christopher Fry.

Jane Eyre

Italy.   1910, 1915 ('The Castle of Thornfield'), 1918.

U.S.A.   1914, 1915, 1918 ('Woman and Wife'), 1921, 1934; 1943 (20th Century-Fox) Orson Welles, Joan Fontaine.

G.B.   1970 (Omnibus Productions) George C. Scott, Susannah York, Ian Bannen.

BBC Television:

29.9.46 Mary Mackenzie, Anthony Hawtrey.

26.9.48 Barbara Mullen, Reginald Tate.

24.2.56 (6-part serial). Daphne Slater, Stanley Baker.

7.4.63 (7-part serial). Ann Bell, Richard Leech.

27.9.73 (5-part serial). Sorcha Cusack, Michael Jayston.

Shirley

G.B.   1922, Carlotta Breese, Clive Brook, Harvey Braban.

The Tenant of Wildfell Hall

BBC Television:

28.12.68 (4-part serial). Janet Munro, Jeremy Burring, Bryan Marshall.

Villette

BBC Television:

17.7.57 (6-part serial). Jill Bennett, Michael Warre.

31.5.70 (5-part serial). Judy Parfitt, Peter Jeffrey.

Wuthering Heights

U.S.A. 1939 (Samuel Goldwyn Productions) Merle Oberon, Laurence Olivier, Flora Robson, David Niven.

Mexico 1953 ('Abismos de Pasion') Jorge Mistral, Irasime Dilian.

G.B. 1920. Milton Rosmer, Colette Brettel, Warwick Ward, Ann Trevor.

1970 (American International Pictures) Anna Calder-Marshall, Timothy Dalton, Harry Andrews.

BBC Television:

7.3.48 Katharine Blake, Kieron Moore.

6.12.53 Yvonne Mitchell, Richard Todd.

11.5.62 Claire Bloom, Keith Michell.

28.10.67 (4-part serial). Angela Scoular, Ian McShane.

Index

Authors included in the Select Bibliography (pp. 351–66) have been omitted unless they are referred to elsewhere in this work.
The Brontë novels are entered independently, not under their authors.
References in bold type at the end of certain entries indicate plates.